SKULLDIGGER
+SKELETON BOY

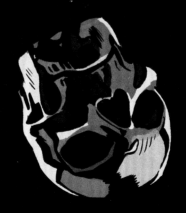

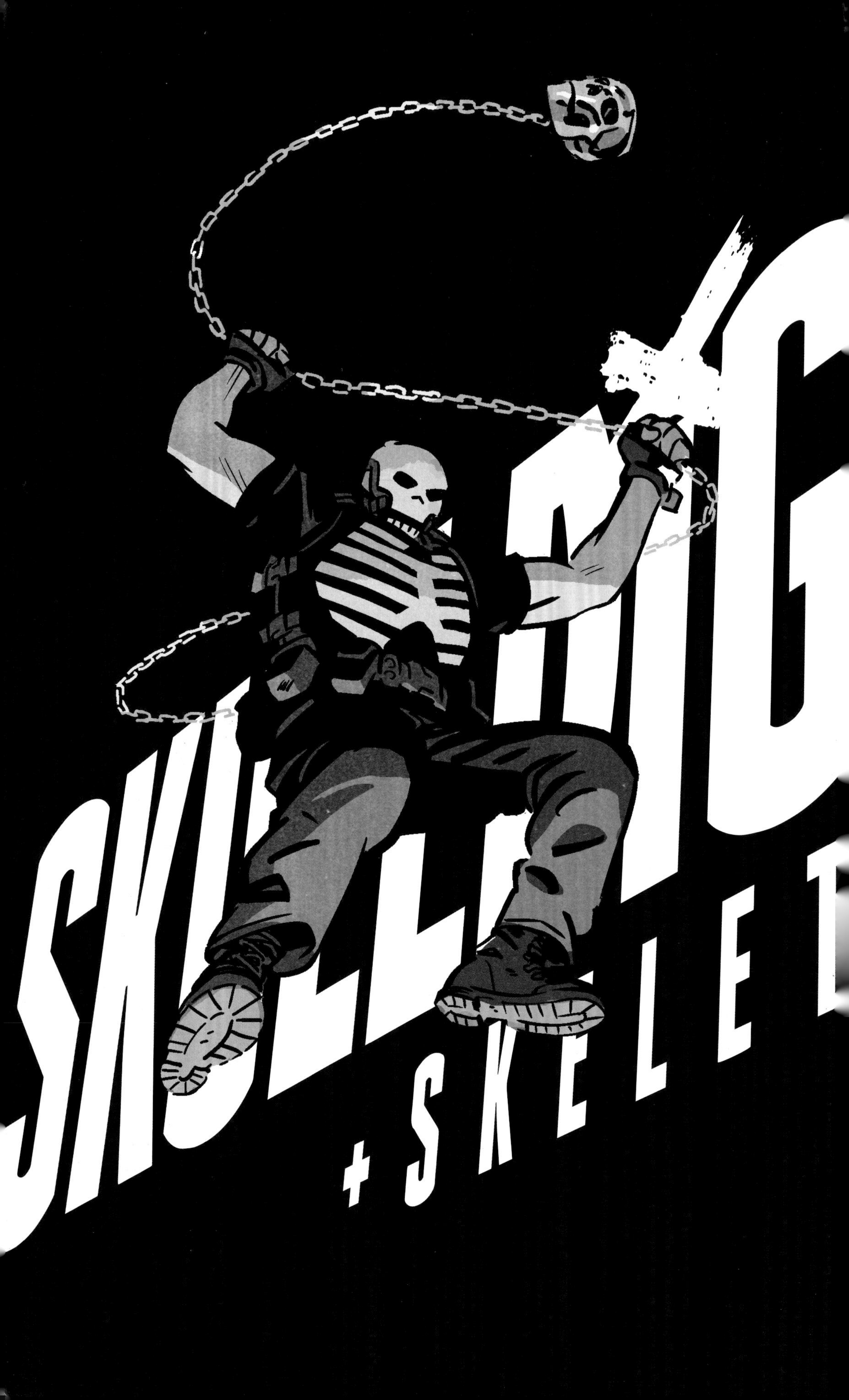
+SKELET

Written by
JEFF LEMIRE

Art by
TONCI ZONJIC

Letters by
STEVE WANDS

Cover by
TONCI ZONJIC

Chapter breaks by
TONCI ZONJIC, MIKE DEODATO JR. with **FRANK MARTIN,
JAMES HARREN, PATRIC REYNOLDS** with **LEE LOUGHRIDGE,
DANIEL WARREN JOHNSON** with **MIKE SPICER,
SAM KIETH,** and **CLIFF CHIANG**

Dark Horse Books

President & Publisher
MIKE RICHARDSON

Editor
DANIEL CHABON

Assistant Editor
CHUCK HOWITT

Designer
PATRICK SATTERFIELD

Digital Art Technician
JOSIE CHRISTENSEN

SKULLDIGGER AND SKELETON BOY

SKULLDIGGER AND SKELETON BOY™ © 2019, 2021 171 Studios, Inc., and Dean Ormston. All rights reserved. Black Hammer™ and all characters prominently featured herein are trademarks of 171 Studios, Inc., and Dean Ormston. All rights reserved. Dark Horse Books® and the Dark Horse logo are registered trademarks of Dark Horse Comics LLC. All rights reserved. No portion of this publication may be reproduced or transmitted, in any form or by any means, without the express written permission of Dark Horse Comics LLC. Names, characters, places, and incidents featured in this publication either are the product of the author's imagination or are used fictitiously. Any resemblance to actual persons (living or dead), events, institutions, or locales, without satiric intent, is coincidental.

Published by
DARK HORSE BOOKS
A division of Dark Horse Comics LLC
10956 SE Main Street
Milwaukie, OR 97222

DarkHorse.com

To find a comics shop in your area, visit comicshoplocator.com

First edition: May 2021
Ebook ISBN 978-1-50671-036-5
Trade Paperback ISBN 978-1-50671-033-4

Collects issues #1–#6 of the Dark Horse Comics series Skulldigger and Skeleton Boy

Library of Congress Cataloging-in-Publication Data

Names: Lemire, Jeff, writer. | Zonjić, Tonči, artist. | Wands, Steve, letterer.
Title: Skulldigger and Skeleton Boy / written by Jeff Lemire ; art by Tonci Zonjic ; letters by Steve Wands.
Description: First edition. | Milwaukie, OR : Dark Horse Books, 2020. | "Collects issues #1–#6 of the Dark Horse Comics series Skulldigger and Skeleton Boy."
Identifiers: LCCN 2020014416 (print) | LCCN 2020014417 (ebook) | ISBN 9781506710334 (trade paperback) | ISBN 9781506710365 (ebook)
Subjects: LCSH: Comic books, strips, etc.
Classification: LCC PN6728.S533 L46 2020 (print) | LCC PN6728.S533 (ebook) | DDC 741.5/973--dc23
LC record available at https://lccn.loc.gov/2020014416
LC ebook record available at https://lccn.loc.gov/2020014417

10 9 8 7 6 5 4 3 2 1
Printed in China

NEIL HANKERSON Executive Vice President • TOM WEDDLE Chief Financial Officer • RANDY STRADLEY Vice President of Publishing • NICK McWHORTER Chief Business Development Officer • DALE LAFOUNTAIN Chief Information Officer • MATT PARKINSON Vice President of Marketing • VANESSA TODD-HOLMES Vice President of Production and Scheduling • MARK BERNARDI Vice President of Book Trade and Digital Sales • KEN LIZZI General Counsel • DAVE MARSHALL Editor in Chief • DAVEY ESTRADA Editorial Director • CHRIS WARNER Senior Books Editor • CARY GRAZZINI Director of Specialty Projects • LIA RIBACCHI Art Director • MATT DRYER Director of Digital Art and Prepress • MICHAEL GOMBOS Senior Director of Licensed Publications • KARI YADRO Director of Custom Programs • KARI TORSON Director of International Licensing • SEAN BRICE Director of Trade Sales

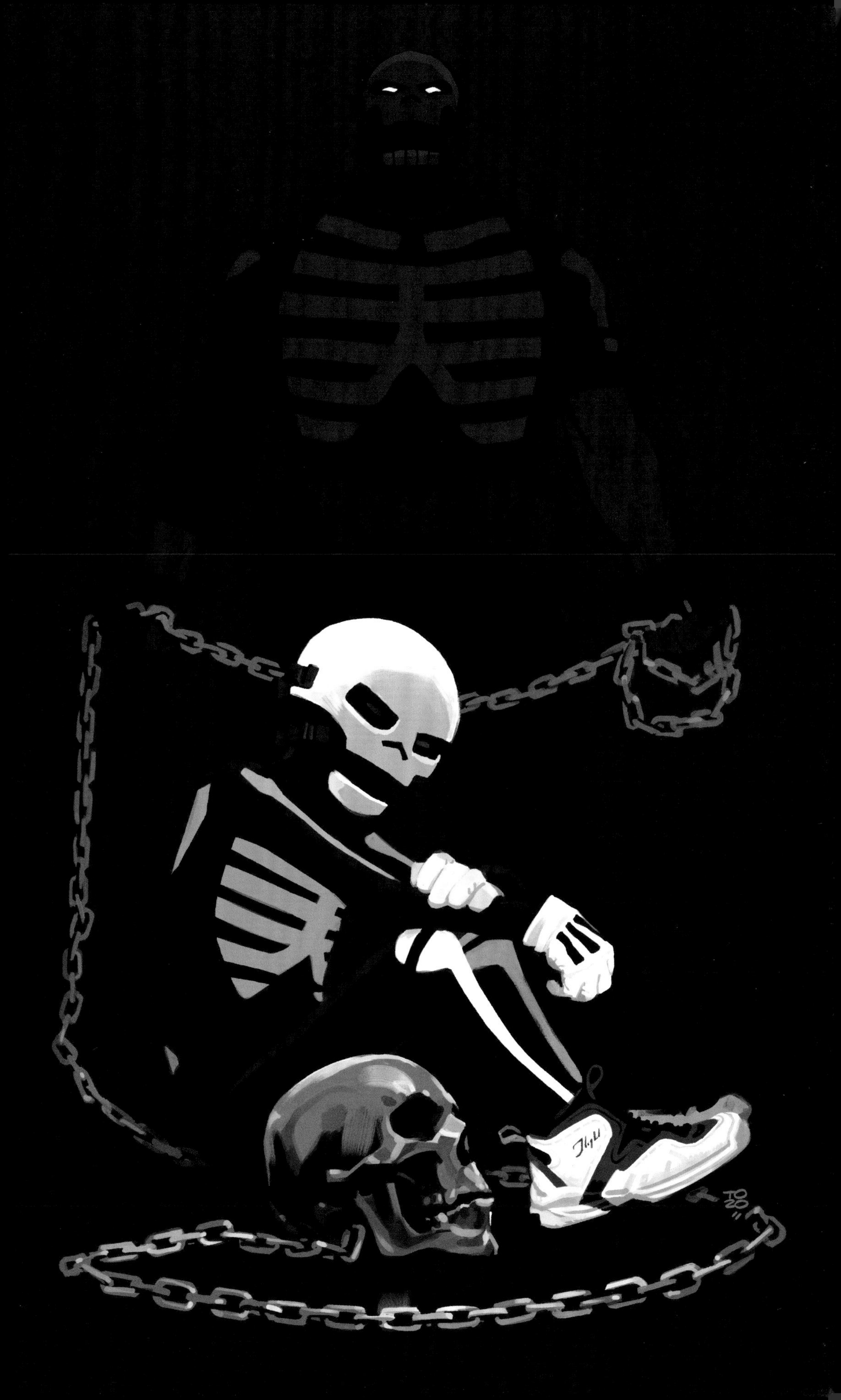

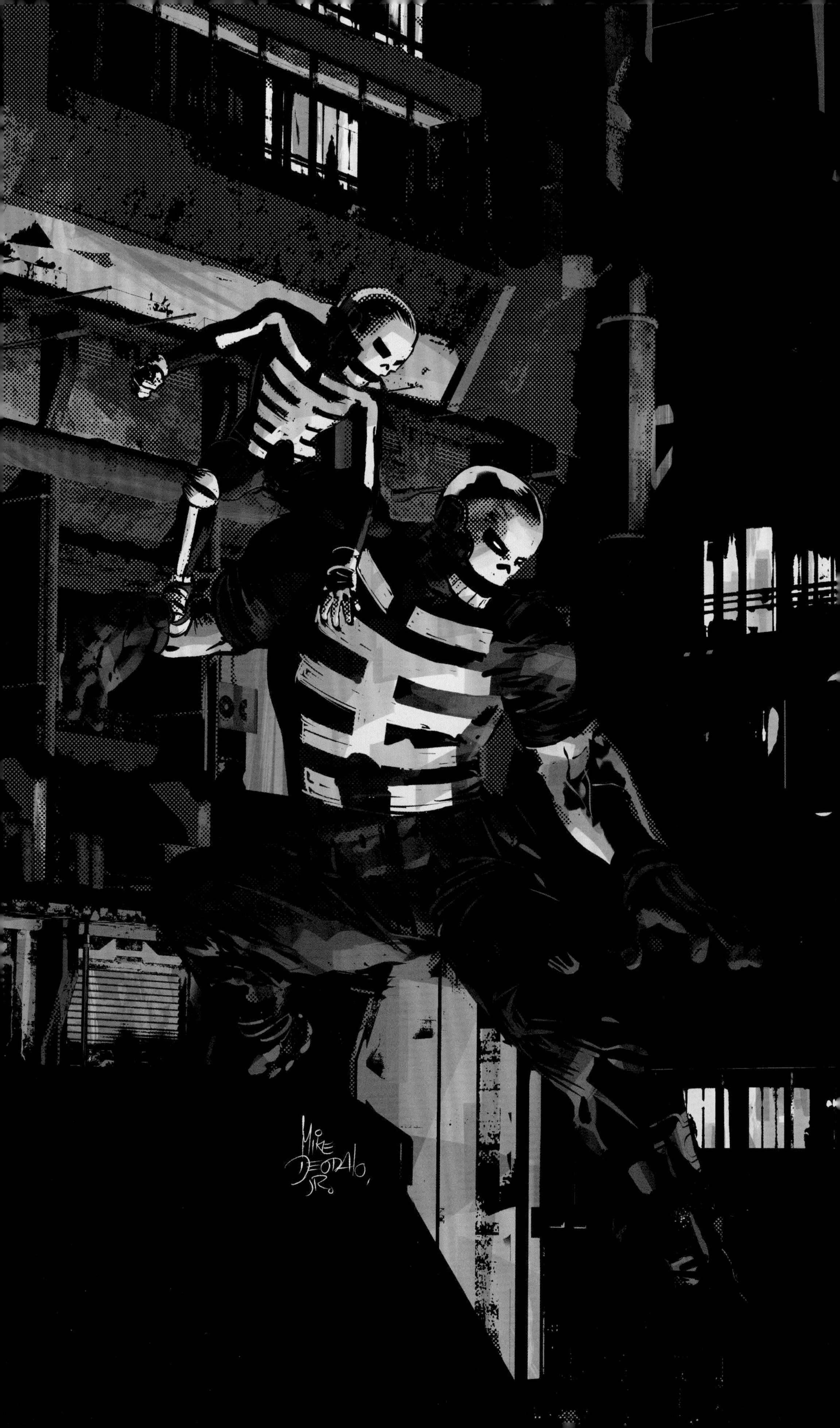
Mike Deodato, Jr.

I'm starting to remember.

I'm starting to remember, but I don't **want** to.

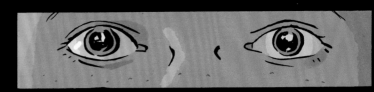

We went to the Italian restaurant I liked. I wanted to have dessert and Mom said no because it was a school night.

But I pouted until she said I could.

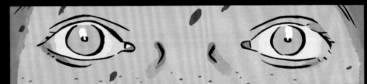

If I hadn't done that we would have left the restaurant a little sooner. Then maybe we wouldn't have been there when he came.

Maybe we would have made it all the way home and everything would be okay.

But I had to have dessert. I had to pout like a baby. And then **I was alone.**

...YOU SAW MY FACE.

CHK

EH?

All alone.

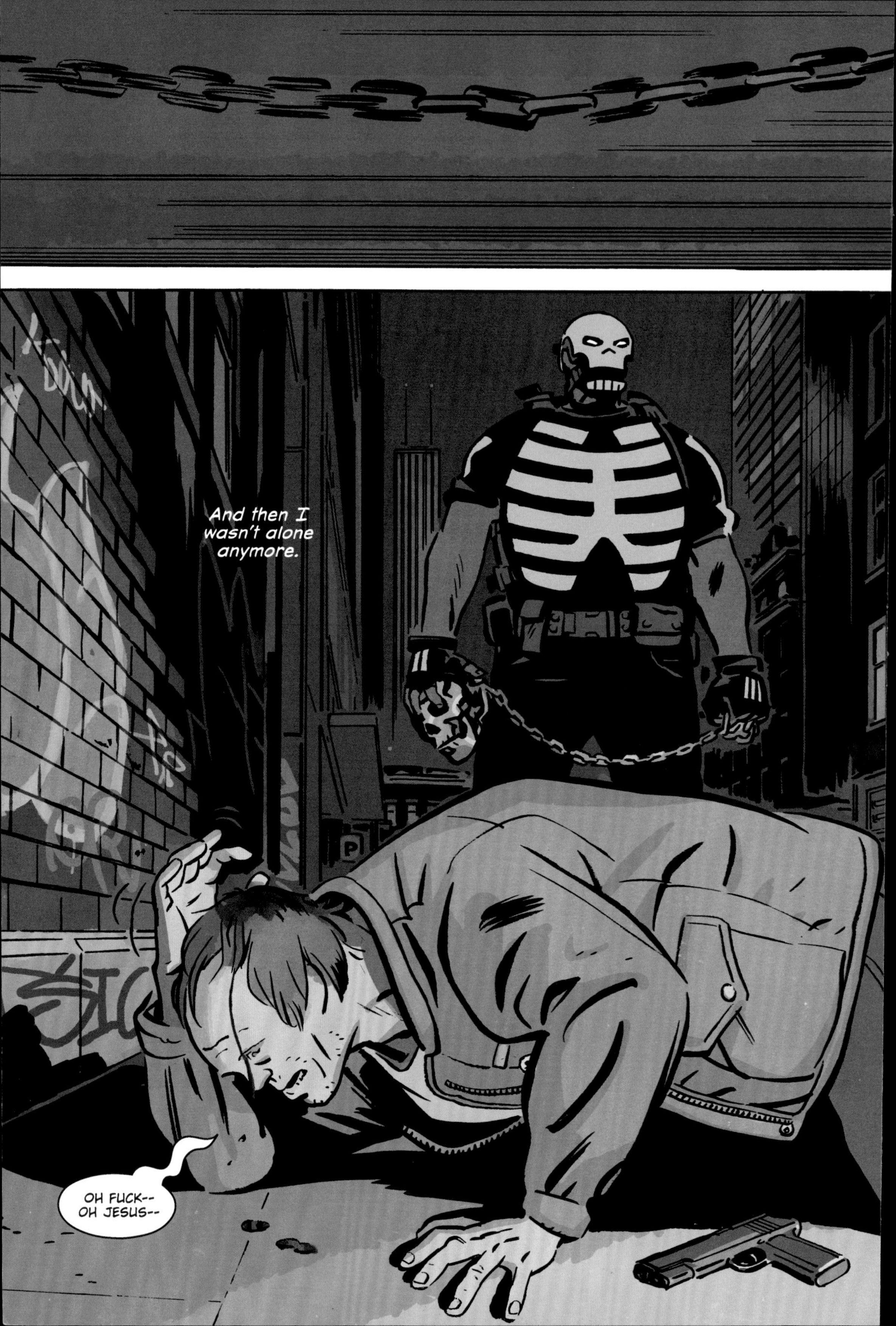
And then I wasn't alone anymore.
OH FUCK-- OH JESUS--

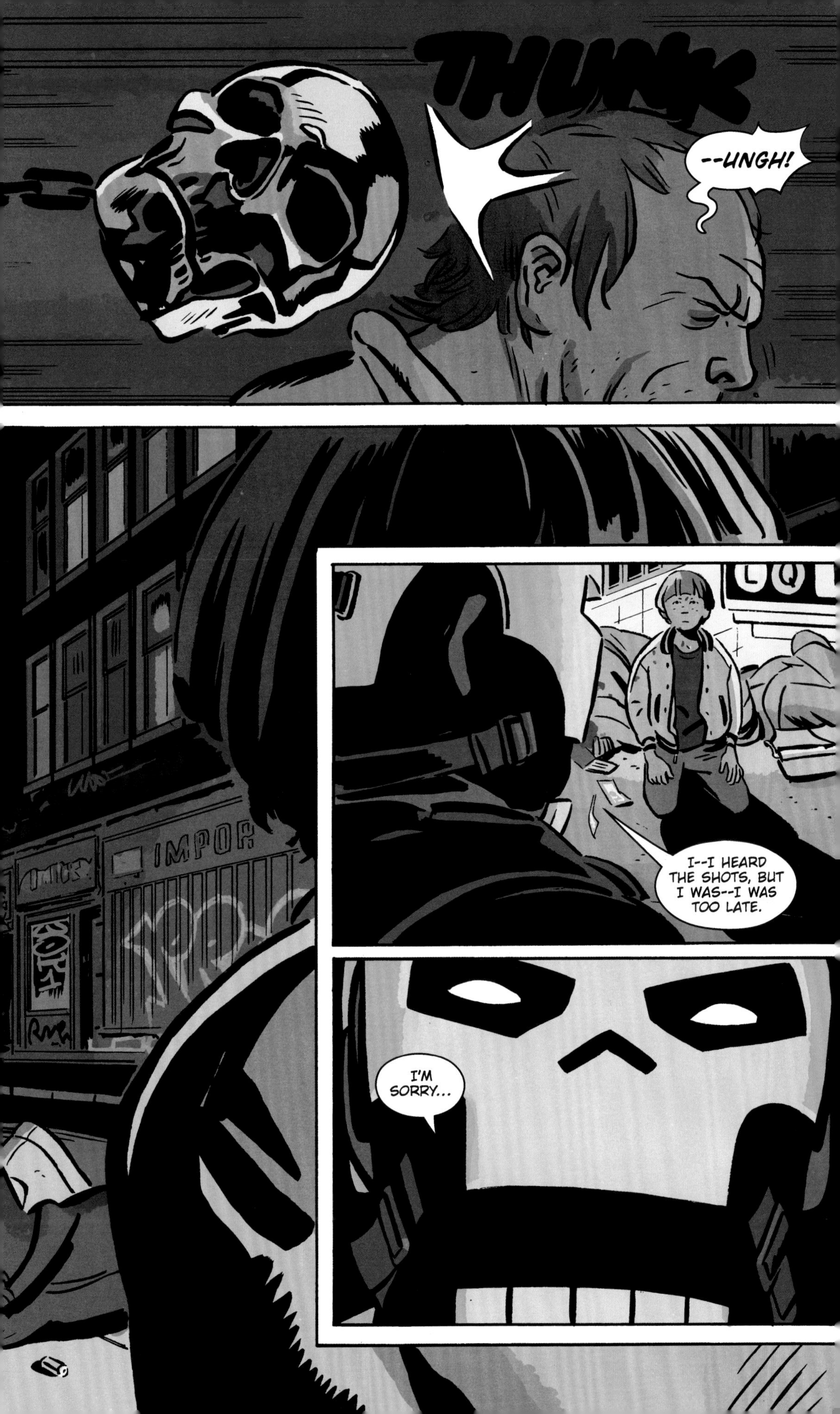
THUNK
--UNGH!
IMPOR
LQ
I--I HEARD THE SHOTS, BUT I WAS--I WAS TOO LATE.
I'M SORRY...

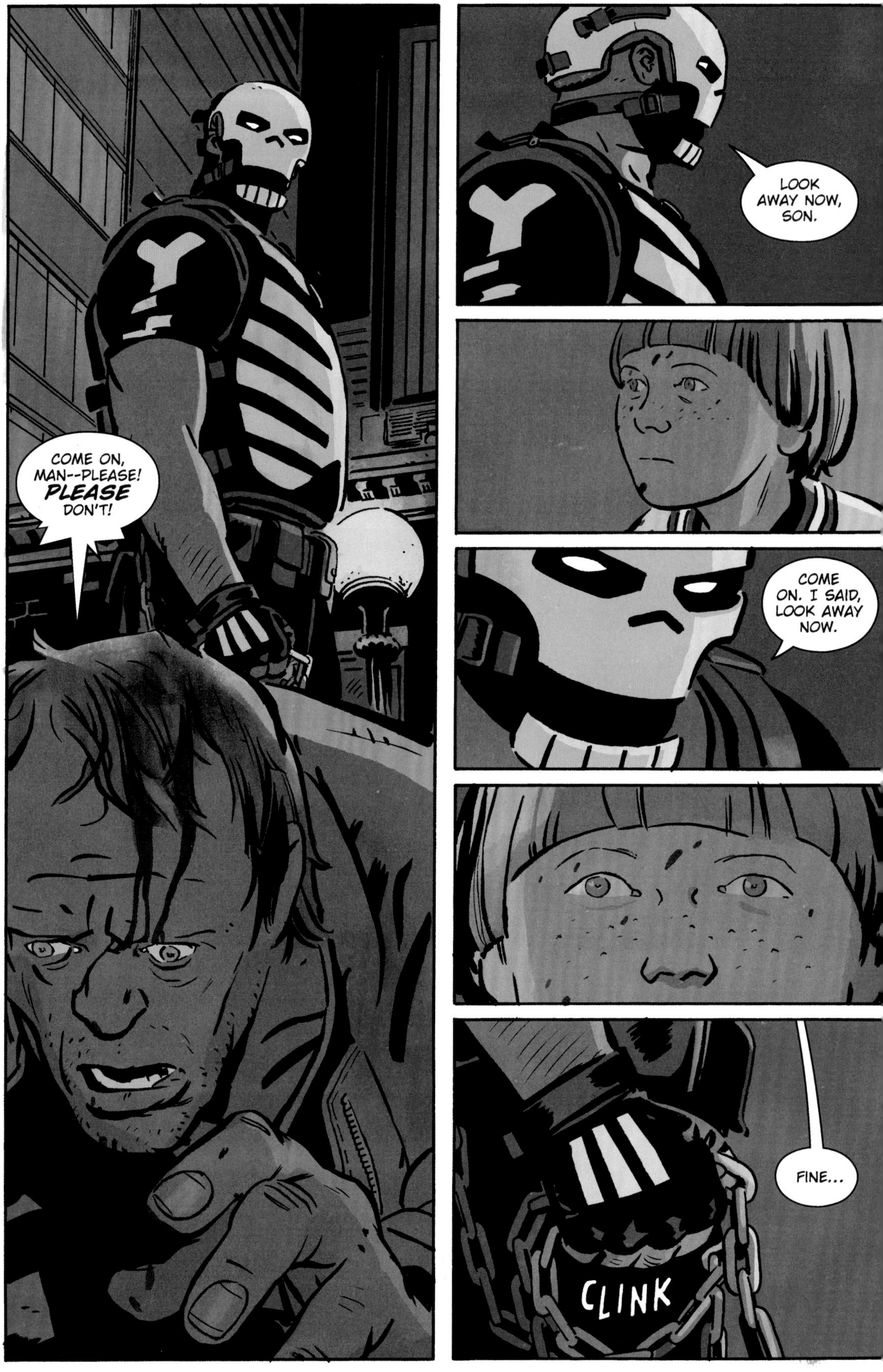
COME ON, MAN--PLEASE! PLEASE DON'T!
LOOK AWAY NOW, SON.
COME ON. I SAID, LOOK AWAY NOW.
FINE...
CLINK

CHUNK

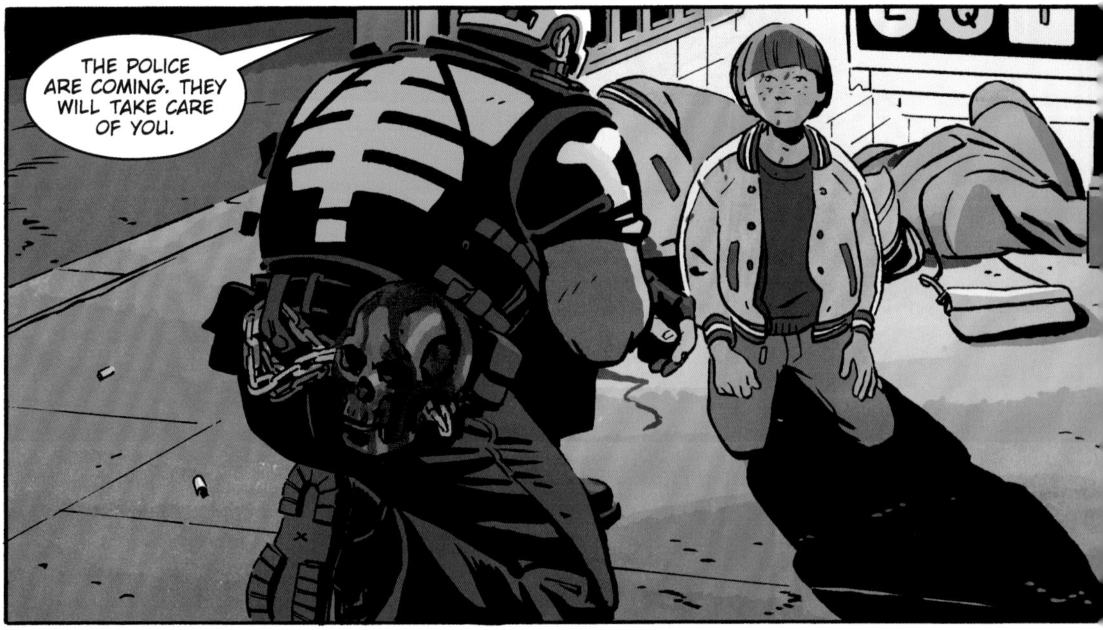
THE POLICE ARE COMING. THEY WILL TAKE CARE OF YOU.

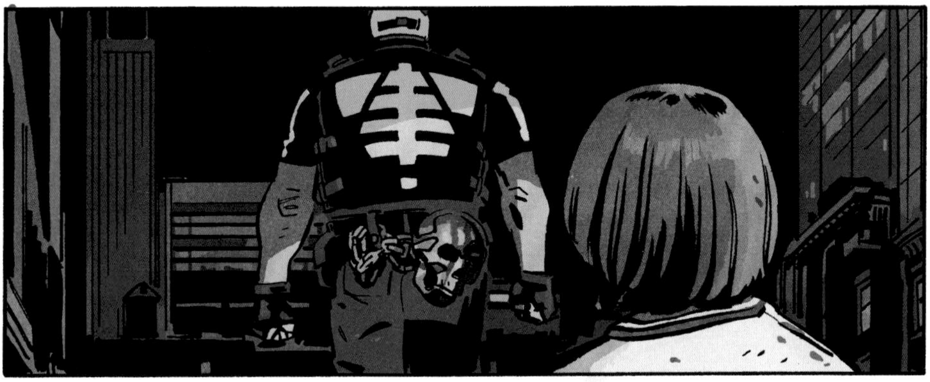

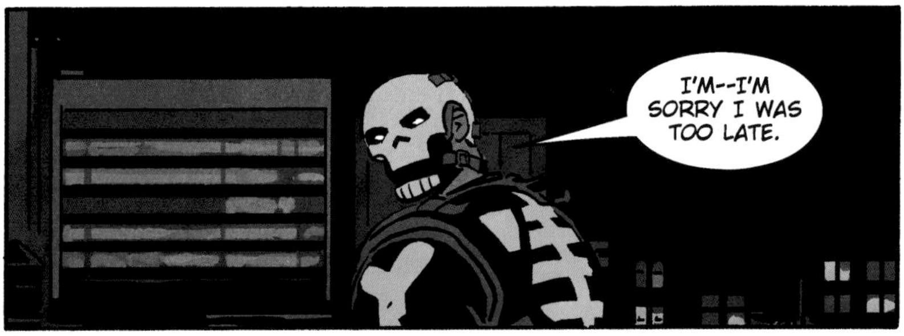
I'M--I'M SORRY I WAS TOO LATE.

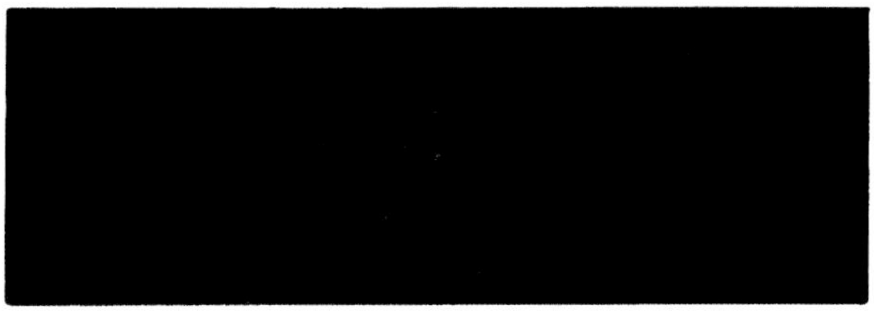

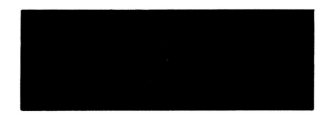

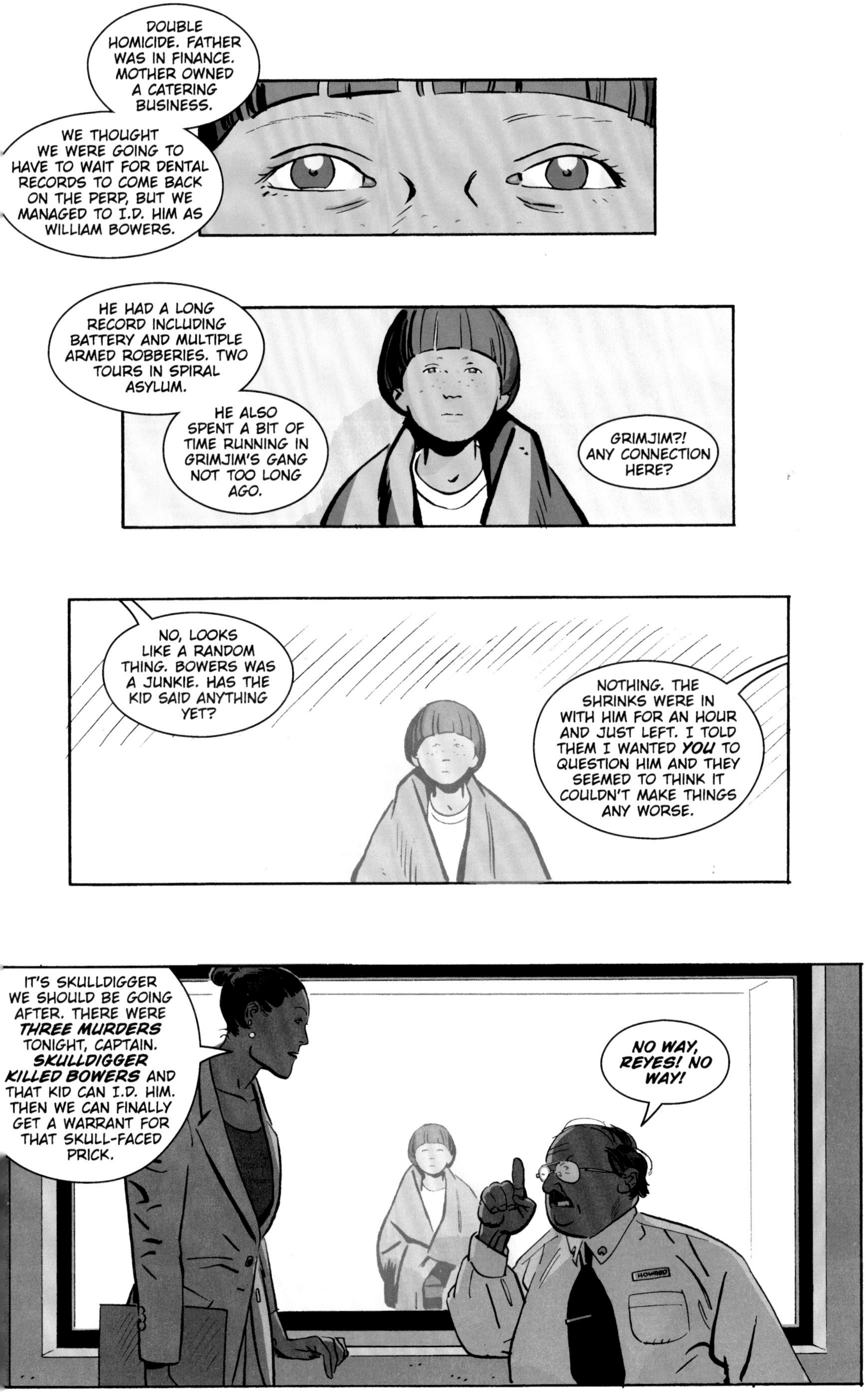
DOUBLE HOMICIDE. FATHER WAS IN FINANCE. MOTHER OWNED A CATERING BUSINESS.
WE THOUGHT WE WERE GOING TO HAVE TO WAIT FOR DENTAL RECORDS TO COME BACK ON THE PERP, BUT WE MANAGED TO I.D. HIM AS WILLIAM BOWERS.
HE HAD A LONG RECORD INCLUDING BATTERY AND MULTIPLE ARMED ROBBERIES. TWO TOURS IN SPIRAL ASYLUM.
HE ALSO SPENT A BIT OF TIME RUNNING IN GRIMJIM'S GANG NOT TOO LONG AGO.
GRIMJIM?! ANY CONNECTION HERE?
NO, LOOKS LIKE A RANDOM THING. BOWERS WAS A JUNKIE. HAS THE KID SAID ANYTHING YET?
NOTHING. THE SHRINKS WERE IN WITH HIM FOR AN HOUR AND JUST LEFT. I TOLD THEM I WANTED ***YOU*** TO QUESTION HIM AND THEY SEEMED TO THINK IT COULDN'T MAKE THINGS ANY WORSE.
IT'S SKULLDIGGER WE SHOULD BE GOING AFTER. THERE WERE ***THREE MURDERS*** TONIGHT, CAPTAIN. ***SKULLDIGGER KILLED BOWERS*** AND THAT KID CAN I.D. HIM. THEN WE CAN FINALLY GET A WARRANT FOR THAT SKULL-FACED PRICK.
NO WAY, REYES! NO WAY!
HOWARD

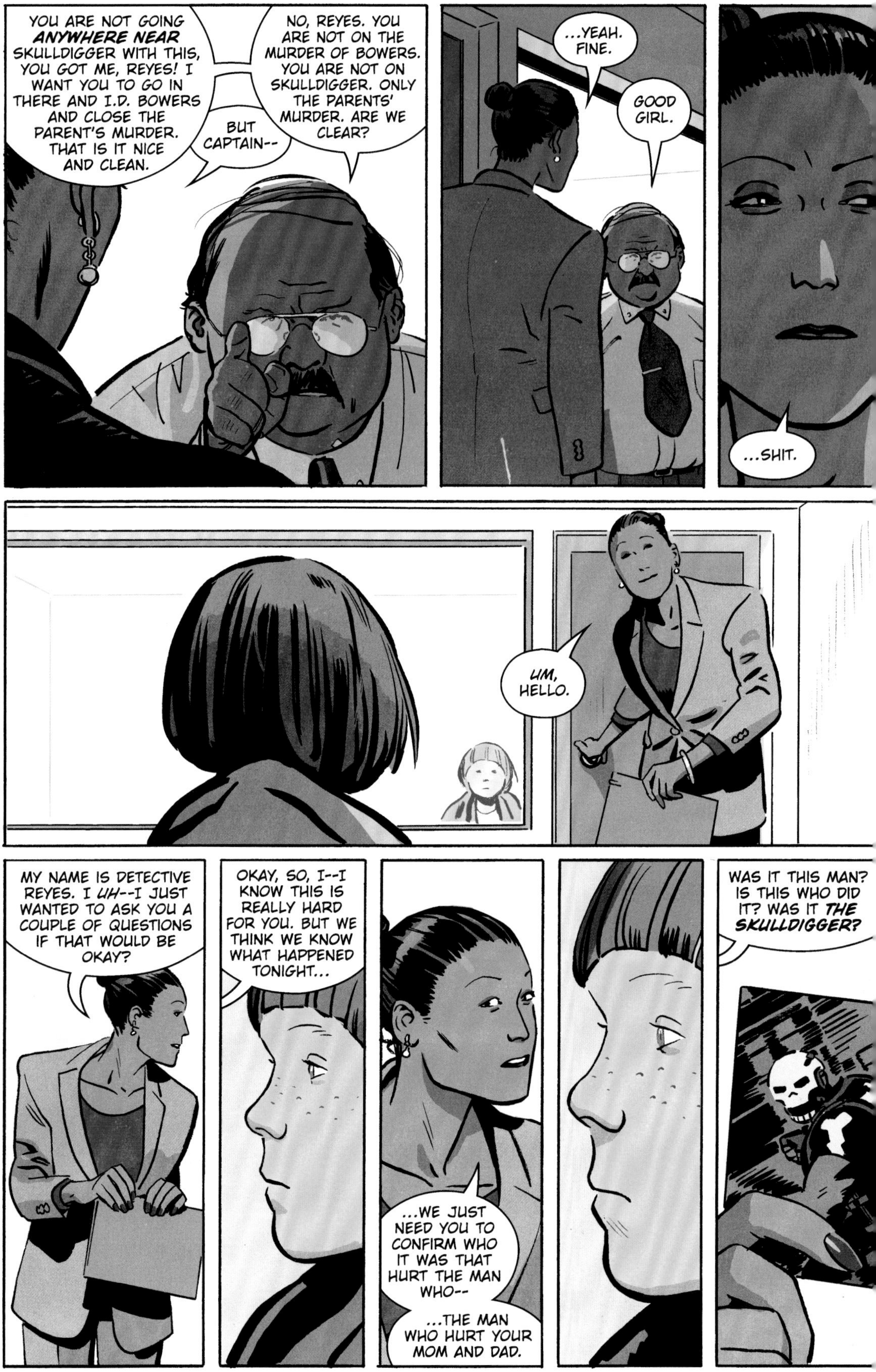
YOU ARE NOT GOING **ANYWHERE NEAR** SKULLDIGGER WITH THIS, YOU GOT ME, REYES! I WANT YOU TO GO IN THERE AND I.D. BOWERS AND CLOSE THE PARENT'S MURDER. THAT IS IT NICE AND CLEAN.
BUT CAPTAIN--
NO, REYES. YOU ARE NOT ON THE MURDER OF BOWERS. YOU ARE NOT ON SKULLDIGGER. ONLY THE PARENTS' MURDER. ARE WE CLEAR?
...YEAH. FINE.
GOOD GIRL.
...SHIT.
UM, HELLO.
MY NAME IS DETECTIVE REYES. I *UH*--I JUST WANTED TO ASK YOU A COUPLE OF QUESTIONS IF THAT WOULD BE OKAY?
OKAY, SO, I--I KNOW THIS IS REALLY HARD FOR YOU. BUT WE THINK WE KNOW WHAT HAPPENED TONIGHT...
...WE JUST NEED YOU TO CONFIRM WHO IT WAS THAT HURT THE MAN WHO--
...THE MAN WHO HURT YOUR MOM AND DAD.
WAS IT THIS MAN? IS THIS WHO DID IT? WAS IT ***THE SKULLDIGGER?***

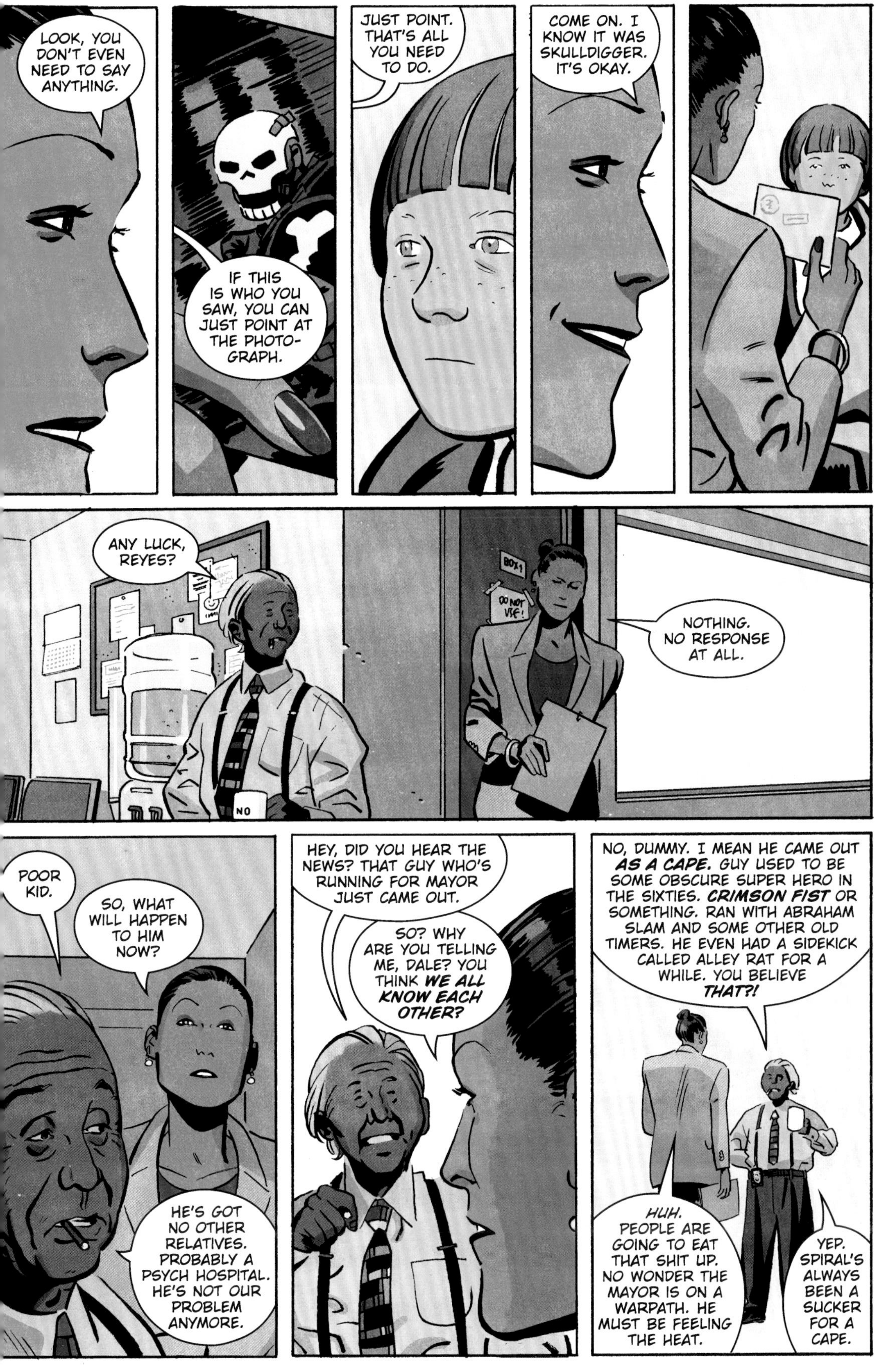
LOOK, YOU DON'T EVEN NEED TO SAY ANYTHING.
IF THIS IS WHO YOU SAW, YOU CAN JUST POINT AT THE PHOTOGRAPH.
JUST POINT. THAT'S ALL YOU NEED TO DO.
COME ON. I KNOW IT WAS SKULLDIGGER. IT'S OKAY.
ANY LUCK, REYES?
NO
BOX 1
DO NOT USE!
NOTHING. NO RESPONSE AT ALL.
POOR KID.
SO, WHAT WILL HAPPEN TO HIM NOW?
HE'S GOT NO OTHER RELATIVES. PROBABLY A PSYCH HOSPITAL. HE'S NOT OUR PROBLEM ANYMORE.
HEY, DID YOU HEAR THE NEWS? THAT GUY WHO'S RUNNING FOR MAYOR JUST CAME OUT.
SO? WHY ARE YOU TELLING ME, DALE? YOU THINK ***WE ALL KNOW EACH OTHER?***
NO, DUMMY. I MEAN HE CAME OUT ***AS A CAPE.*** GUY USED TO BE SOME OBSCURE SUPER HERO IN THE SIXTIES. ***CRIMSON FIST*** OR SOMETHING. RAN WITH ABRAHAM SLAM AND SOME OTHER OLD TIMERS. HE EVEN HAD A SIDEKICK CALLED ALLEY RAT FOR A WHILE. YOU BELIEVE ***THAT?!***
HUH. PEOPLE ARE GOING TO EAT THAT SHIT UP. NO WONDER THE MAYOR IS ON A WARPATH. HE MUST BE FEELING THE HEAT.
YEP. SPIRAL'S ALWAYS BEEN A SUCKER FOR A CAPE.

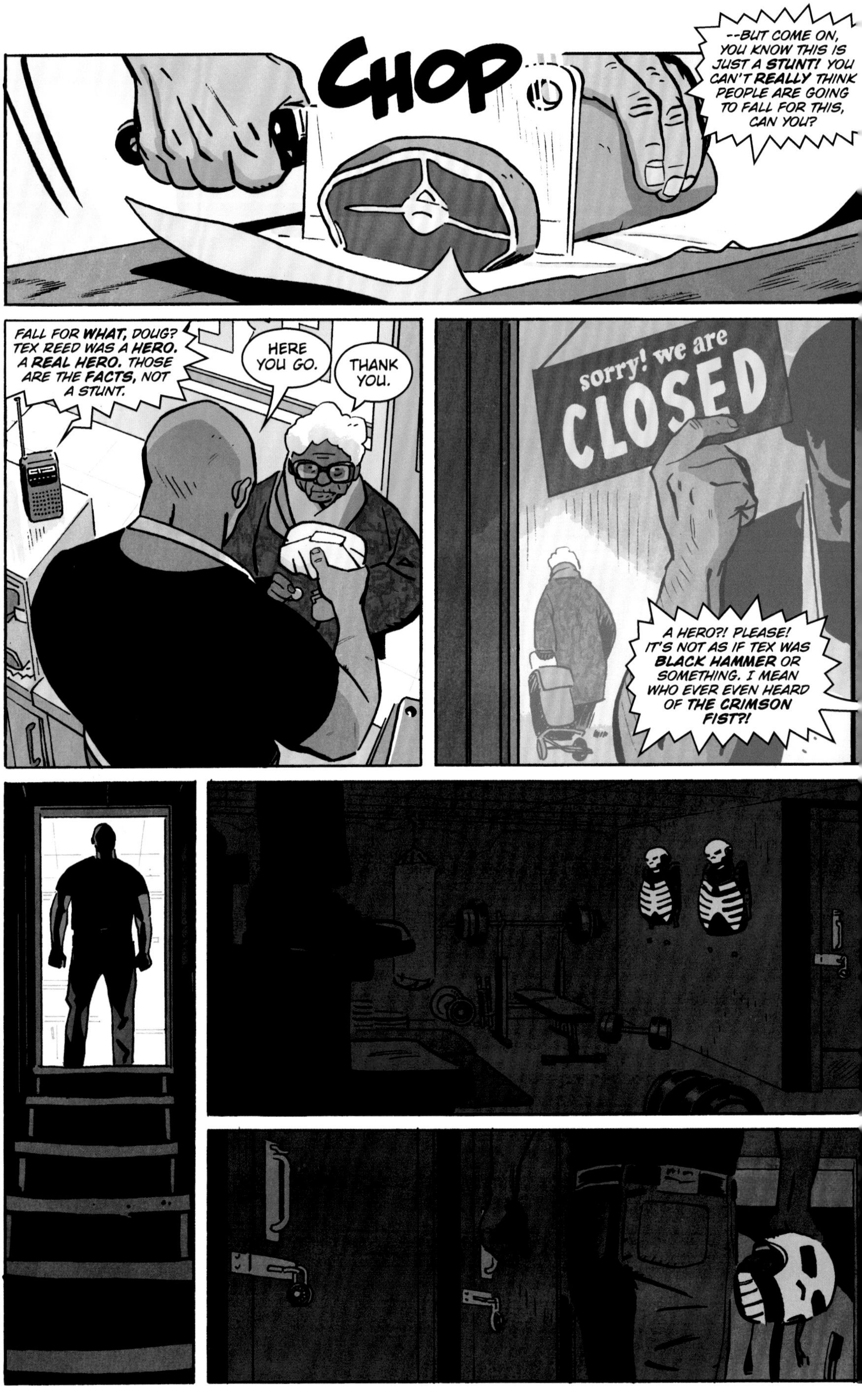
CHOP
--BUT COME ON, YOU KNOW THIS IS JUST A STUNT! YOU CAN'T REALLY THINK PEOPLE ARE GOING TO FALL FOR THIS, CAN YOU?
FALL FOR WHAT, DOUG? TEX REED WAS A HERO. A REAL HERO. THOSE ARE THE FACTS, NOT A STUNT.
HERE YOU GO.
THANK YOU.
sorry! we are CLOSED
A HERO?! PLEASE! IT'S NOT AS IF TEX WAS BLACK HAMMER OR SOMETHING. I MEAN WHO EVER EVEN HEARD OF THE CRIMSON FIST?!

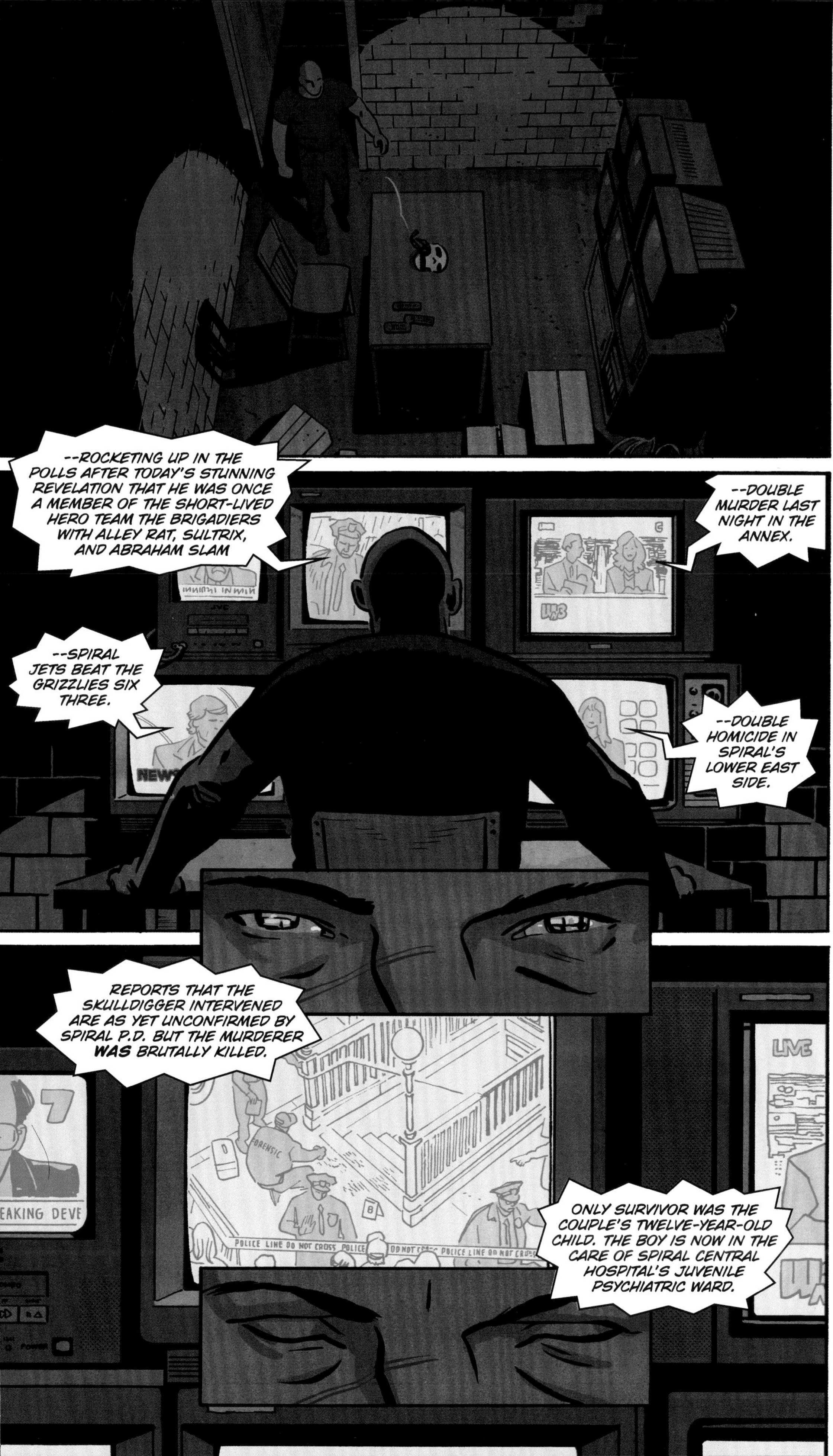
--ROCKETING UP IN THE POLLS AFTER TODAY'S STUNNING REVELATION THAT HE WAS ONCE A MEMBER OF THE SHORT-LIVED HERO TEAM THE BRIGADIERS WITH ALLEY RAT, SULTRIX, AND ABRAHAM SLAM
--DOUBLE MURDER LAST NIGHT IN THE ANNEX.
--SPIRAL JETS BEAT THE GRIZZLIES SIX THREE.
--DOUBLE HOMICIDE IN SPIRAL'S LOWER EAST SIDE.
REPORTS THAT THE SKULLDIGGER INTERVENED ARE AS YET UNCONFIRMED BY SPIRAL P.D. BUT THE MURDERER **WAS** BRUTALLY KILLED.
ONLY SURVIVOR WAS THE COUPLE'S TWELVE-YEAR-OLD CHILD. THE BOY IS NOW IN THE CARE OF SPIRAL CENTRAL HOSPITAL'S JUVENILE PSYCHIATRIC WARD.
FORENSIC
POLICE LINE DO NOT CROSS POLICE
LIVE
EAKING DEVE

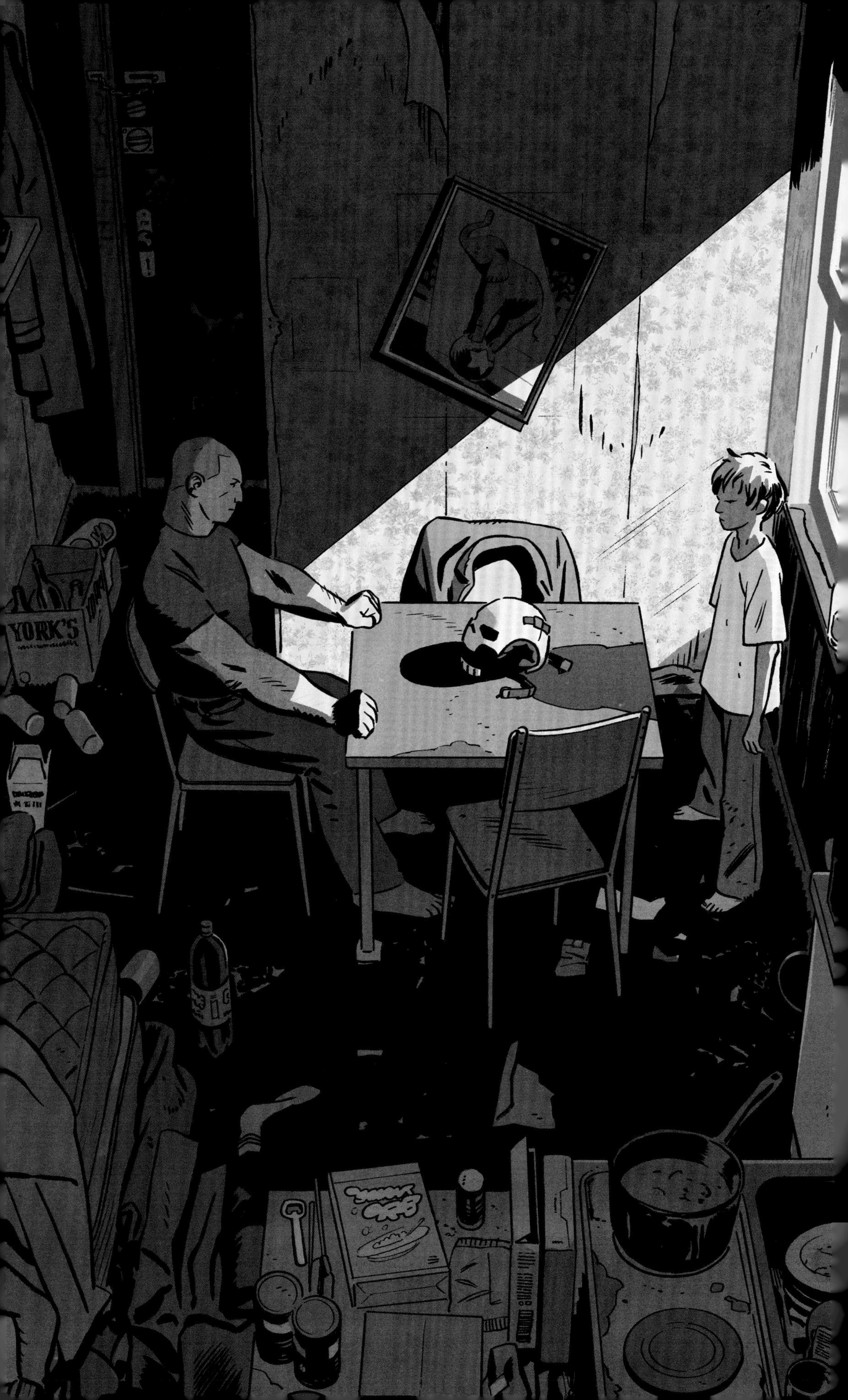
YORK'S

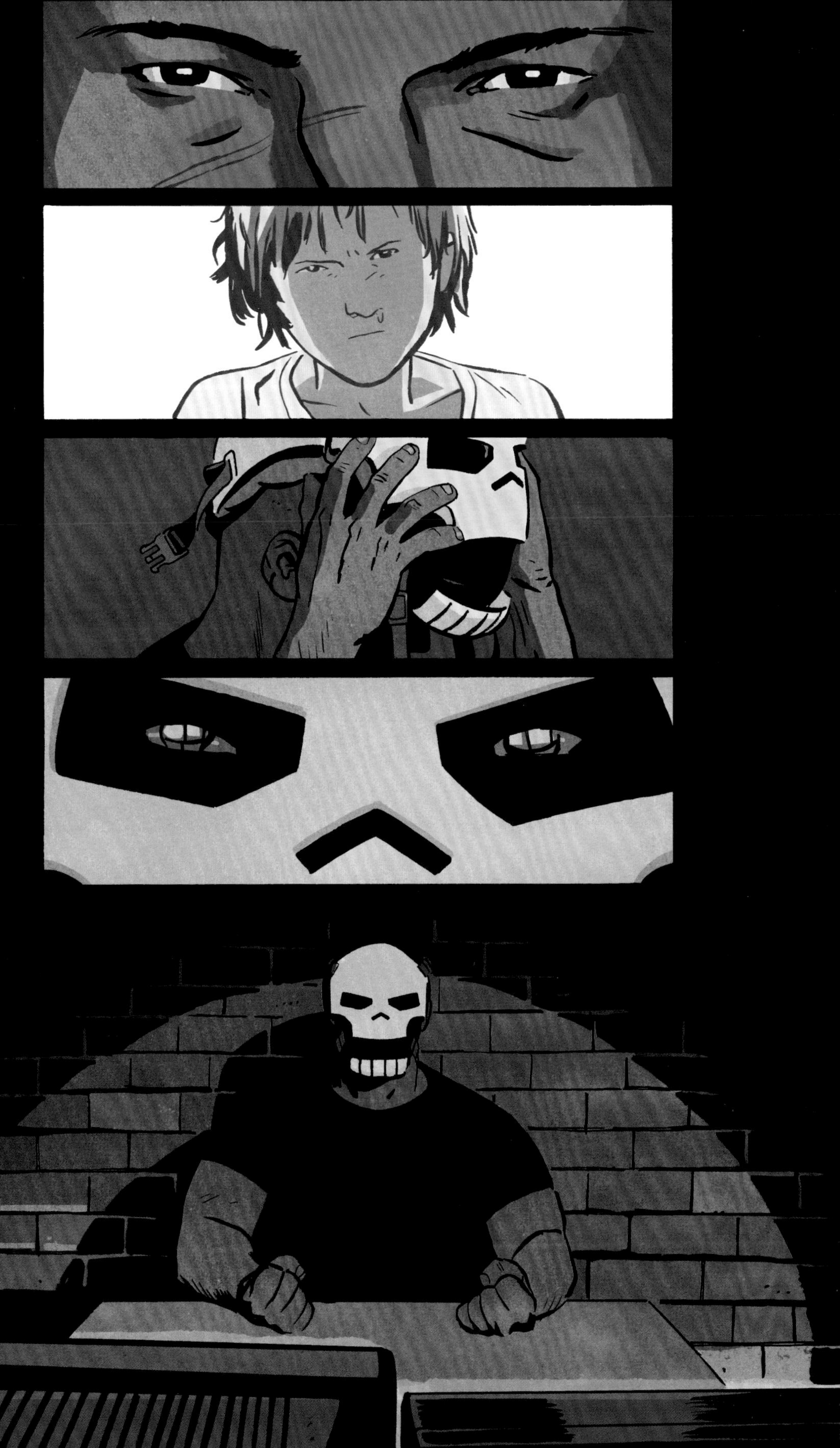

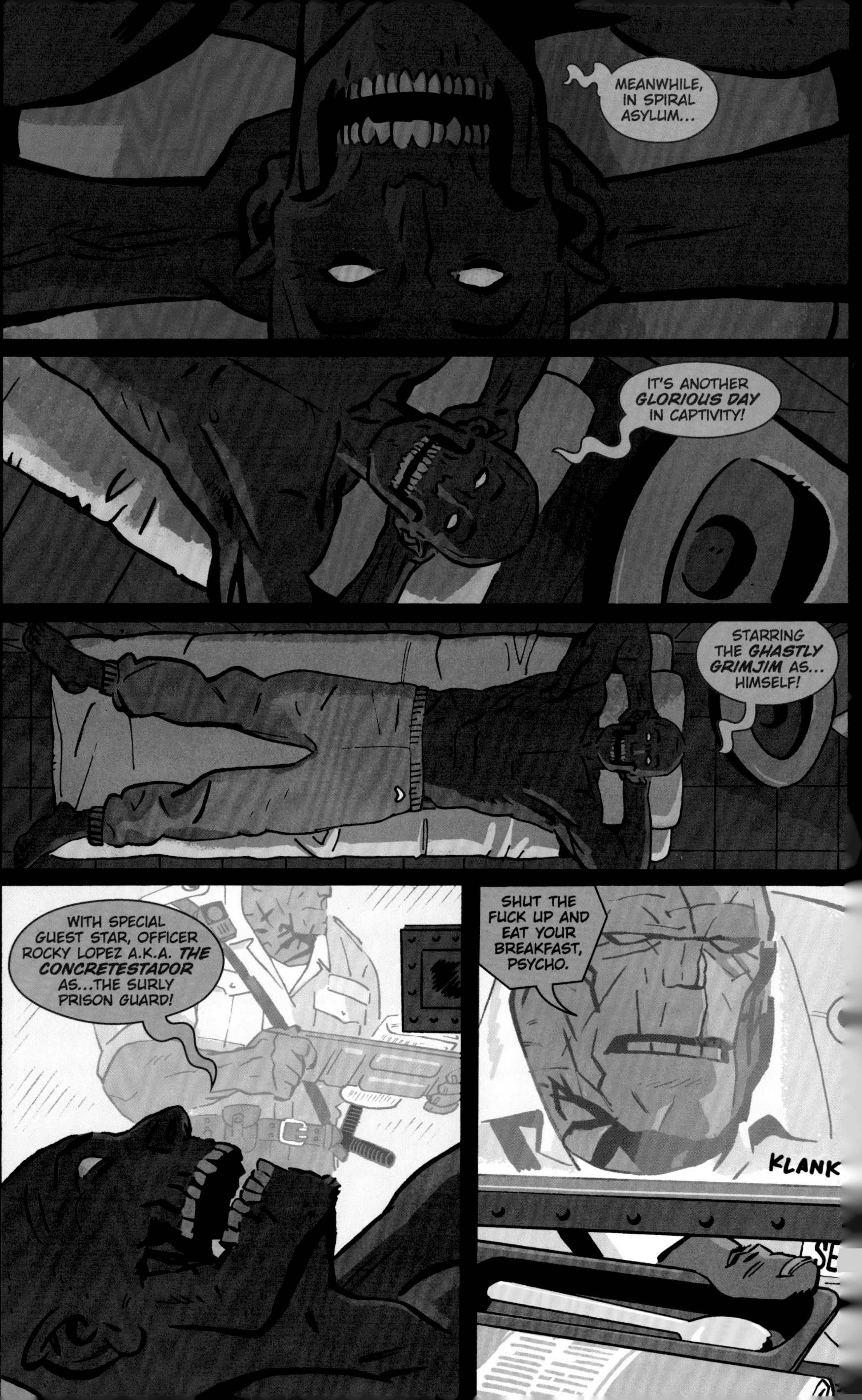
MEANWHILE, IN SPIRAL ASYLUM...
IT'S ANOTHER GLORIOUS DAY IN CAPTIVITY!
STARRING THE GHASTLY GRIMJIM AS... HIMSELF!
WITH SPECIAL GUEST STAR, OFFICER ROCKY LOPEZ A.K.A. THE CONCRETESTADOR AS...THE SURLY PRISON GUARD!
SHUT THE FUCK UP AND EAT YOUR BREAKFAST, PSYCHO.
KLANK

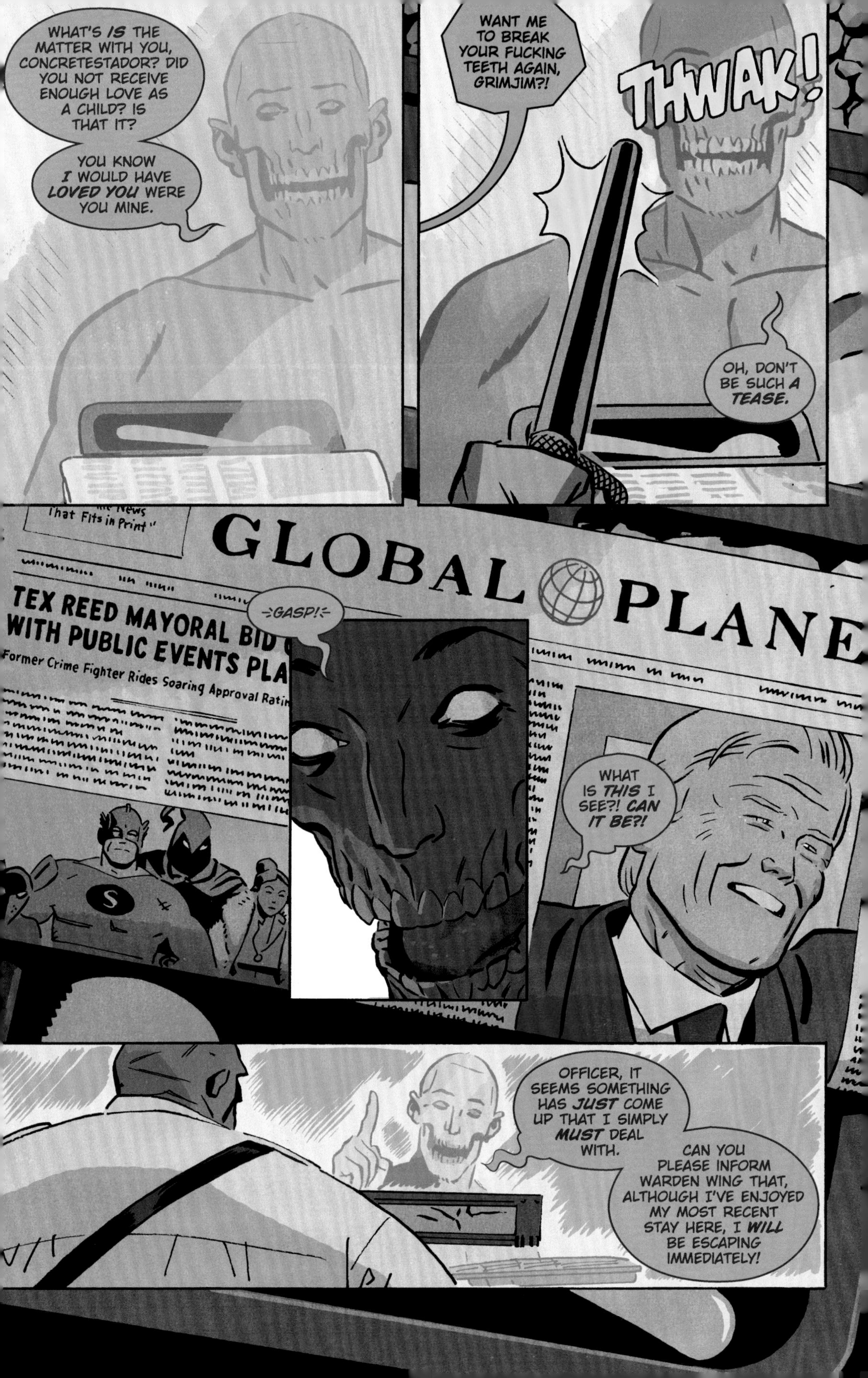
WHAT'S *IS* THE MATTER WITH YOU, CONCRETESTADOR? DID YOU NOT RECEIVE ENOUGH LOVE AS A CHILD? IS THAT IT?
YOU KNOW *I* WOULD HAVE *LOVED YOU* WERE YOU MINE.
WANT ME TO BREAK YOUR FUCKING TEETH AGAIN, GRIMJIM?!
THWAK!
OH, DON'T BE SUCH *A TEASE.*
"That Fits in Print"
GLOBAL PLANE
TEX REED MAYORAL BID
WITH PUBLIC EVENTS PLA
Former Crime Fighter Rides Soaring Approval Ratin
GASP!
WHAT IS *THIS* I SEE?! *CAN IT BE?!*
OFFICER, IT SEEMS SOMETHING HAS *JUST* COME UP THAT I SIMPLY *MUST* DEAL WITH.
CAN YOU PLEASE INFORM WARDEN WING THAT, ALTHOUGH I'VE ENJOYED MY MOST RECENT STAY HERE, I *WILL* BE ESCAPING IMMEDIATELY!

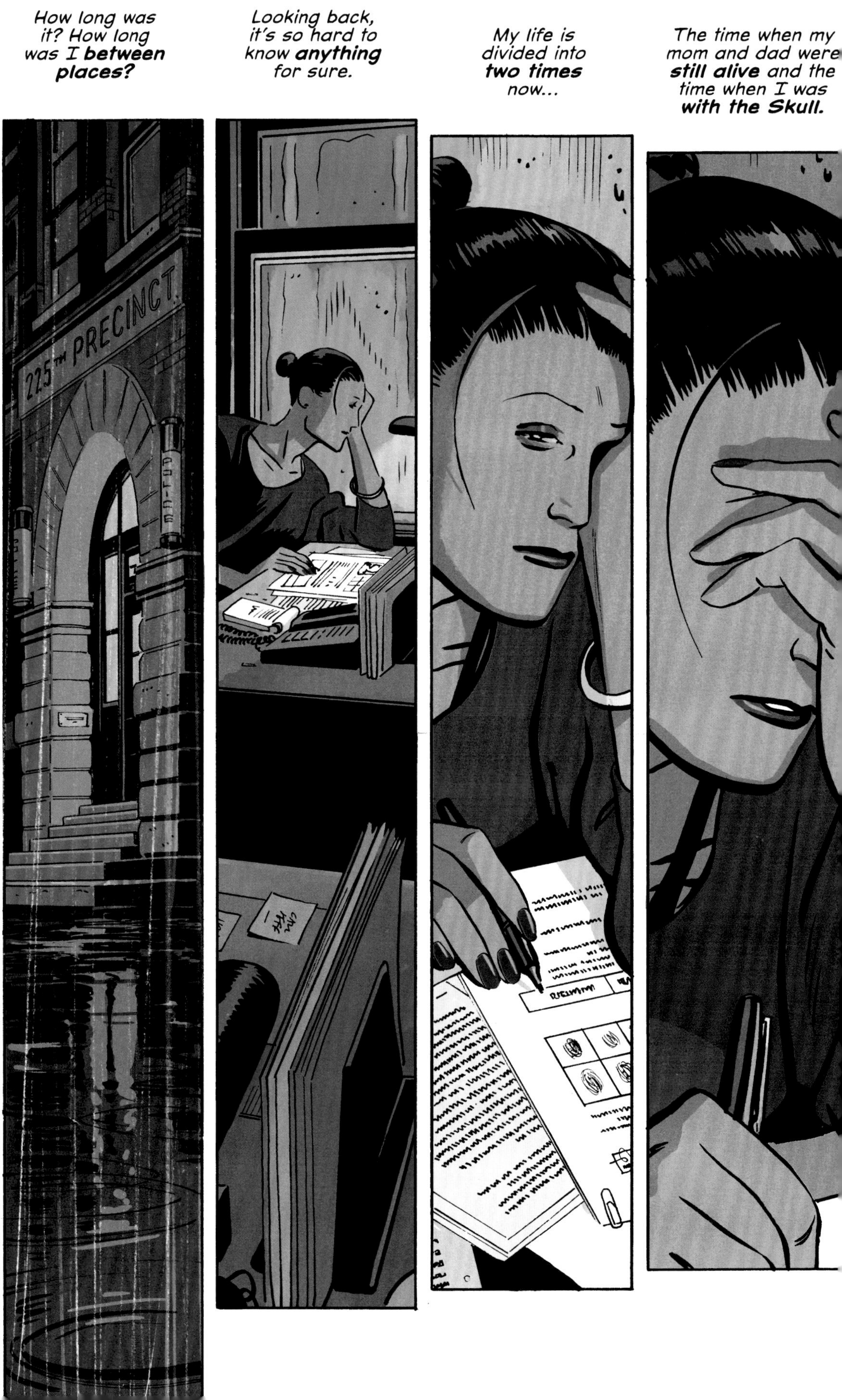
How long was it? How long was I **between places?**
225TH PRECINCT
Looking back, it's so hard to know **anything** for sure.
My life is divided into **two times** now...
The time when my mom and dad were **still alive** and the time when I was **with the Skull.**

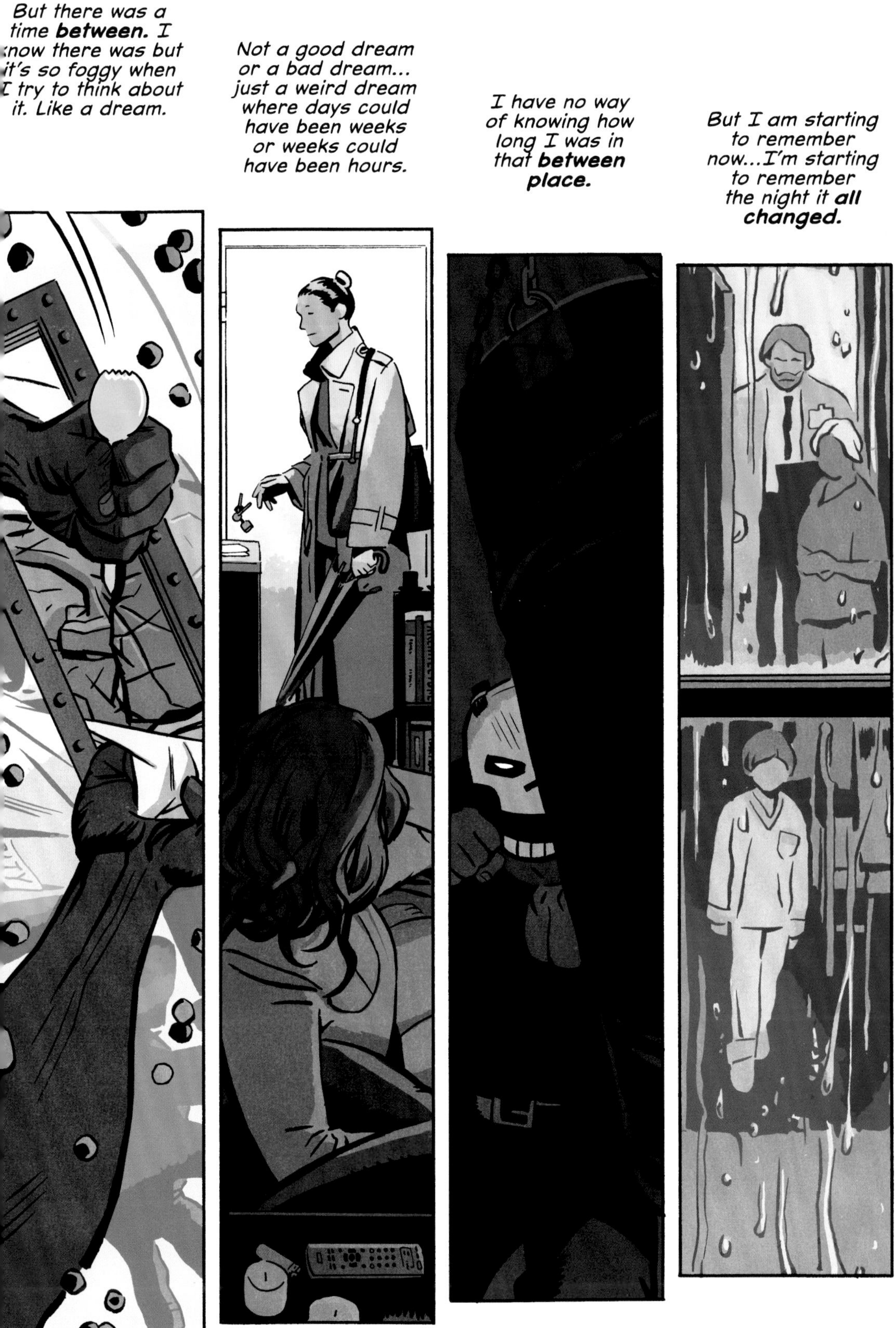
But there was a time **between.** I know there was but it's so foggy when I try to think about it. Like a dream.
Not a good dream or a bad dream... just a weird dream where days could have been weeks or weeks could have been hours.
I have no way of knowing how long I was in that **between place.**
But I am starting to remember now...I'm starting to remember the night it **all changed.**

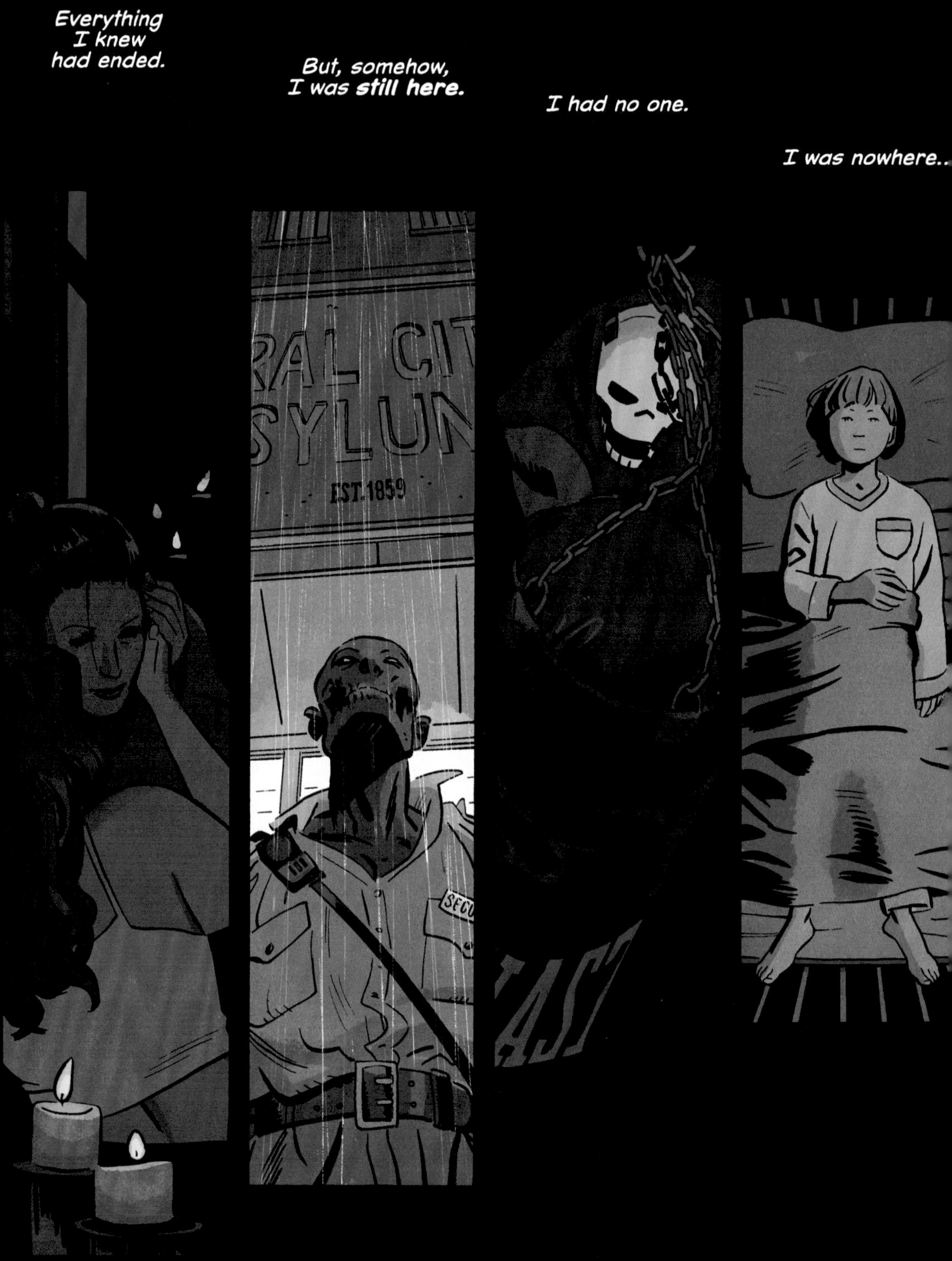
Everything I knew had ended.
But, somehow, I was **still here.**
I had no one.
I was nowhere...
EST.1859

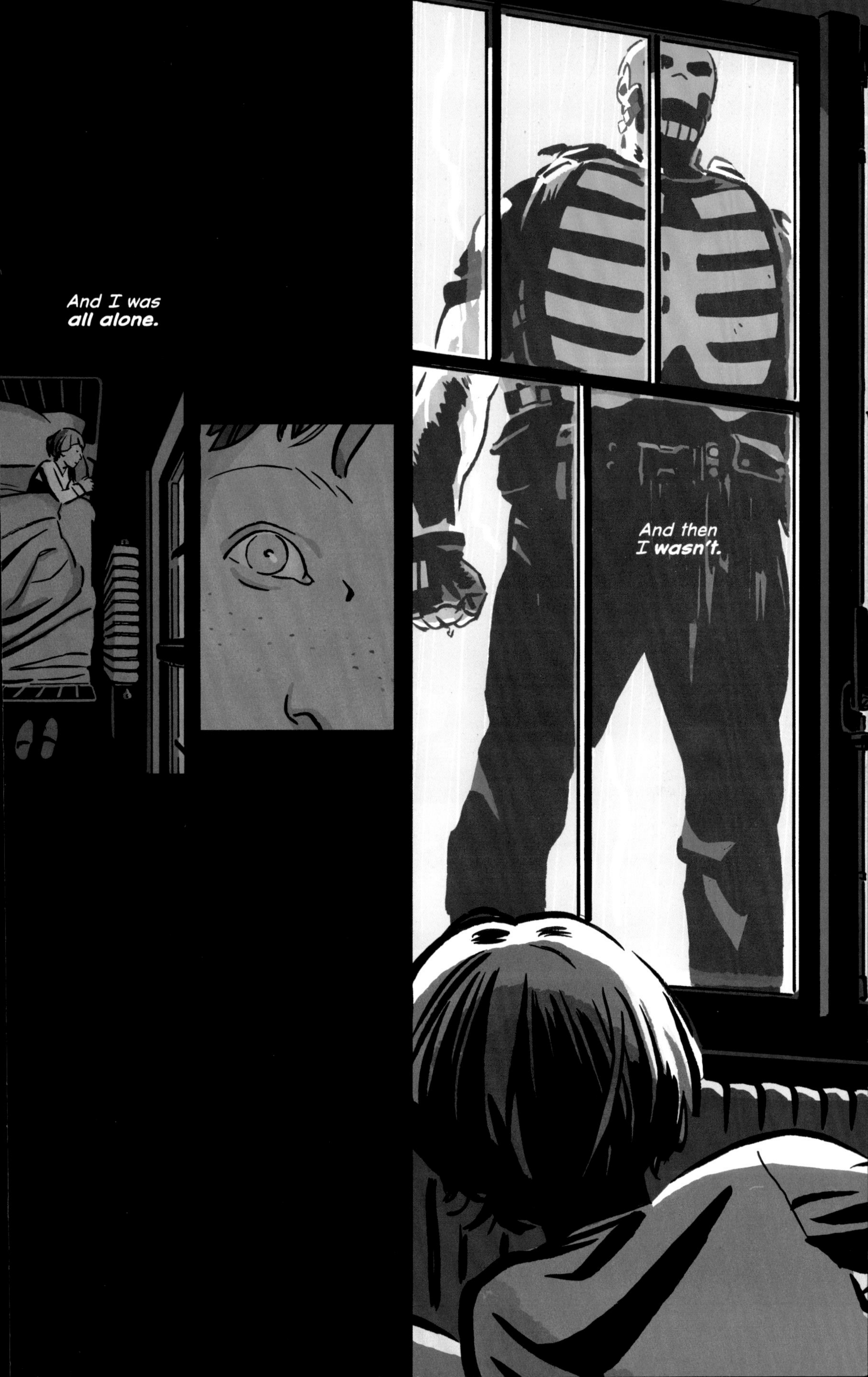
And I was all alone.
And then I wasn't.

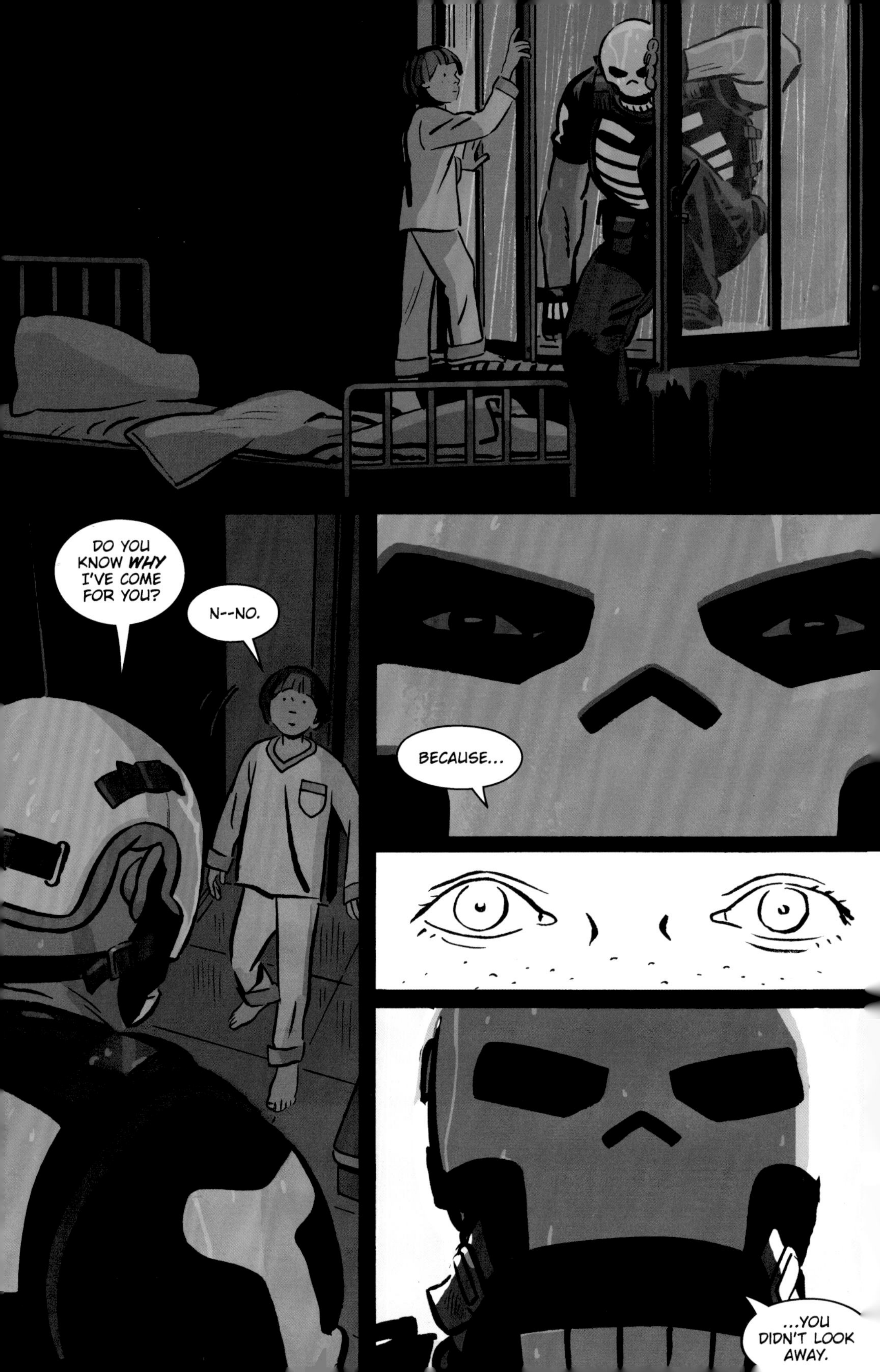
DO YOU KNOW WHY I'VE COME FOR YOU?
N--NO.
BECAUSE...
...YOU DIDN'T LOOK AWAY.

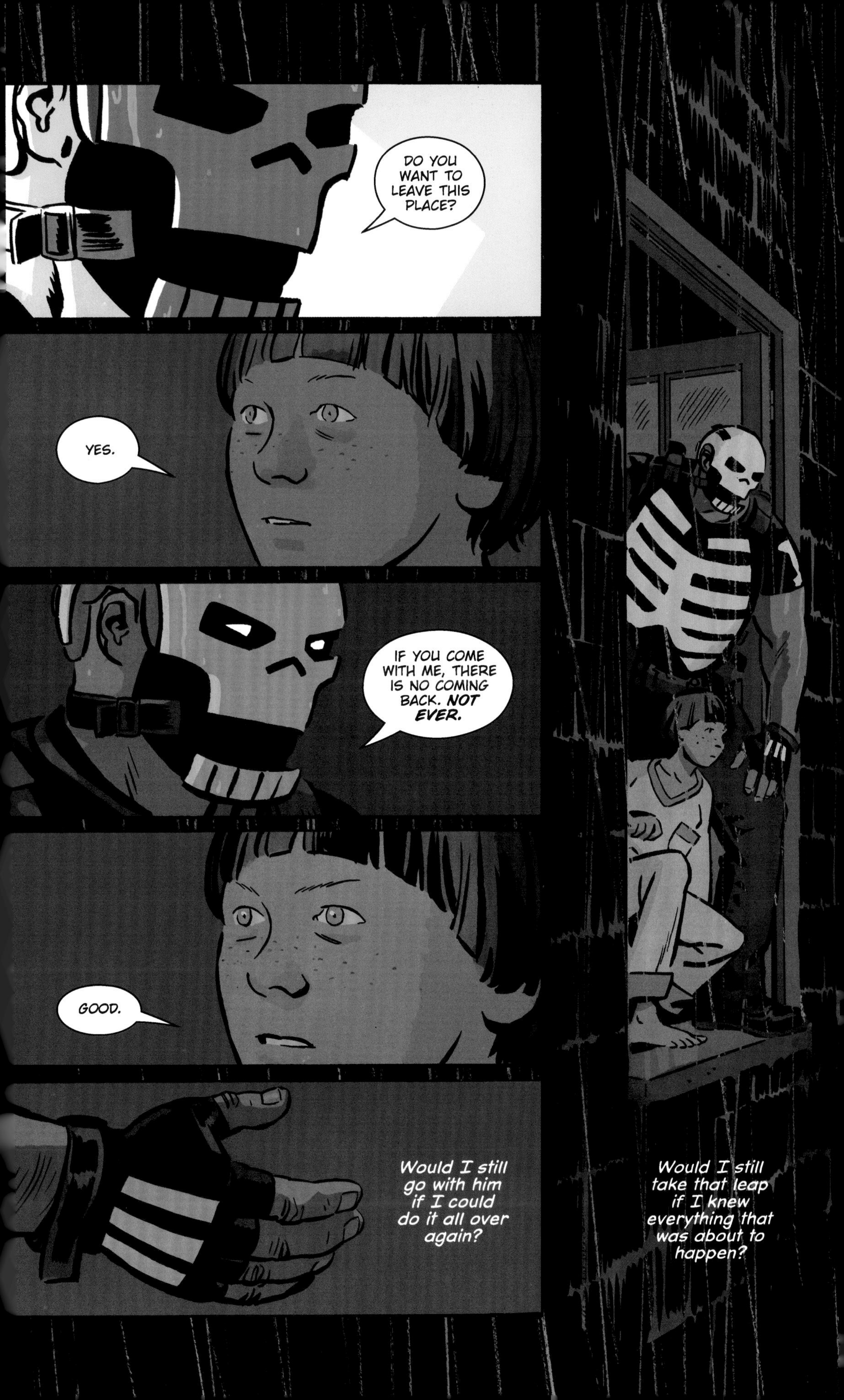
DO YOU WANT TO LEAVE THIS PLACE?
YES.
IF YOU COME WITH ME, THERE IS NO COMING BACK. **NOT EVER.**
GOOD.
Would I still go with him if I could do it all over again?
Would I still take that leap if I knew everything that was about to happen?

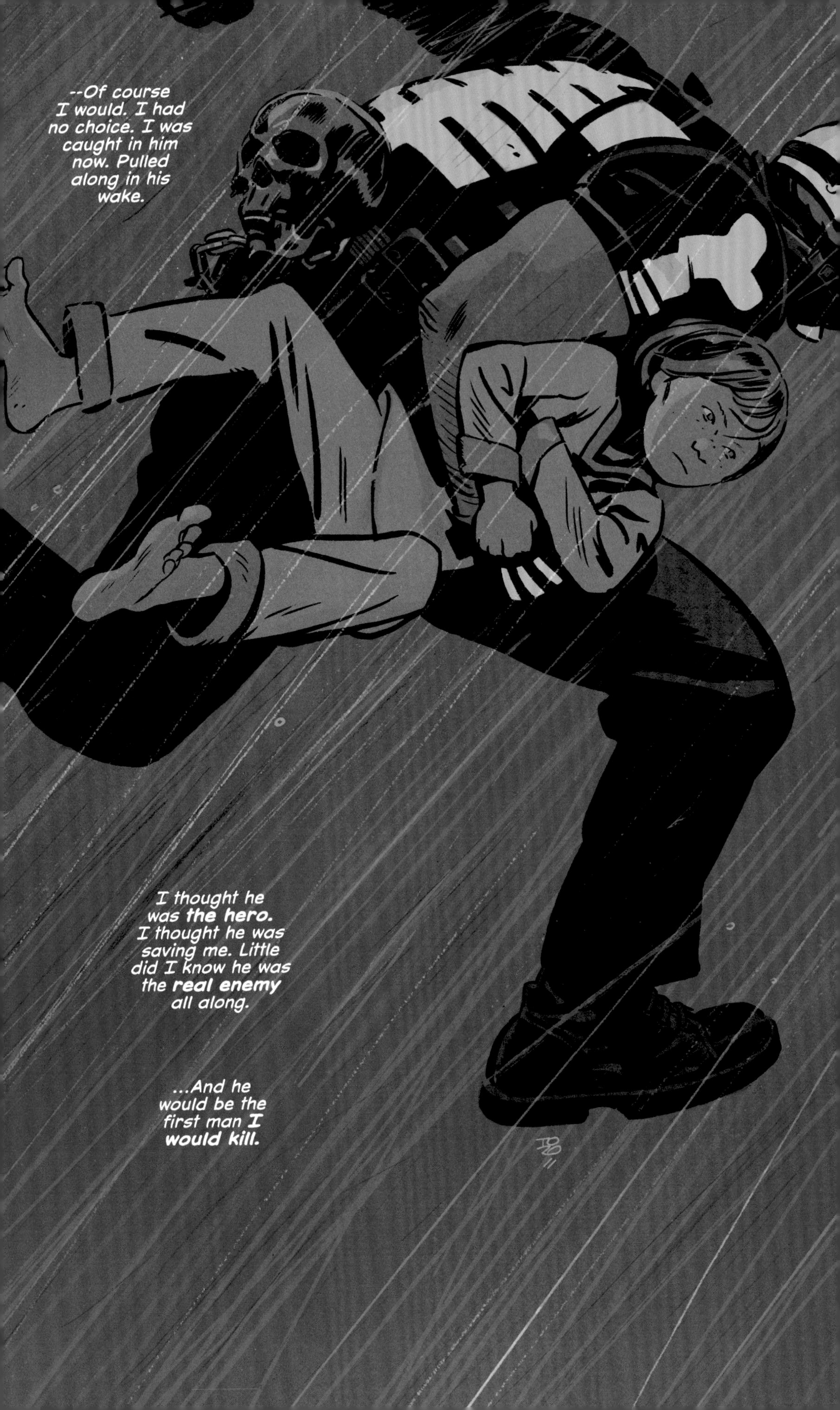
--Of course I would. I had no choice. I was caught in him now. Pulled along in his wake.
I thought he was **the hero.** I thought he was saving me. Little did I know he was the **real enemy** all along.
...And he would be the first man **I would kill.**

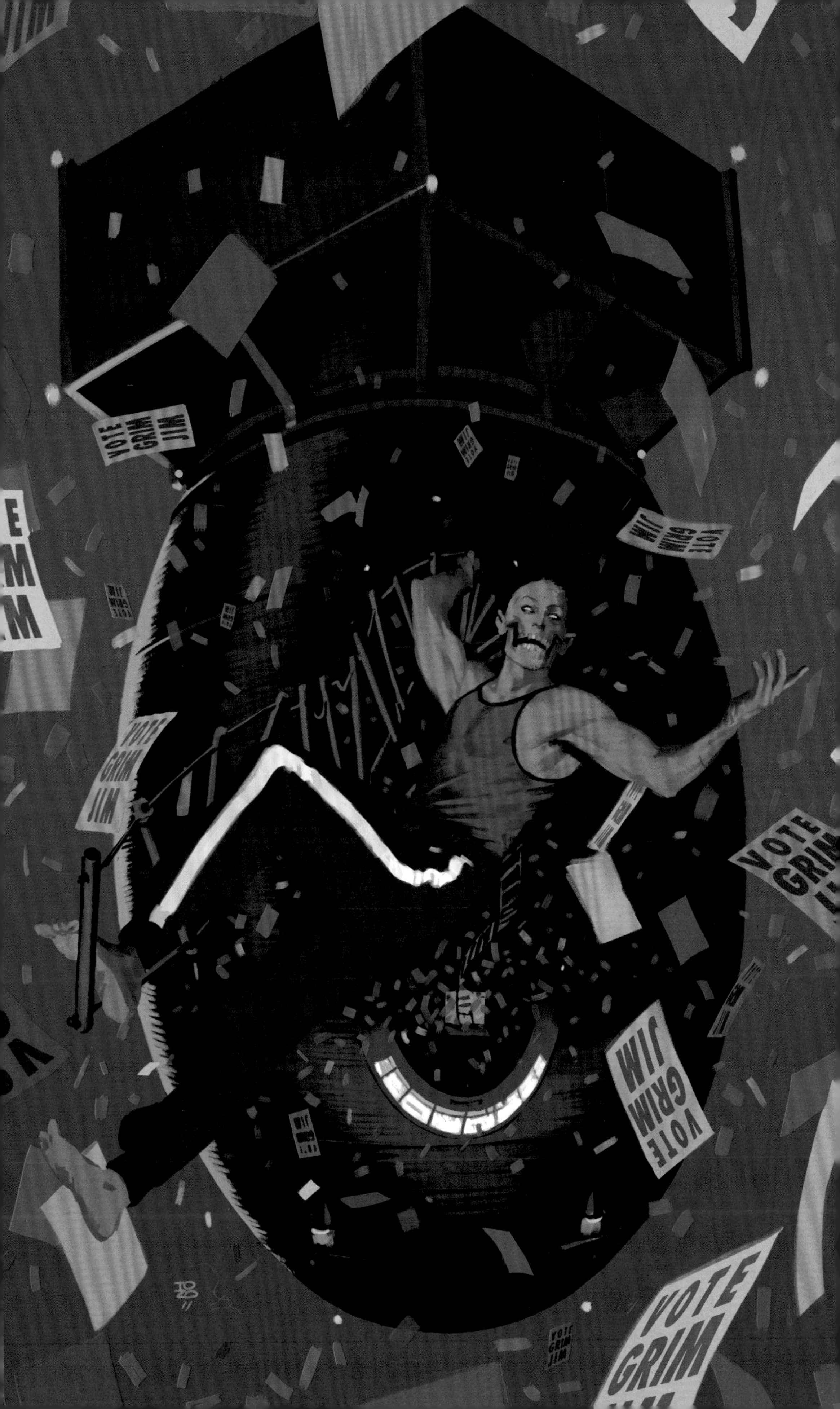
VOTE GRIM JIM
VOTE GRIM JIM
VOTE GRIM JIM
VOTE GRIM JIM
VOTE GRIM

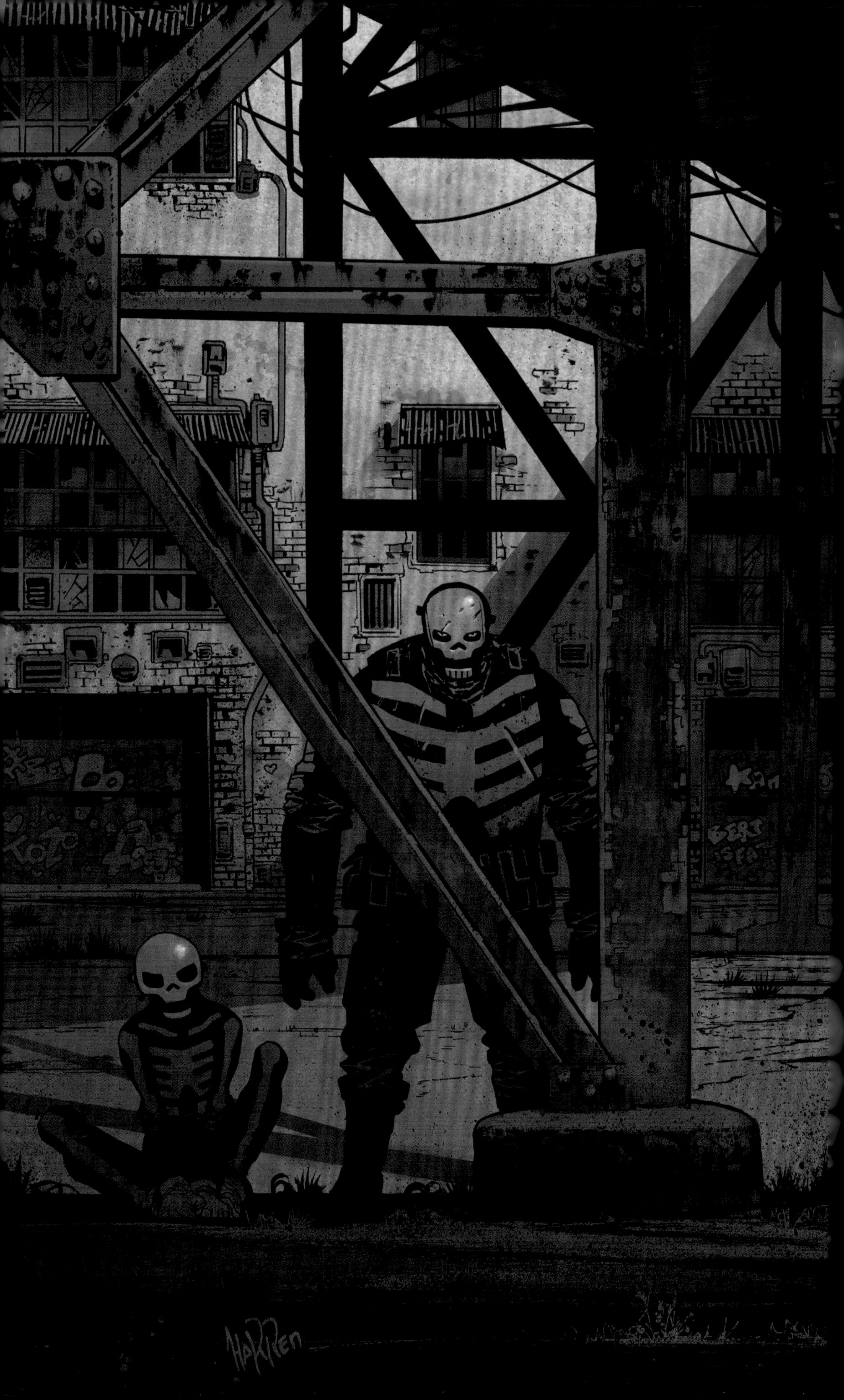

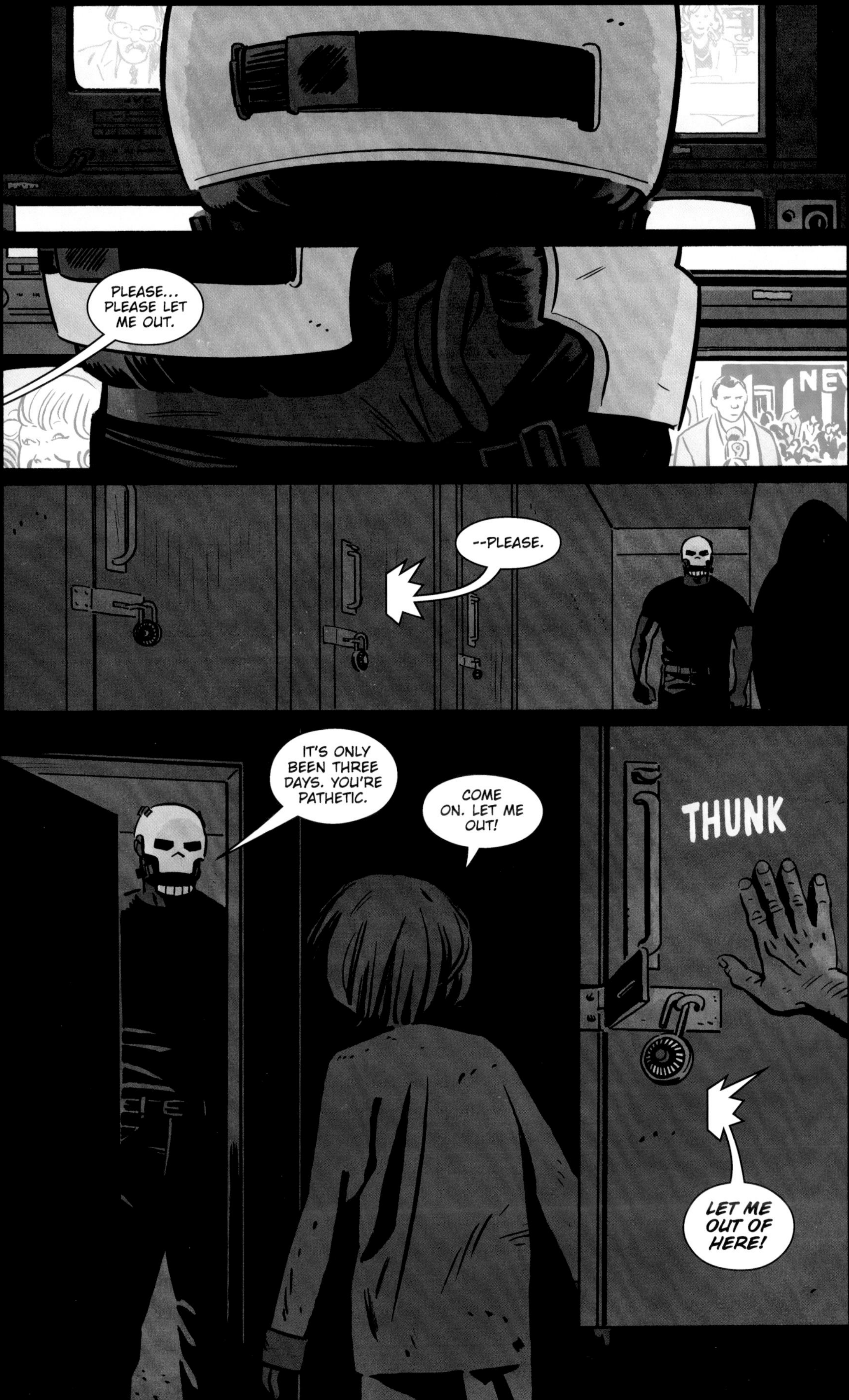
PLEASE... PLEASE LET ME OUT.
--PLEASE.
IT'S ONLY BEEN THREE DAYS. YOU'RE PATHETIC.
COME ON. LET ME OUT!
THUNK
LET ME OUT OF HERE!

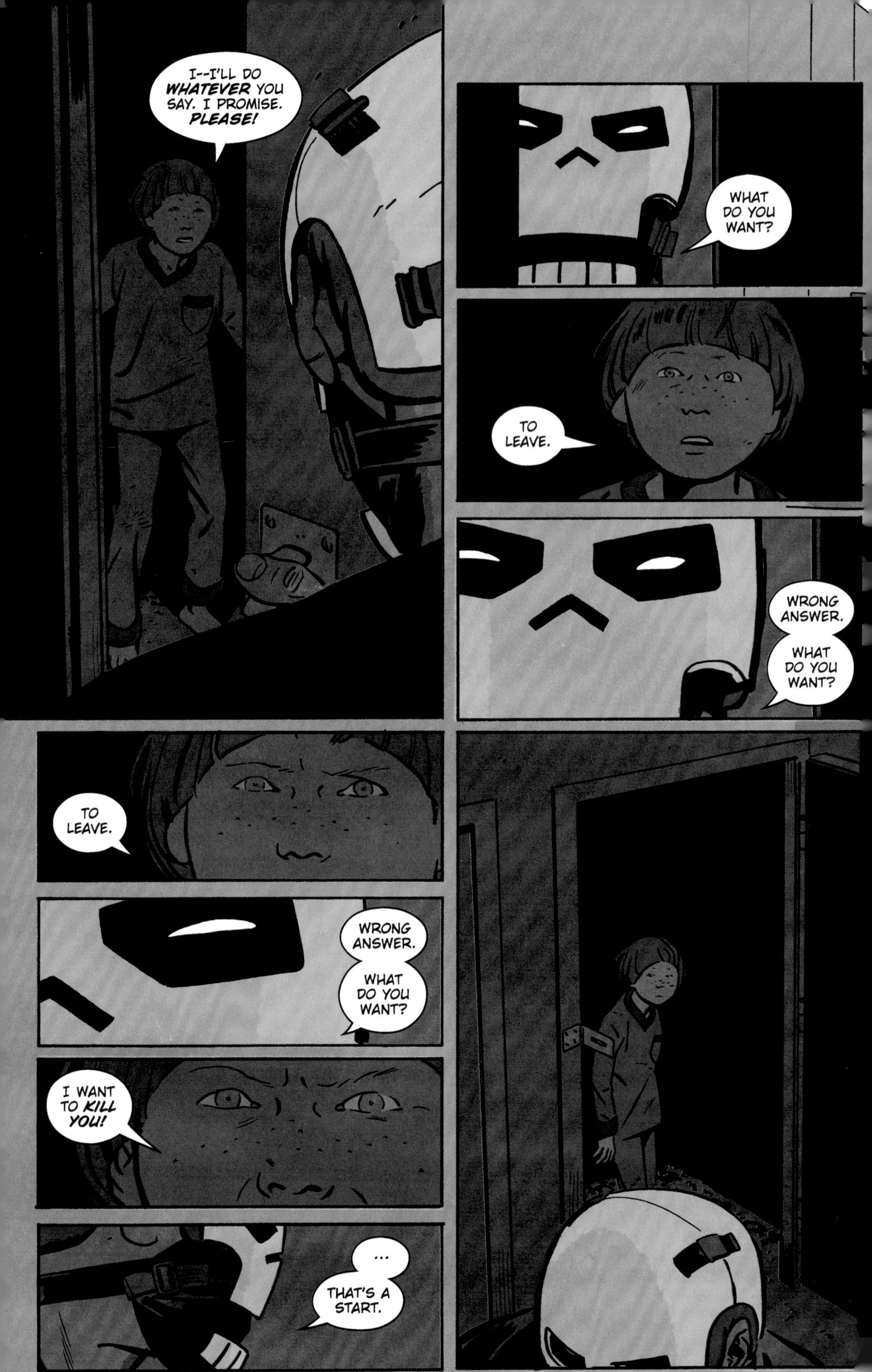
I--I'LL DO *WHATEVER* YOU SAY. I PROMISE. *PLEASE!*
WHAT DO YOU WANT?
TO LEAVE.
WRONG ANSWER.
WHAT DO YOU WANT?
TO LEAVE.
WRONG ANSWER.
WHAT DO YOU WANT?
I WANT TO *KILL YOU!*
...
THAT'S A START.

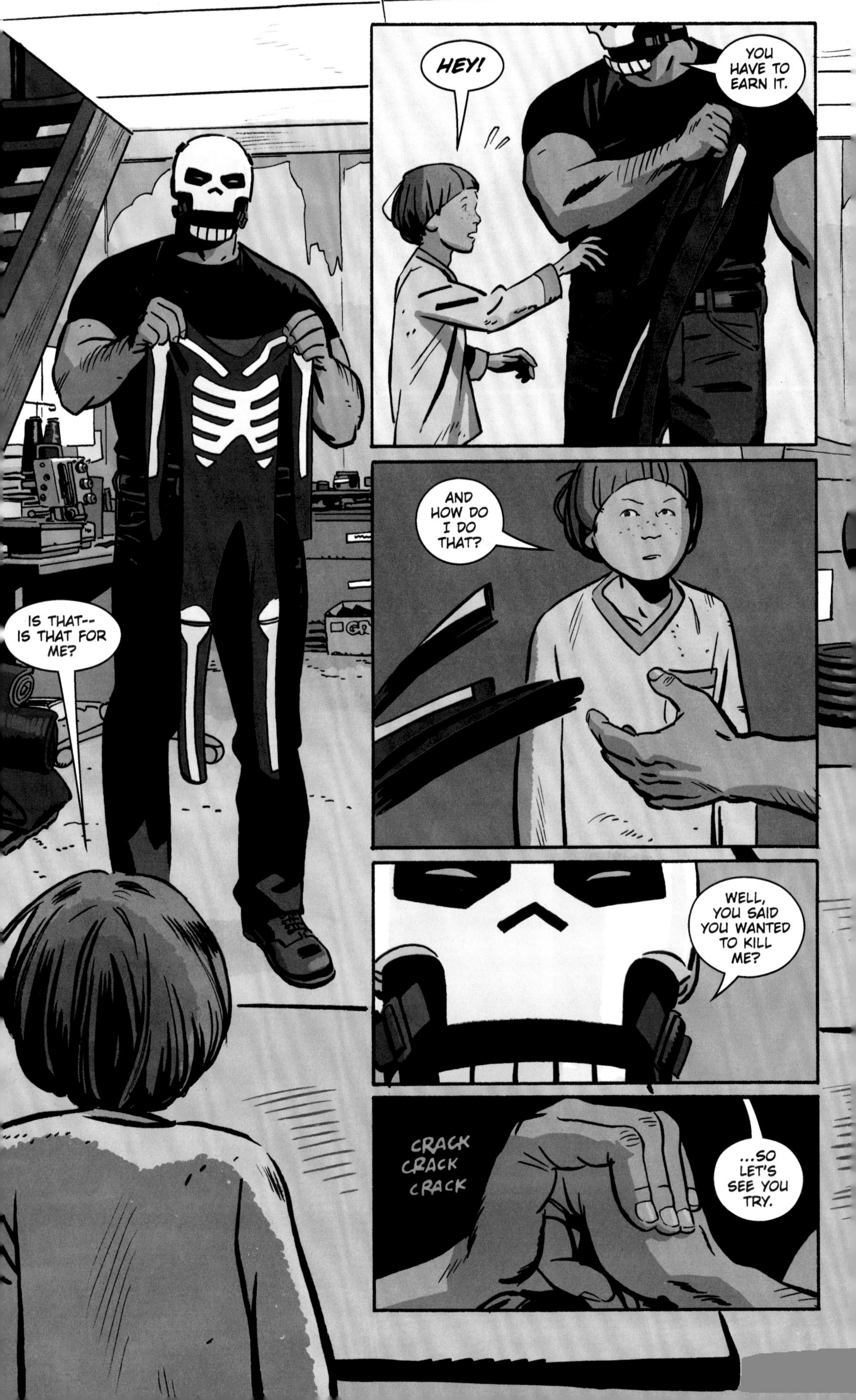
IS THAT-- IS THAT FOR ME?
HEY!
YOU HAVE TO EARN IT.
AND HOW DO I DO THAT?
WELL, YOU SAID YOU WANTED TO KILL ME?
CRACK CRACK CRACK
...SO LET'S SEE YOU TRY.

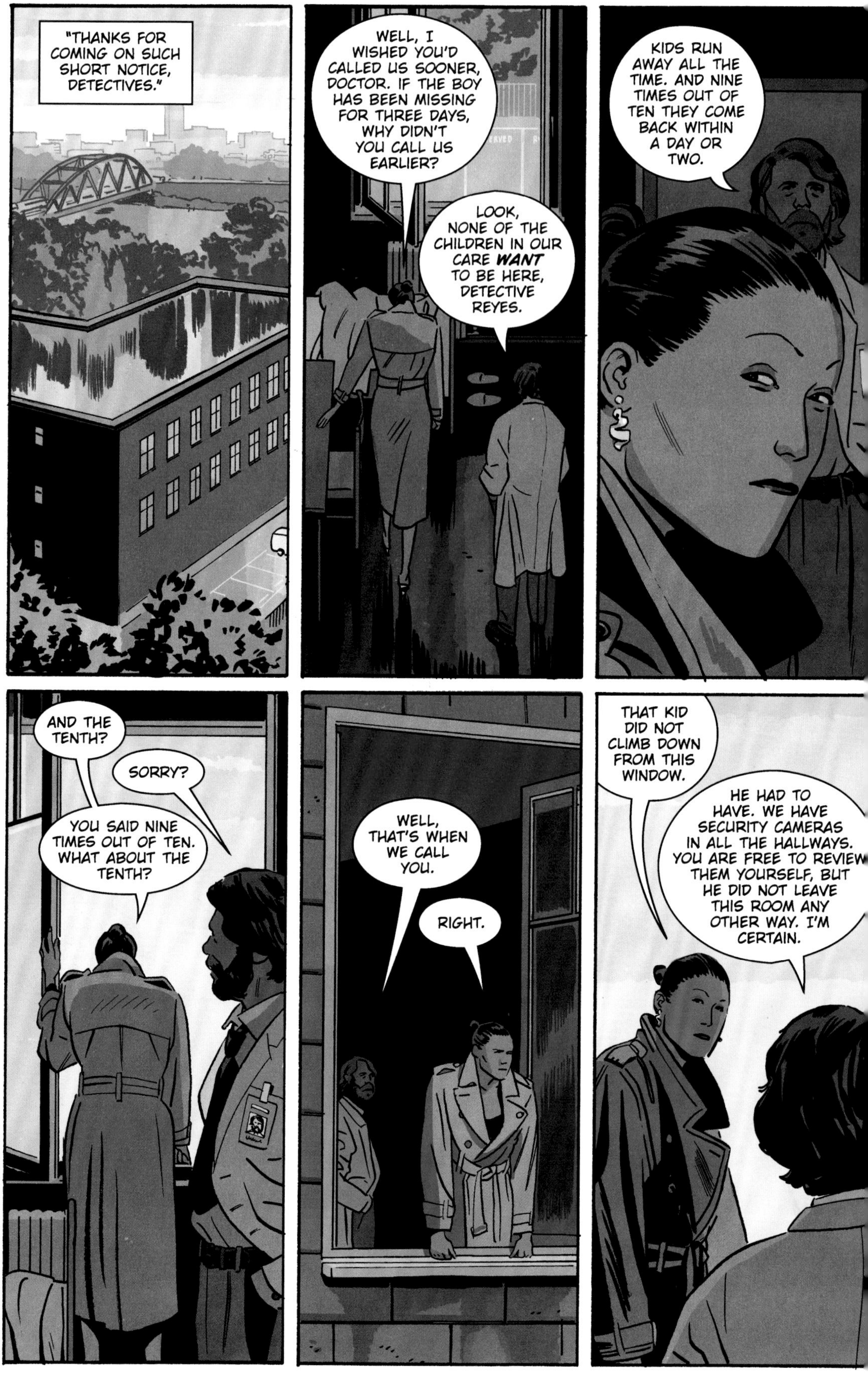
"THANKS FOR COMING ON SUCH SHORT NOTICE, DETECTIVES."
WELL, I WISHED YOU'D CALLED US SOONER, DOCTOR. IF THE BOY HAS BEEN MISSING FOR THREE DAYS, WHY DIDN'T YOU CALL US EARLIER?
LOOK, NONE OF THE CHILDREN IN OUR CARE **WANT** TO BE HERE, DETECTIVE REYES.
KIDS RUN AWAY ALL THE TIME. AND NINE TIMES OUT OF TEN THEY COME BACK WITHIN A DAY OR TWO.
AND THE TENTH?
SORRY?
YOU SAID NINE TIMES OUT OF TEN. WHAT ABOUT THE TENTH?
WELL, THAT'S WHEN WE CALL YOU.
RIGHT.
THAT KID DID NOT CLIMB DOWN FROM THIS WINDOW.
HE HAD TO HAVE. WE HAVE SECURITY CAMERAS IN ALL THE HALLWAYS. YOU ARE FREE TO REVIEW THEM YOURSELF, BUT HE DID NOT LEAVE THIS ROOM ANY OTHER WAY. I'M CERTAIN.

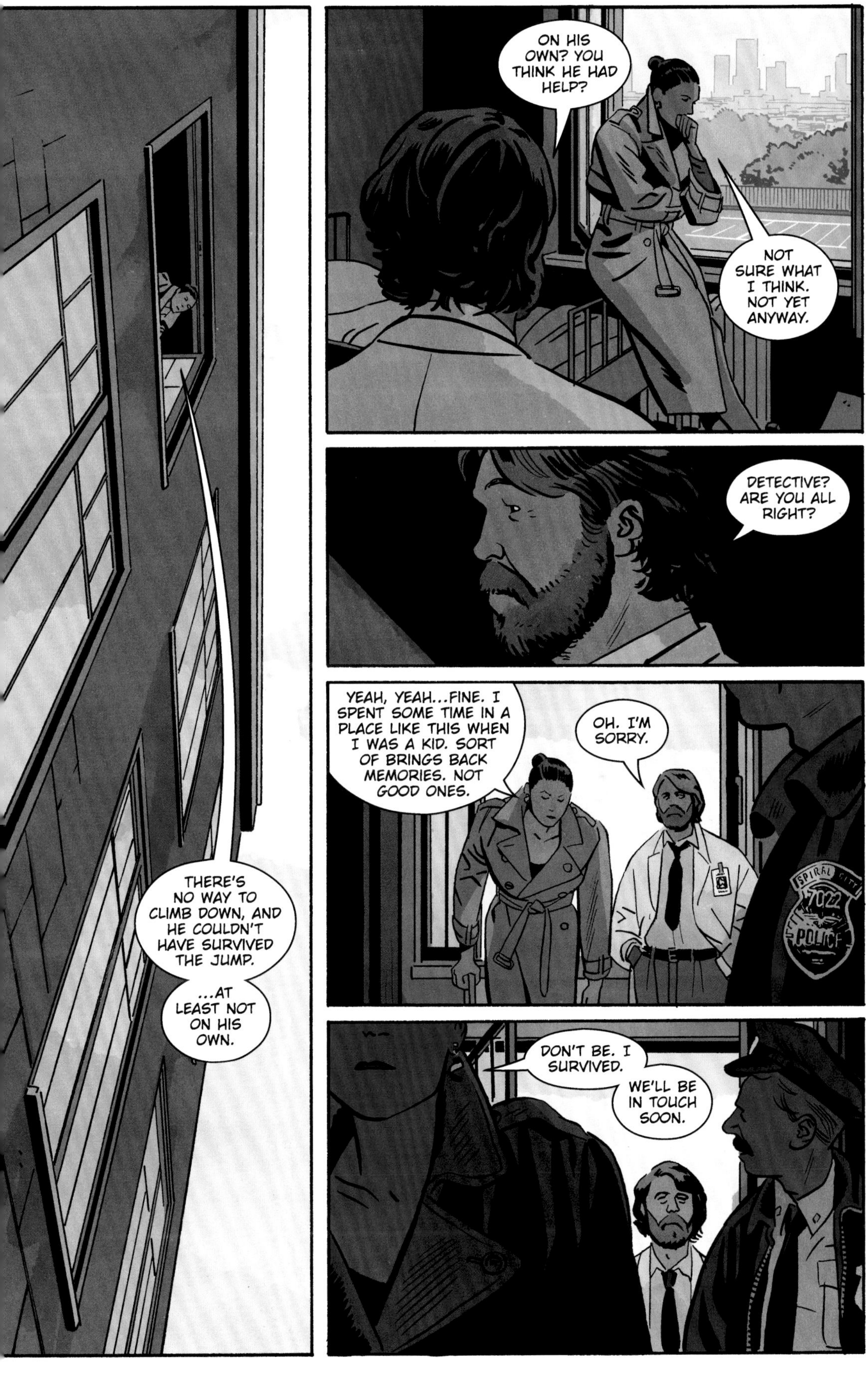
THERE'S NO WAY TO CLIMB DOWN, AND HE COULDN'T HAVE SURVIVED THE JUMP.
...AT LEAST NOT ON HIS OWN.
ON HIS OWN? YOU THINK HE HAD HELP?
NOT SURE WHAT I THINK. NOT YET ANYWAY.
DETECTIVE? ARE YOU ALL RIGHT?
YEAH, YEAH...FINE. I SPENT SOME TIME IN A PLACE LIKE THIS WHEN I WAS A KID. SORT OF BRINGS BACK MEMORIES. NOT GOOD ONES.
OH. I'M SORRY.
SPIRAL CITY 7022 POLICE
DON'T BE. I SURVIVED.
WE'LL BE IN TOUCH SOON.

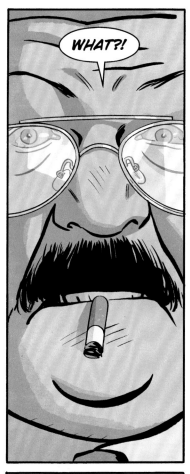

WHAT?!

YOU HEARD ME. I THINK SKULLDIGGER **TOOK THE KID.**

AND WHAT ON EARTH DO YOU HAVE TO BACK THIS LITTLE THEORY OF YOURS, REYES?

ABSOLUTELY NOTHING, CHIEF. IT'S JUST A GUT FEELING. BUT I SWEAR, I THINK THAT SKULL-HEADED PRICK CAME AND GOT THE KID.

CPT HOWARD

LOOK, AMANDA, YOU ARE SUPPOSED TO BE CLOSING THIS MURDER CASE AS QUICKLY AS POSSIBLE, **NOT** INVESTIGATING A MISSING CHILD. AND **DEFINITELY** NOT GETTING ANYWHERE **NEAR** SKULLDIGGER. I MADE THAT VERY, **VERY** CLEAR TO YOU.

COME ON, CAP. THAT ASSHOLE HAS BEEN RUNNING AROUND UNCHECKED FOR WAY TOO LONG! WE CAN FINALLY DO SOMETHING ABOUT IT! BESIDES, NOW A KID'S INVOLVED. THIS IS DIFFERENT THAN HIM JUST KILLING RAPISTS AND MURDERERS.

YOU HAVE ZERO PROOF THAT SKULLDIGGER HAD ANYTHING TO DO WITH THE KID GOING MISSING. LISTEN TO ME, THE KID RAN AWAY **ON HIS OWN.** THAT IS WHAT IS GOING IN YOUR REPORT.

NOW CLOSE THE CASE AND FILE IT. I WANT IT ON MY DESK BY THE END OF THE DAY.

CPT HO

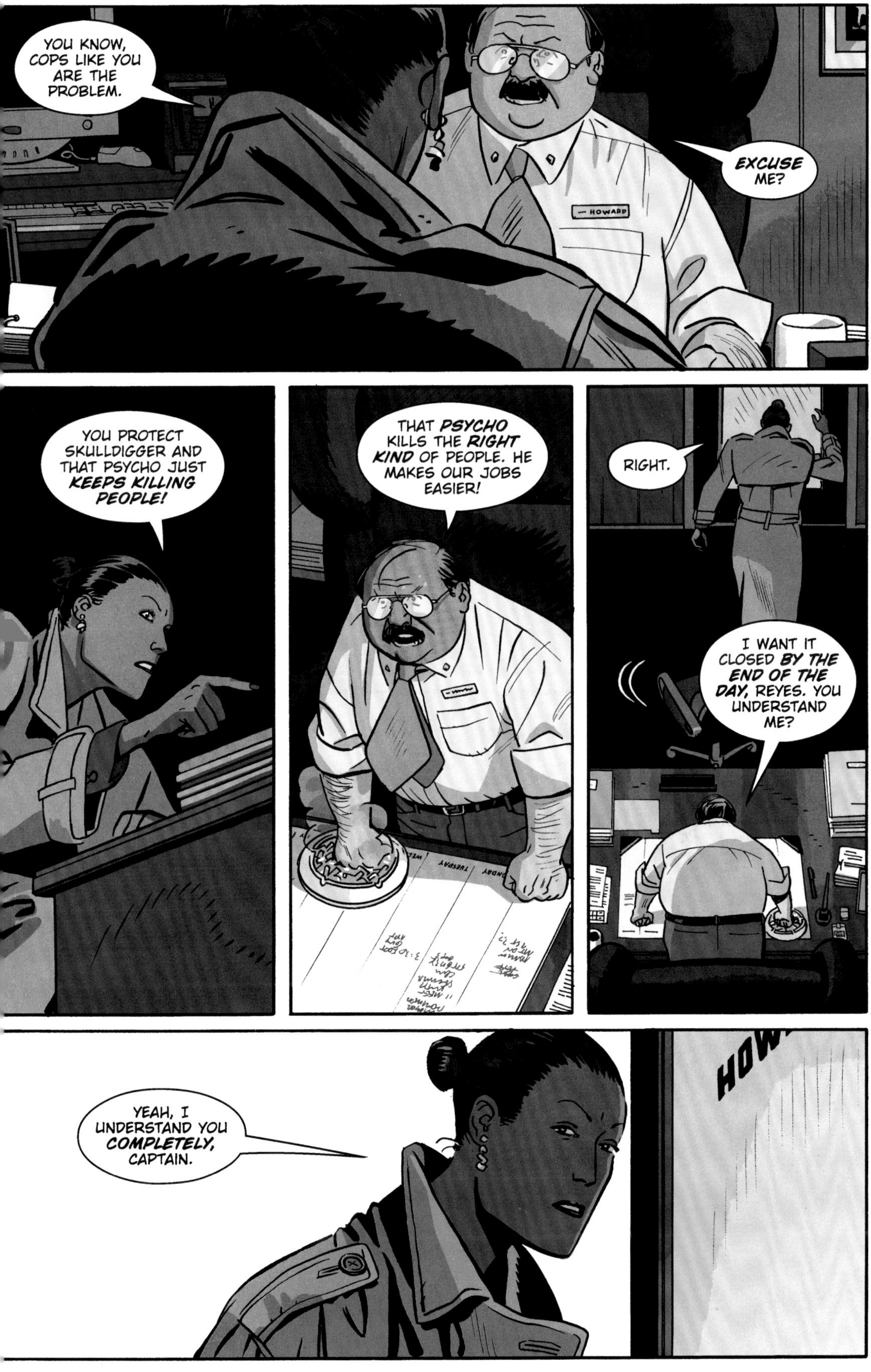
YOU KNOW, COPS LIKE YOU ARE THE PROBLEM.
EXCUSE ME?
HOWARD
YOU PROTECT SKULLDIGGER AND THAT PSYCHO JUST KEEPS KILLING PEOPLE!
THAT PSYCHO KILLS THE RIGHT KIND OF PEOPLE. HE MAKES OUR JOBS EASIER!
RIGHT.
I WANT IT CLOSED BY THE END OF THE DAY, REYES. YOU UNDERSTAND ME?
YEAH, I UNDERSTAND YOU COMPLETELY, CAPTAIN.
HOW

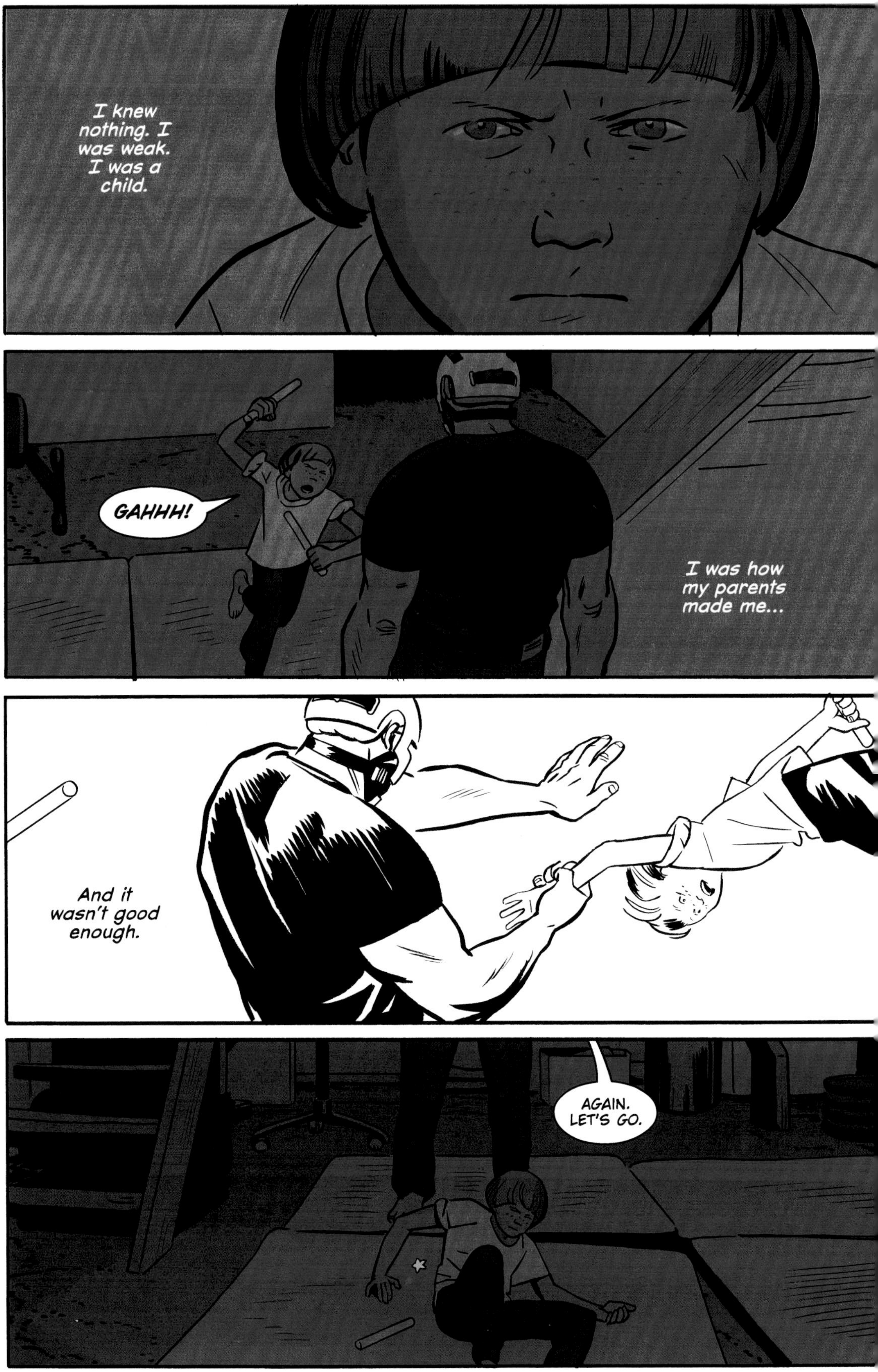
I knew nothing. I was weak. I was a child.
GAHHH!
I was how my parents made me...
And it wasn't good enough.
AGAIN. LET'S GO.

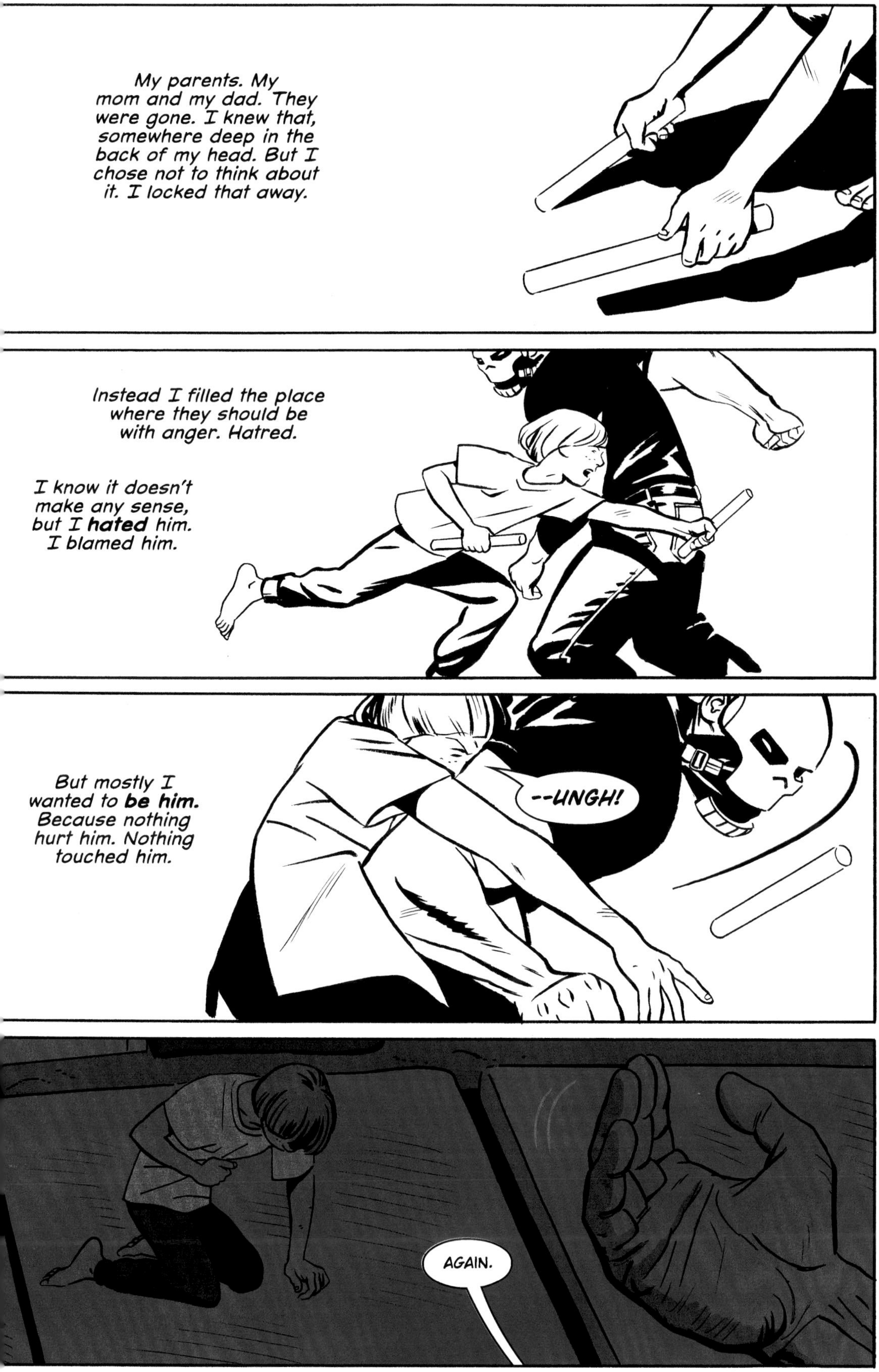
My parents. My mom and my dad. They were gone. I knew that, somewhere deep in the back of my head. But I chose not to think about it. I locked that away.
Instead I filled the place where they should be with anger. Hatred.
I know it doesn't make any sense, but I **hated** him. I blamed him.
But mostly I wanted to **be him.** Because nothing hurt him. Nothing touched him.
--UNGH!
AGAIN.

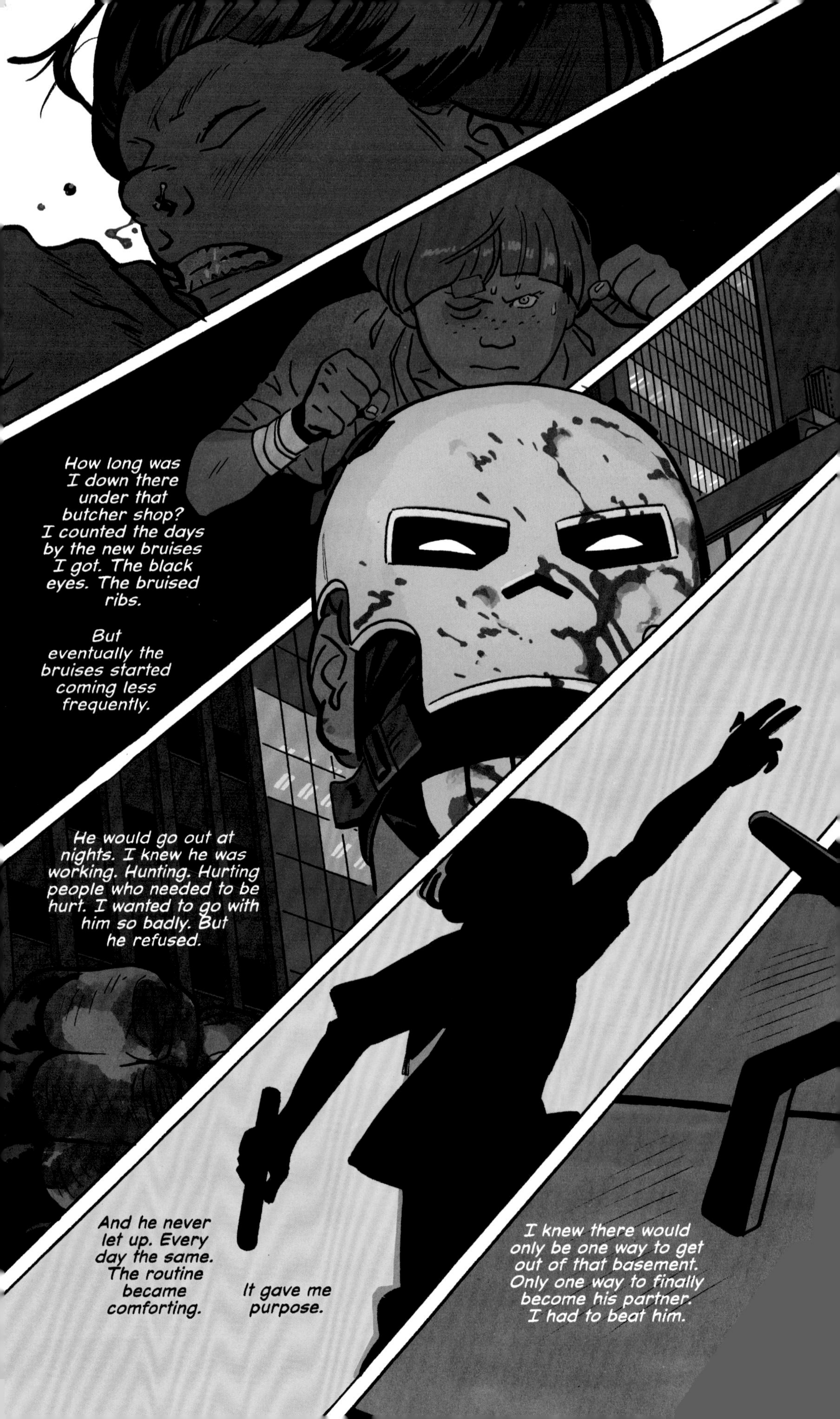
How long was I down there under that butcher shop? I counted the days by the new bruises I got. The black eyes. The bruised ribs.
But eventually the bruises started coming less frequently.
He would go out at nights. I knew he was working. Hunting. Hurting people who needed to be hurt. I wanted to go with him so badly. But he refused.
And he never let up. Every day the same. The routine became comforting.
It gave me purpose.
I knew there would only be one way to get out of that basement. Only one way to finally become his partner. I had to beat him.

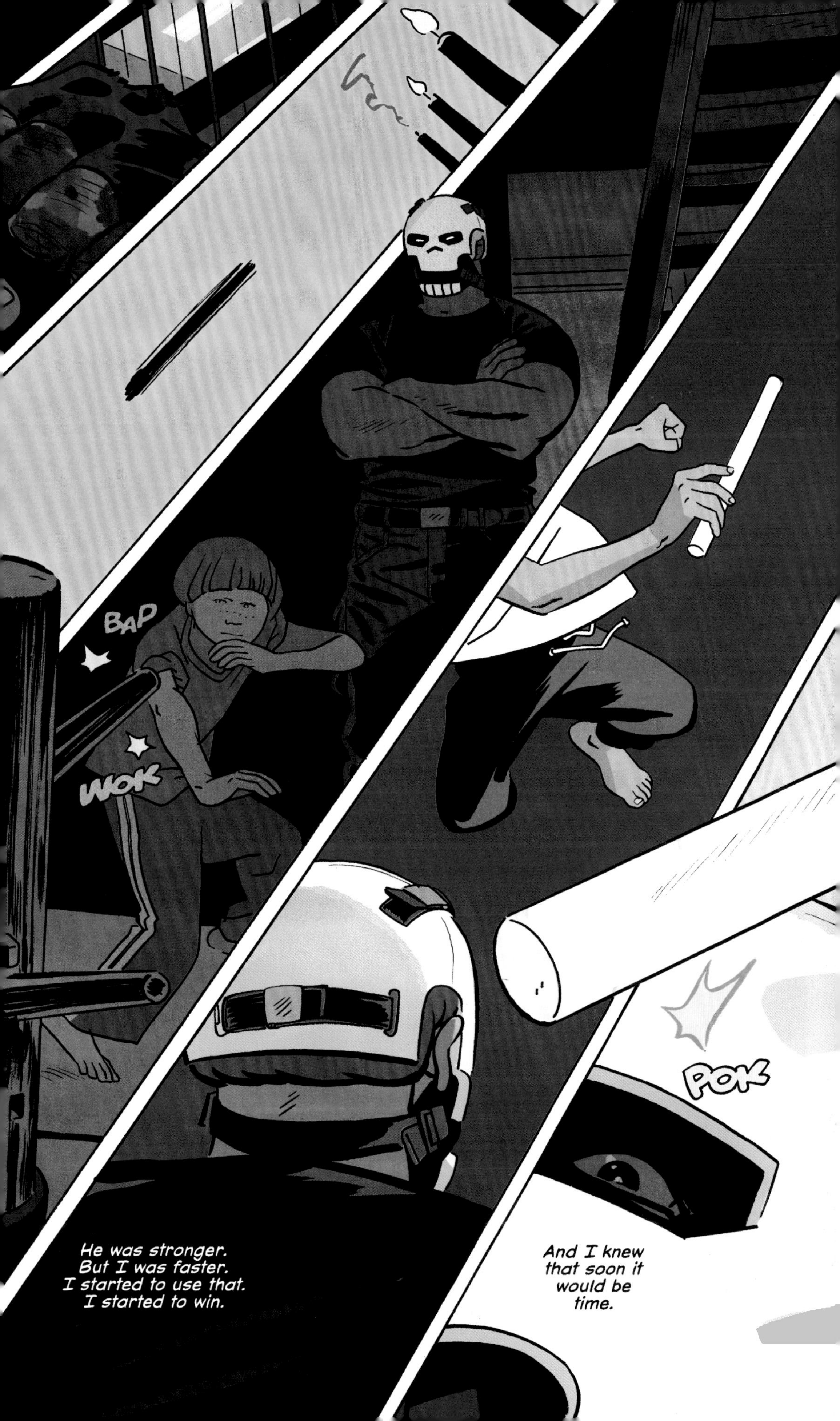
BAP
WOK
POK
He was stronger.
But I was faster.
I started to use that.
I started to win.
And I knew
that soon it
would be
time.

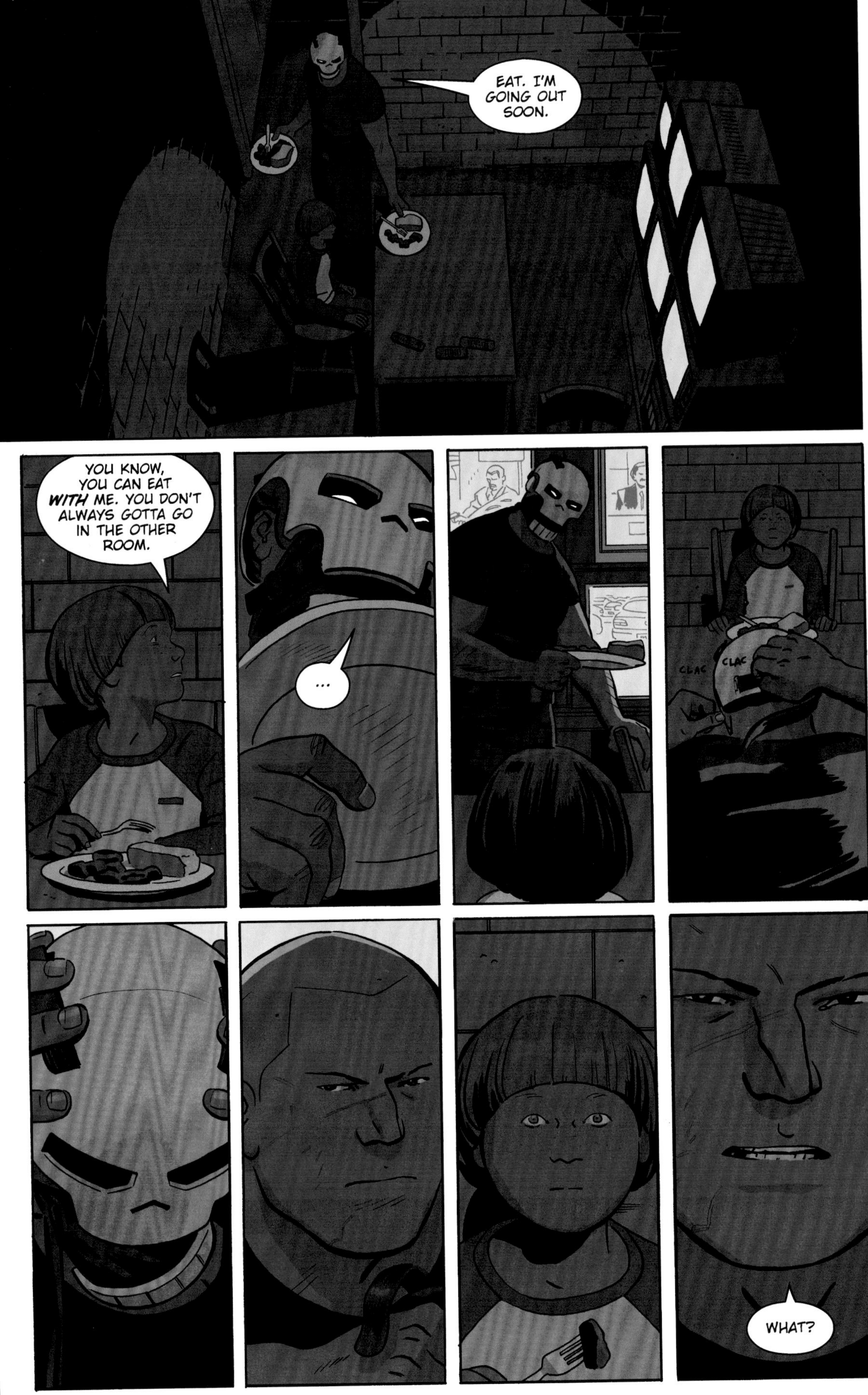
EAT. I'M GOING OUT SOON.
YOU KNOW, YOU CAN EAT *WITH* ME. YOU DON'T ALWAYS GOTTA GO IN THE OTHER ROOM.
...
CLAC CLAC
WHAT?

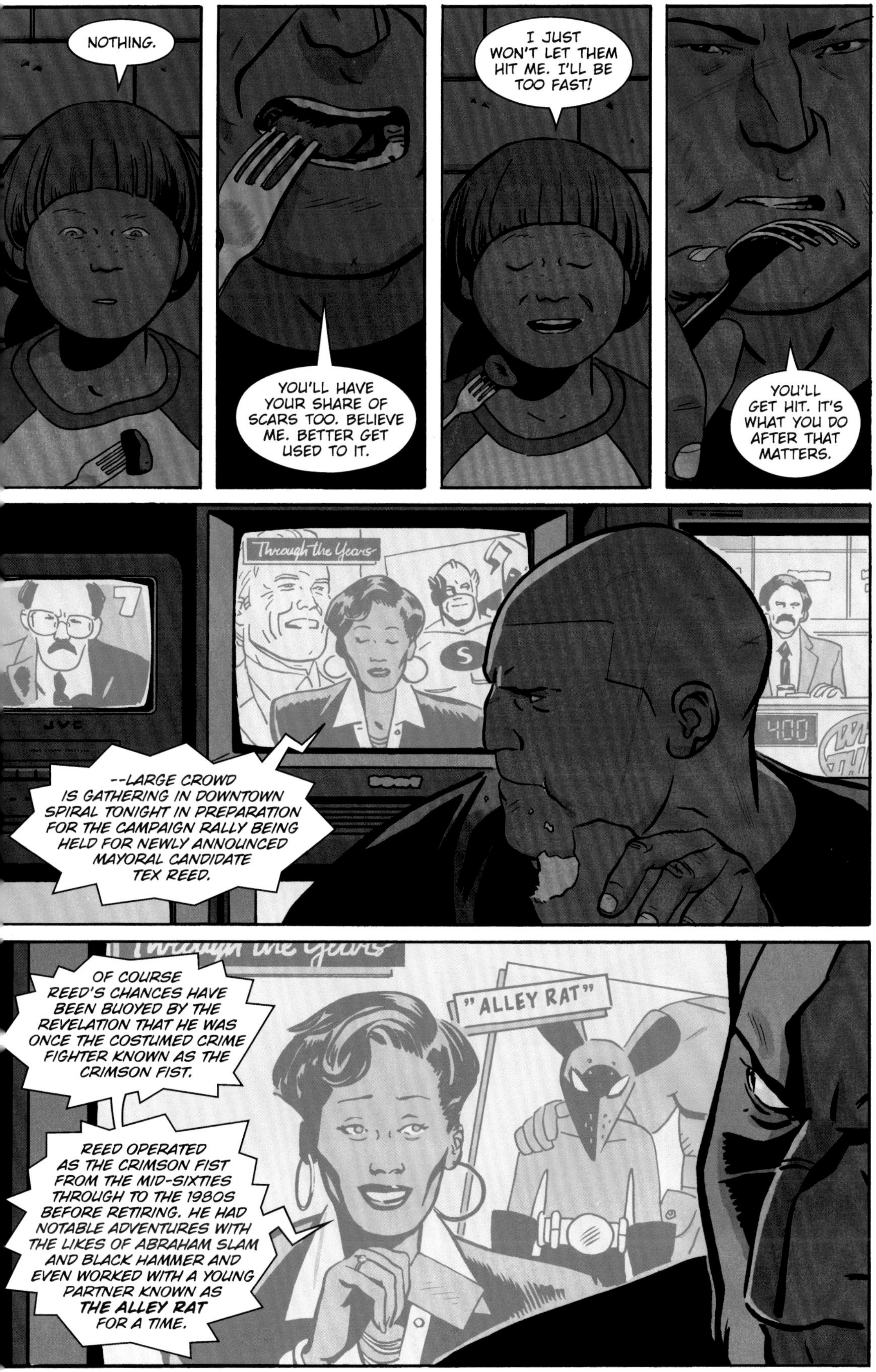

NOTHING.
YOU'LL HAVE YOUR SHARE OF SCARS TOO. BELIEVE ME. BETTER GET USED TO IT.
I JUST WON'T LET THEM HIT ME. I'LL BE TOO FAST!
YOU'LL GET HIT. IT'S WHAT YOU DO AFTER THAT MATTERS.
Through the Years
--LARGE CROWD IS GATHERING IN DOWNTOWN SPIRAL TONIGHT IN PREPARATION FOR THE CAMPAIGN RALLY BEING HELD FOR NEWLY ANNOUNCED MAYORAL CANDIDATE TEX REED.
"ALLEY RAT"
OF COURSE REED'S CHANCES HAVE BEEN BUOYED BY THE REVELATION THAT HE WAS ONCE THE COSTUMED CRIME FIGHTER KNOWN AS THE CRIMSON FIST.
REED OPERATED AS THE CRIMSON FIST FROM THE MID-SIXTIES THROUGH TO THE 1980S BEFORE RETIRING. HE HAD NOTABLE ADVENTURES WITH THE LIKES OF ABRAHAM SLAM AND BLACK HAMMER AND EVEN WORKED WITH A YOUNG PARTNER KNOWN AS **THE ALLEY RAT** FOR A TIME.

SO WHEN DO YOU THINK I CAN PUT THE COSTUME ON? I'VE BEEN THINKING OF A FEW NAMES. WHATTA YOU THINK ABOUT BONE CRUSHER.

BONE CRUSHER. FOR MY NAME?

UP TO YOU.

REALLY?

OF COURSE. IT'S *YOUR* NAME. *YOUR* COSTUME.

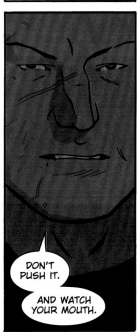

DON'T PUSH IT.

AND WATCH YOUR MOUTH.

YOU BEAT PEOPLE TO DEATH WITH A METAL SKULL, AND YOU'RE WORRIED ABOUT MY LANGUAGE?

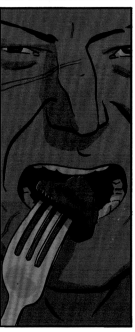

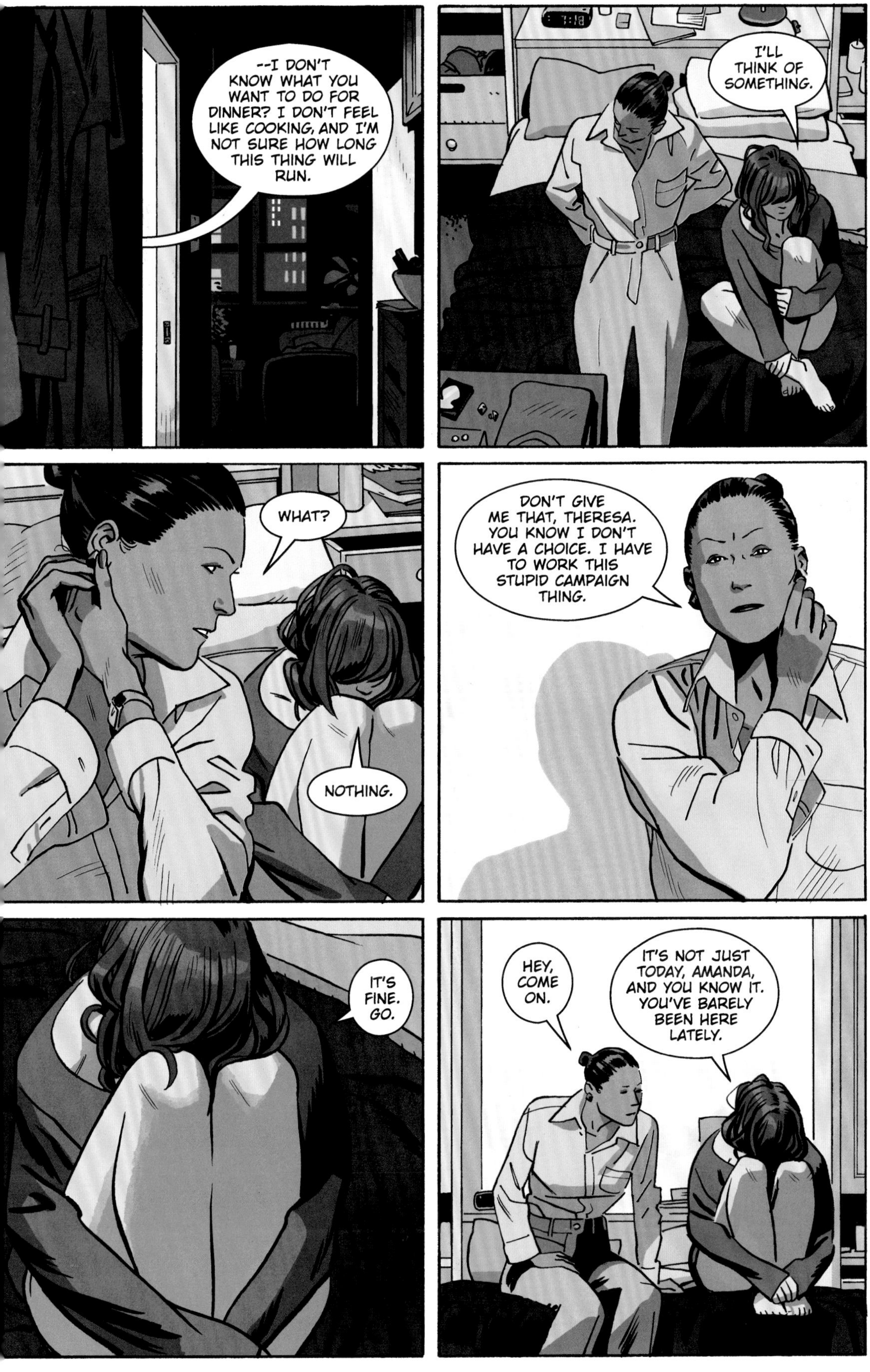
--I DON'T KNOW WHAT YOU WANT TO DO FOR DINNER? I DON'T FEEL LIKE COOKING, AND I'M NOT SURE HOW LONG THIS THING WILL RUN.
I'LL THINK OF SOMETHING.
WHAT?
NOTHING.
DON'T GIVE ME THAT, THERESA. YOU KNOW I DON'T HAVE A CHOICE. I HAVE TO WORK THIS STUPID CAMPAIGN THING.
IT'S FINE. GO.
HEY, COME ON.
IT'S NOT JUST TODAY, AMANDA, AND YOU KNOW IT. YOU'VE BARELY BEEN HERE LATELY.

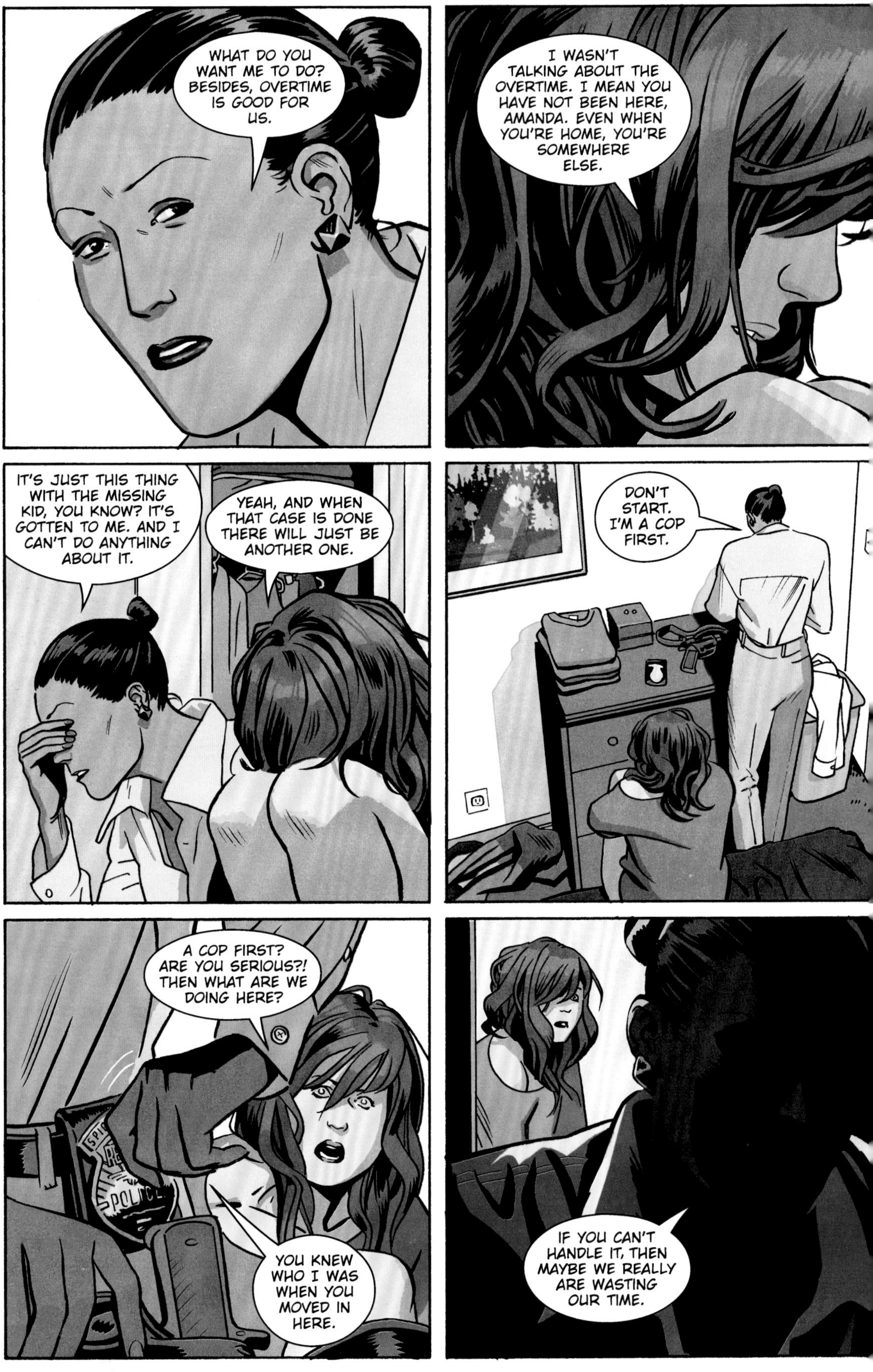
WHAT DO YOU WANT ME TO DO? BESIDES, OVERTIME IS GOOD FOR US.
I WASN'T TALKING ABOUT THE OVERTIME. I MEAN YOU HAVE NOT BEEN HERE, AMANDA. EVEN WHEN YOU'RE HOME, YOU'RE SOMEWHERE ELSE.
IT'S JUST THIS THING WITH THE MISSING KID, YOU KNOW? IT'S GOTTEN TO ME. AND I CAN'T DO ANYTHING ABOUT IT.
YEAH, AND WHEN THAT CASE IS DONE THERE WILL JUST BE ANOTHER ONE.
DON'T START. I'M A COP FIRST.
A COP FIRST? ARE YOU SERIOUS?! THEN WHAT ARE WE DOING HERE?
YOU KNEW WHO I WAS WHEN YOU MOVED IN HERE.
IF YOU CAN'T HANDLE IT, THEN MAYBE WE REALLY ARE WASTING OUR TIME.

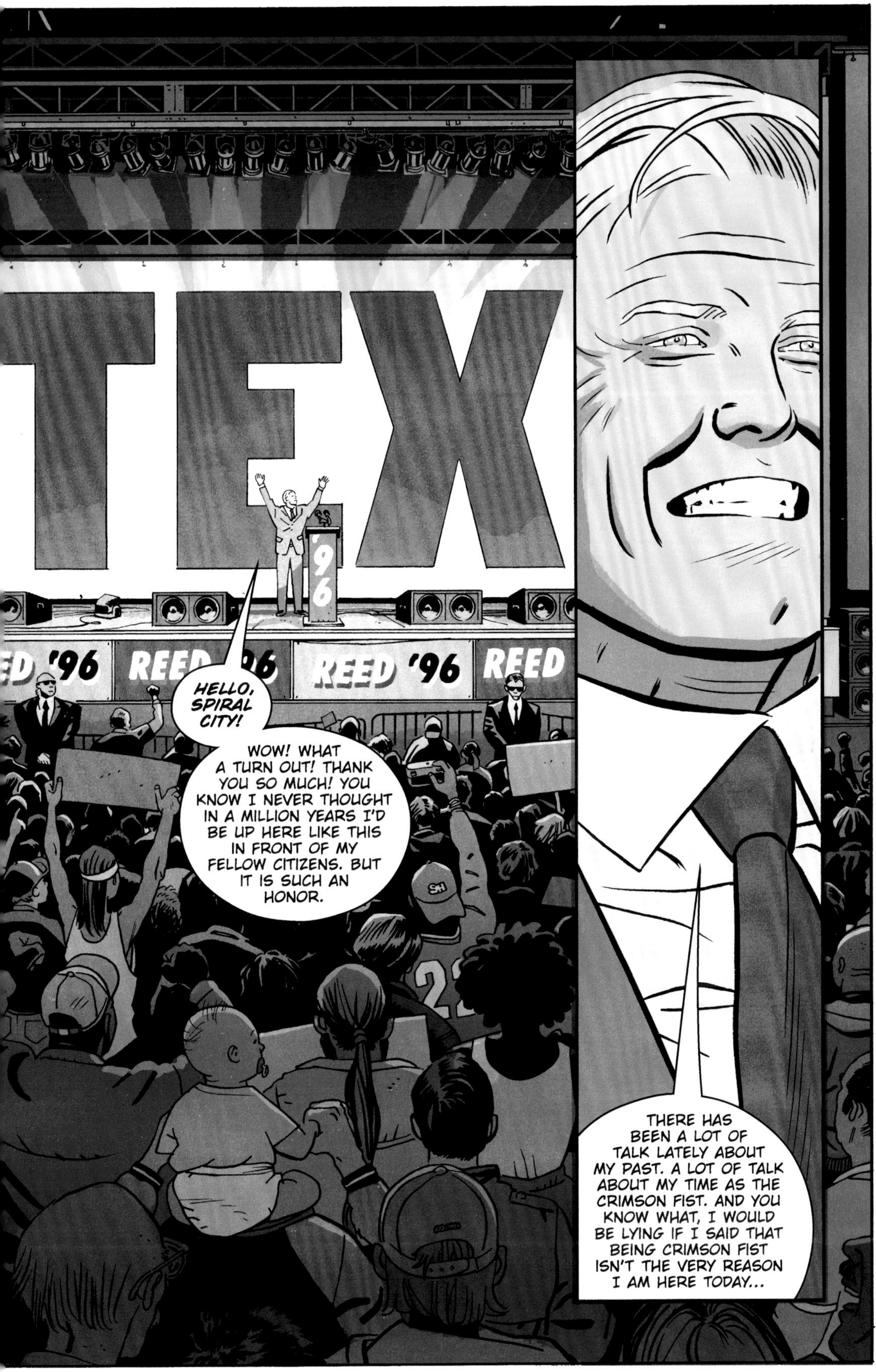
TEX
'96
ED '96
REED '96
REED '96
REED
HELLO, SPIRAL CITY!
WOW! WHAT A TURN OUT! THANK YOU SO MUCH! YOU KNOW I NEVER THOUGHT IN A MILLION YEARS I'D BE UP HERE LIKE THIS IN FRONT OF MY FELLOW CITIZENS. BUT IT IS SUCH AN HONOR.
THERE HAS BEEN A LOT OF TALK LATELY ABOUT MY PAST. A LOT OF TALK ABOUT MY TIME AS THE CRIMSON FIST. AND YOU KNOW WHAT, I WOULD BE LYING IF I SAID THAT BEING CRIMSON FIST ISN'T THE VERY REASON I AM HERE TODAY...

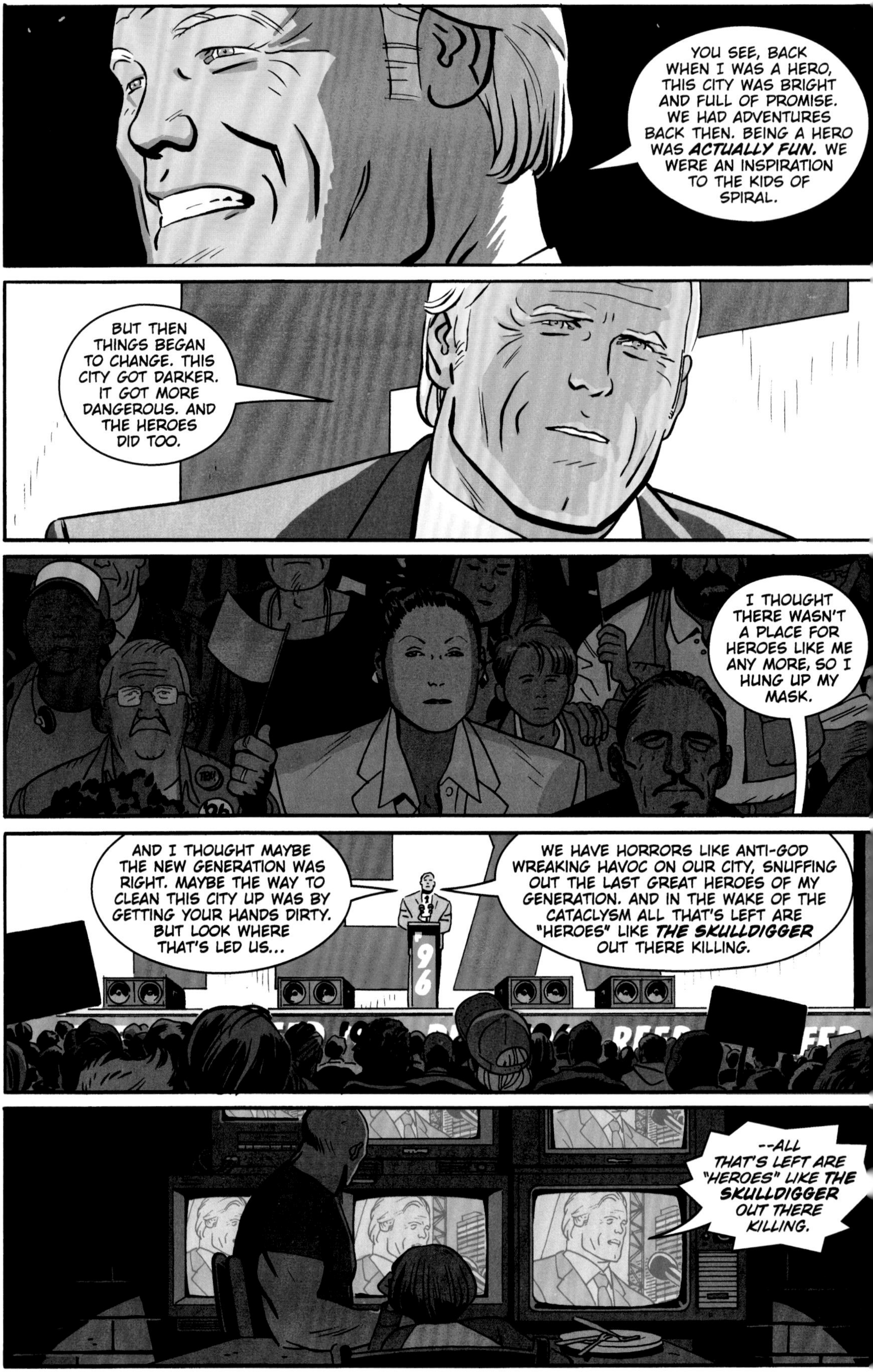
YOU SEE, BACK WHEN I WAS A HERO, THIS CITY WAS BRIGHT AND FULL OF PROMISE. WE HAD ADVENTURES BACK THEN. BEING A HERO WAS ACTUALLY FUN. WE WERE AN INSPIRATION TO THE KIDS OF SPIRAL.
BUT THEN THINGS BEGAN TO CHANGE. THIS CITY GOT DARKER. IT GOT MORE DANGEROUS. AND THE HEROES DID TOO.
I THOUGHT THERE WASN'T A PLACE FOR HEROES LIKE ME ANY MORE, SO I HUNG UP MY MASK.
AND I THOUGHT MAYBE THE NEW GENERATION WAS RIGHT. MAYBE THE WAY TO CLEAN THIS CITY UP WAS BY GETTING YOUR HANDS DIRTY. BUT LOOK WHERE THAT'S LED US...
WE HAVE HORRORS LIKE ANTI-GOD WREAKING HAVOC ON OUR CITY, SNUFFING OUT THE LAST GREAT HEROES OF MY GENERATION. AND IN THE WAKE OF THE CATACLYSM ALL THAT'S LEFT ARE "HEROES" LIKE THE SKULLDIGGER OUT THERE KILLING.
'96
--ALL THAT'S LEFT ARE "HEROES" LIKE THE SKULLDIGGER OUT THERE KILLING.

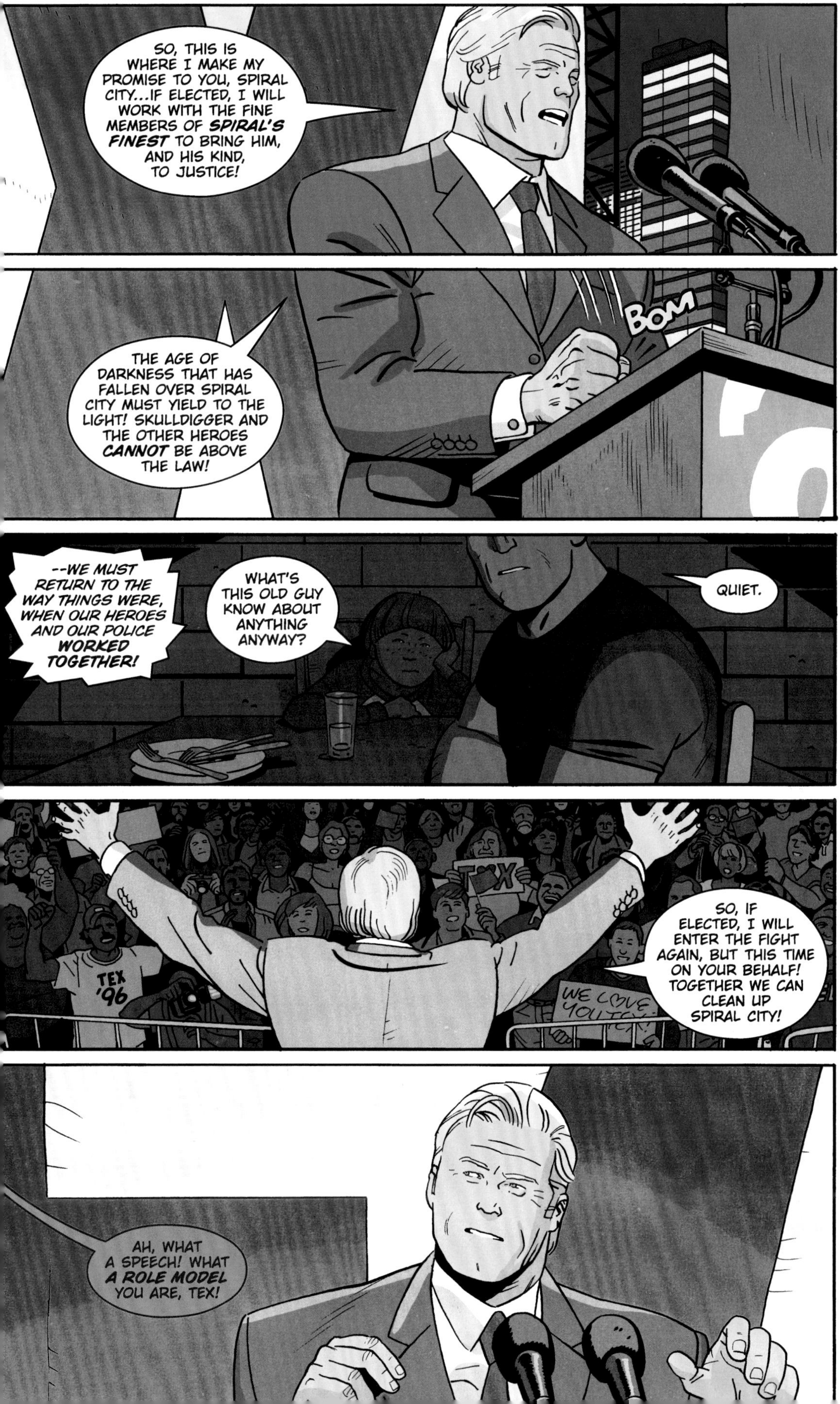
SO, THIS IS WHERE I MAKE MY PROMISE TO YOU, SPIRAL CITY...IF ELECTED, I WILL WORK WITH THE FINE MEMBERS OF SPIRAL'S FINEST TO BRING HIM, AND HIS KIND, TO JUSTICE!
BOM
THE AGE OF DARKNESS THAT HAS FALLEN OVER SPIRAL CITY MUST YIELD TO THE LIGHT! SKULLDIGGER AND THE OTHER HEROES CANNOT BE ABOVE THE LAW!
--WE MUST RETURN TO THE WAY THINGS WERE, WHEN OUR HEROES AND OUR POLICE WORKED TOGETHER!
WHAT'S THIS OLD GUY KNOW ABOUT ANYTHING ANYWAY?
QUIET.
TEX '96
SO, IF ELECTED, I WILL ENTER THE FIGHT AGAIN, BUT THIS TIME ON YOUR BEHALF! TOGETHER WE CAN CLEAN UP SPIRAL CITY!
AH, WHAT A SPEECH! WHAT A ROLE MODEL YOU ARE, TEX!

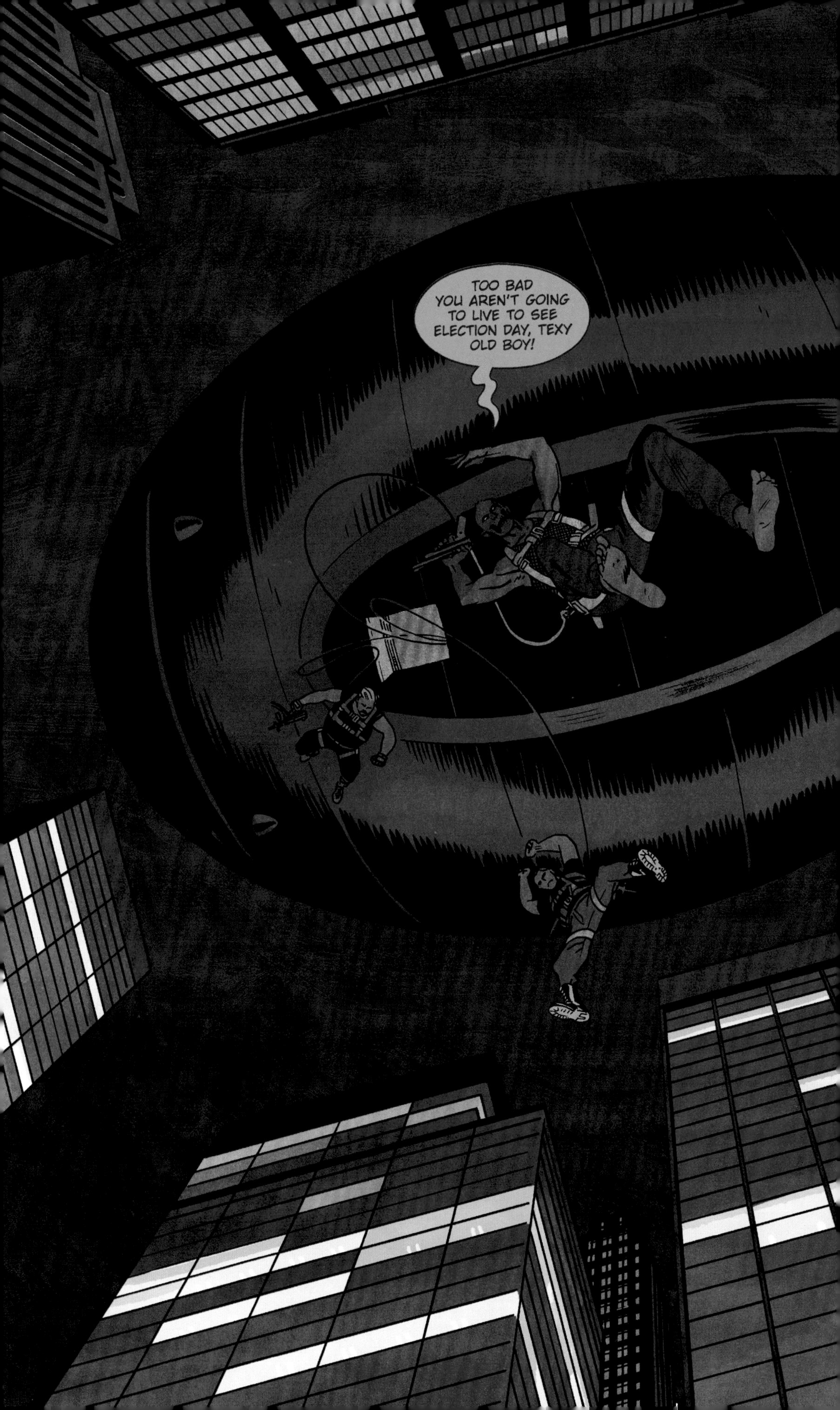
TOO BAD YOU AREN'T GOING TO LIVE TO SEE ELECTION DAY, TEXY OLD BOY!

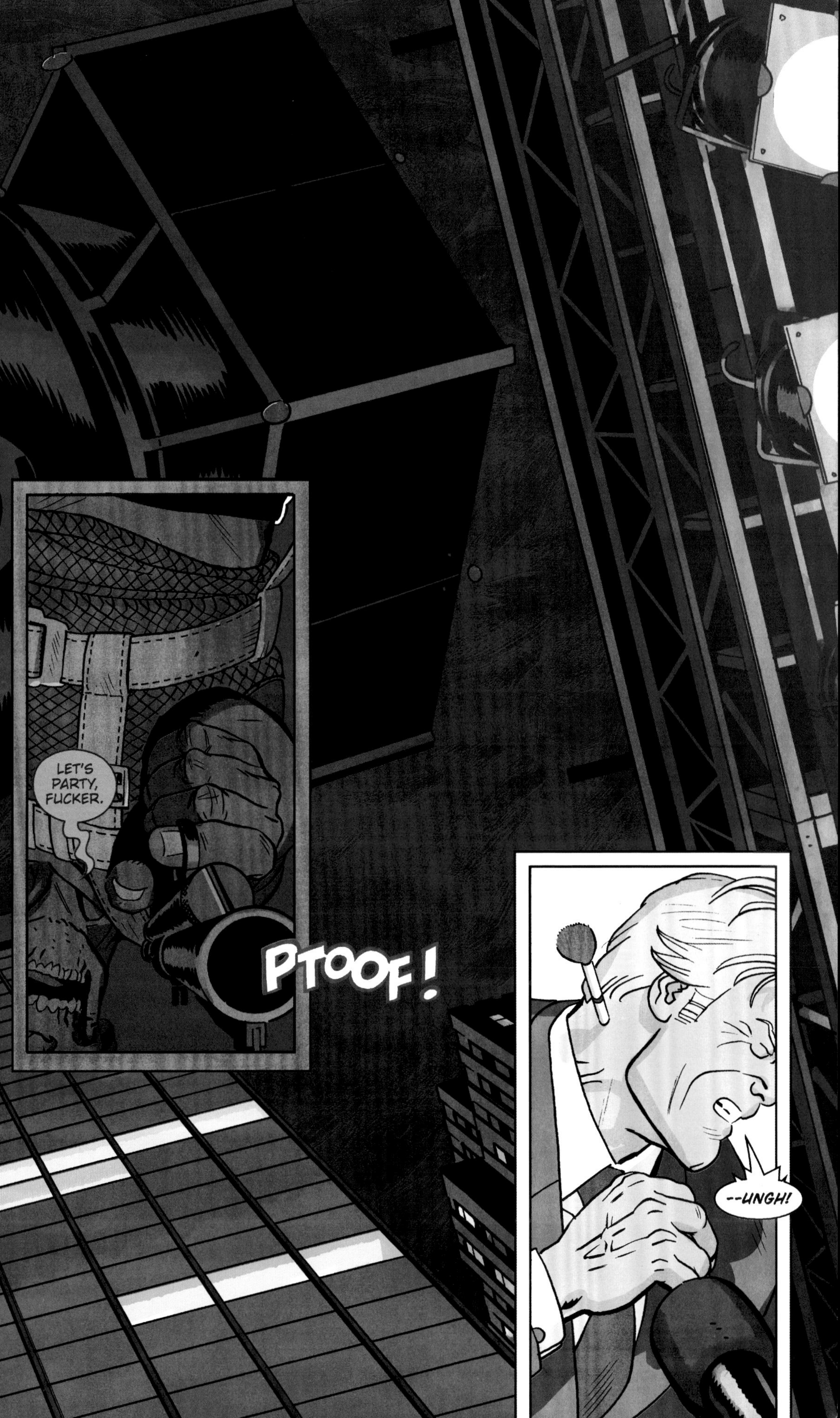
LET'S PARTY, FUCKER.
PTOOF!
--UNGH!

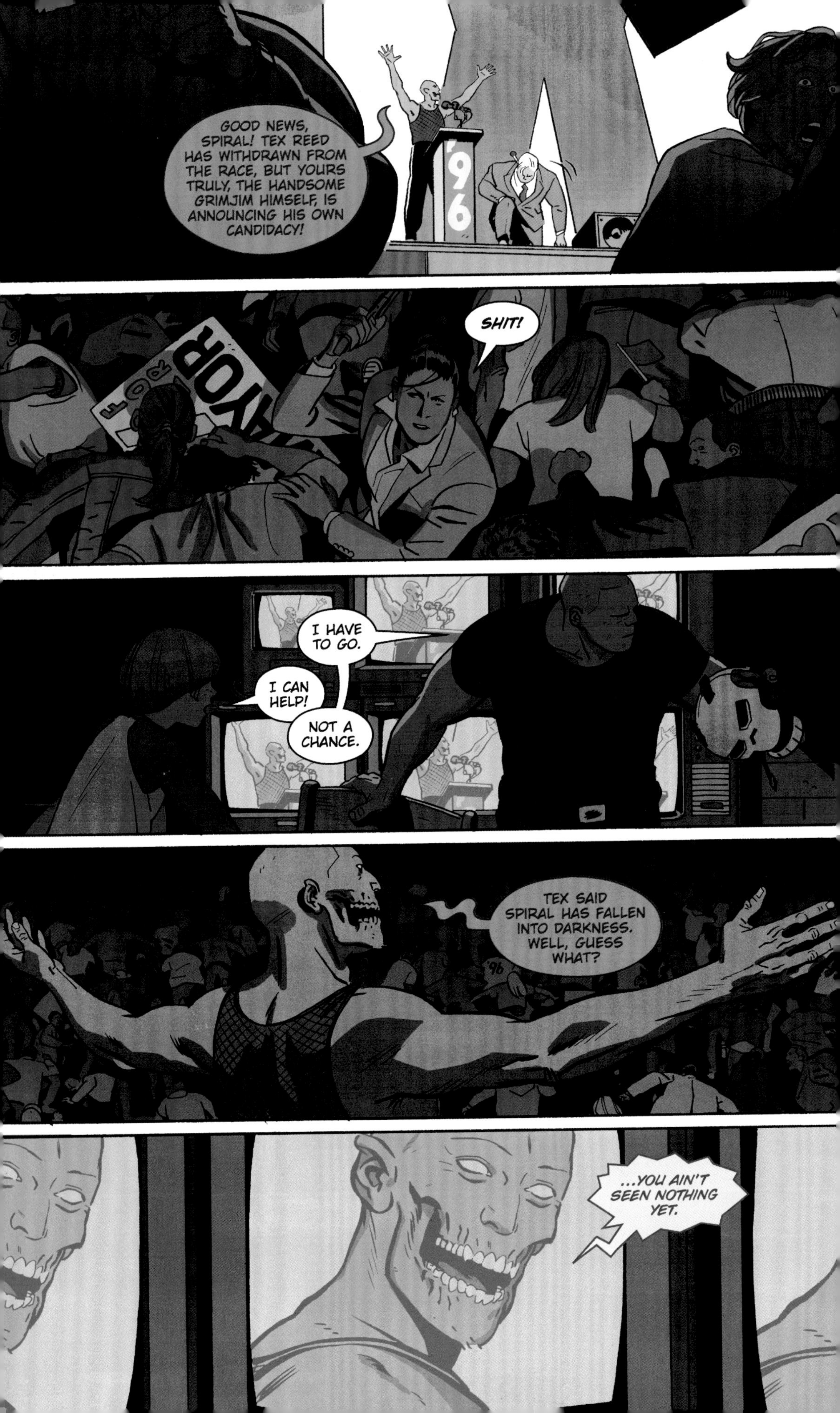
GOOD NEWS, SPIRAL! TEX REED HAS WITHDRAWN FROM THE RACE, BUT YOURS TRULY, THE HANDSOME GRIMJIM HIMSELF, IS ANNOUNCING HIS OWN CANDIDACY!
'96
SHIT!
I HAVE TO GO.
I CAN HELP!
NOT A CHANCE.
TEX SAID SPIRAL HAS FALLEN INTO DARKNESS. WELL, GUESS WHAT?
...YOU AIN'T SEEN NOTHING YET.

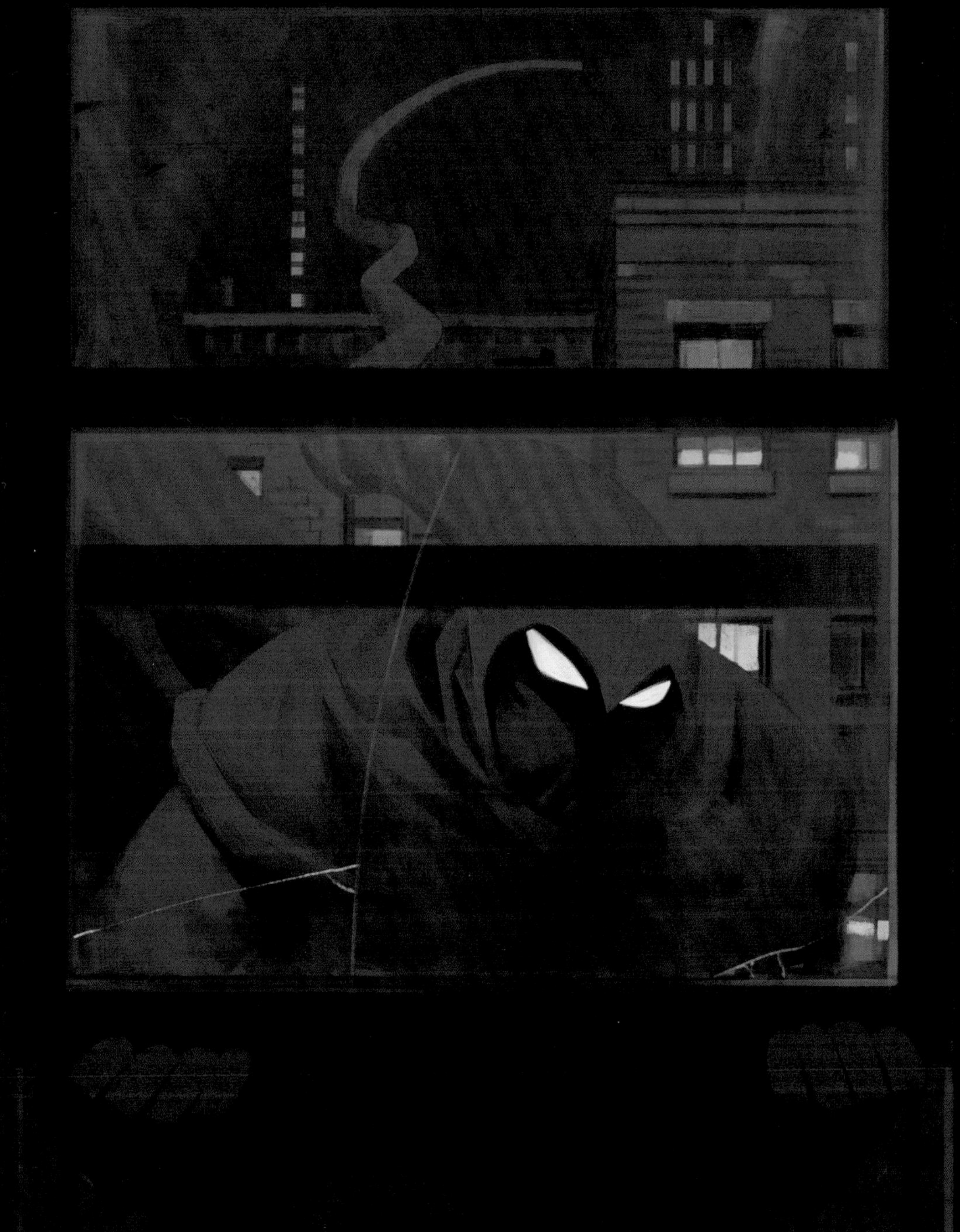

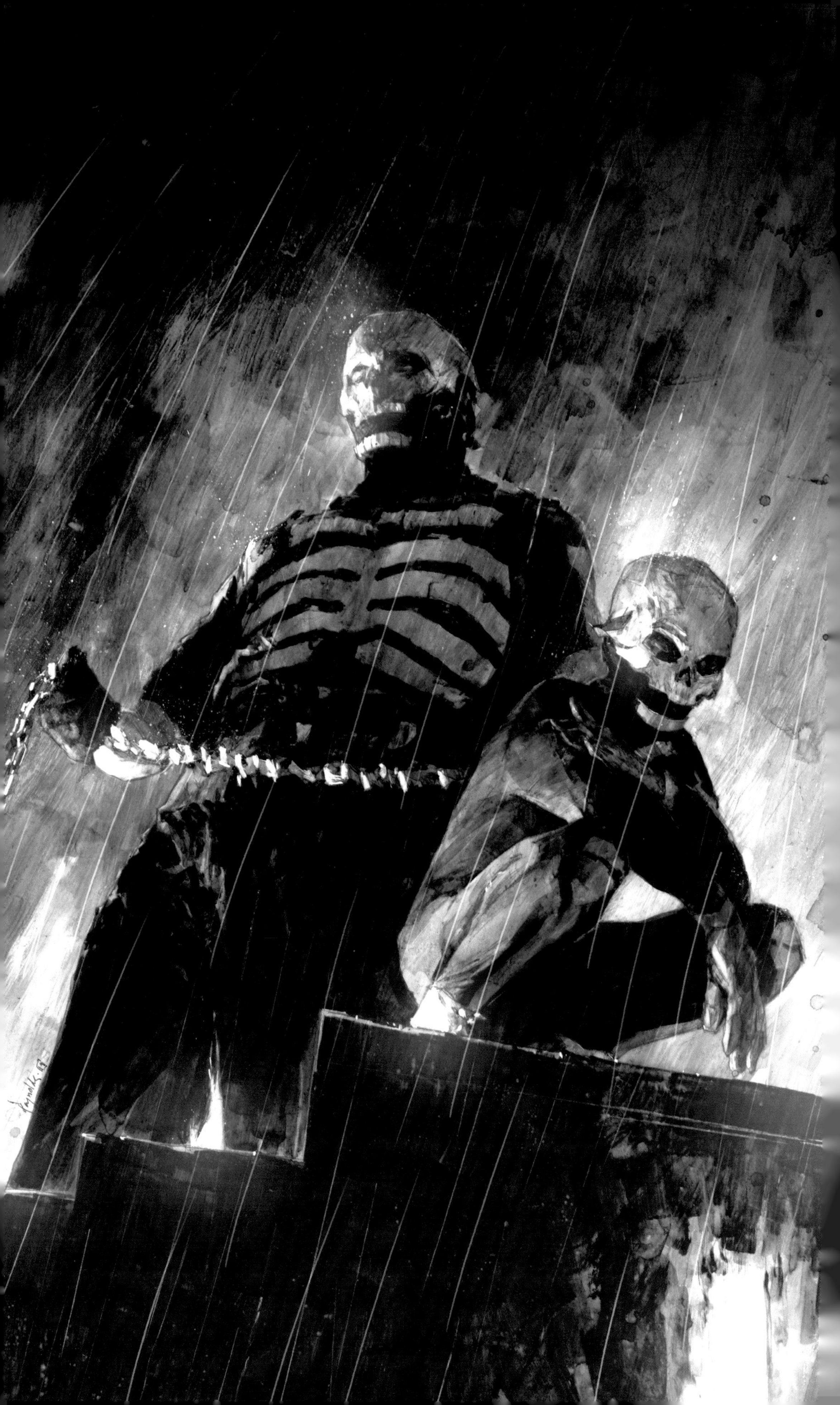

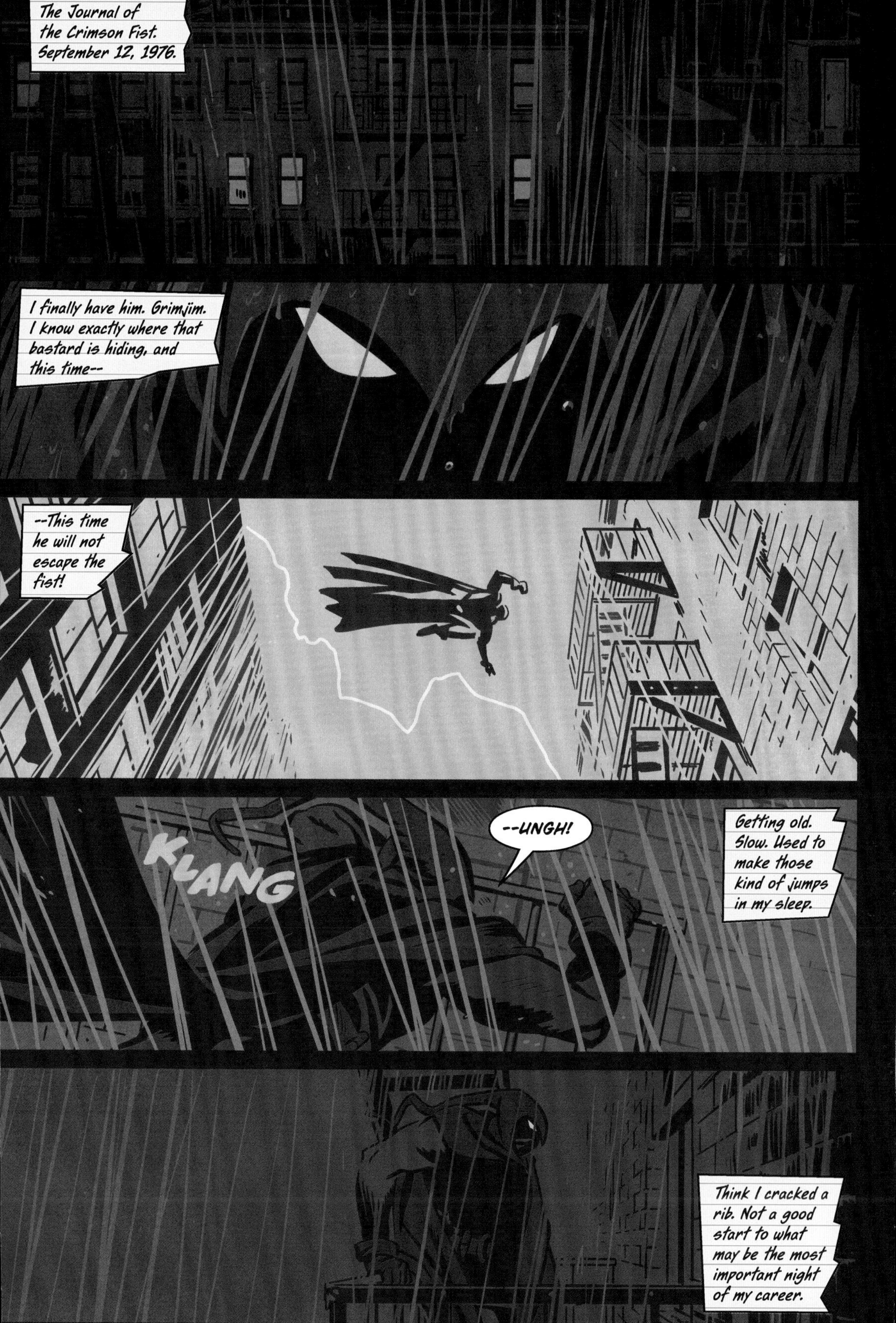
The Journal of the Crimson Fist. September 12, 1976.
I finally have him. Grimjim. I know exactly where that bastard is hiding, and this time--
--This time he will not escape the fist!
KLANG
--UNGH!
Getting old. Slow. Used to make those kind of jumps in my sleep.
Think I cracked a rib. Not a good start to what may be the most important night of my career.

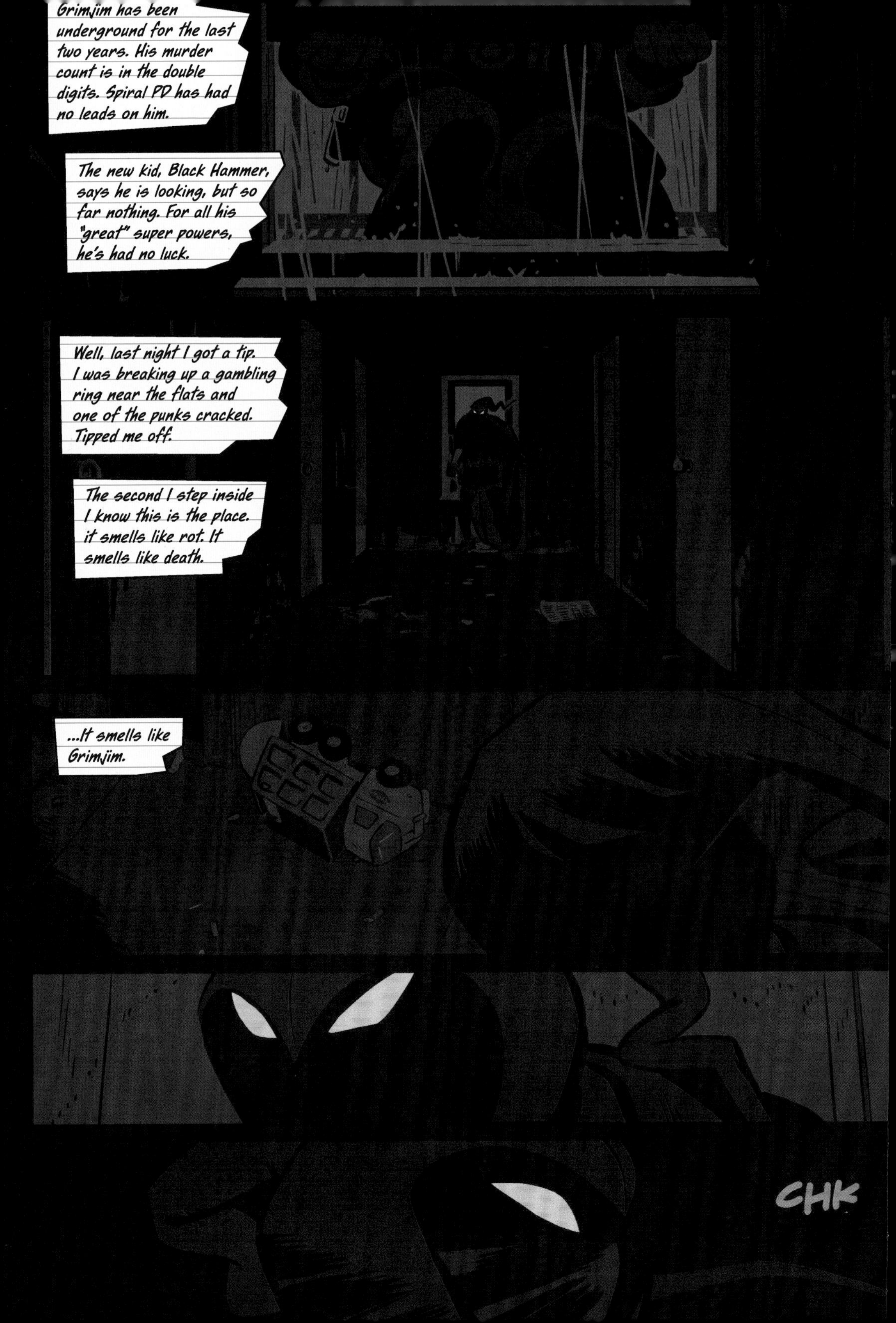
Grimjim has been underground for the last two years. His murder count is in the double digits. Spiral PD has had no leads on him.
The new kid, Black Hammer, says he is looking, but so far nothing. For all his "great" super powers, he's had no luck.
Well, last night I got a tip. I was breaking up a gambling ring near the flats and one of the punks cracked. Tipped me off.
The second I step inside I know this is the place. it smells like rot. It smells like death.
...It smells like Grimjim.
CHK

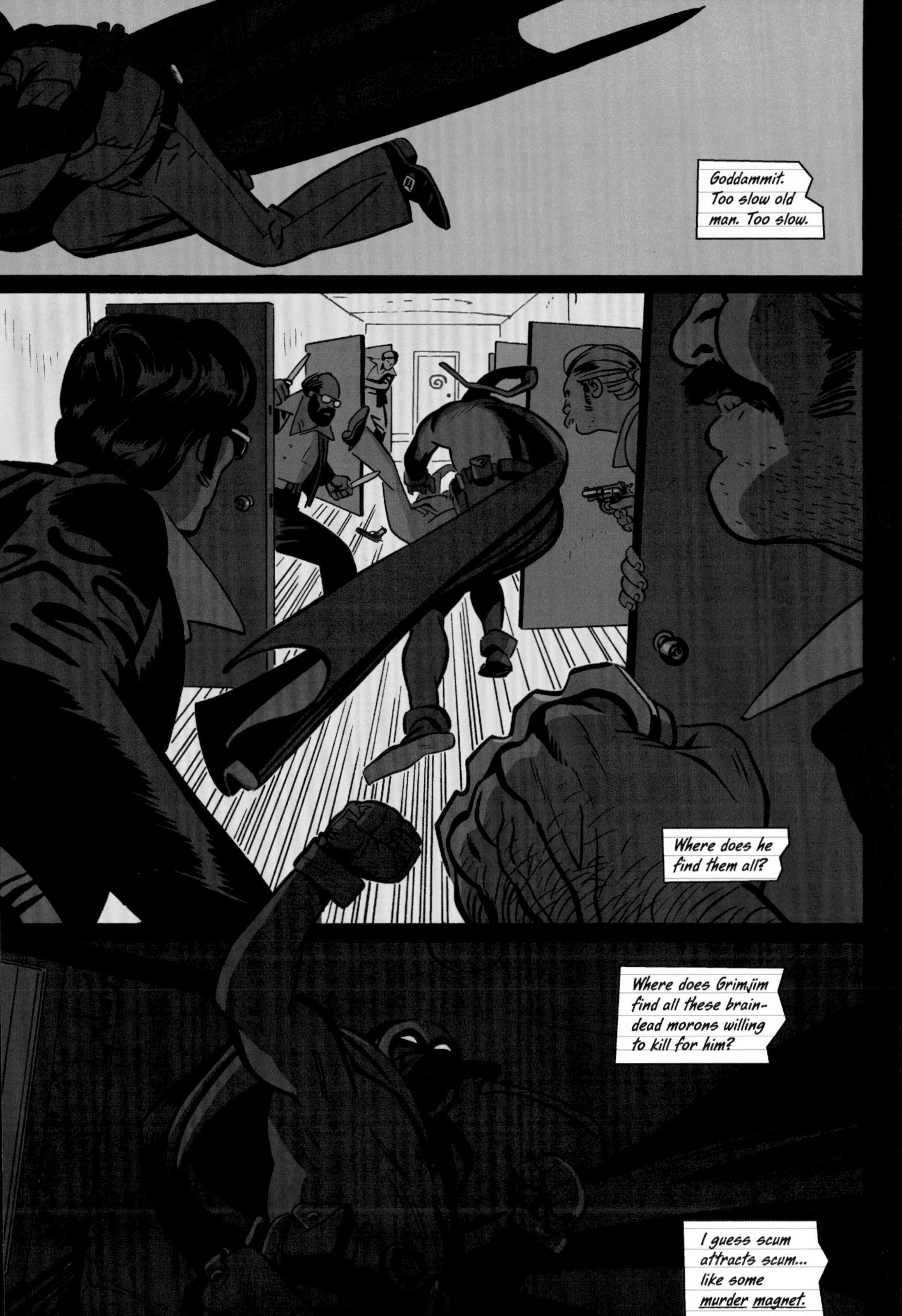
Goddammit. Too slow old man. Too slow.
Where does he find them all?
Where does Grimjim find all these brain-dead morons willing to kill for him?
I guess scum attracts scum... like some murder magnet.

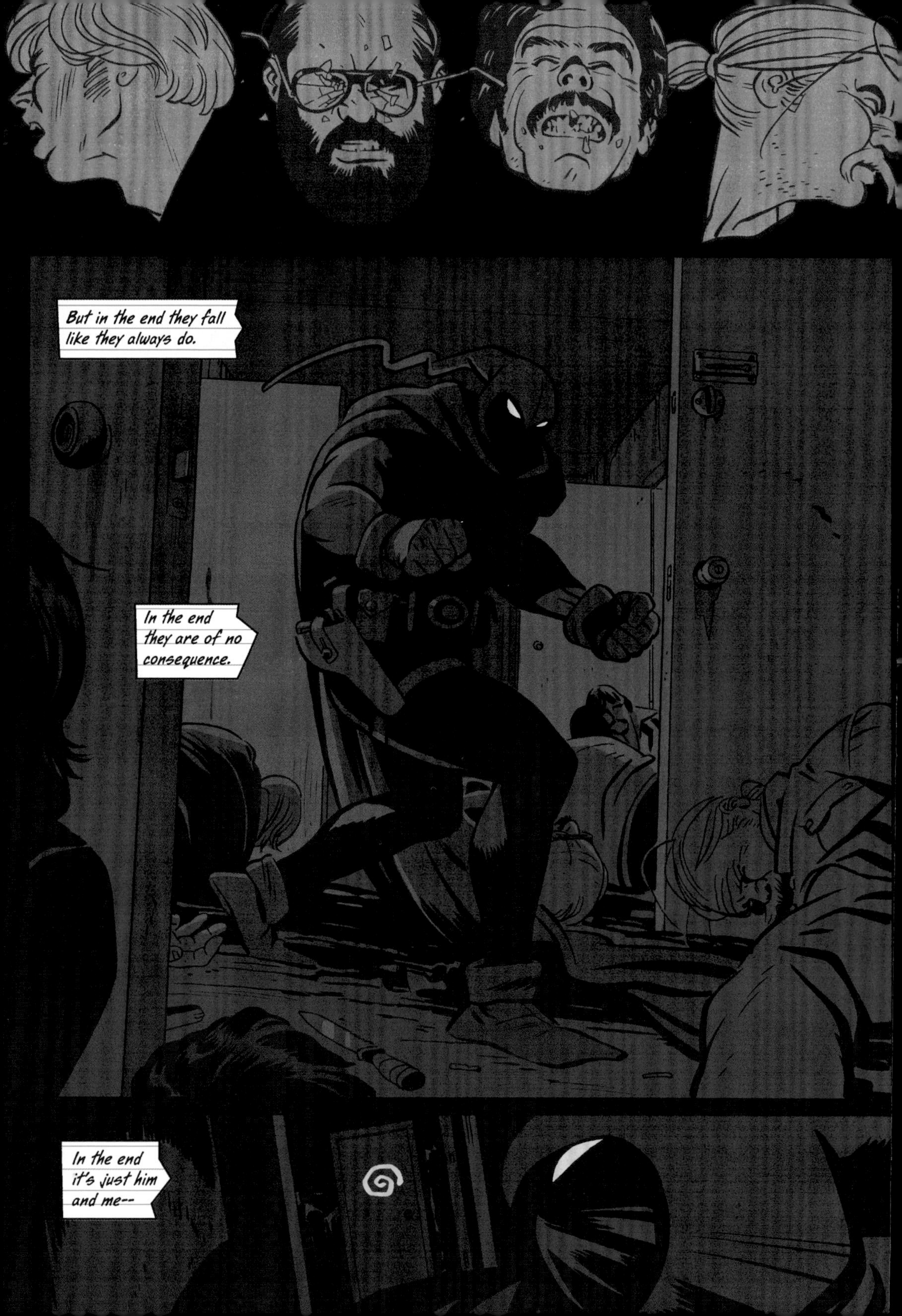
But in the end they fall like they always do.
In the end they are of no consequence.
In the end it's just him and me--

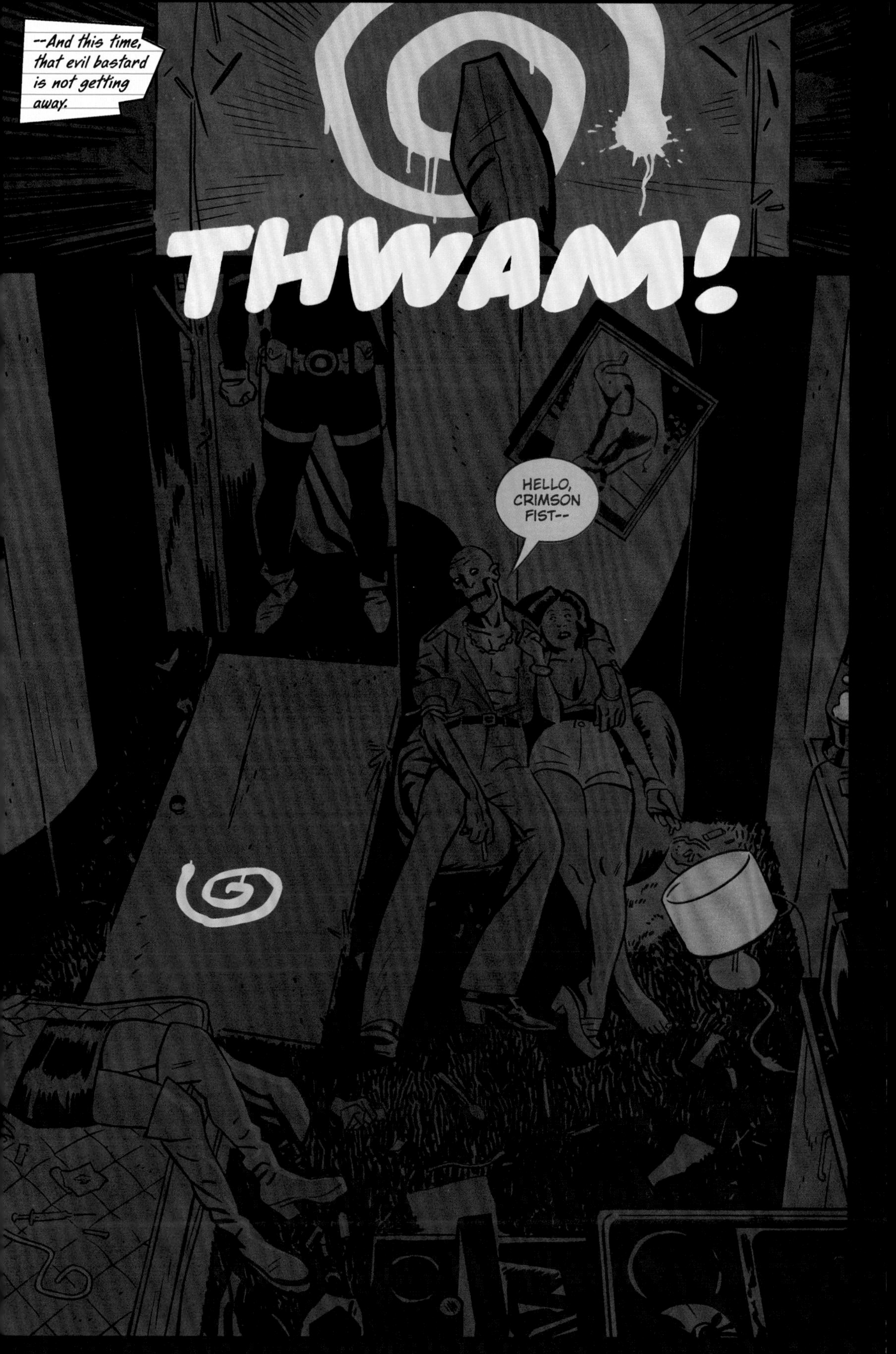
--And this time, that evil bastard is not getting away.
THWAM!
HELLO, CRIMSON FIST--

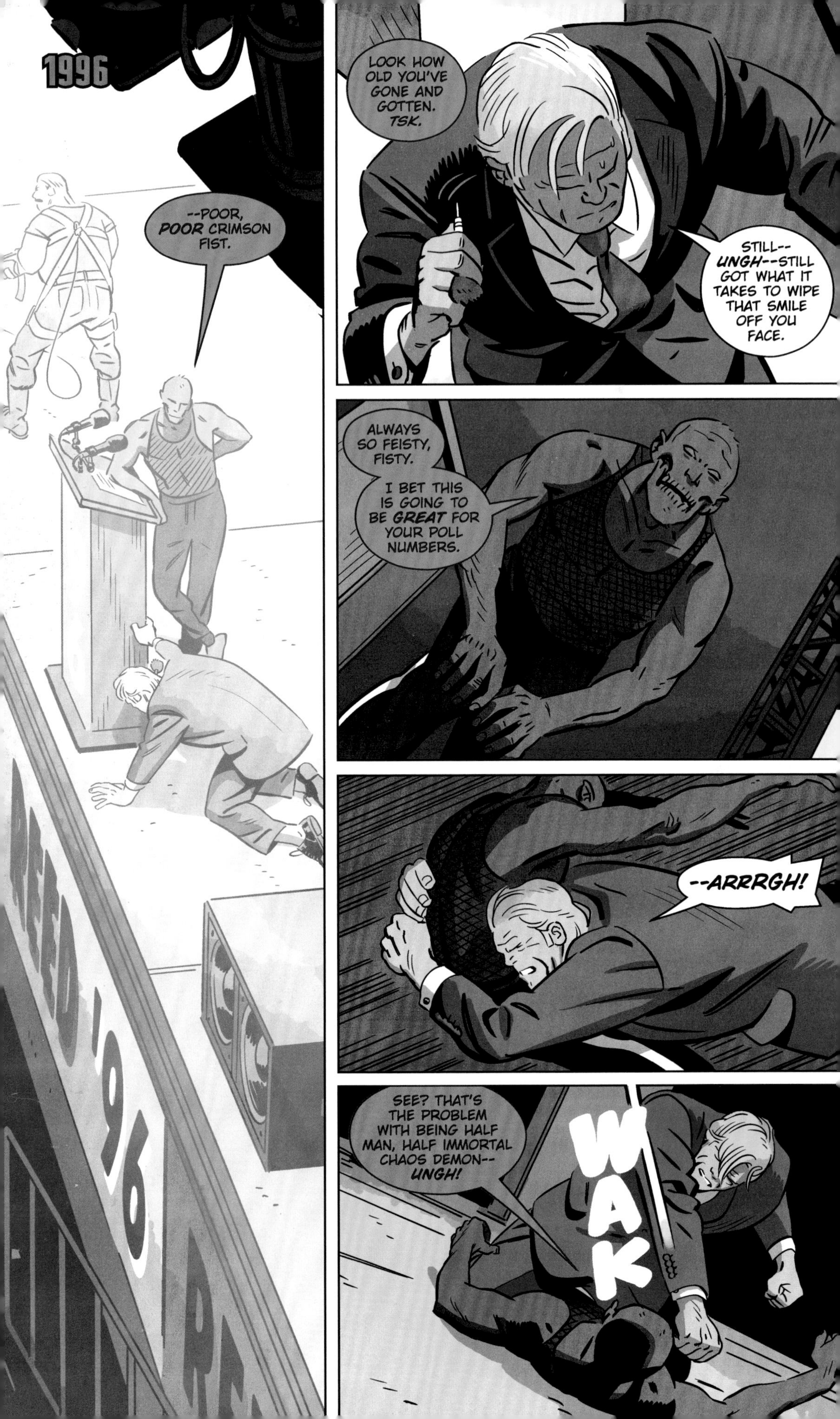
1996
--POOR, POOR CRIMSON FIST.
REED 1996
LOOK HOW OLD YOU'VE GONE AND GOTTEN. TSK.
STILL-- UNGH--STILL GOT WHAT IT TAKES TO WIPE THAT SMILE OFF YOU FACE.
ALWAYS SO FEISTY, FISTY.
I BET THIS IS GOING TO BE GREAT FOR YOUR POLL NUMBERS.
--ARRRGH!
SEE? THAT'S THE PROBLEM WITH BEING HALF MAN, HALF IMMORTAL CHAOS DEMON-- UNGH!
WAK

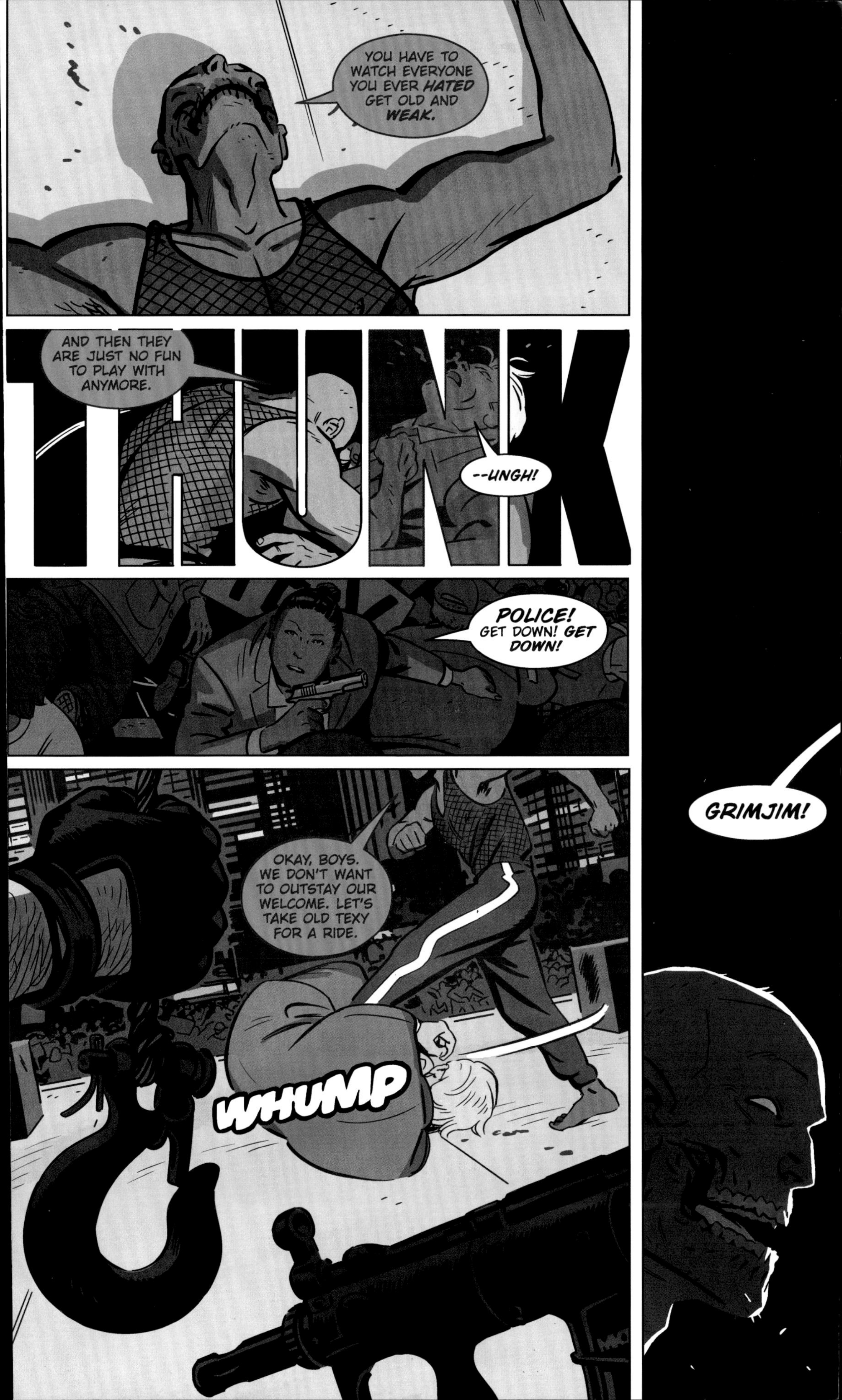
YOU HAVE TO WATCH EVERYONE YOU EVER HATED GET OLD AND WEAK.
AND THEN THEY ARE JUST NO FUN TO PLAY WITH ANYMORE.
THUNK
--UNGH!
POLICE! GET DOWN! GET DOWN!
OKAY, BOYS. WE DON'T WANT TO OUTSTAY OUR WELCOME. LET'S TAKE OLD TEXY FOR A RIDE.
WHUMP
GRIMJIM!

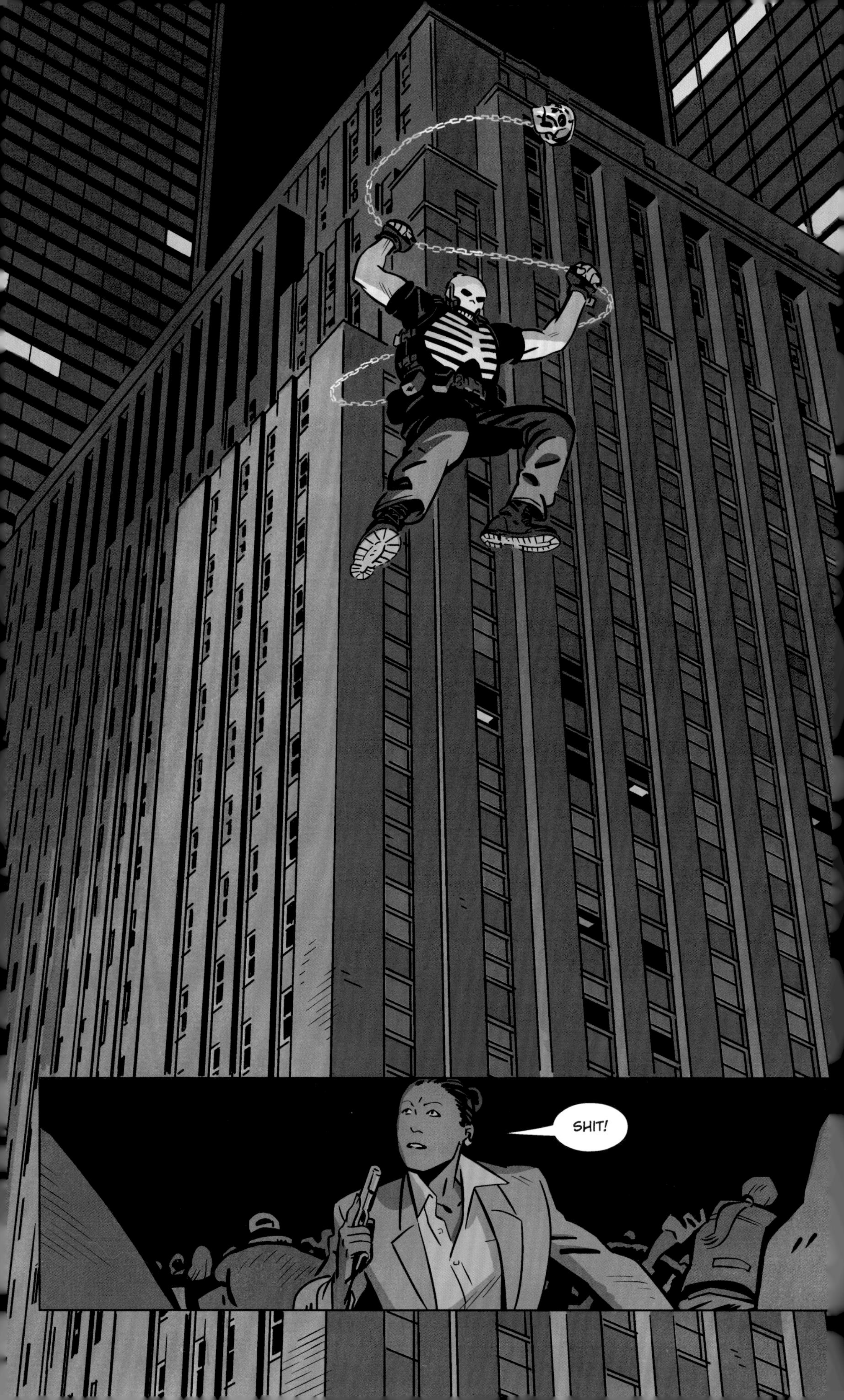
SHIT!

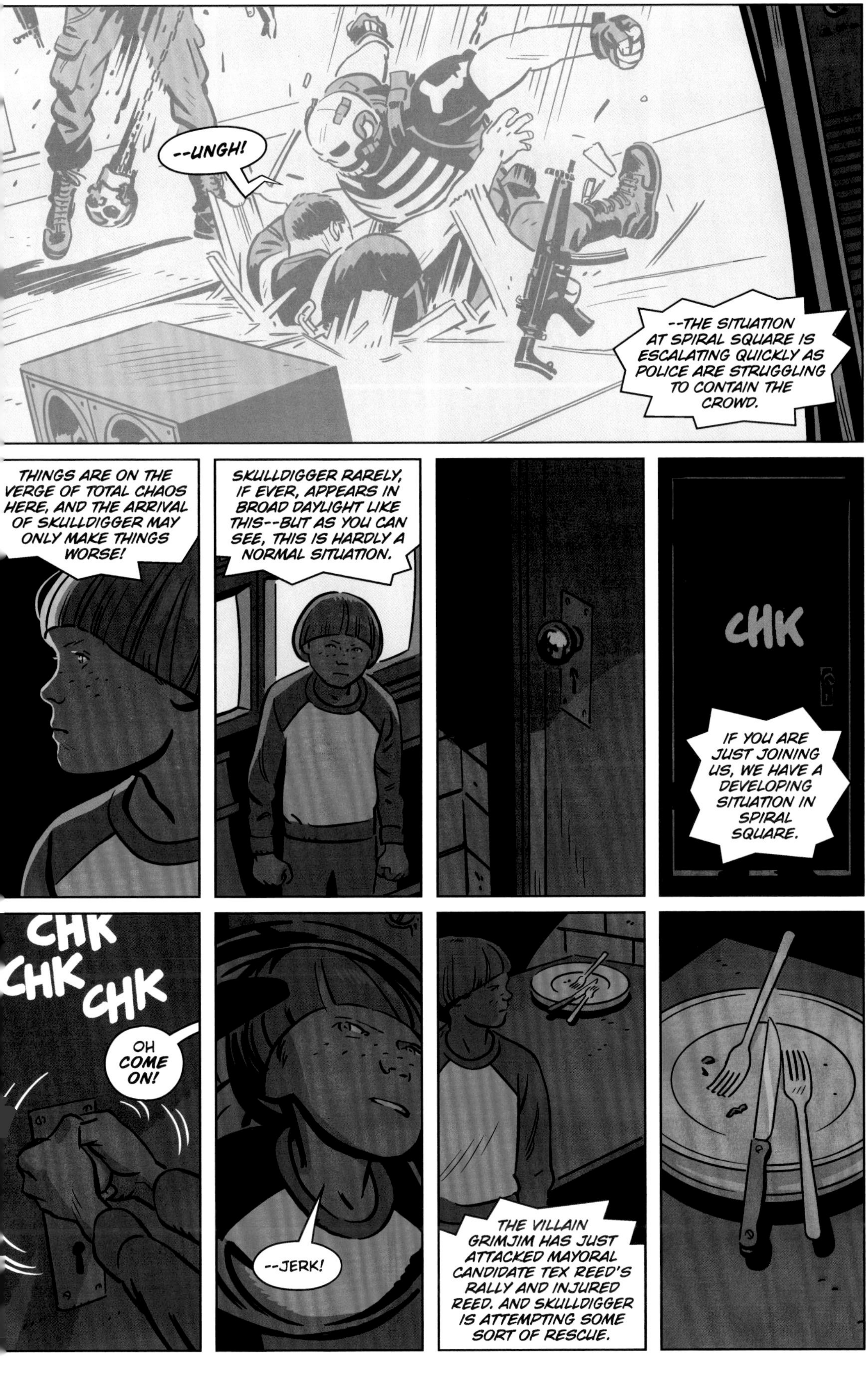
--UNGH!
--THE SITUATION AT SPIRAL SQUARE IS ESCALATING QUICKLY AS POLICE ARE STRUGGLING TO CONTAIN THE CROWD.
THINGS ARE ON THE VERGE OF TOTAL CHAOS HERE, AND THE ARRIVAL OF SKULLDIGGER MAY ONLY MAKE THINGS WORSE!
SKULLDIGGER RARELY, IF EVER, APPEARS IN BROAD DAYLIGHT LIKE THIS--BUT AS YOU CAN SEE, THIS IS HARDLY A NORMAL SITUATION.
CHK
IF YOU ARE JUST JOINING US, WE HAVE A DEVELOPING SITUATION IN SPIRAL SQUARE.
CHK CHK CHK
OH COME ON!
--JERK!
THE VILLAIN GRIMJIM HAS JUST ATTACKED MAYORAL CANDIDATE TEX REED'S RALLY AND INJURED REED. AND SKULLDIGGER IS ATTEMPTING SOME SORT OF RESCUE.

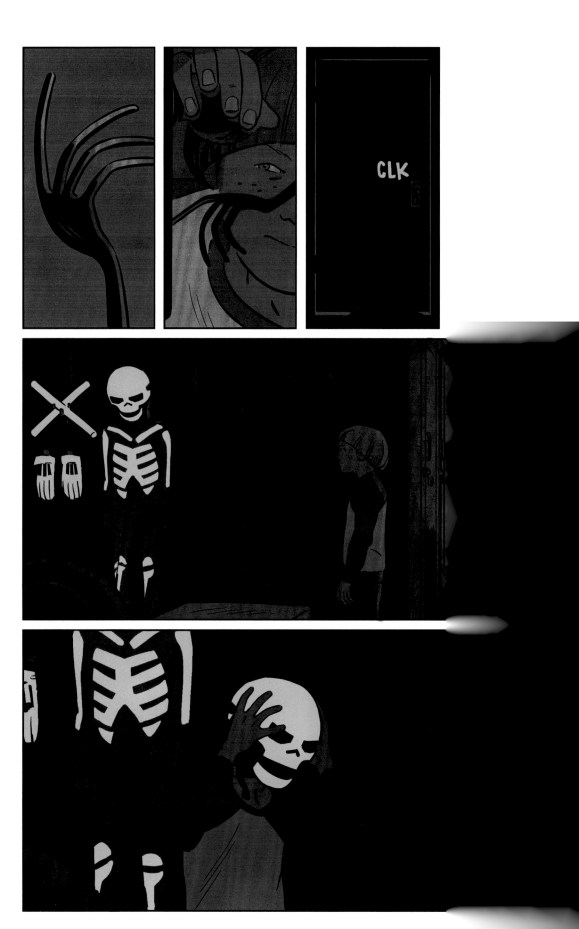

CLK

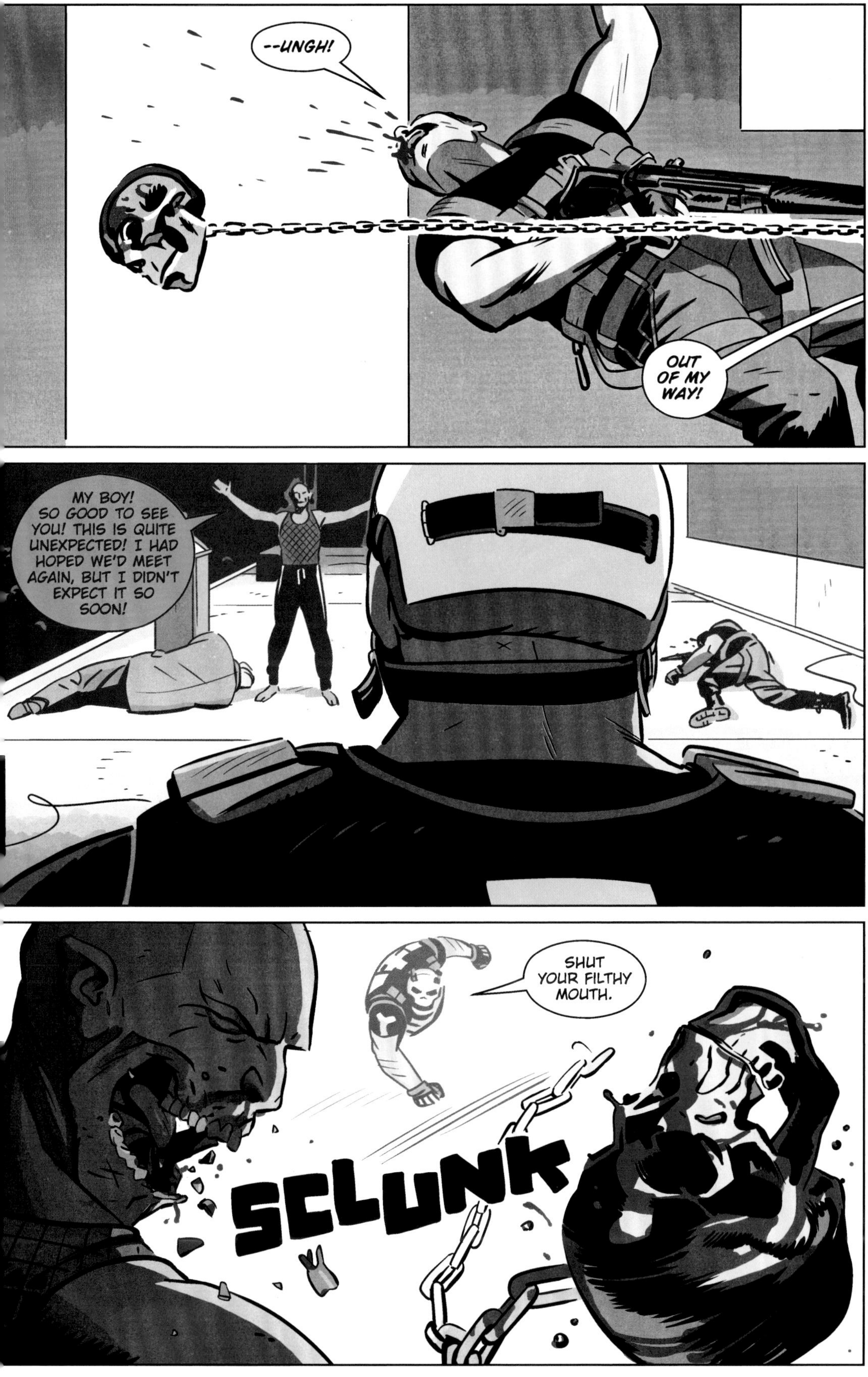
--UNGH!
OUT OF MY WAY!
MY BOY! SO GOOD TO SEE YOU! THIS IS QUITE UNEXPECTED! I HAD HOPED WE'D MEET AGAIN, BUT I DIDN'T EXPECT IT SO SOON!
SHUT YOUR FILTHY MOUTH.
SCLUNK

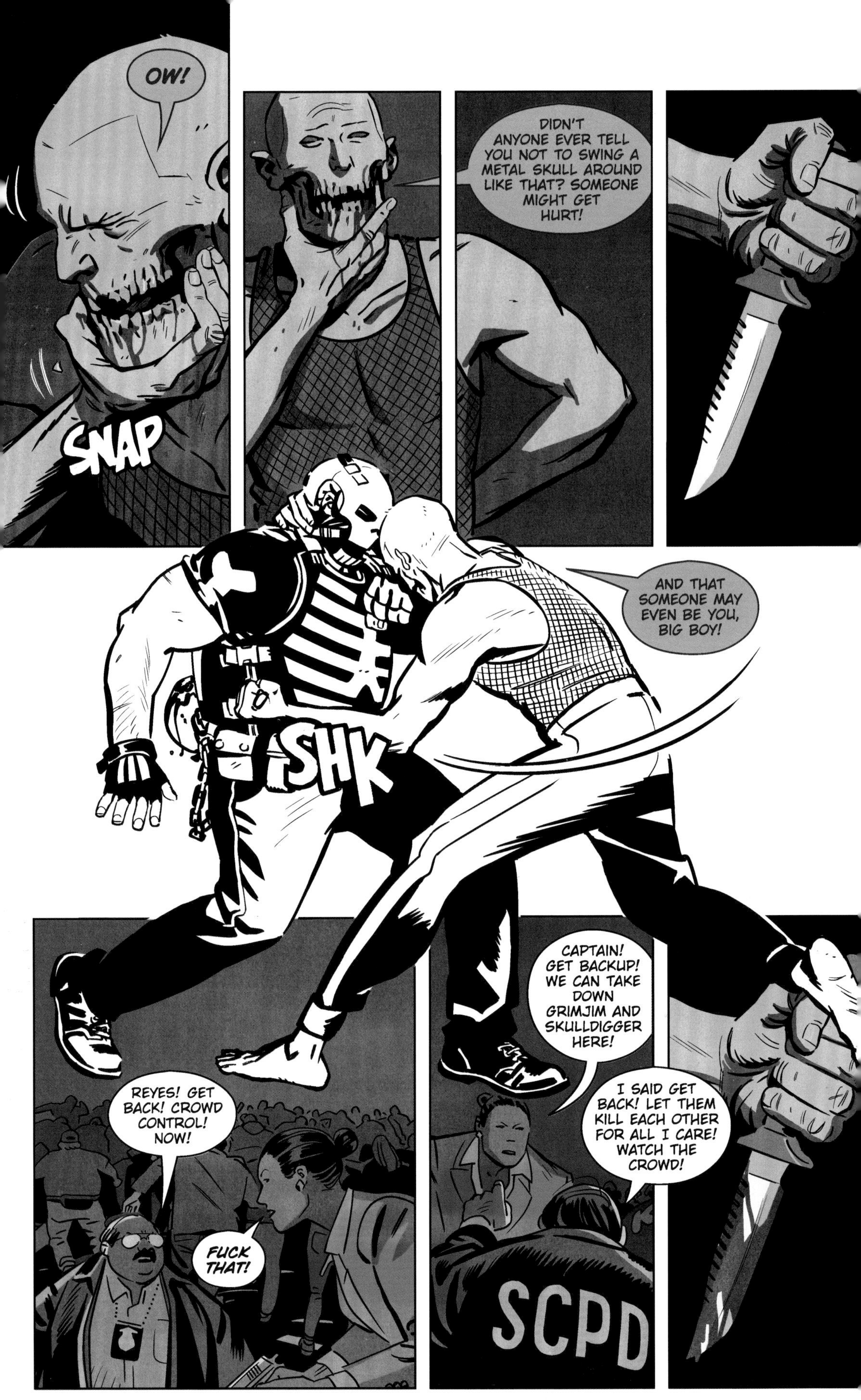
OW!
SNAP
DIDN'T ANYONE EVER TELL YOU NOT TO SWING A METAL SKULL AROUND LIKE THAT? SOMEONE MIGHT GET HURT!
AND THAT SOMEONE MAY EVEN BE YOU, BIG BOY!
SHK
REYES! GET BACK! CROWD CONTROL! NOW!
FUCK THAT!
CAPTAIN! GET BACKUP! WE CAN TAKE DOWN GRIMJIM AND SKULLDIGGER HERE!
I SAID GET BACK! LET THEM KILL EACH OTHER FOR ALL I CARE! WATCH THE CROWD!
SCPD

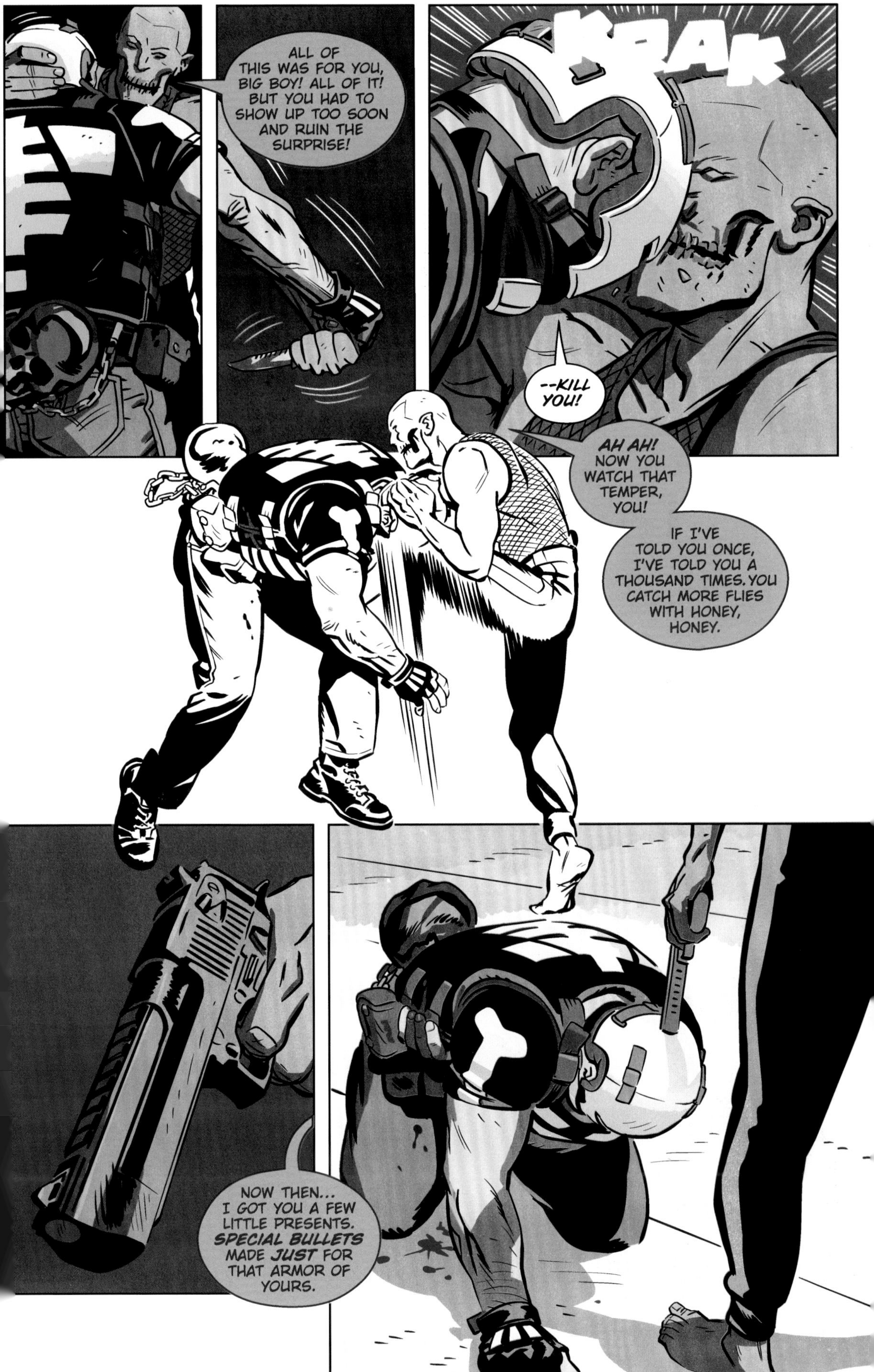
ALL OF THIS WAS FOR YOU, BIG BOY! ALL OF IT! BUT YOU HAD TO SHOW UP TOO SOON AND RUIN THE SURPRISE!
KRAK
--KILL YOU!
AH AH! NOW YOU WATCH THAT TEMPER, YOU!
IF I'VE TOLD YOU ONCE, I'VE TOLD YOU A THOUSAND TIMES. YOU CATCH MORE FLIES WITH HONEY, HONEY.
NOW THEN... I GOT YOU A FEW LITTLE PRESENTS. SPECIAL BULLETS MADE JUST FOR THAT ARMOR OF YOURS.

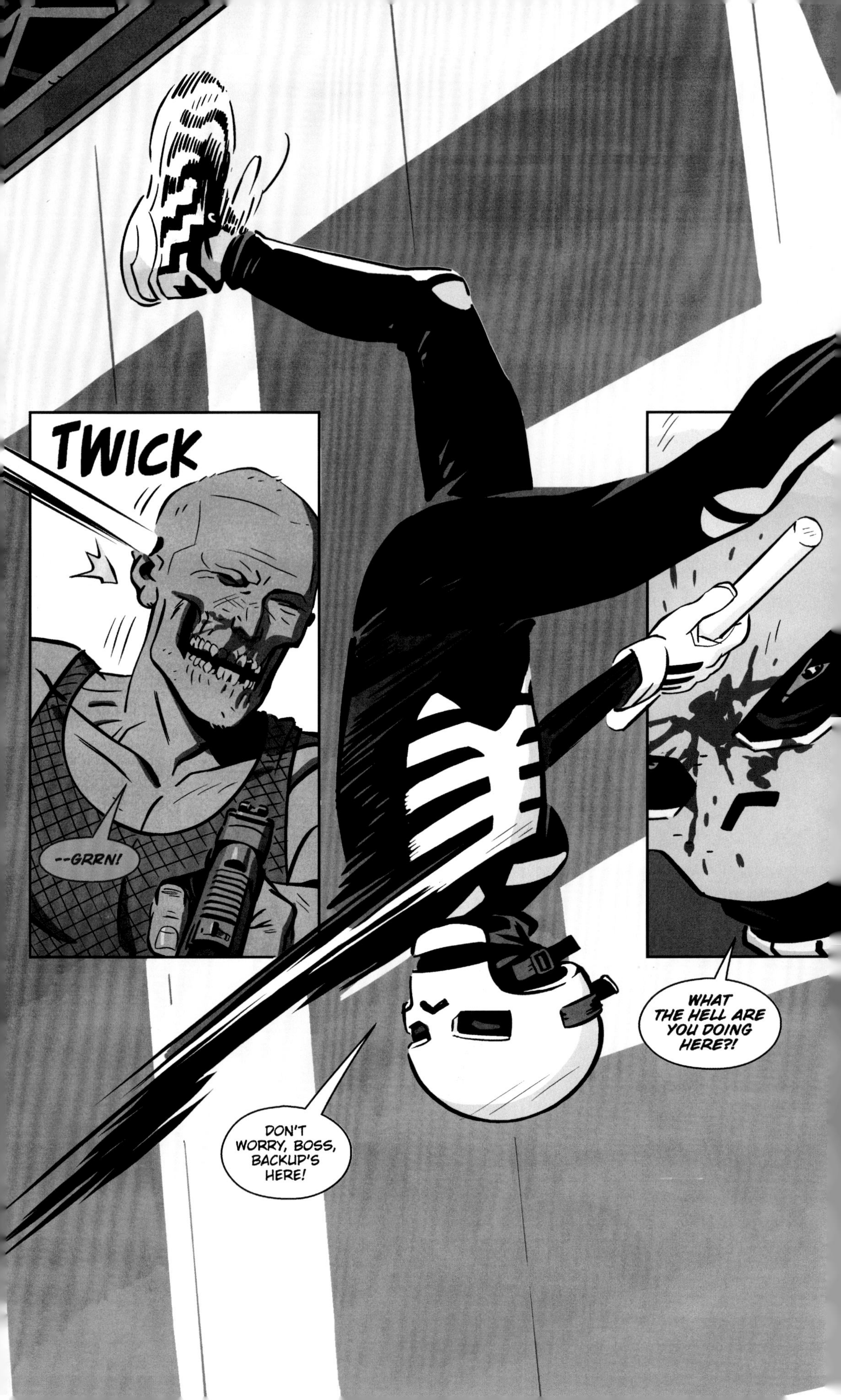
TWICK
--GRRN!
WHAT THE HELL ARE YOU DOING HERE?!
DON'T WORRY, BOSS, BACKUP'S HERE!

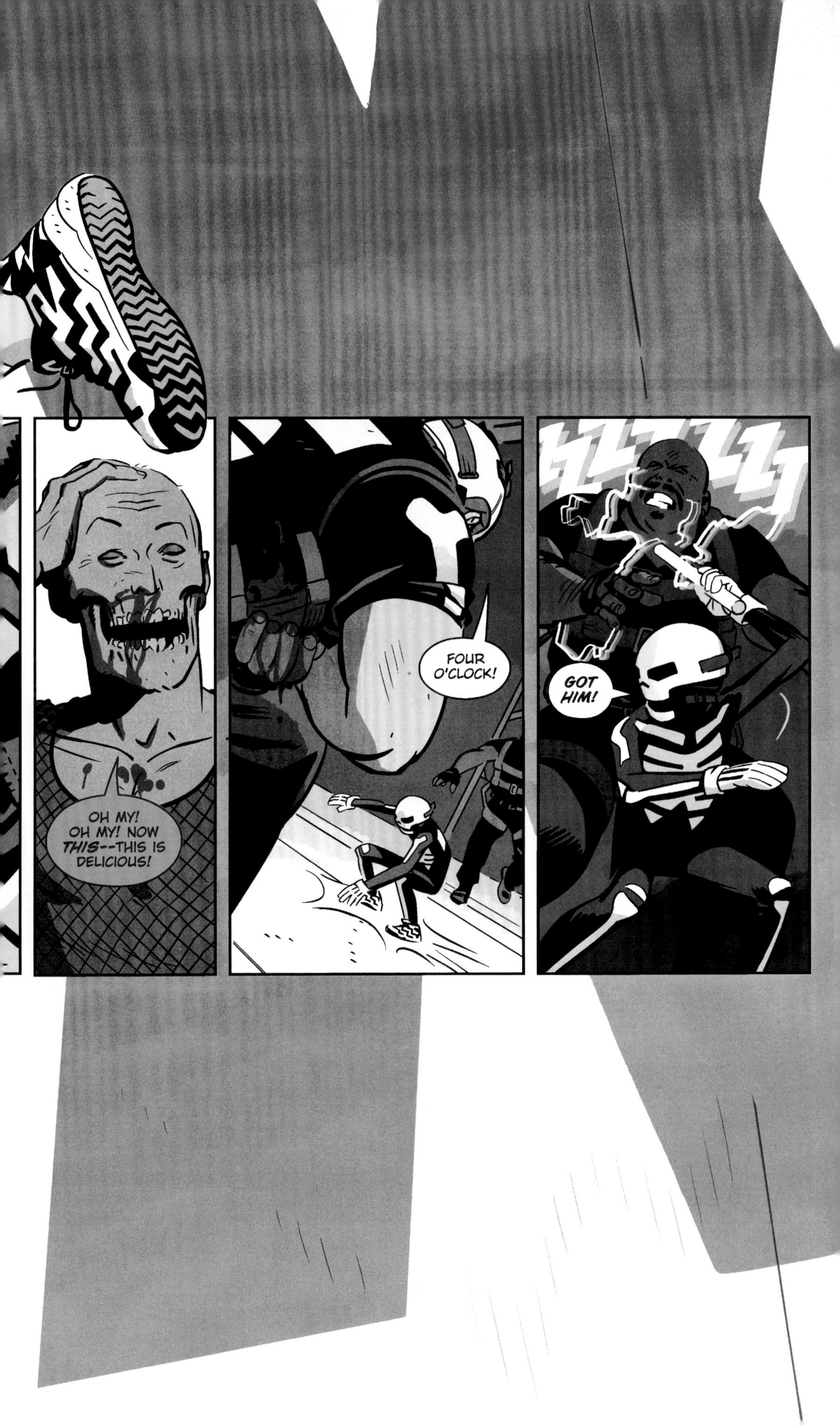
OH MY! OH MY! NOW THIS--THIS IS DELICIOUS!
FOUR O'CLOCK!
GOT HIM!

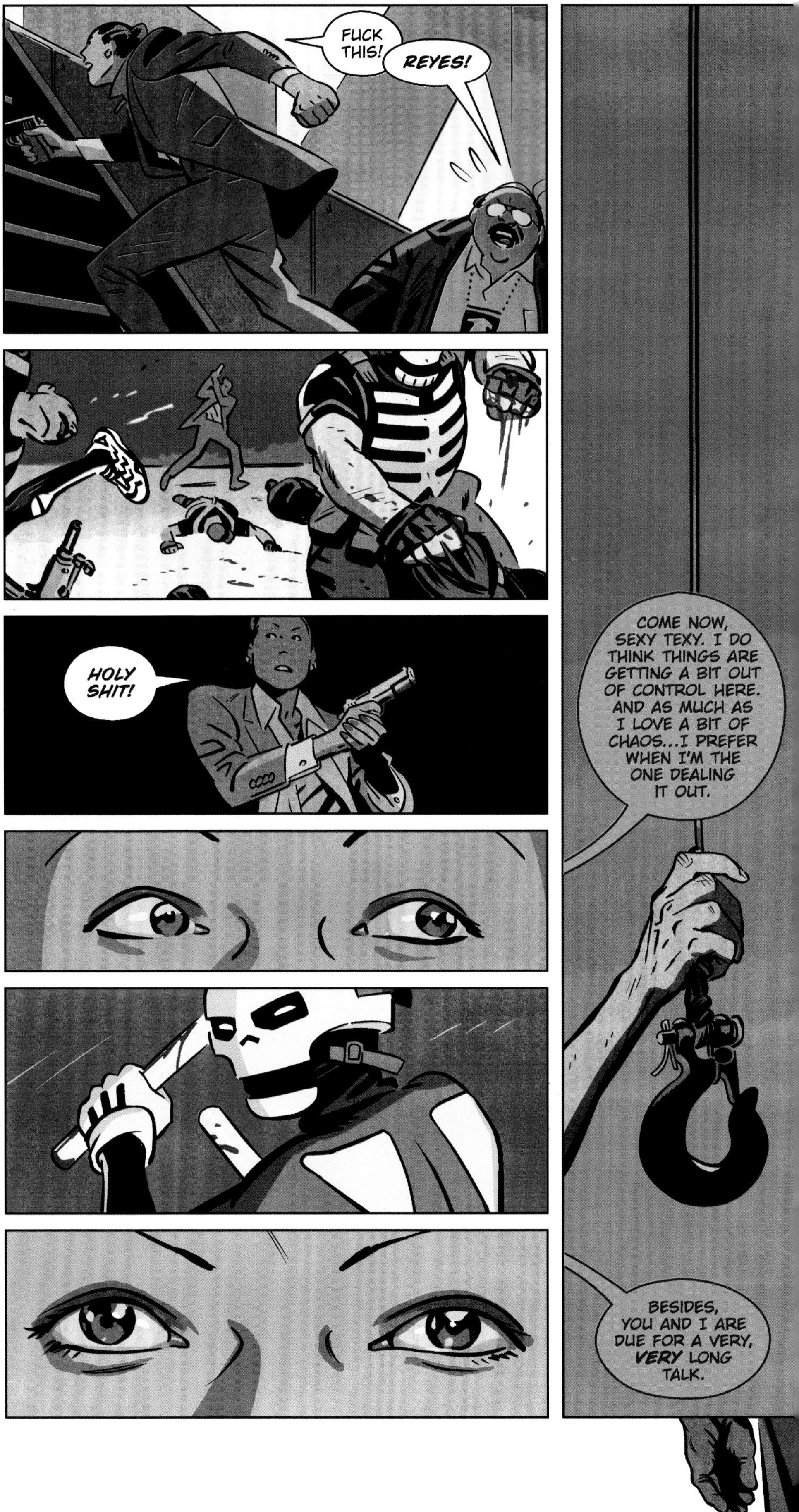

FUCK THIS!
REYES!
HOLY SHIT!
COME NOW, SEXY TEXY. I DO THINK THINGS ARE GETTING A BIT OUT OF CONTROL HERE. AND AS MUCH AS I LOVE A BIT OF CHAOS...I PREFER WHEN I'M THE ONE DEALING IT OUT.
BESIDES, YOU AND I ARE DUE FOR A VERY, VERY LONG TALK.

FREEZE! DO NOT MOVE, SKULLDIGGER! I SWEAR TO GOD, I WILL PUT YOU DOWN!

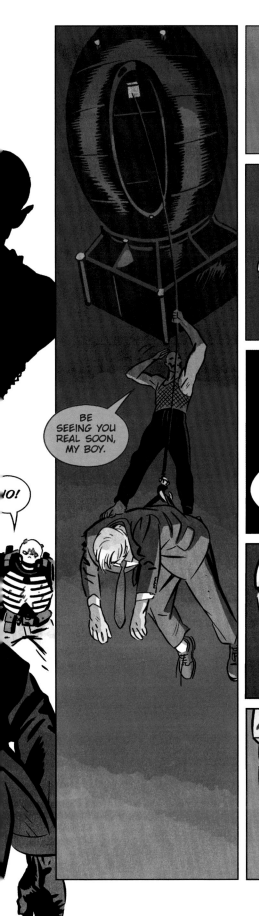

BE SEEING YOU REAL SOON, MY BOY.

NO!

IT'S OKAY-- I CAN HELP YOU. JUST STEP AWAY FROM HIM.

IT'S ALL GOING TO BE OKAY. I CAN HELP YOU--I--I *KNOW WHO YOU ARE.* JUST COME HERE. COME WITH ME.

WITH YOU? WHY WOULD I GO WITH *YOU?* YOU HAVE NO IDEA *WHO* I AM...

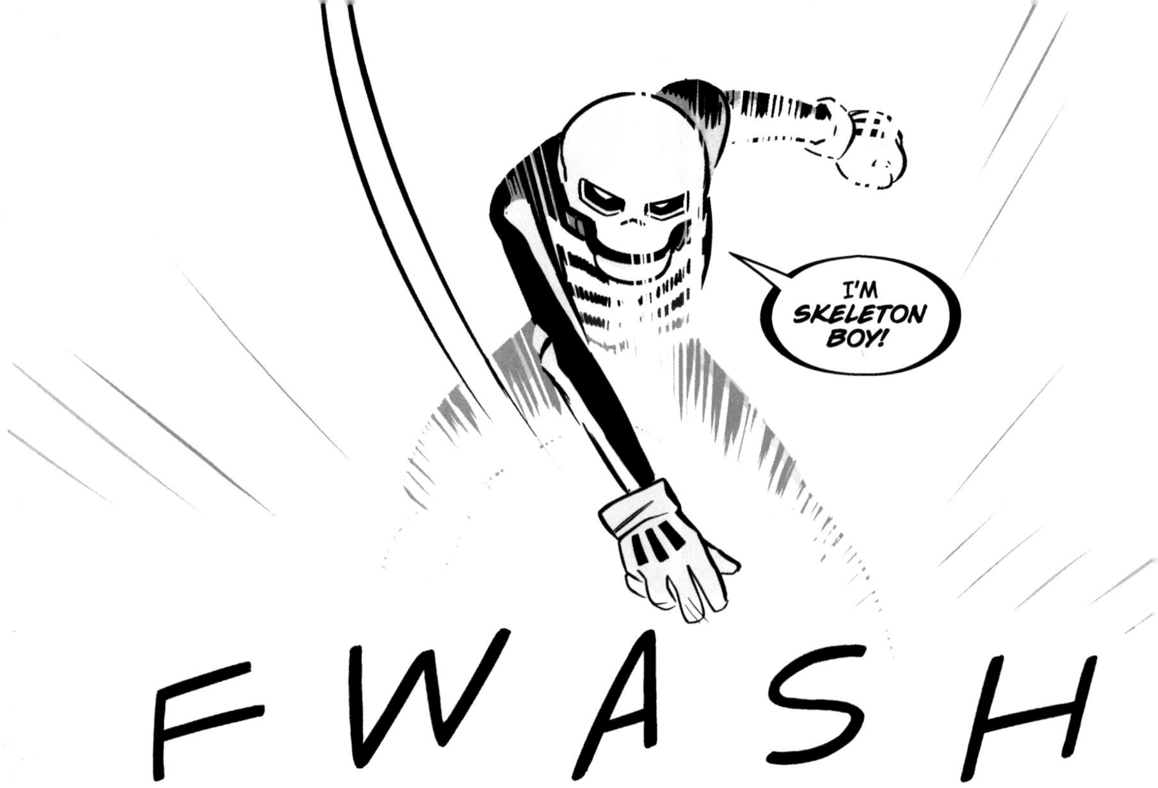
I'M SKELETON BOY!
FWASH

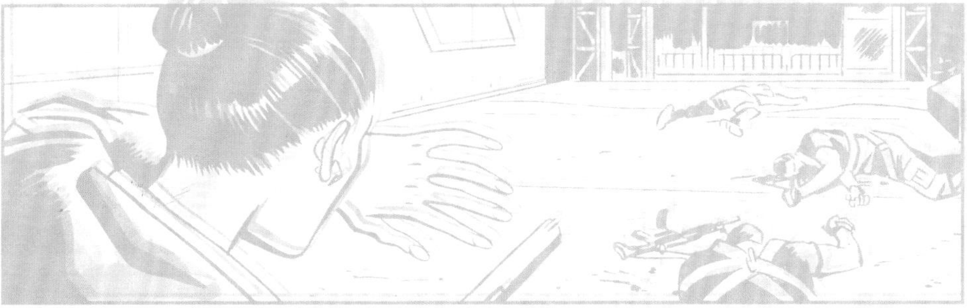

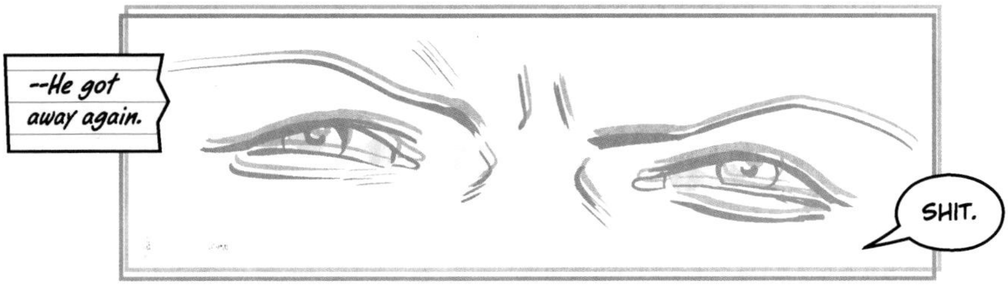
--He got away again.
SHIT.

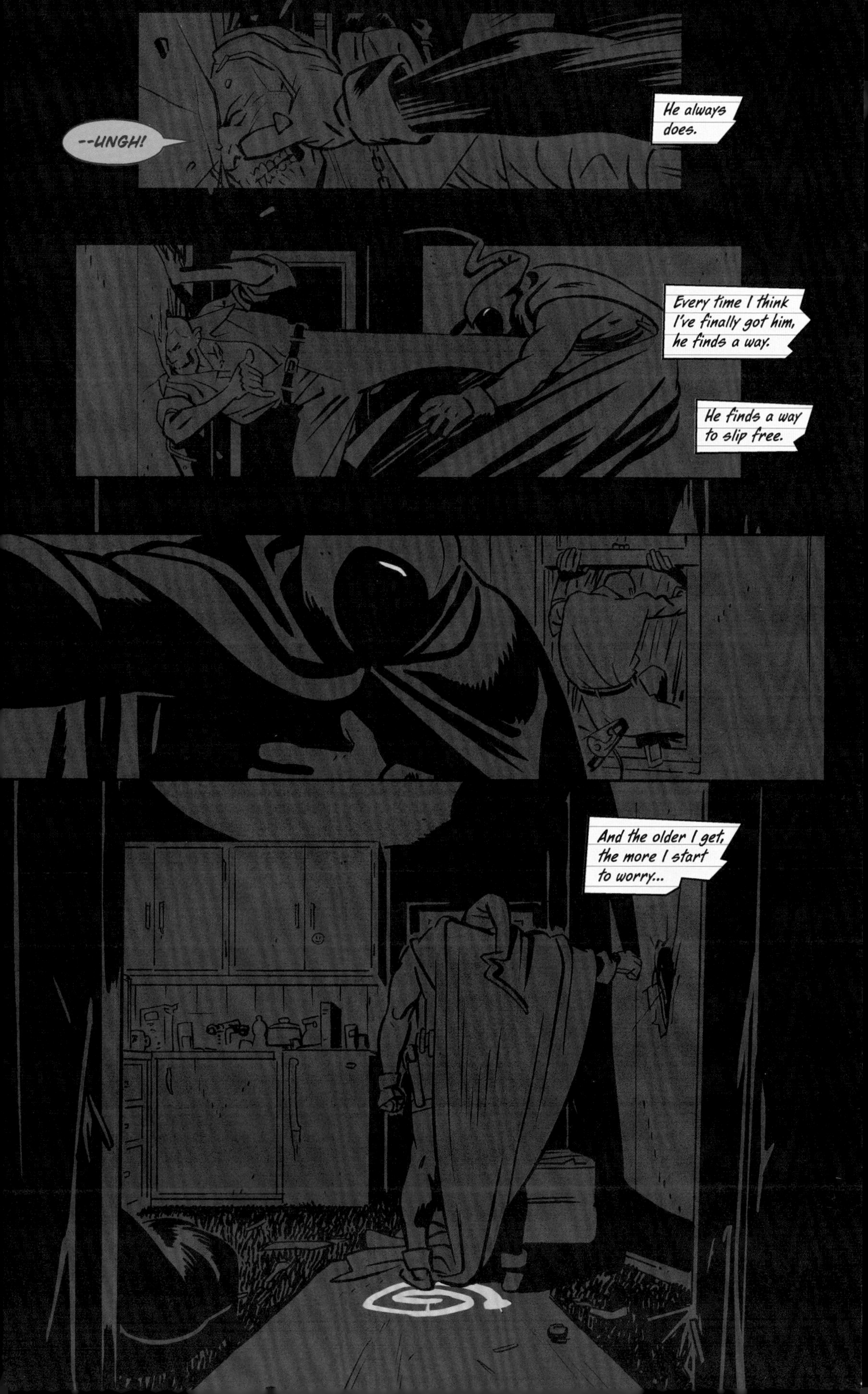
--UNGH!
He always does.
Every time I think I've finally got him, he finds a way.
He finds a way to slip free.
And the older I get, the more I start to worry...

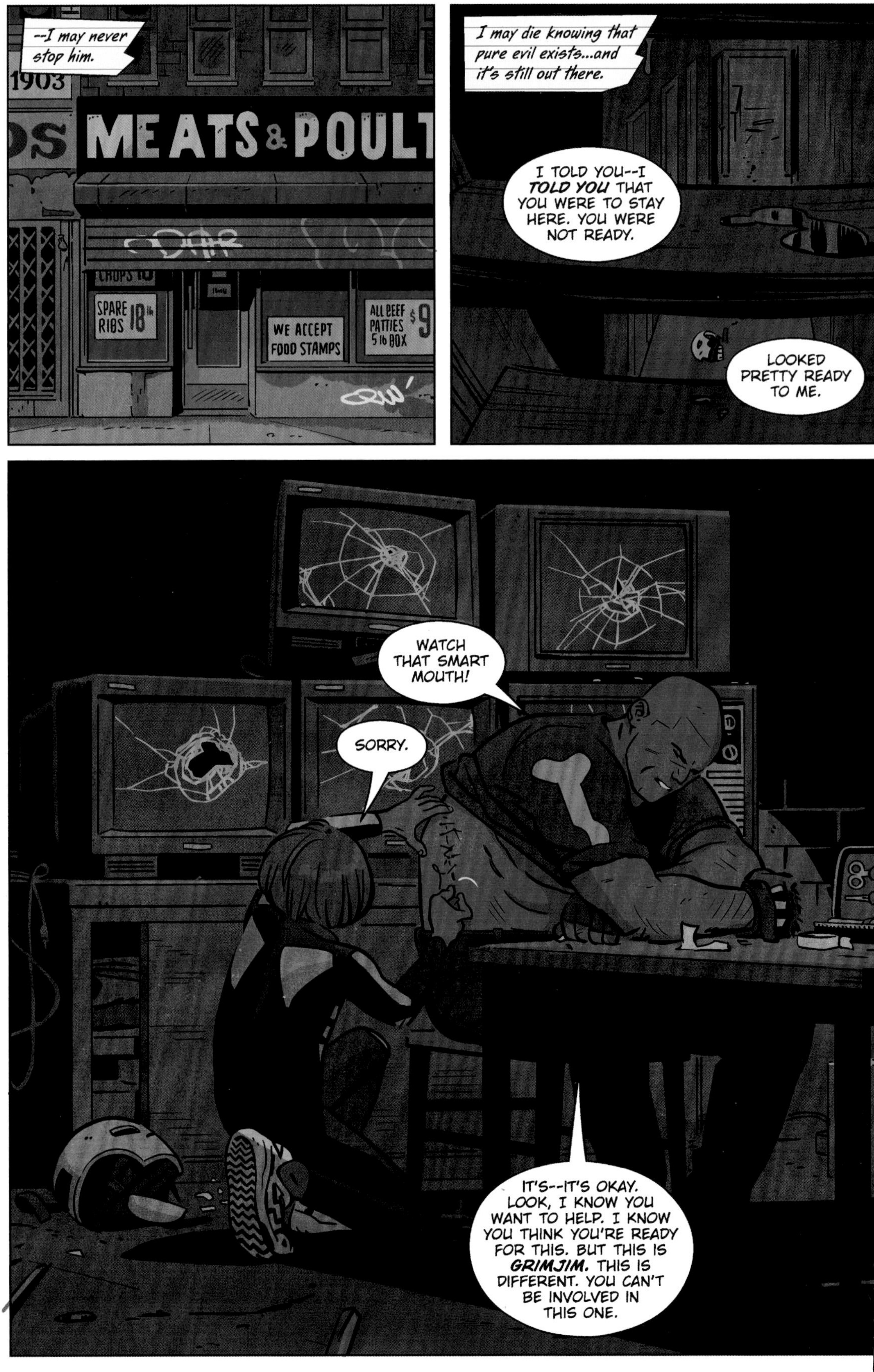
--I may never stop him.
1903
MEATS & POULT
CHOPS
SPARE RIBS 18 lb
WE ACCEPT FOOD STAMPS
ALL BEEF PATTIES 5 lb BOX $9
I may die knowing that pure evil exists...and it's still out there.
I TOLD YOU--I TOLD YOU THAT YOU WERE TO STAY HERE. YOU WERE NOT READY.
LOOKED PRETTY READY TO ME.
WATCH THAT SMART MOUTH!
SORRY.
IT'S--IT'S OKAY. LOOK, I KNOW YOU WANT TO HELP. I KNOW YOU THINK YOU'RE READY FOR THIS. BUT THIS IS GRIMJIM. THIS IS DIFFERENT. YOU CAN'T BE INVOLVED IN THIS ONE.

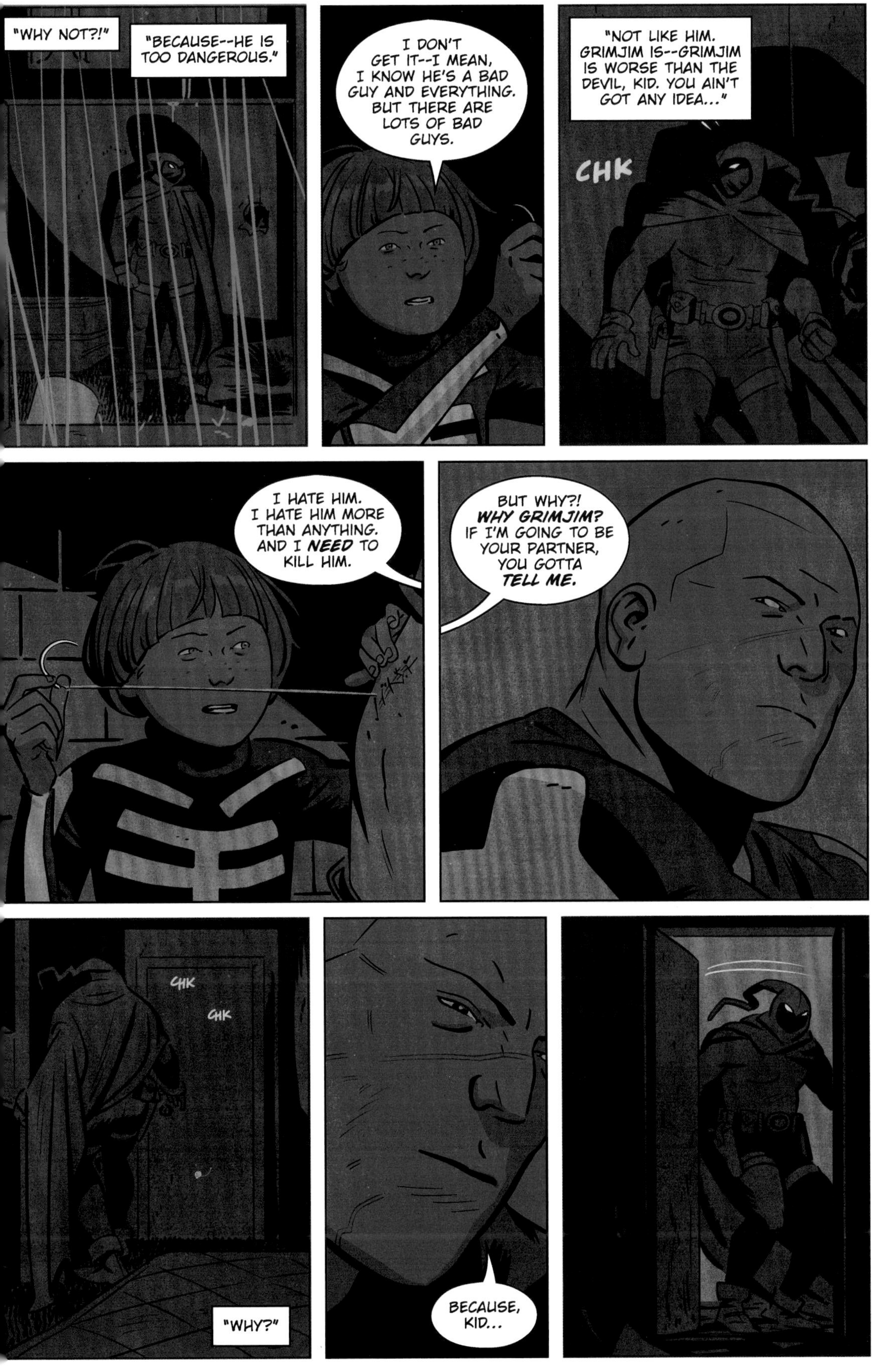
"WHY NOT?!"
"BECAUSE--HE IS TOO DANGEROUS."
I DON'T GET IT--I MEAN, I KNOW HE'S A BAD GUY AND EVERYTHING. BUT THERE ARE LOTS OF BAD GUYS.
"NOT LIKE HIM. GRIMJIM IS--GRIMJIM IS WORSE THAN THE DEVIL, KID. YOU AIN'T GOT ANY IDEA..."
CHK
I HATE HIM. I HATE HIM MORE THAN ANYTHING. AND I NEED TO KILL HIM.
BUT WHY?! WHY GRIMJIM? IF I'M GOING TO BE YOUR PARTNER, YOU GOTTA TELL ME.
CHK
CHK
"WHY?"
BECAUSE, KID...

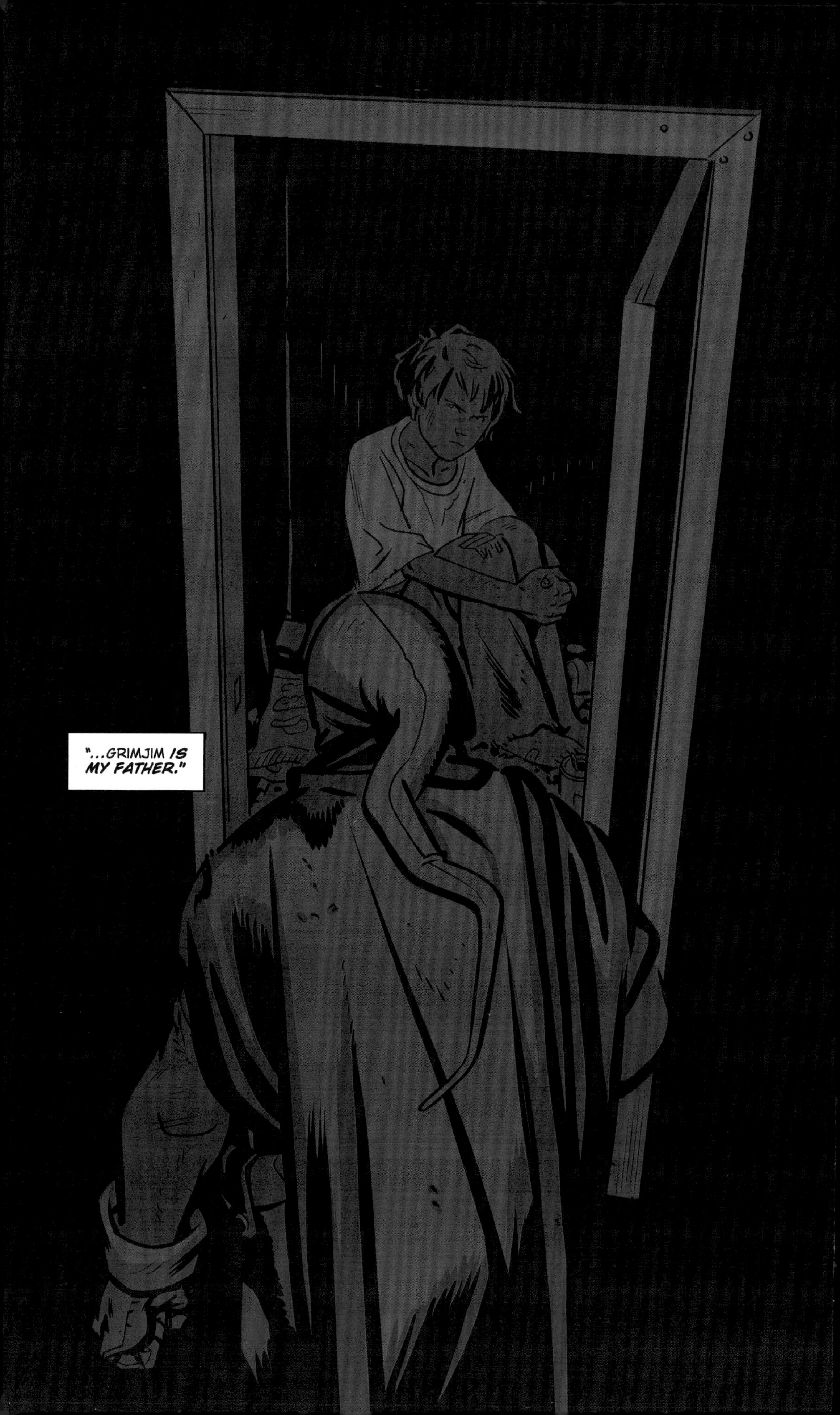
"...GRIMJIM IS MY FATHER."

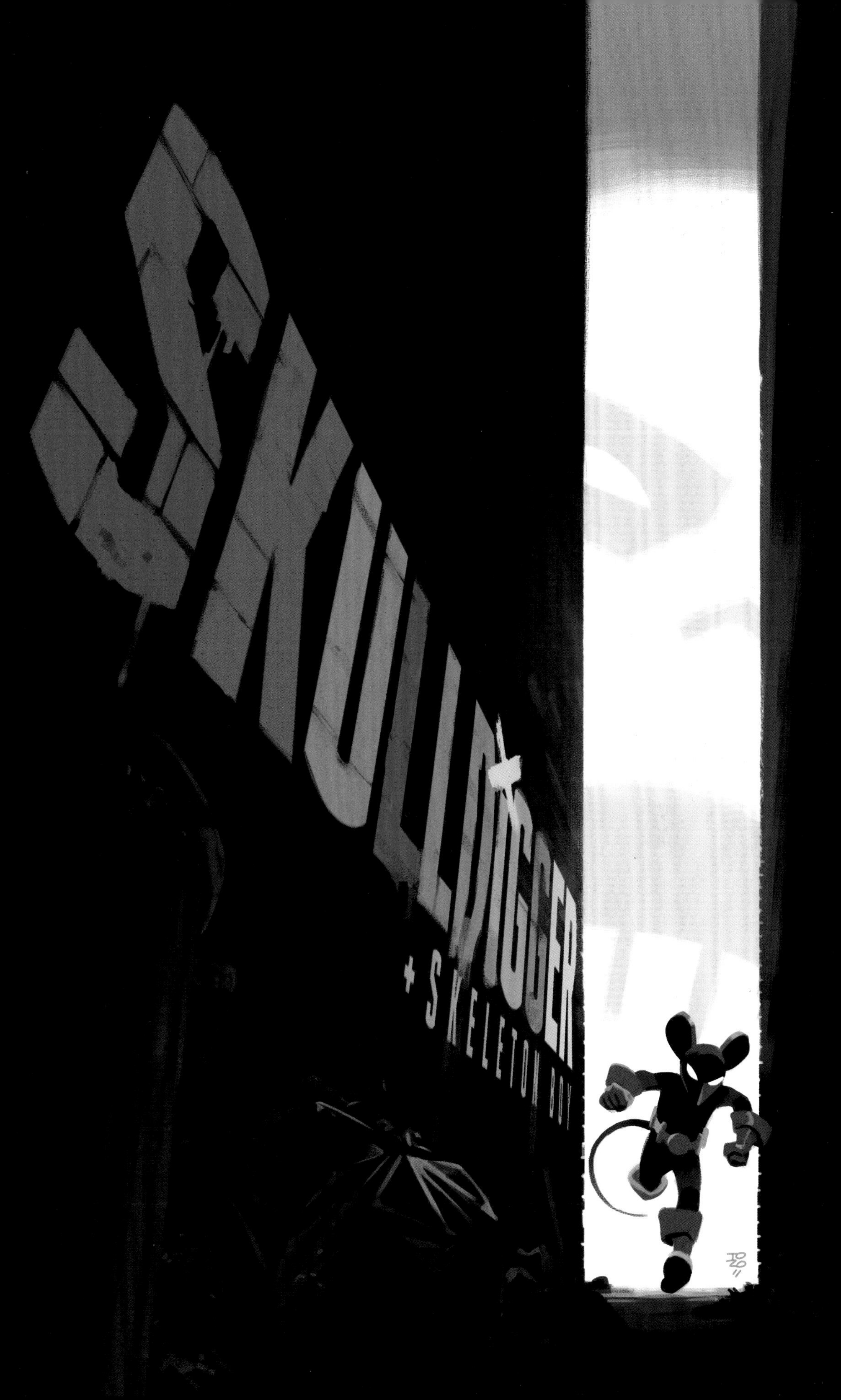
SKULLDIGGER
+ SKELETON BOY

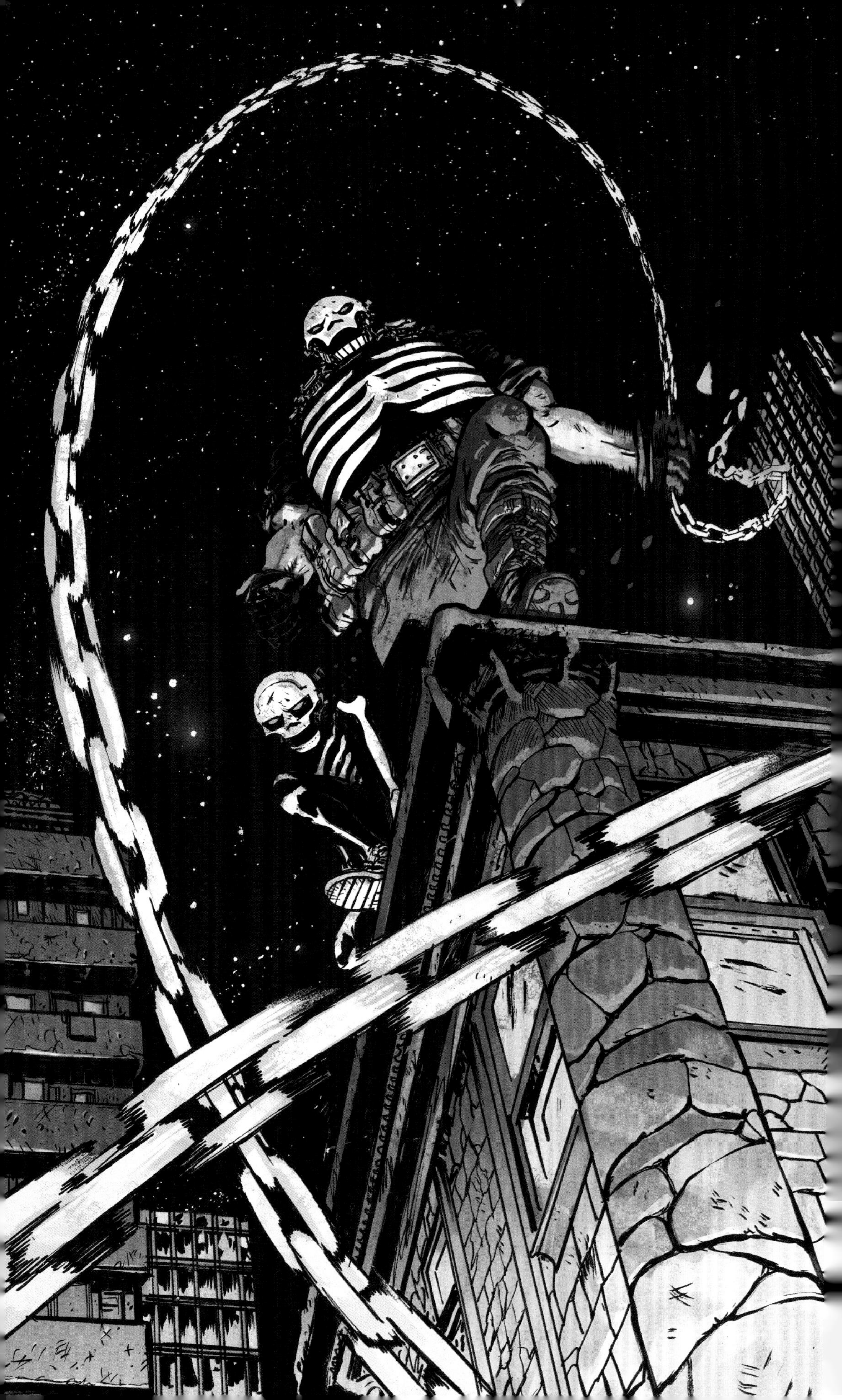

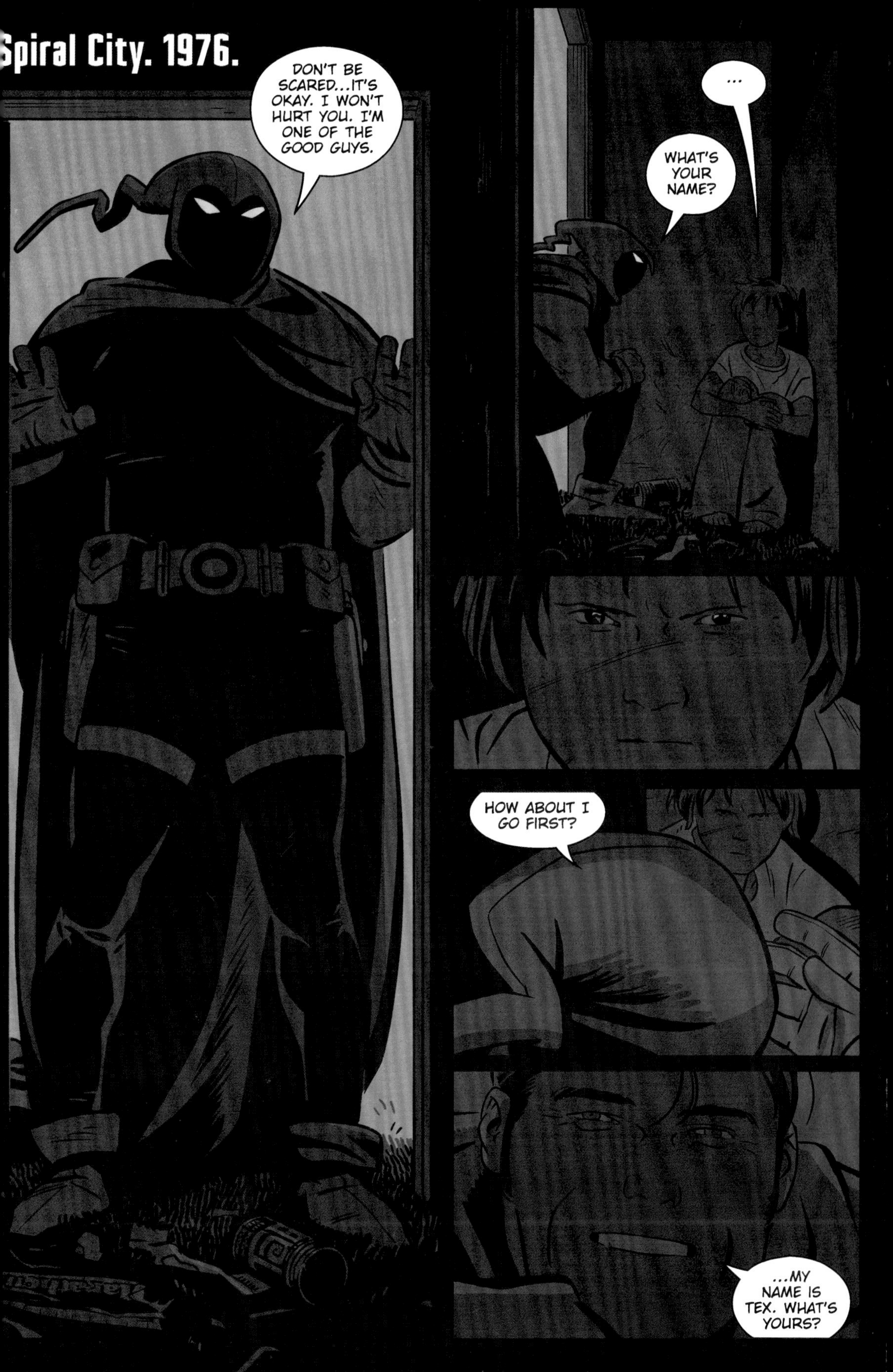
Spiral City. 1976.
DON'T BE SCARED...IT'S OKAY. I WON'T HURT YOU. I'M ONE OF THE GOOD GUYS.
...
WHAT'S YOUR NAME?
HOW ABOUT I GO FIRST?
...MY NAME IS TEX. WHAT'S YOURS?

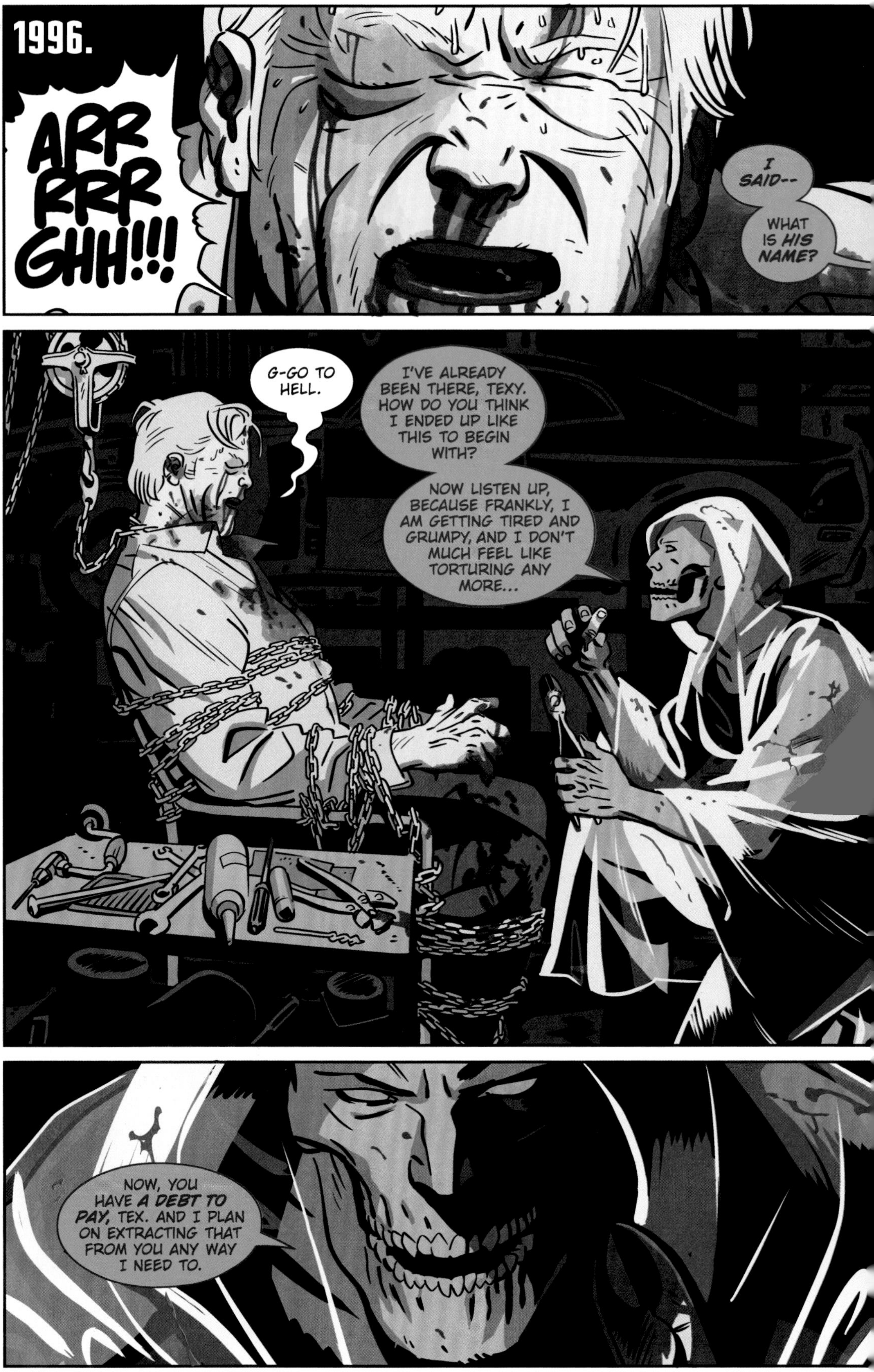
1996.
ARR RRR GHH!!!
I SAID--
WHAT IS HIS NAME?
G-GO TO HELL.
I'VE ALREADY BEEN THERE, TEXY. HOW DO YOU THINK I ENDED UP LIKE THIS TO BEGIN WITH?
NOW LISTEN UP, BECAUSE FRANKLY, I AM GETTING TIRED AND GRUMPY, AND I DON'T MUCH FEEL LIKE TORTURING ANY MORE...
NOW, YOU HAVE A DEBT TO PAY, TEX. AND I PLAN ON EXTRACTING THAT FROM YOU ANY WAY I NEED TO.

A DEBT? WHAT KIND OF DEBT DO I OWE *YOU*?!

YOU. STOLE. MY. SON.

THAT BOY WAS STARVING...FILTHY. I DON'T KNOW WHO HE BELONGED TO. MAYBE YOU, MAYBE ONE OF THOSE CRACK WHORES YOU HAD WITH YOU.

I--I *SAVED* HIM.

SAVED HIM? *SAVED* HIM?!

YOU KNOW THAT'S NOT TRUE. YOU *RUINED HIM...*

"YOU TRIED TO MAKE HIM LIKE YOU, DIDN'T YOU? YOUR LITTLE PARTNER. YOUR LITTLE SIDEKICK. WHAT WAS THAT RIDICULOUS NAME YOU GAVE HIM? *THE ALLEY RAT?*

BUT HE HAD TOO MUCH OF HIS DADDY IN HIM, DIDN'T HE? HE WENT ROGUE. DROPPED YOUR SILLY COSTUME AND PUT ON THE SKULL.

LET'S BE HONEST, I WOULD BE DOING THIS CITY A FAVOR...HE NEEDS TO *BE PUT DOWN* LIKE THE BAD LITTLE DOGGY THAT HE IS. DEEP DOWN, *I KNOW* THAT YOU KNOW THAT.

P-PLEASE-- PLEASE DON'T--

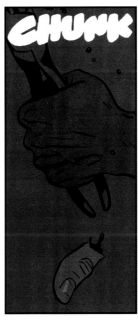

CHUNK

B-BUTCHER SHOP...

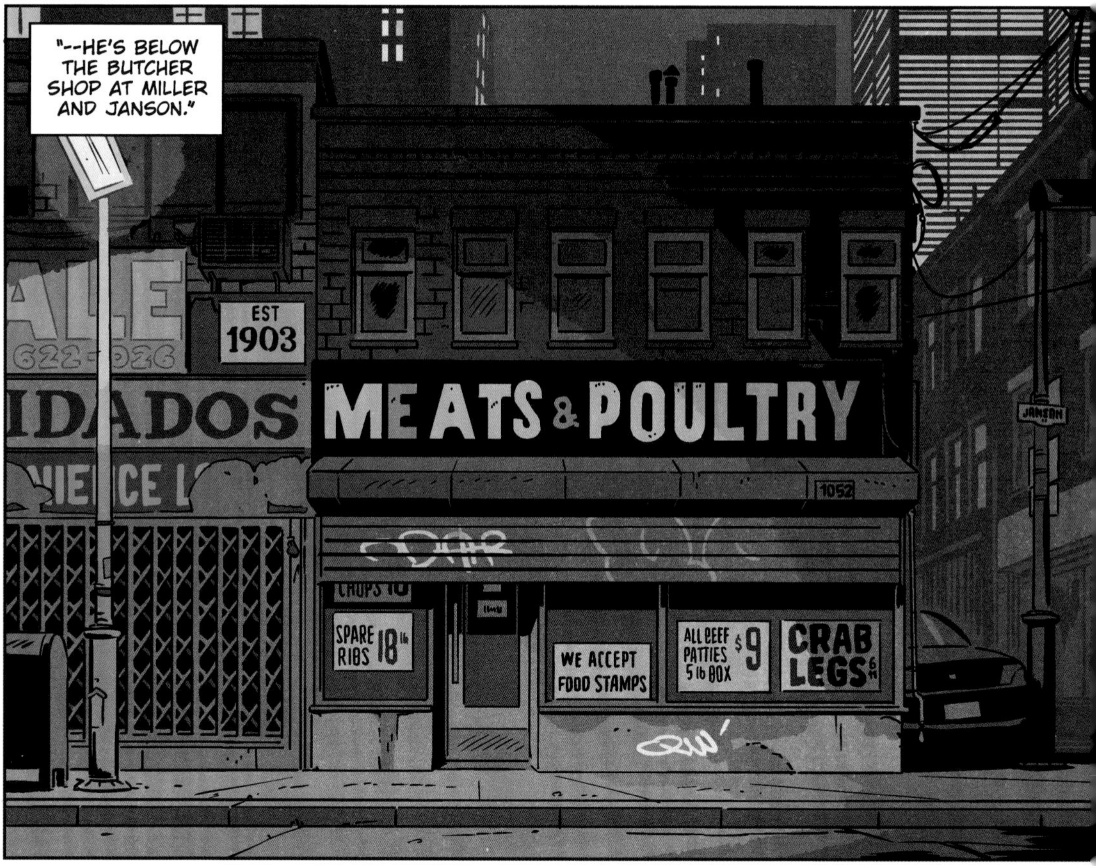
"--HE'S BELOW THE BUTCHER SHOP AT MILLER AND JANSON."
EST 1903
MEATS & POULTRY
1052
SPARE RIBS 18
WE ACCEPT FOOD STAMPS
ALL BEEF PATTIES 5 lb BOX $9
CRAB LEGS
JANSON

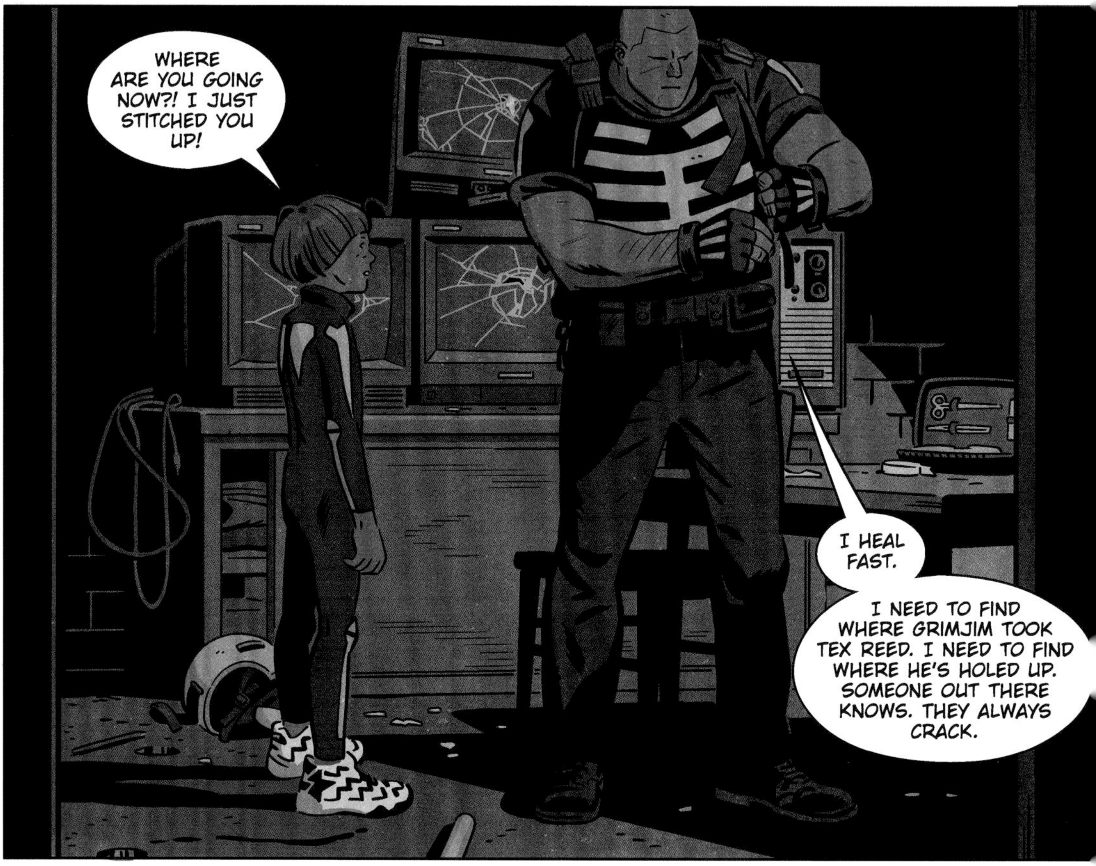
WHERE ARE YOU GOING NOW?! I JUST STITCHED YOU UP!
I HEAL FAST.
I NEED TO FIND WHERE GRIMJIM TOOK TEX REED. I NEED TO FIND WHERE HE'S HOLED UP. SOMEONE OUT THERE KNOWS. THEY ALWAYS CRACK.

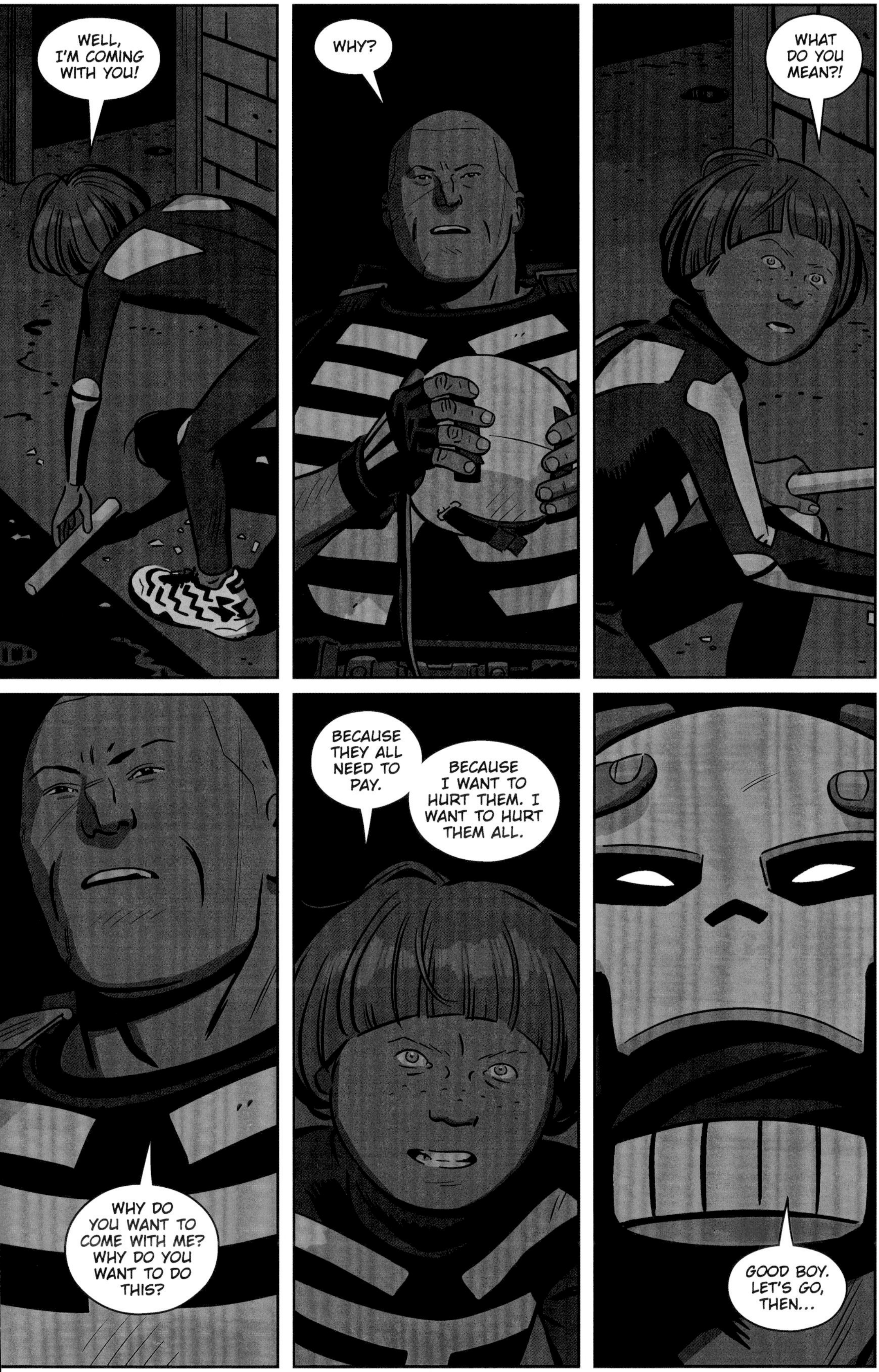
WELL, I'M COMING WITH YOU!
WHY?
WHAT DO YOU MEAN?!
WHY DO YOU WANT TO COME WITH ME? WHY DO YOU WANT TO DO THIS?
BECAUSE THEY ALL NEED TO PAY.
BECAUSE I WANT TO HURT THEM. I WANT TO HURT THEM ALL.
GOOD BOY. LET'S GO, THEN...

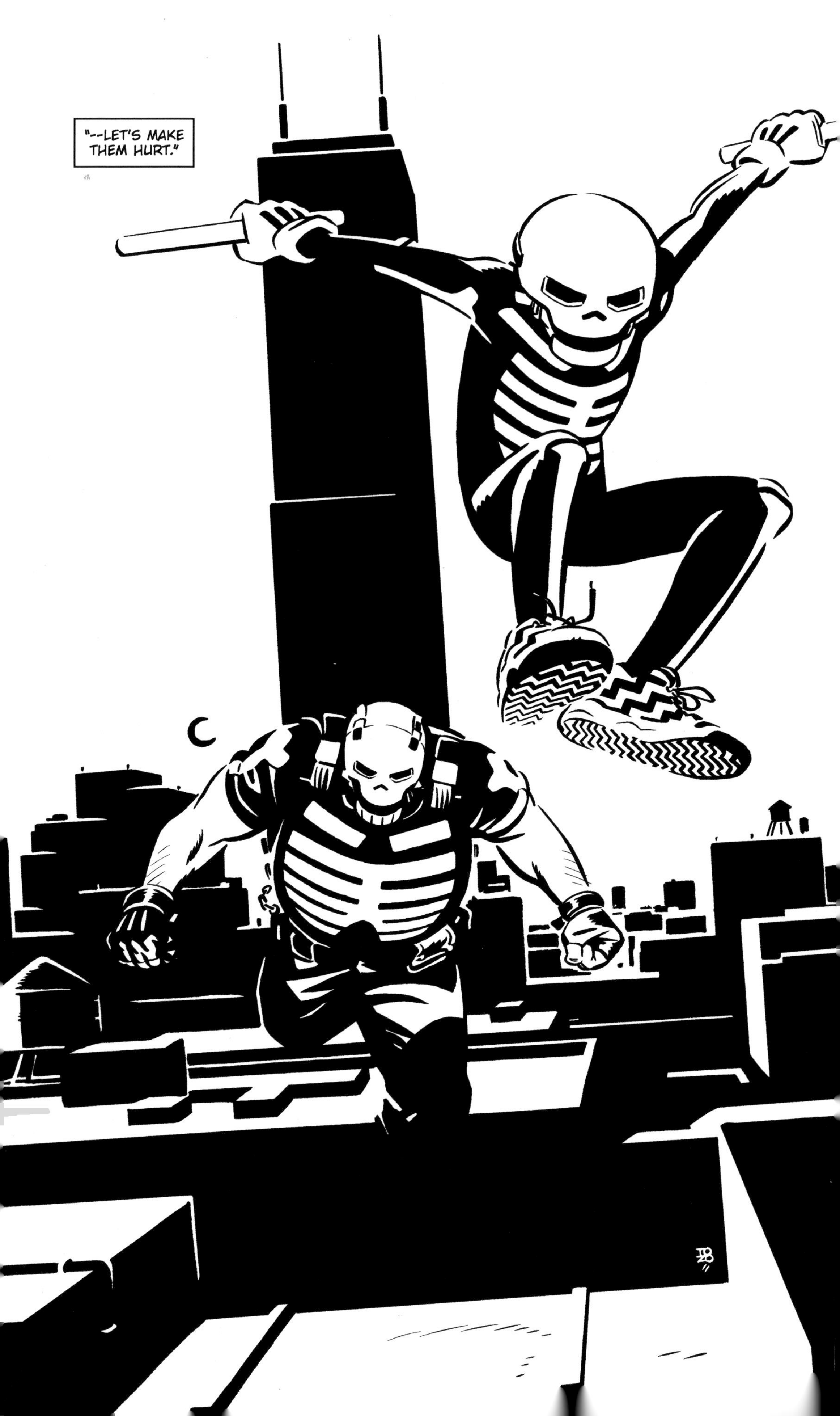
"--LET'S MAKE THEM HURT."

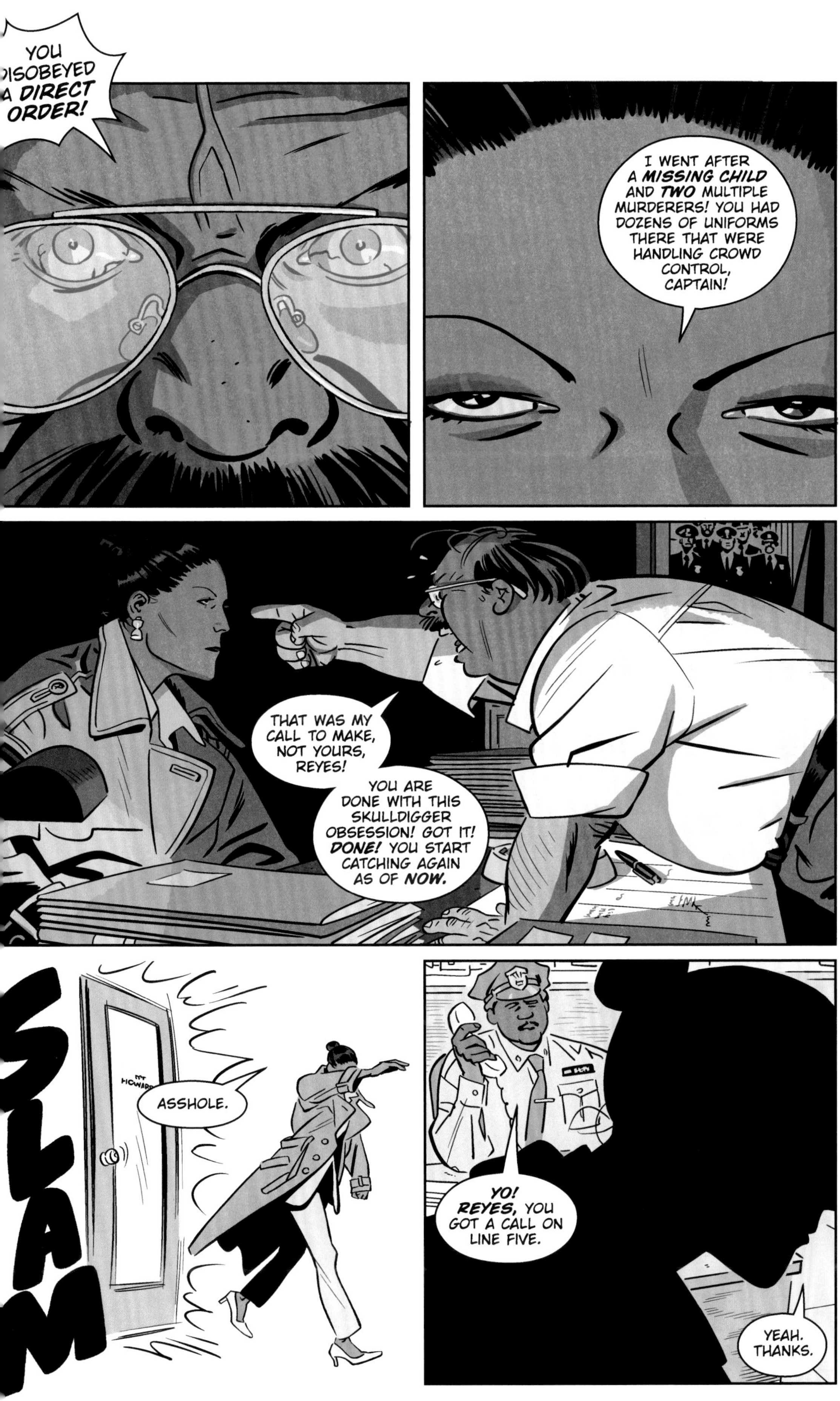
YOU DISOBEYED A DIRECT ORDER!
I WENT AFTER A MISSING CHILD AND TWO MULTIPLE MURDERERS! YOU HAD DOZENS OF UNIFORMS THERE THAT WERE HANDLING CROWD CONTROL, CAPTAIN!
THAT WAS MY CALL TO MAKE, NOT YOURS, REYES!
YOU ARE DONE WITH THIS SKULLDIGGER OBSESSION! GOT IT! DONE! YOU START CATCHING AGAIN AS OF NOW.
SLAM
ASSHOLE.
YO! REYES, YOU GOT A CALL ON LINE FIVE.
YEAH. THANKS.

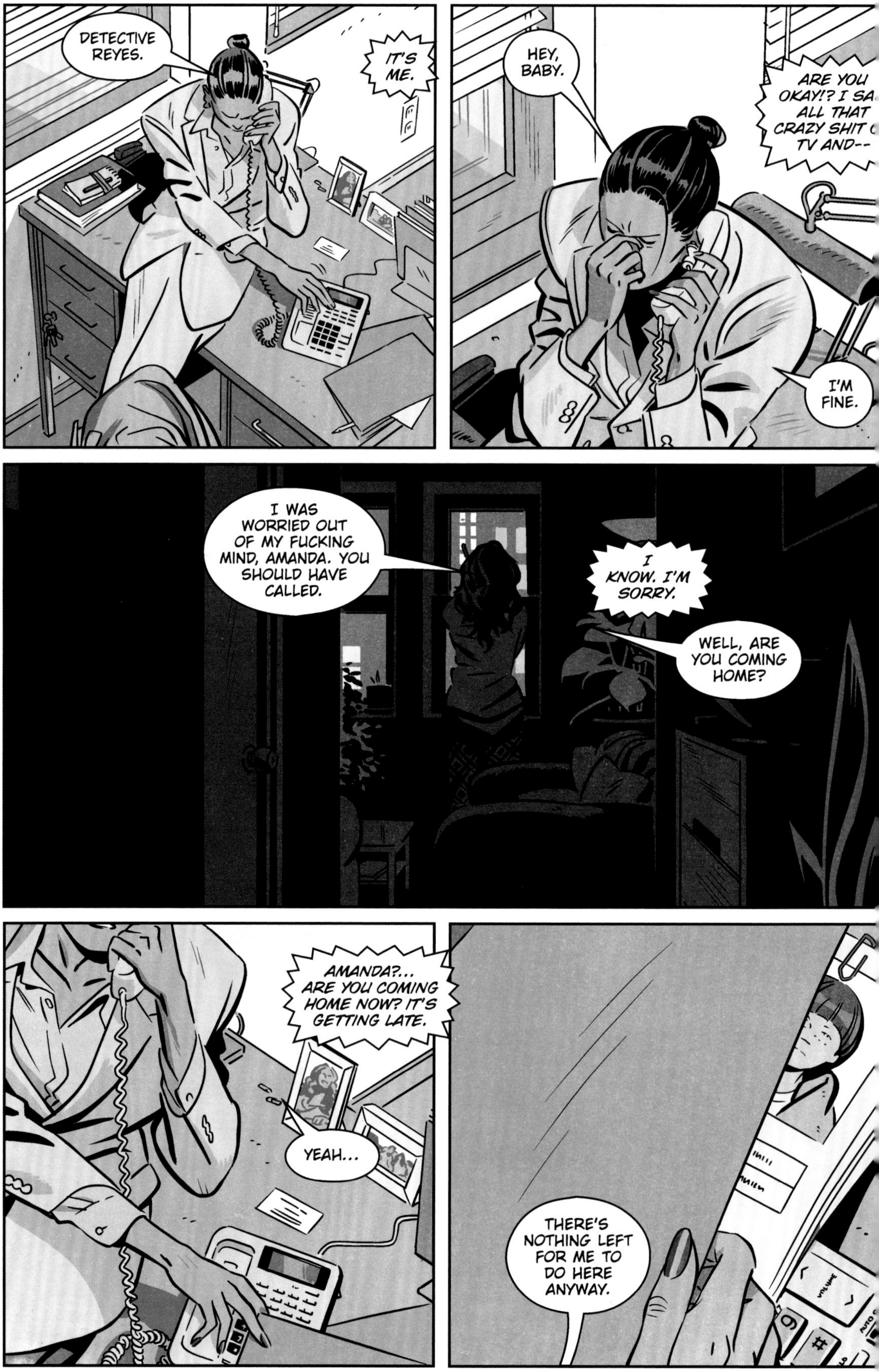
DETECTIVE REYES.
IT'S ME.
HEY, BABY.
ARE YOU OKAY!? I SA ALL THAT CRAZY SHIT TV AND--
I'M FINE.
I WAS WORRIED OUT OF MY FUCKING MIND, AMANDA. YOU SHOULD HAVE CALLED.
I KNOW. I'M SORRY.
WELL, ARE YOU COMING HOME?
AMANDA?... ARE YOU COMING HOME NOW? IT'S GETTING LATE.
YEAH...
THERE'S NOTHING LEFT FOR ME TO DO HERE ANYWAY.

Well, now they are both dead...

They believed in turning the other cheek. They believed there was always another way to deal with problems.

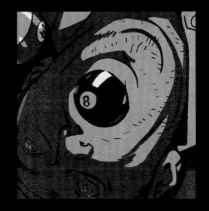

I never got in a fight before. I was beat up twice at school, but my mom and dad said they were proud of me for not fighting back.

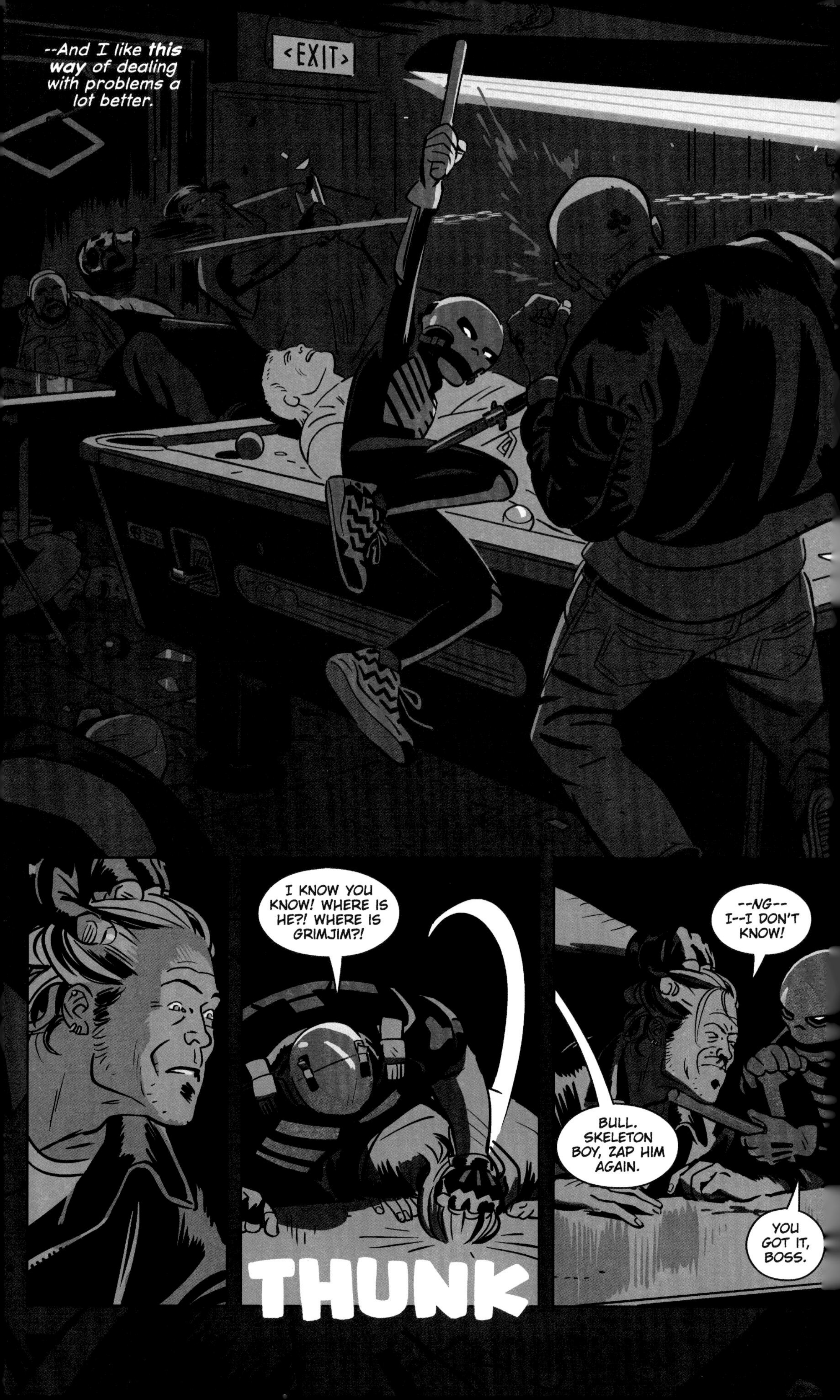
--And I like this way of dealing with problems a lot better.
EXIT
I KNOW YOU KNOW! WHERE IS HE?! WHERE IS GRIMJIM?!
THUNK
--NG-- I--I DON'T KNOW!
BULL. SKELETON BOY, ZAP HIM AGAIN.
YOU GOT IT, BOSS.

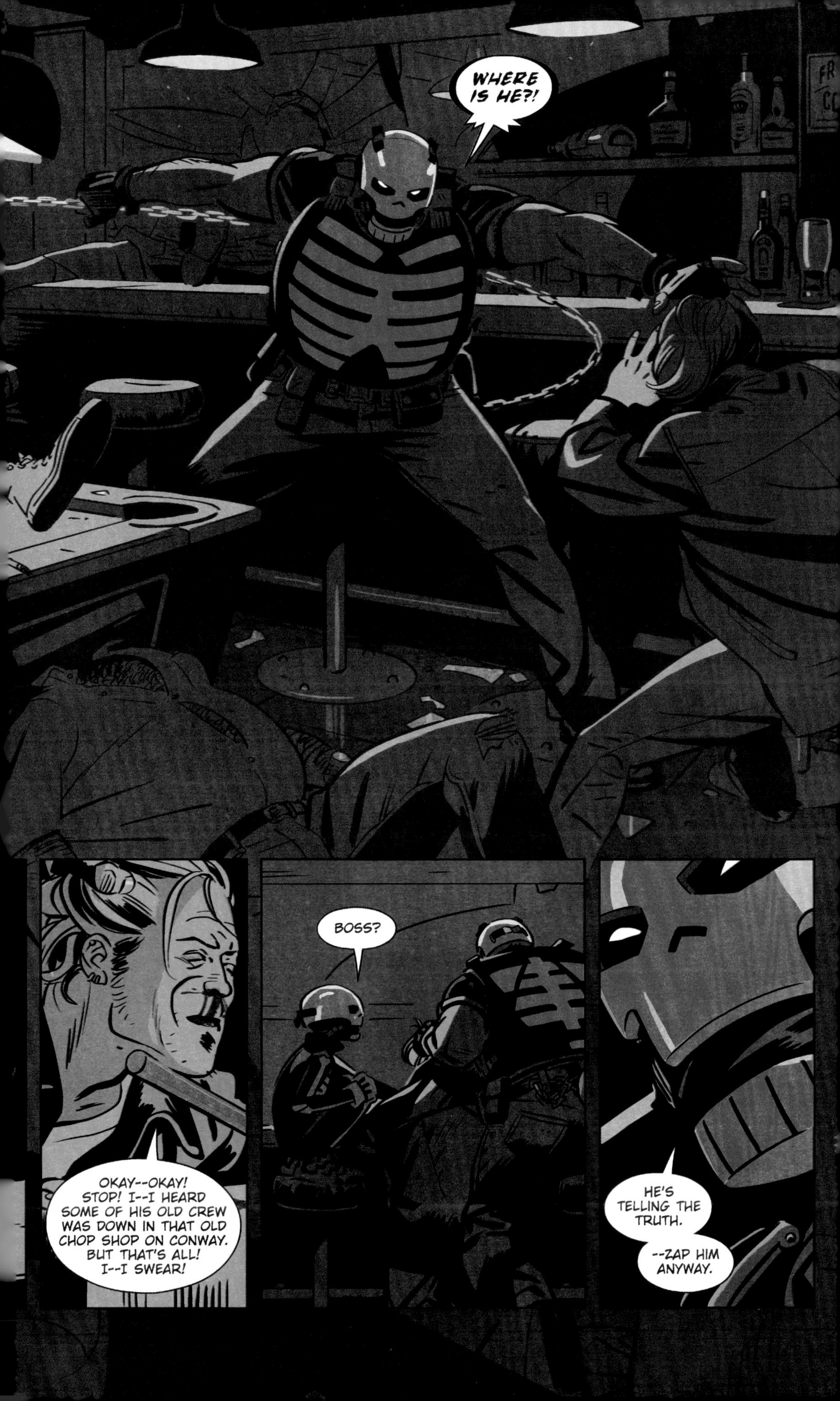
WHERE IS HE?!
OKAY--OKAY! STOP! I--I HEARD SOME OF HIS OLD CREW WAS DOWN IN THAT OLD CHOP SHOP ON CONWAY. BUT THAT'S ALL! I--I SWEAR!
BOSS?
HE'S TELLING THE TRUTH.
--ZAP HIM ANYWAY.

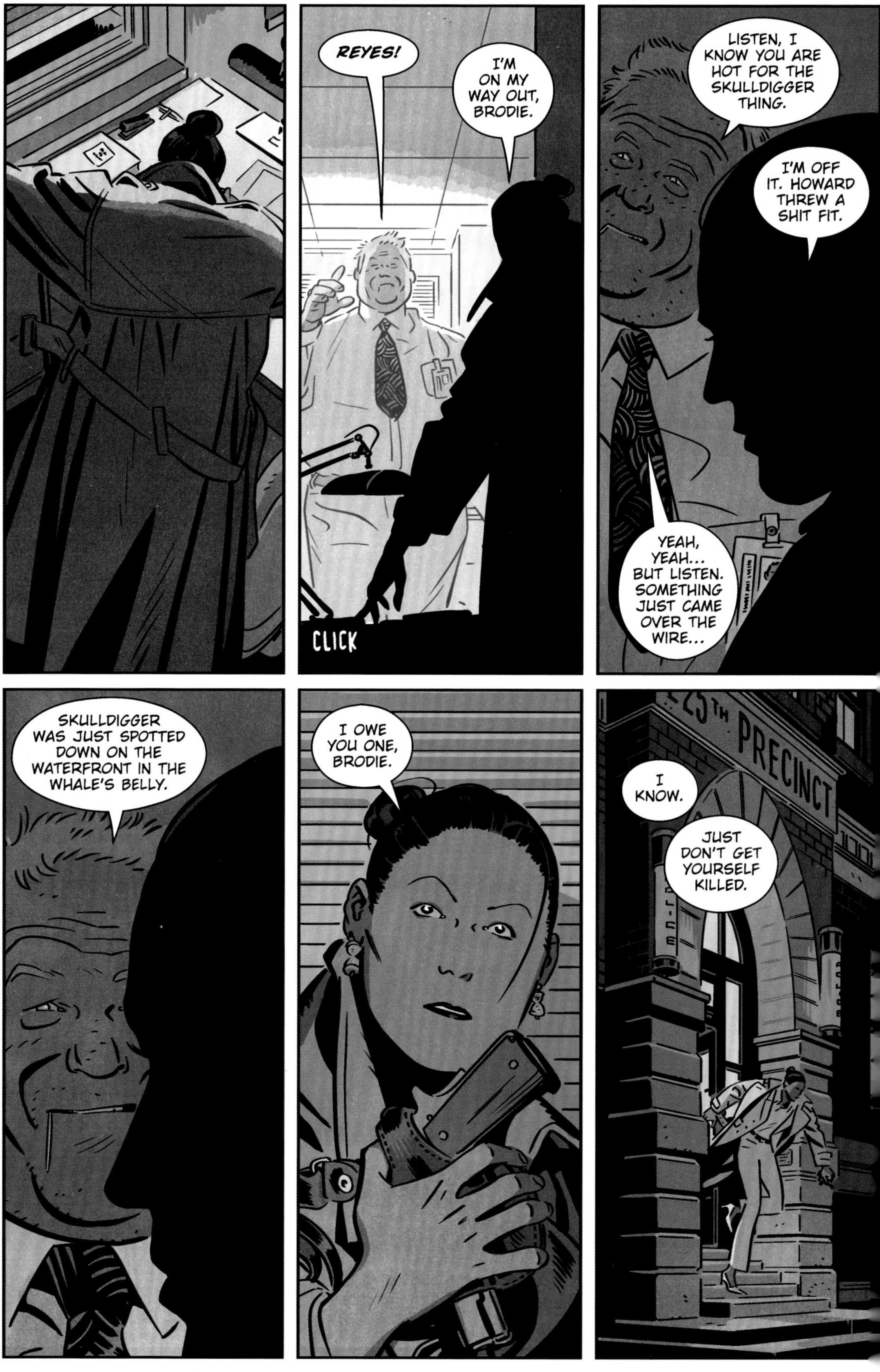
REYES!
I'M ON MY WAY OUT, BRODIE.
CLICK
LISTEN, I KNOW YOU ARE HOT FOR THE SKULLDIGGER THING.
I'M OFF IT. HOWARD THREW A SHIT FIT.
YEAH, YEAH... BUT LISTEN. SOMETHING JUST CAME OVER THE WIRE...
SKULLDIGGER WAS JUST SPOTTED DOWN ON THE WATERFRONT IN THE WHALE'S BELLY.
I OWE YOU ONE, BRODIE.
25TH PRECINCT
I KNOW.
JUST DON'T GET YOURSELF KILLED.

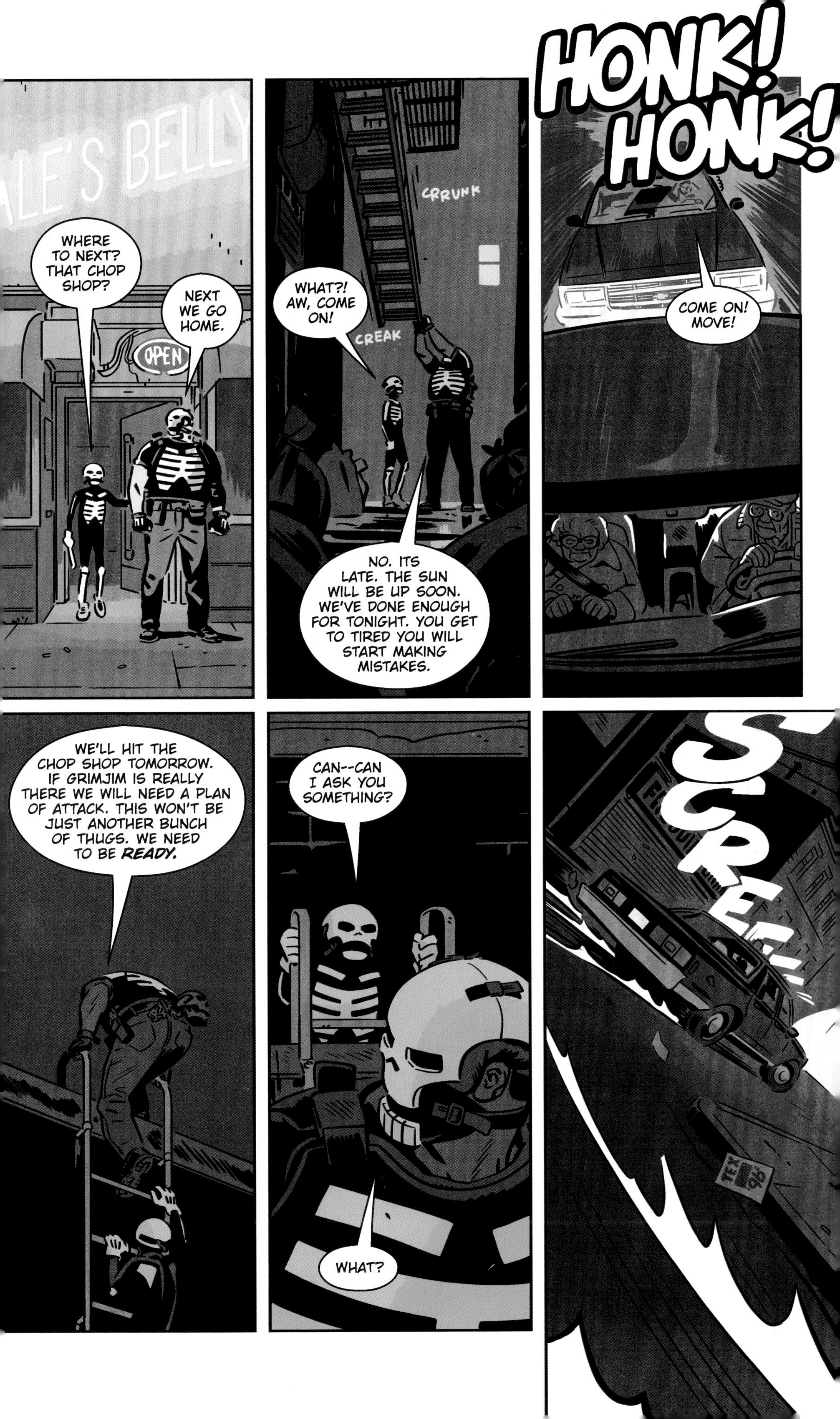
ALE'S BELLY
WHERE TO NEXT? THAT CHOP SHOP?
NEXT WE GO HOME.
OPEN
WHAT?! AW, COME ON!
CRRUNK
CREAK
NO. ITS LATE. THE SUN WILL BE UP SOON. WE'VE DONE ENOUGH FOR TONIGHT. YOU GET TO TIRED YOU WILL START MAKING MISTAKES.
HONK! HONK!
COME ON! MOVE!
WE'LL HIT THE CHOP SHOP TOMORROW. IF GRIMJIM IS REALLY THERE WE WILL NEED A PLAN OF ATTACK. THIS WON'T BE JUST ANOTHER BUNCH OF THUGS. WE NEED TO BE *READY.*
CAN--CAN I ASK YOU SOMETHING?
WHAT?
SCREE
TEX '96

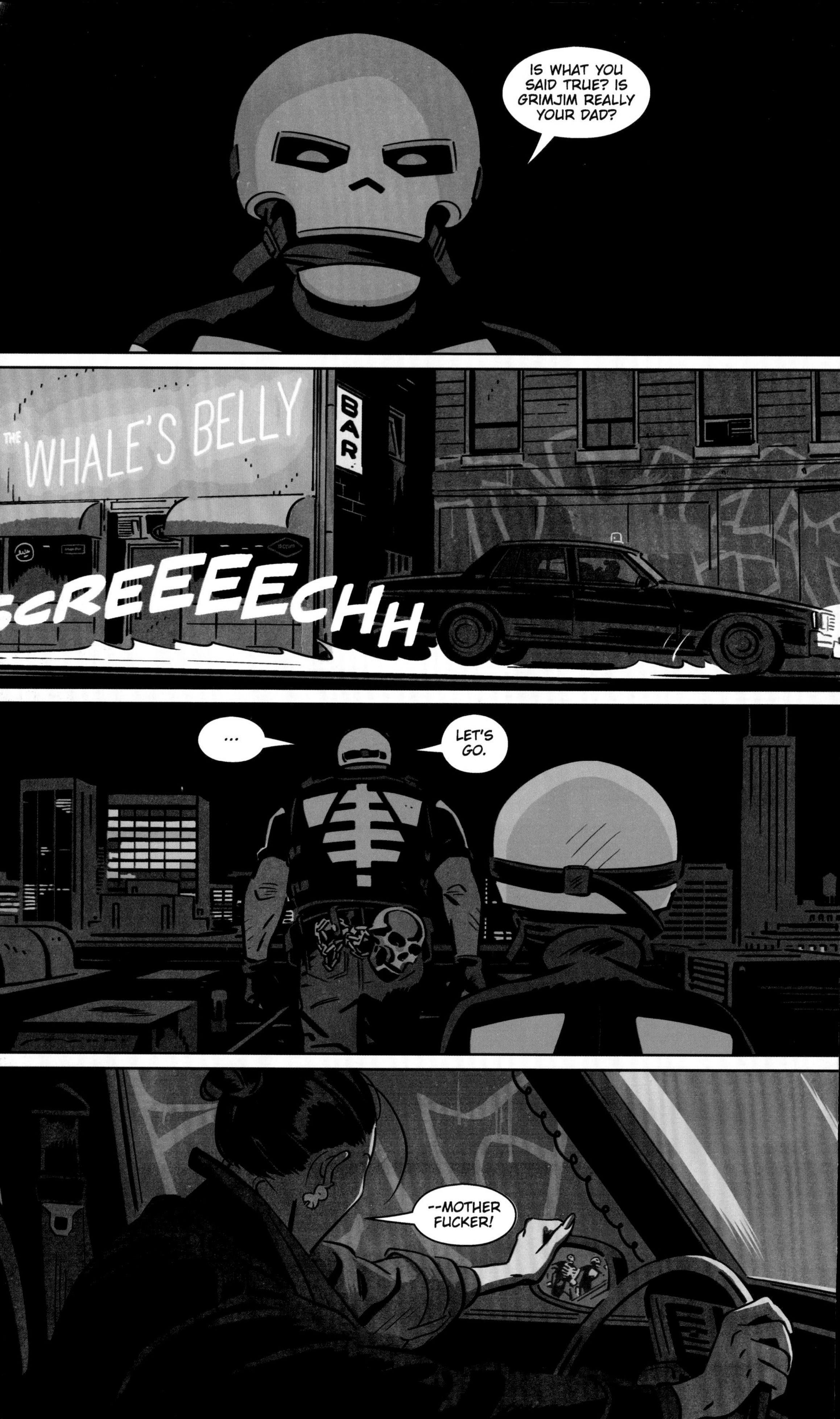
IS WHAT YOU SAID TRUE? IS GRIMJIM REALLY YOUR DAD?
THE WHALE'S BELLY
BAR
SCREEEECHH
...
LET'S GO.
--MOTHER FUCKER!

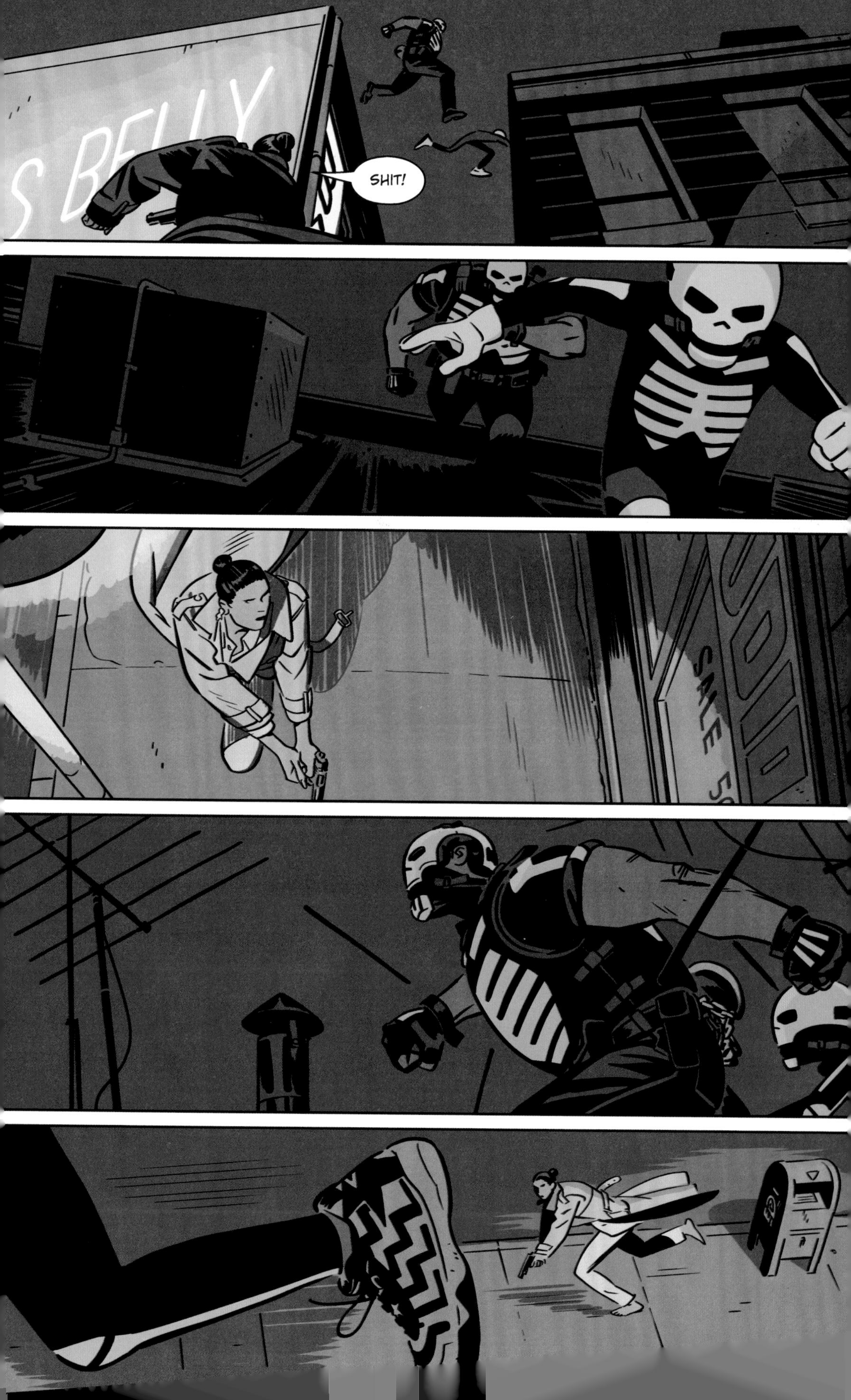
SHIT!

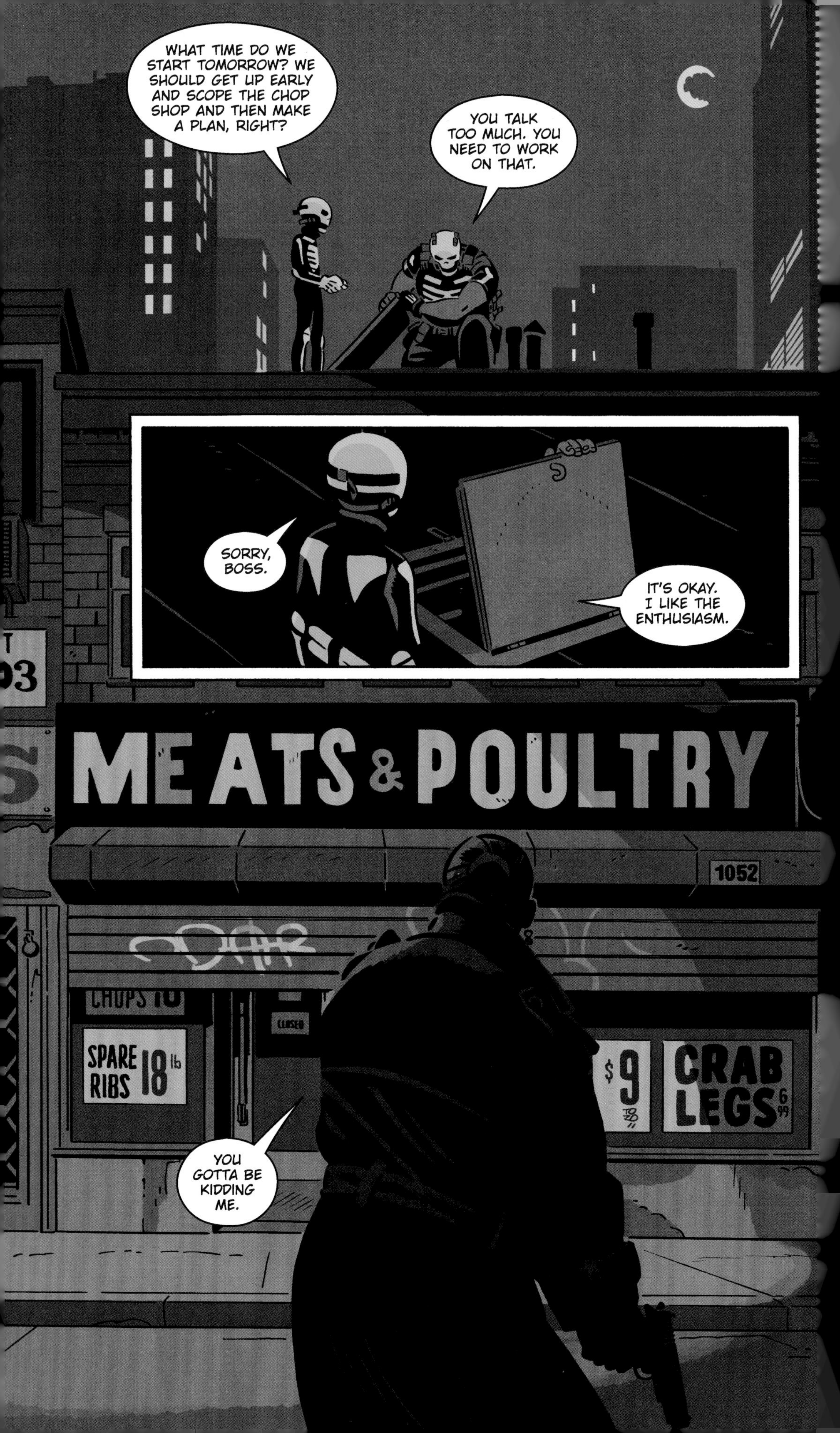
WHAT TIME DO WE START TOMORROW? WE SHOULD GET UP EARLY AND SCOPE THE CHOP SHOP AND THEN MAKE A PLAN, RIGHT?
YOU TALK TOO MUCH. YOU NEED TO WORK ON THAT.
SORRY, BOSS.
IT'S OKAY. I LIKE THE ENTHUSIASM.
MEATS & POULTRY
1052
CLOSED
SPARE RIBS 18 lb
$9
CRAB LEGS 6.99
YOU GOTTA BE KIDDING ME.

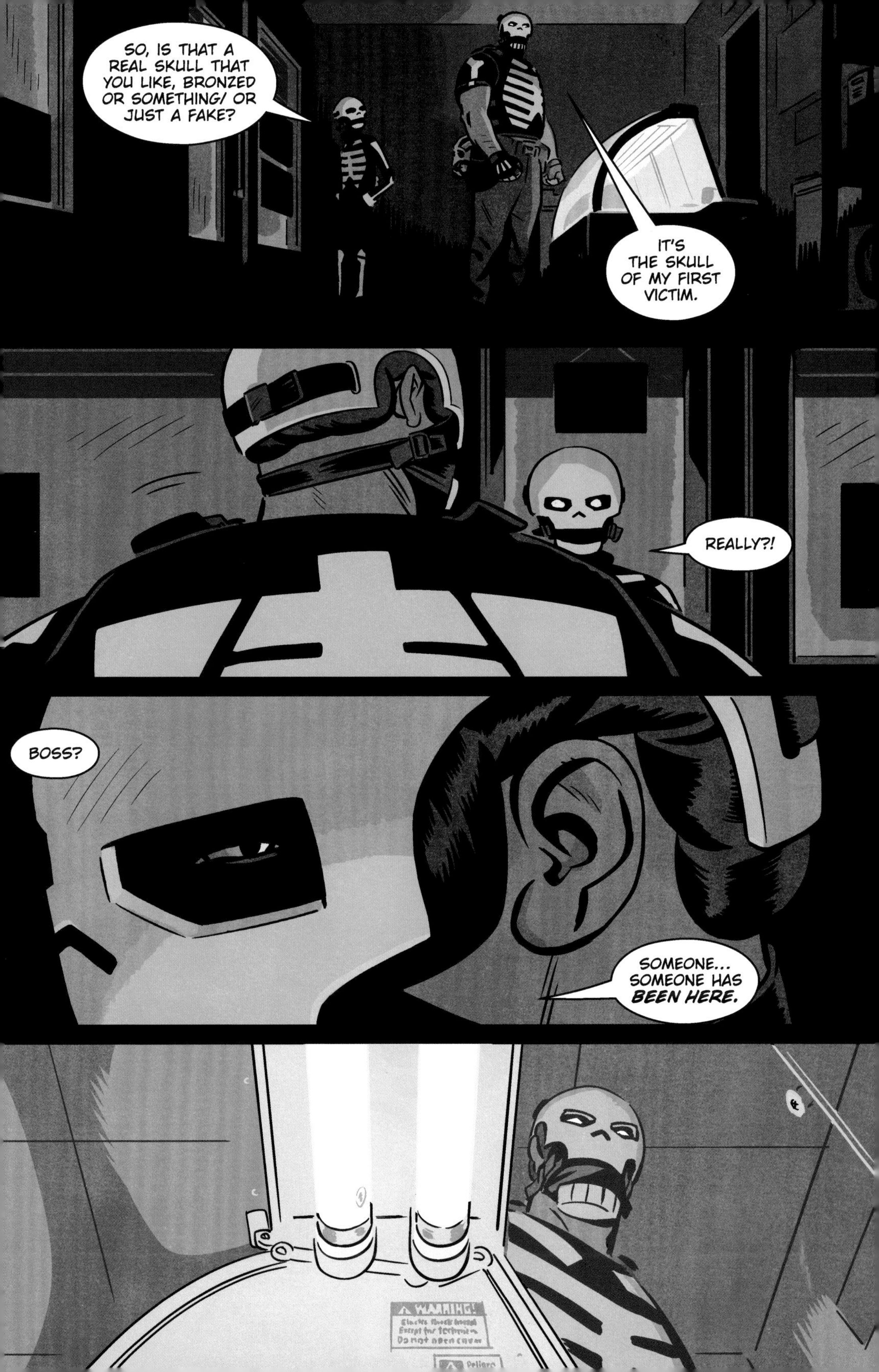
SO, IS THAT A REAL SKULL THAT YOU LIKE, BRONZED OR SOMETHING/ OR JUST A FAKE?
IT'S THE SKULL OF MY FIRST VICTIM.
REALLY?!
BOSS?
SOMEONE... SOMEONE HAS *BEEN HERE.*

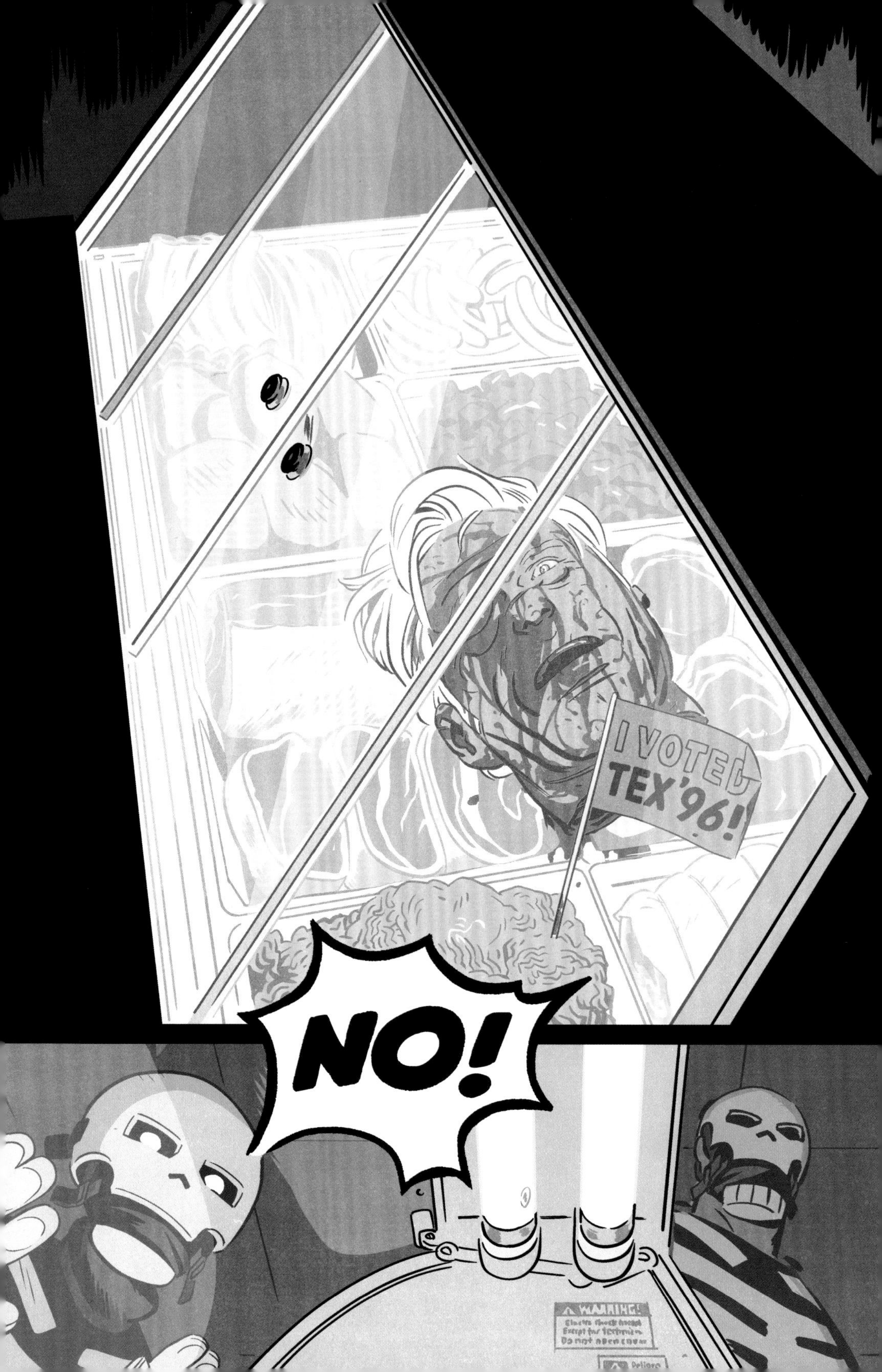
I VOTED TEX '96!
NO!

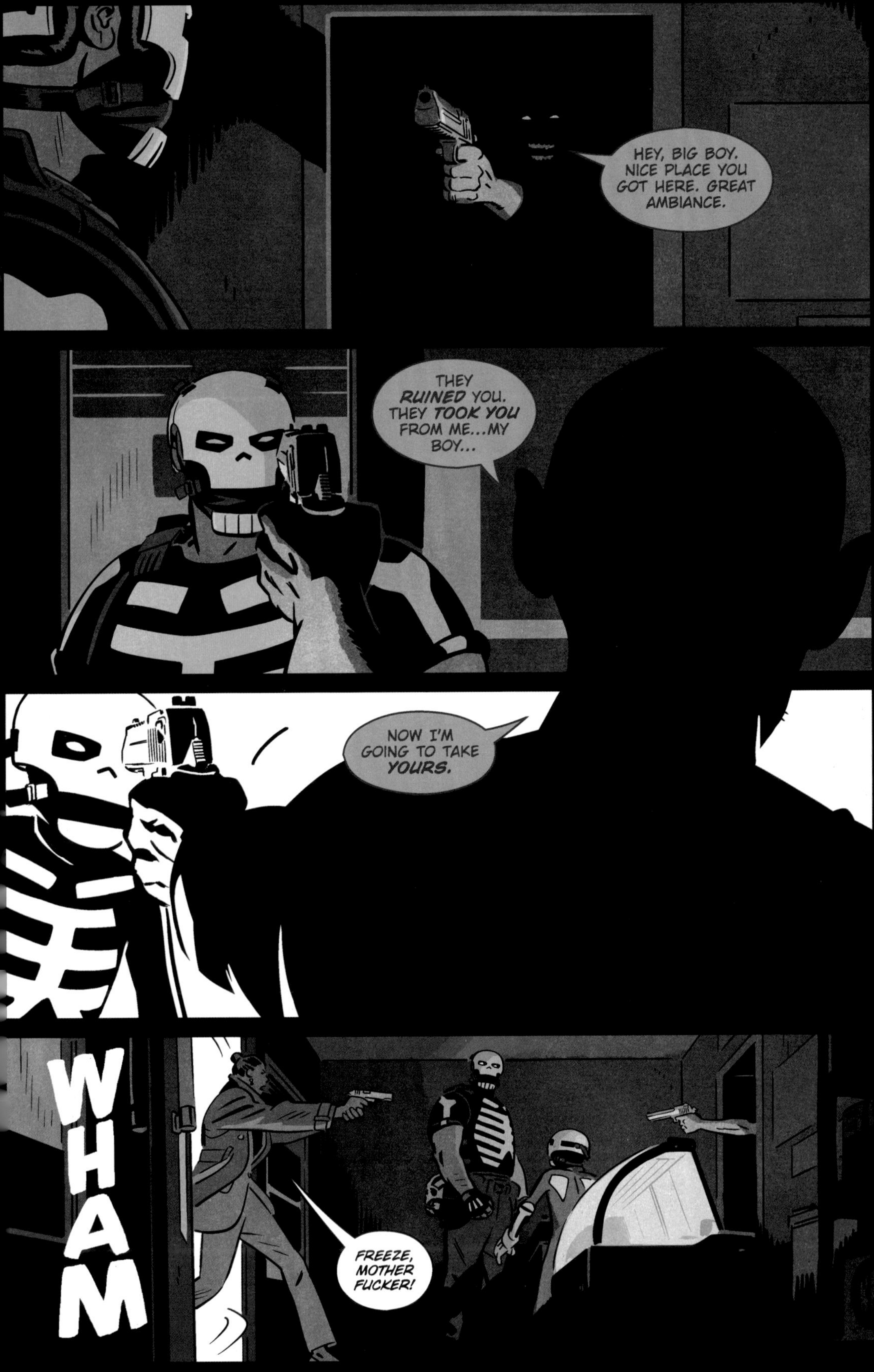
HEY, BIG BOY. NICE PLACE YOU GOT HERE. GREAT AMBIANCE.
THEY *RUINED* YOU. THEY *TOOK YOU* FROM ME...MY BOY...
NOW I'M GOING TO TAKE *YOURS.*
WHAM
FREEZE, MOTHER FUCKER!

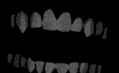

YOU, MY DEAR, ARE *RUINING* OUR REUNION.

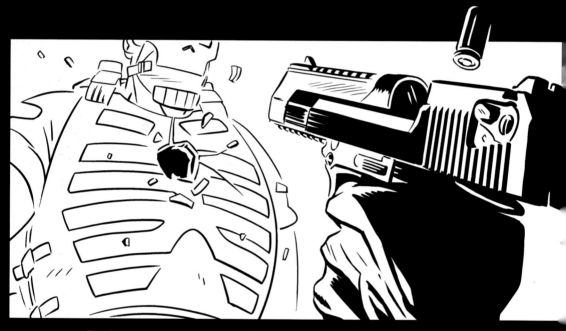

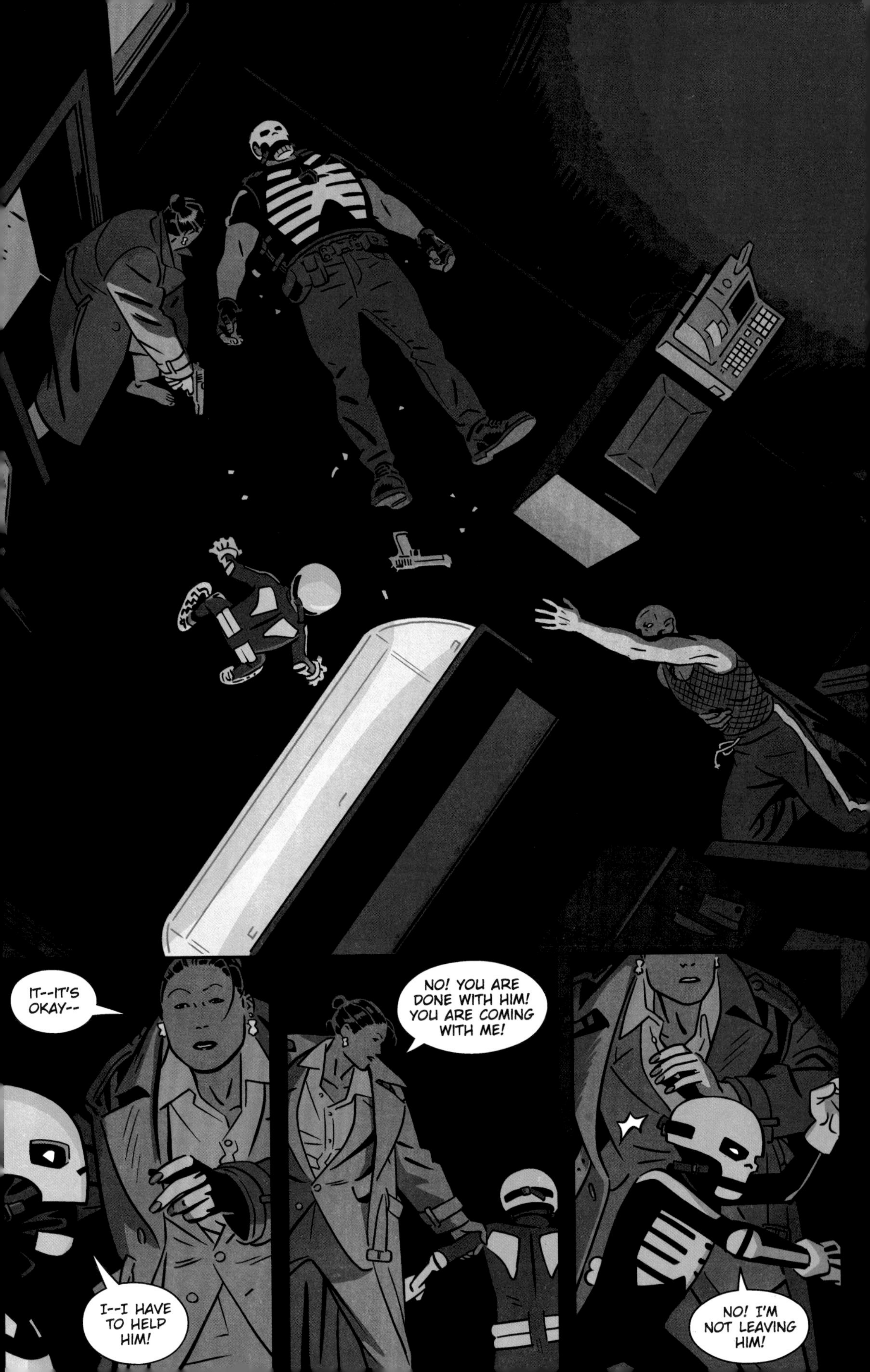
IT--IT'S OKAY--
I--I HAVE TO HELP HIM!
NO! YOU ARE DONE WITH HIM! YOU ARE COMING WITH ME!
NO! I'M NOT LEAVING HIM!

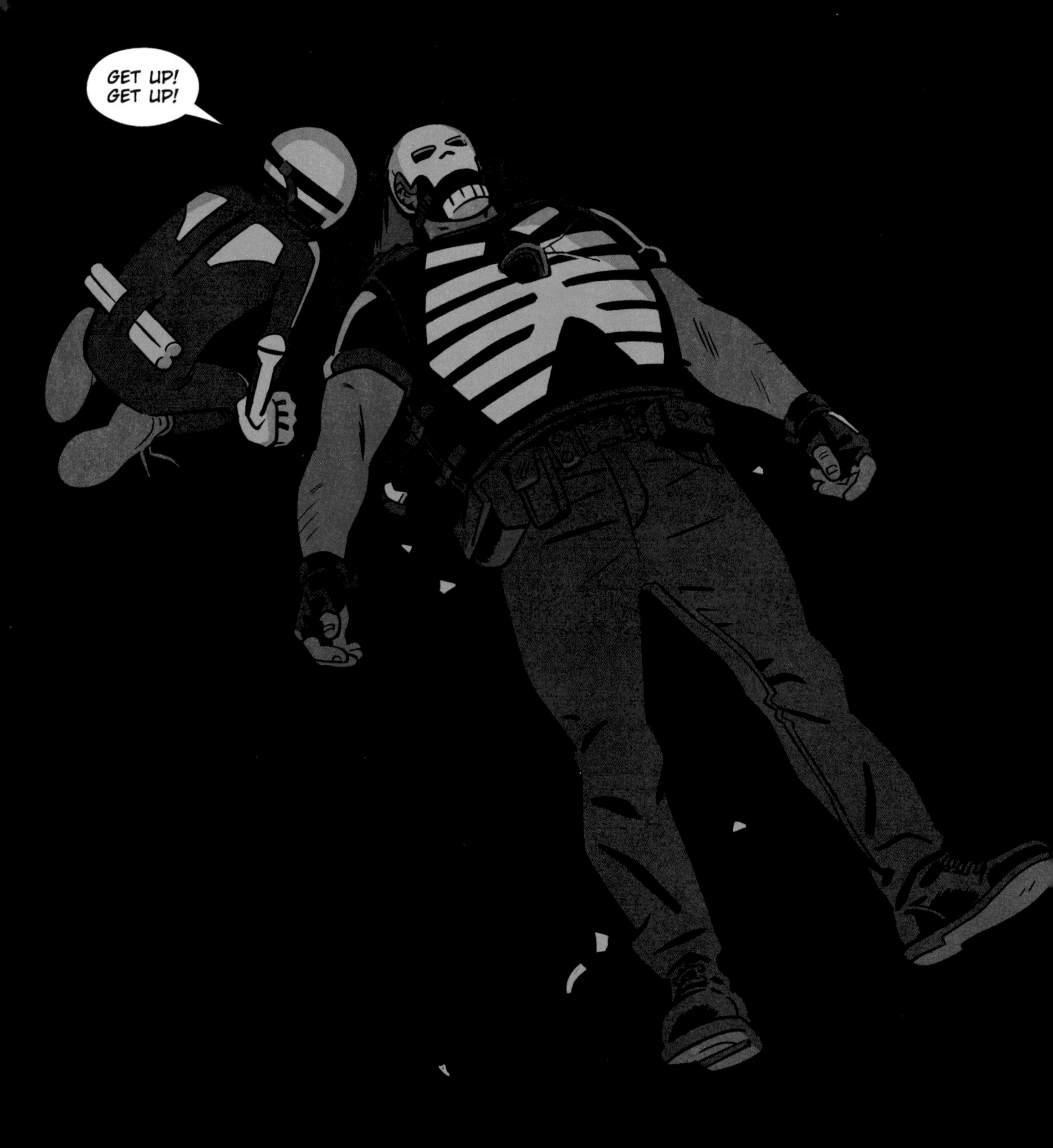
GET UP!
GET UP!

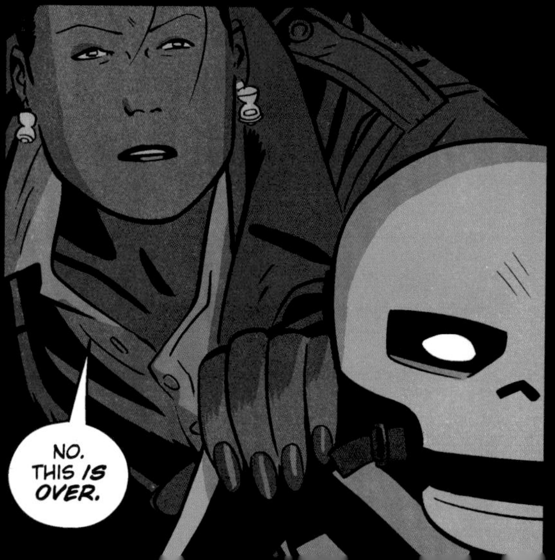
NO. THIS *IS* OVER.

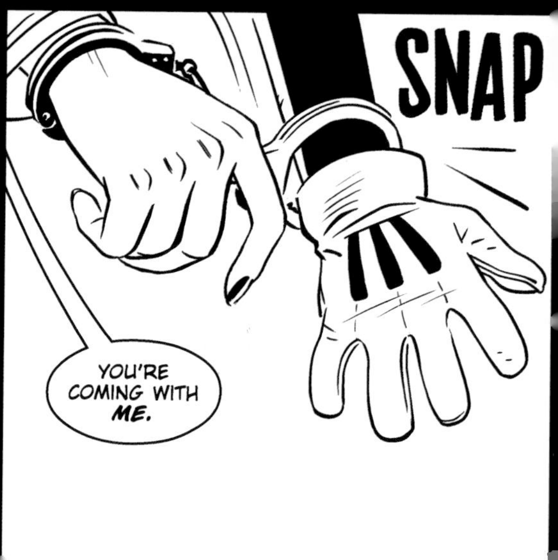
SNAP
YOU'RE COMING WITH *ME*.

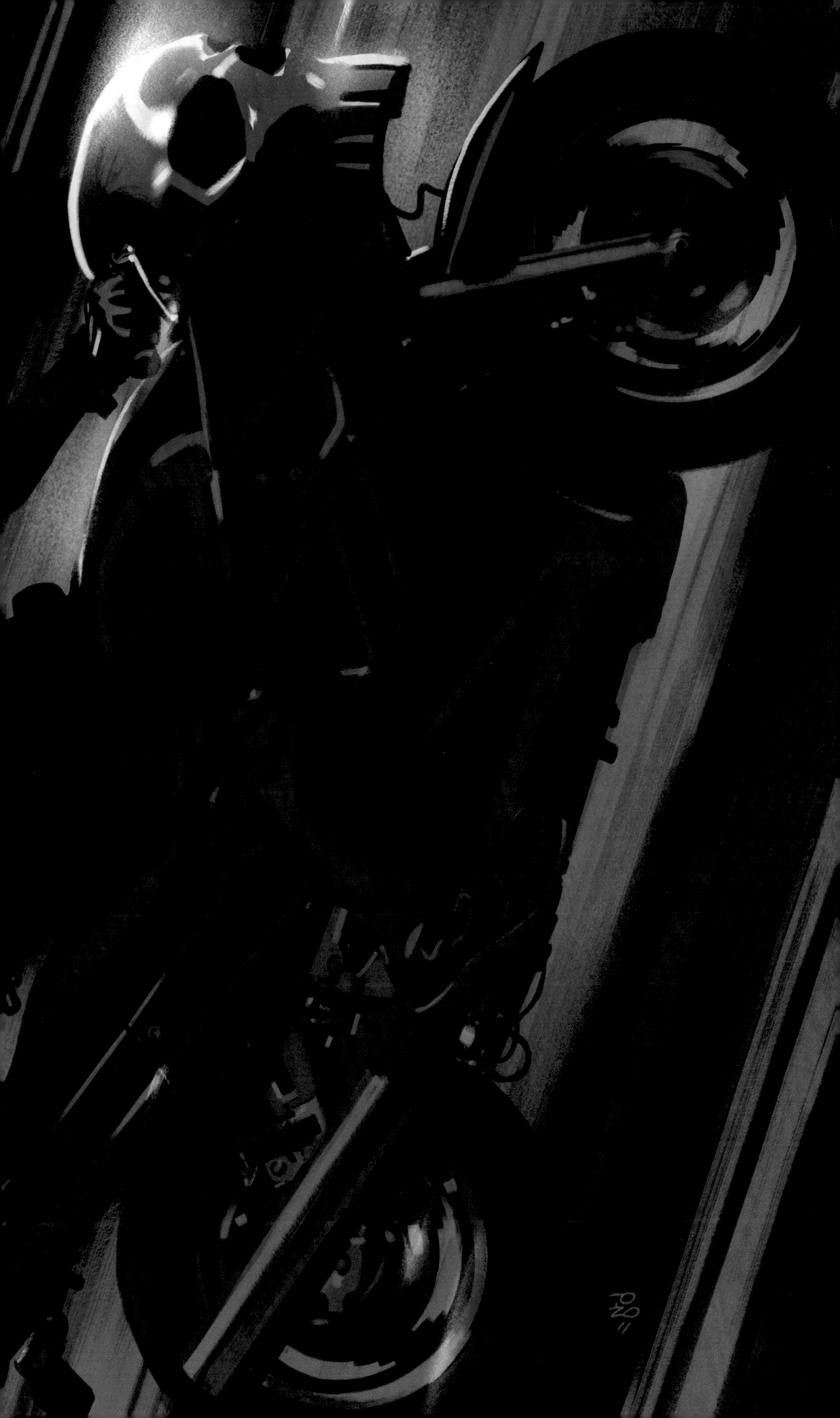

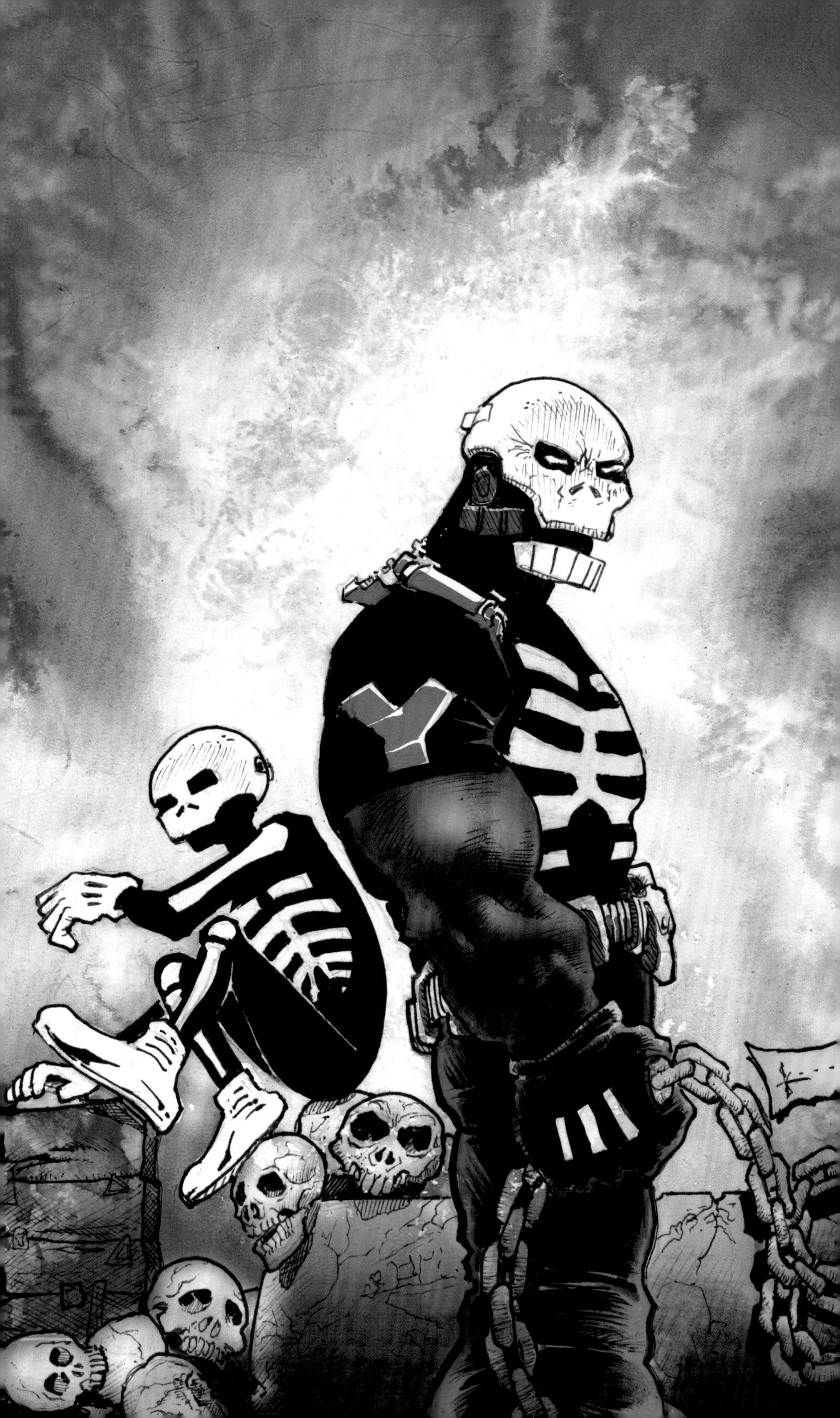

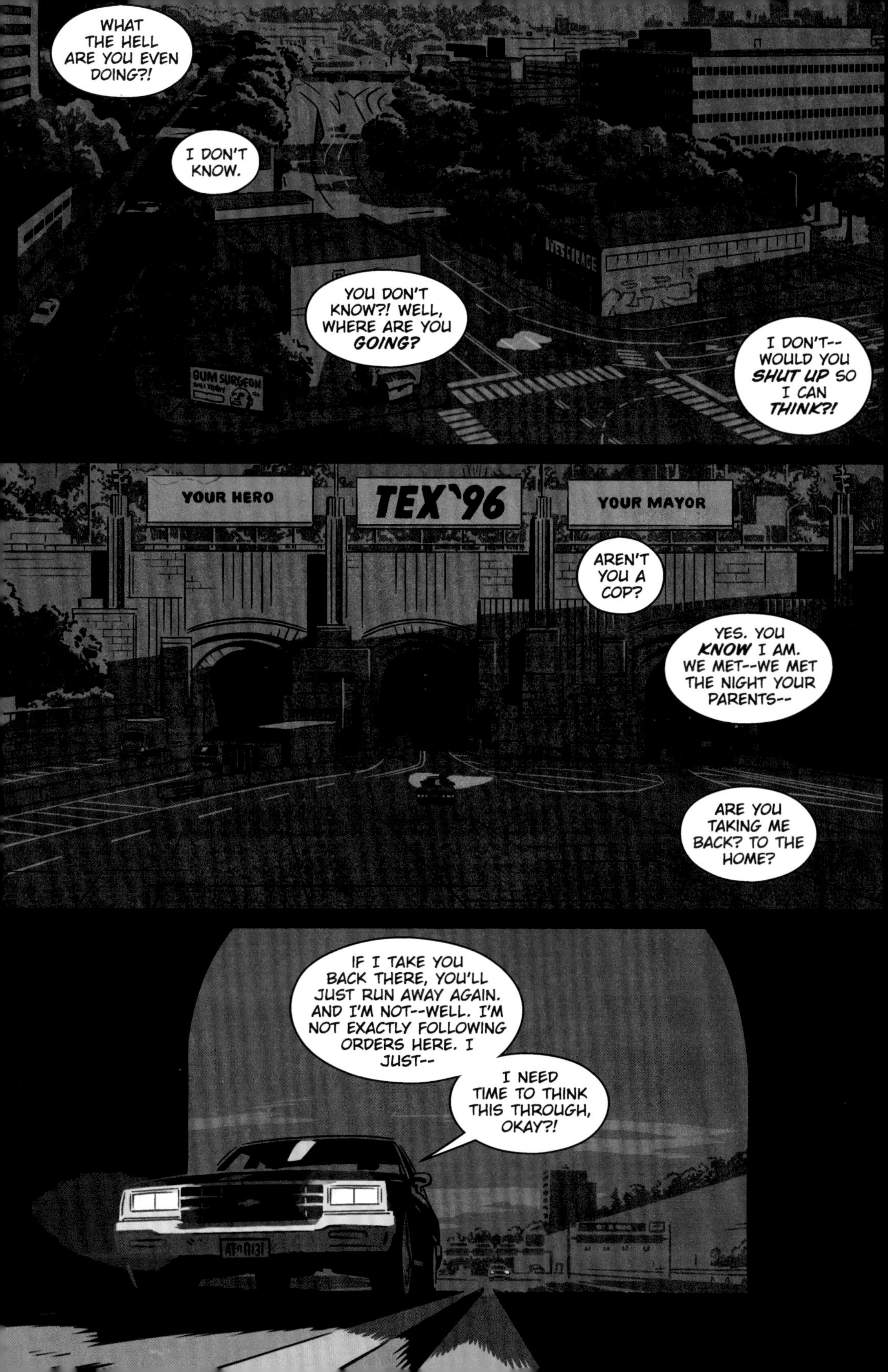

WHAT THE HELL ARE YOU EVEN DOING?!
I DON'T KNOW.
GUM SURGEON
YOU DON'T KNOW?! WELL, WHERE ARE YOU *GOING?*
I DON'T-- WOULD YOU ***SHUT UP*** SO I CAN ***THINK?!***
YOUR HERO
TEX`96
YOUR MAYOR
AREN'T YOU A COP?
YES. YOU ***KNOW*** I AM. WE MET--WE MET THE NIGHT YOUR PARENTS--
ARE YOU TAKING ME BACK? TO THE HOME?
IF I TAKE YOU BACK THERE, YOU'LL JUST RUN AWAY AGAIN. AND I'M NOT--WELL. I'M NOT EXACTLY FOLLOWING ORDERS HERE. I JUST--
I NEED TIME TO THINK THIS THROUGH, OKAY?!

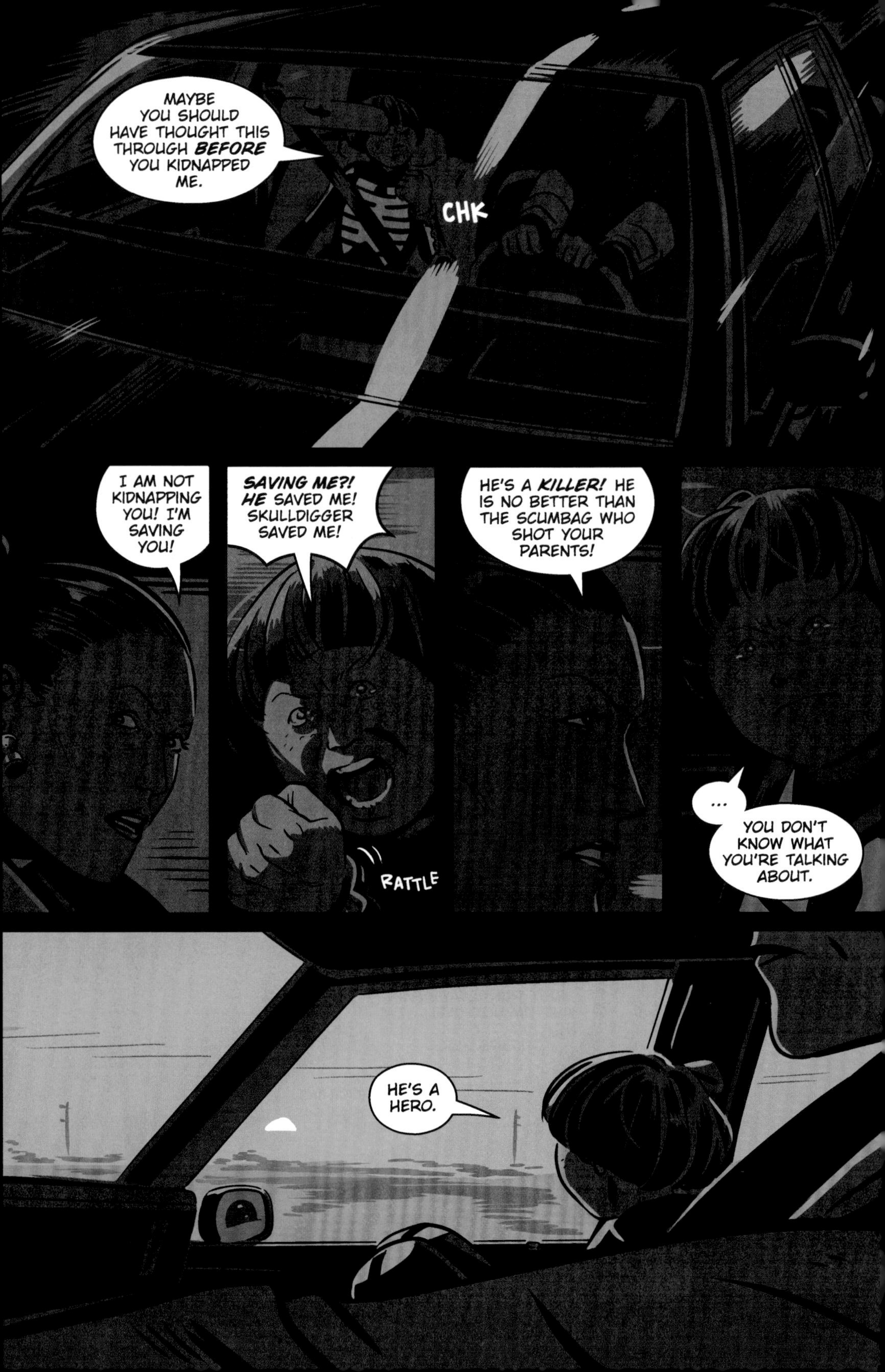
MAYBE YOU SHOULD HAVE THOUGHT THIS THROUGH **BEFORE** YOU KIDNAPPED ME.
CHK
I AM NOT KIDNAPPING YOU! I'M SAVING YOU!
SAVING ME?! HE SAVED ME! SKULLDIGGER SAVED ME!
RATTLE
HE'S A **KILLER!** HE IS NO BETTER THAN THE SCUMBAG WHO SHOT YOUR PARENTS!
...
YOU DON'T KNOW WHAT YOU'RE TALKING ABOUT.
HE'S A HERO.

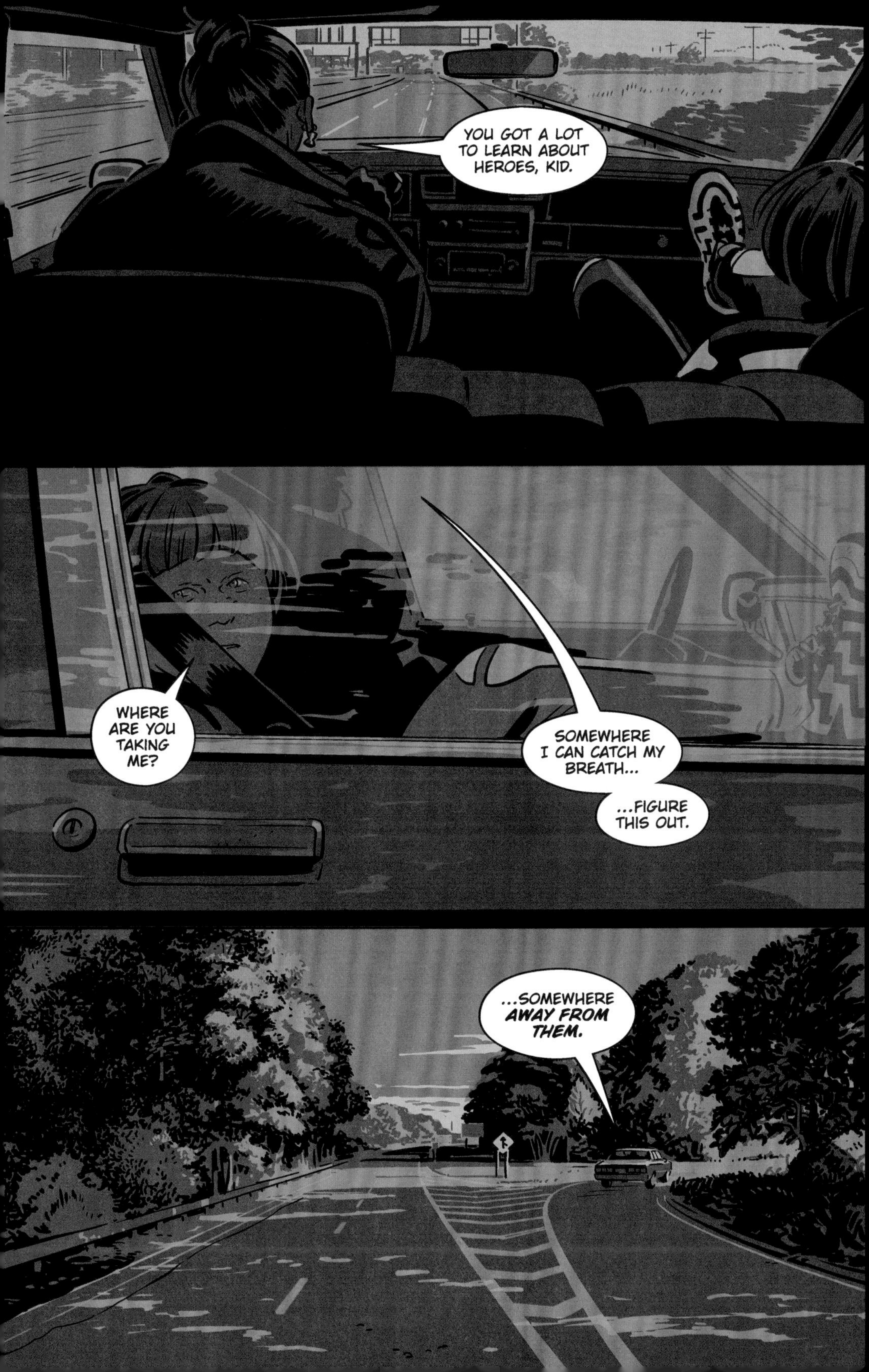
YOU GOT A LOT TO LEARN ABOUT HEROES, KID.
WHERE ARE YOU TAKING ME?
SOMEWHERE I CAN CATCH MY BREATH...
...FIGURE THIS OUT.
...SOMEWHERE AWAY FROM THEM.

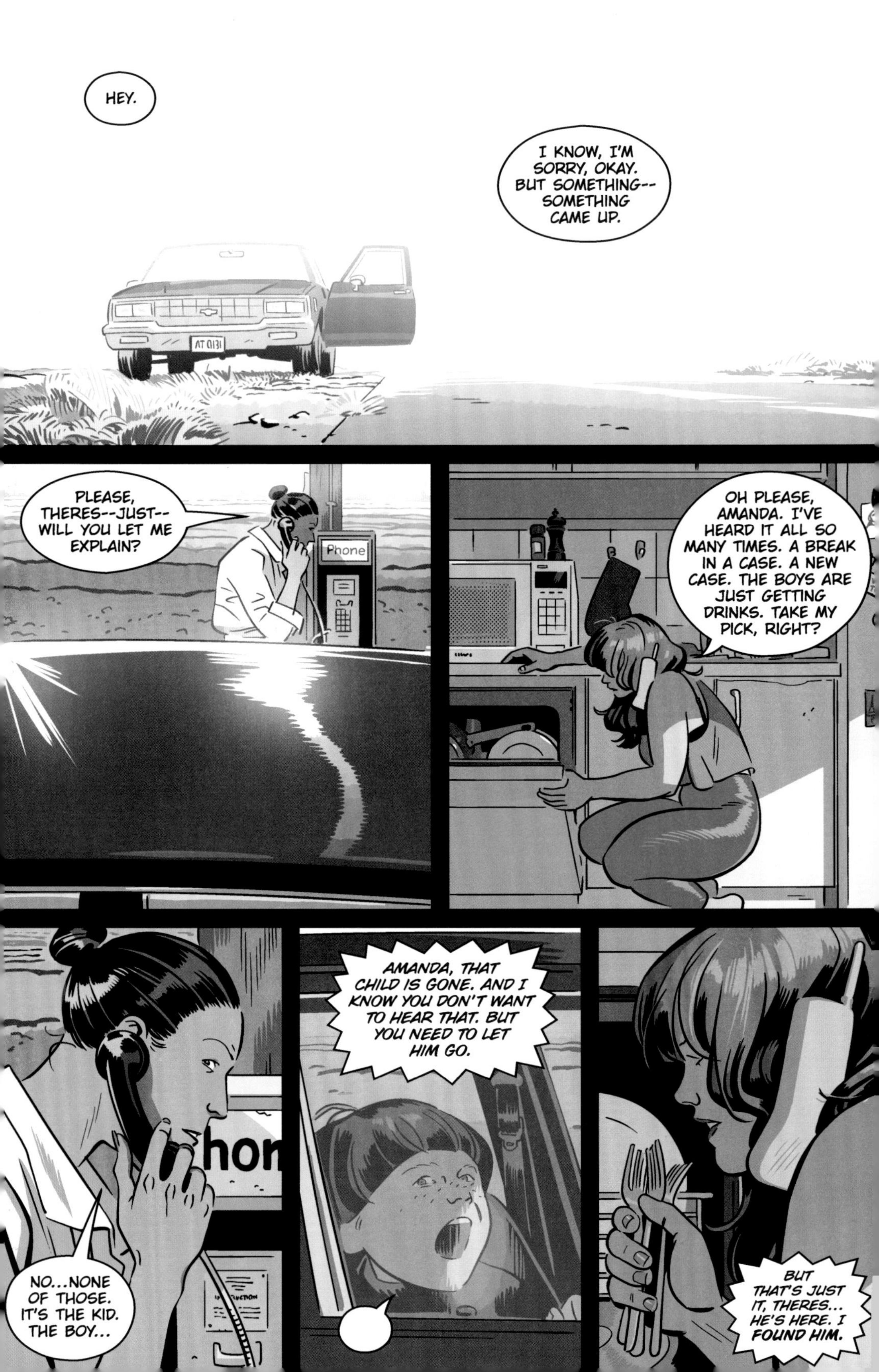
HEY.
I KNOW, I'M SORRY, OKAY. BUT SOMETHING-- SOMETHING CAME UP.
AT 0131
PLEASE, THERES--JUST-- WILL YOU LET ME EXPLAIN?
Phone
OH PLEASE, AMANDA. I'VE HEARD IT ALL SO MANY TIMES. A BREAK IN A CASE. A NEW CASE. THE BOYS ARE JUST GETTING DRINKS. TAKE MY PICK, RIGHT?
NO...NONE OF THOSE. IT'S THE KID. THE BOY...
AMANDA, THAT CHILD IS GONE. AND I KNOW YOU DON'T WANT TO HEAR THAT. BUT YOU NEED TO LET HIM GO.
BUT THAT'S JUST IT, THERES... HE'S HERE. I **FOUND HIM.**

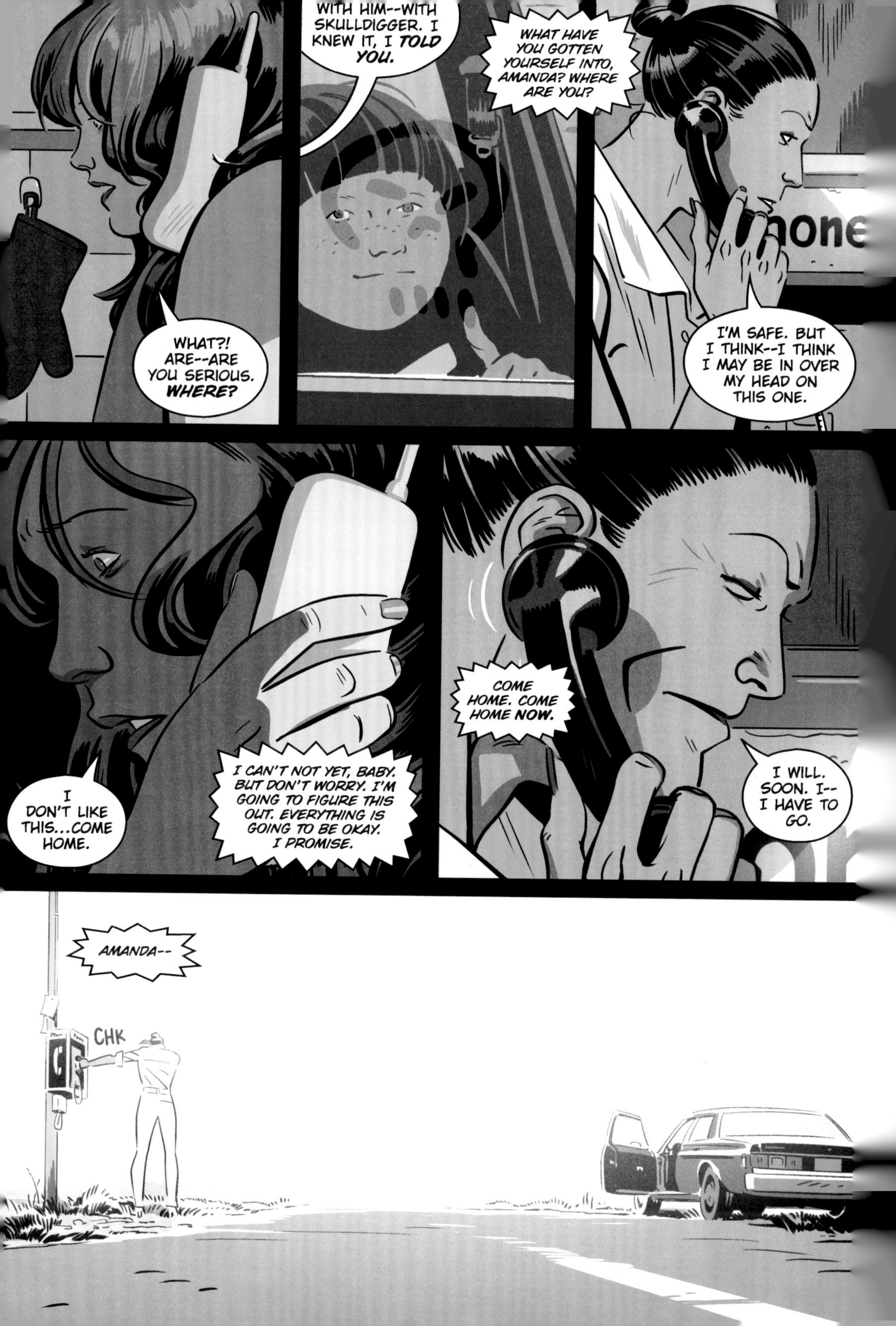
WITH HIM--WITH SKULLDIGGER. I KNEW IT, I TOLD YOU.
WHAT?! ARE--ARE YOU SERIOUS. WHERE?
WHAT HAVE YOU GOTTEN YOURSELF INTO, AMANDA? WHERE ARE YOU?
I'M SAFE. BUT I THINK--I THINK I MAY BE IN OVER MY HEAD ON THIS ONE.
I DON'T LIKE THIS...COME HOME.
I CAN'T NOT YET, BABY. BUT DON'T WORRY. I'M GOING TO FIGURE THIS OUT. EVERYTHING IS GOING TO BE OKAY. I PROMISE.
COME HOME. COME HOME NOW.
I WILL. SOON. I-- I HAVE TO GO.
AMANDA--
CHK

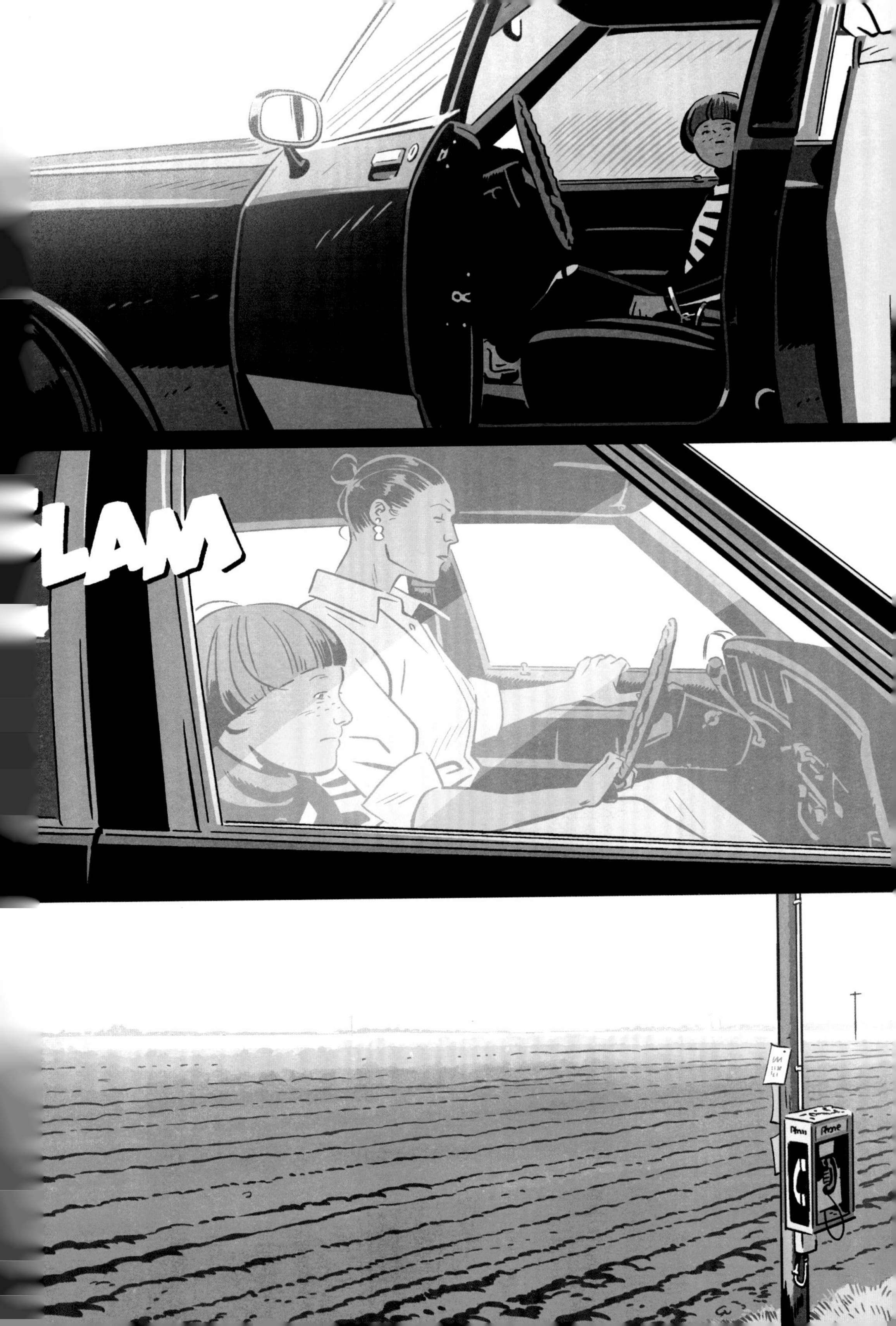
LAM

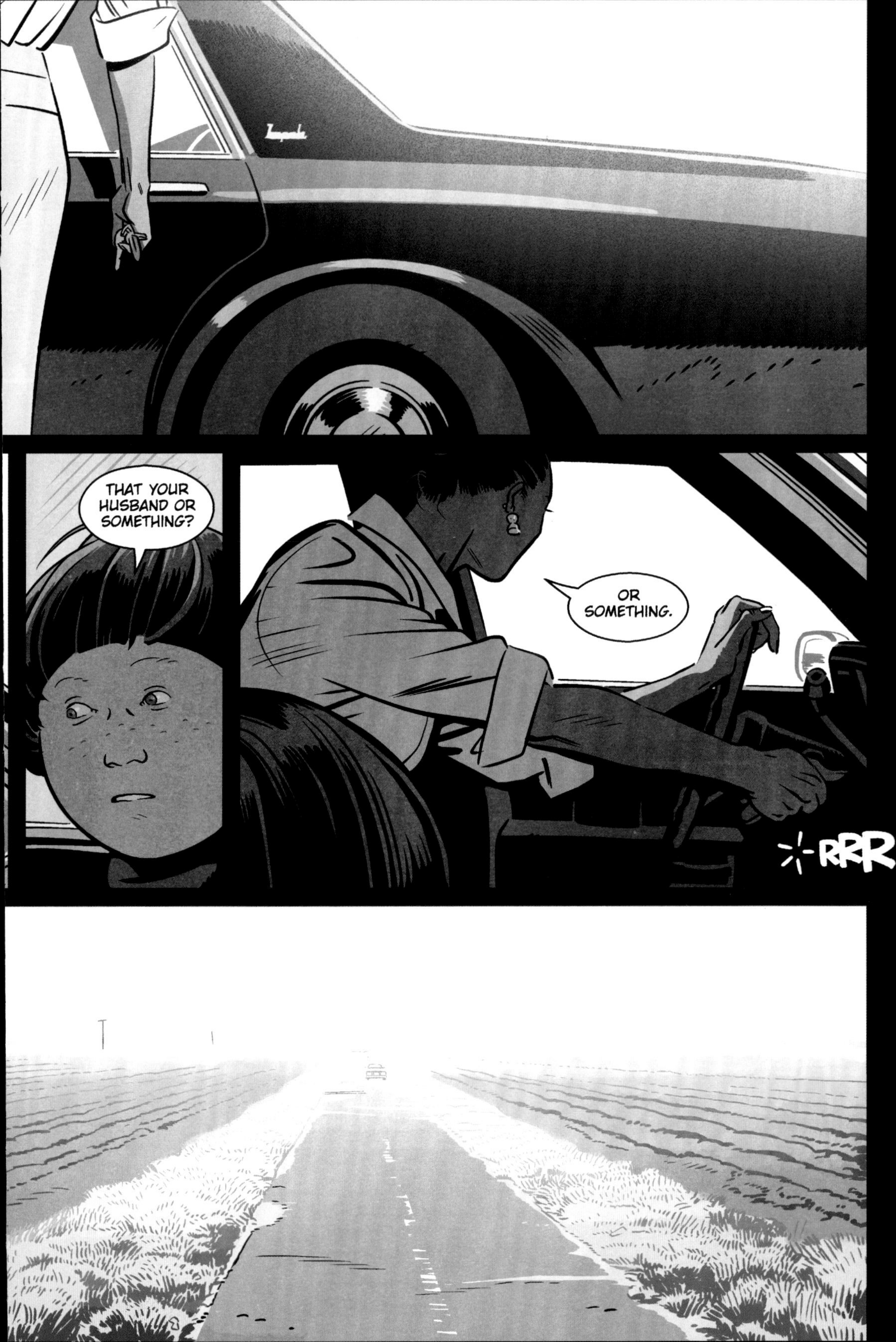
THAT YOUR HUSBAND OR SOMETHING?
OR SOMETHING.
RRR

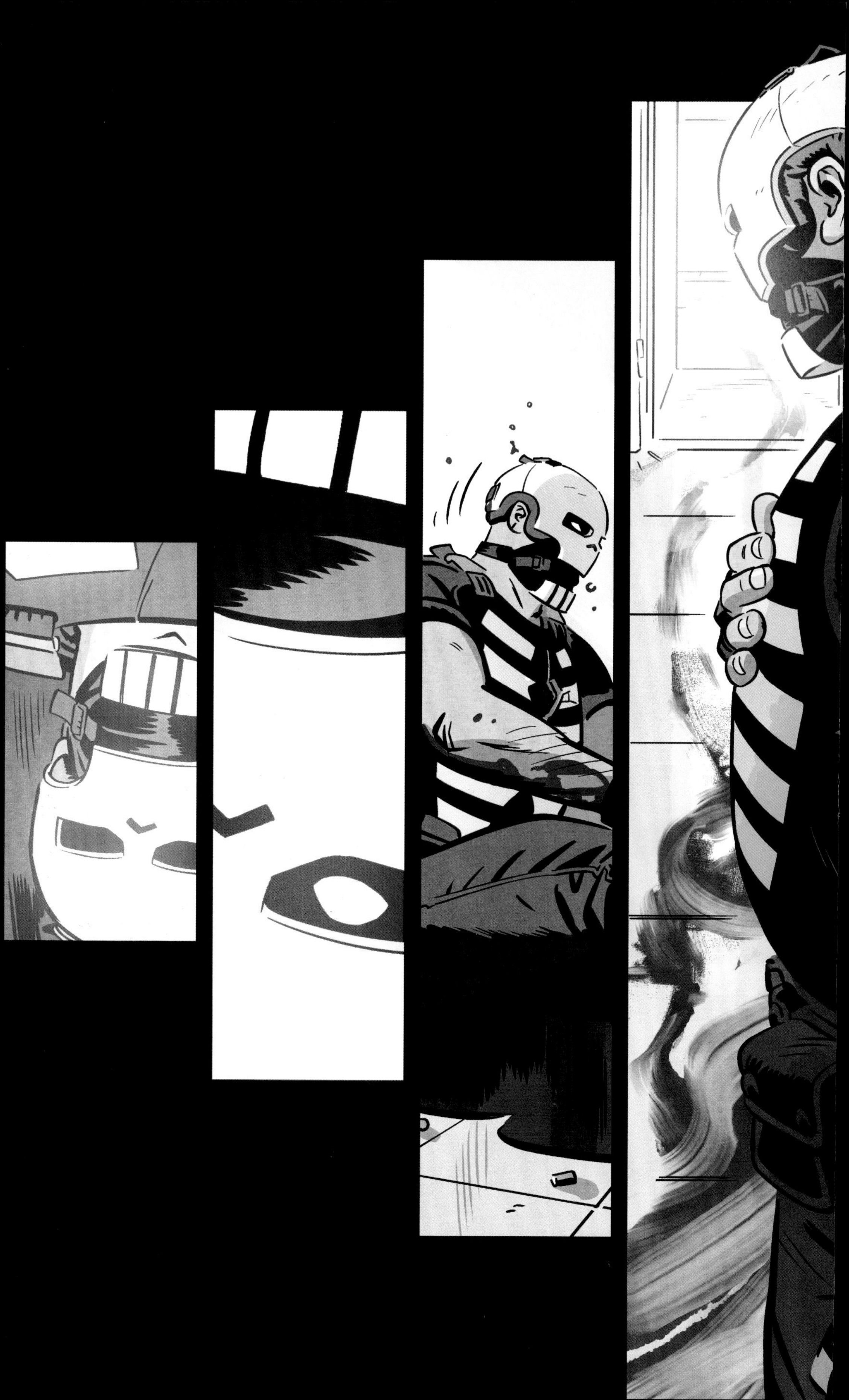

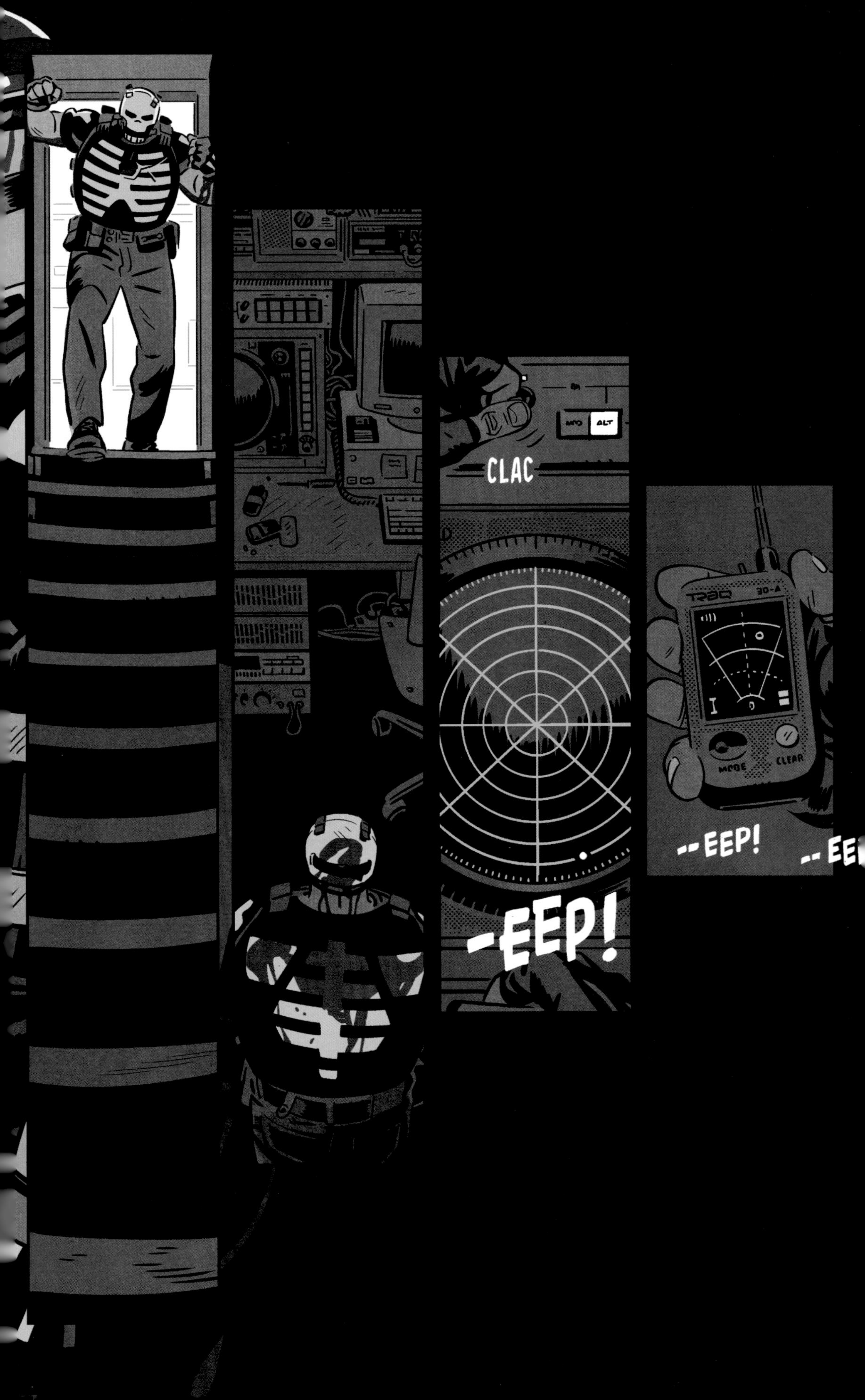
CLAC
-EEP!
TRAQ
3D-A
MODE
CLEAR
--EEP!

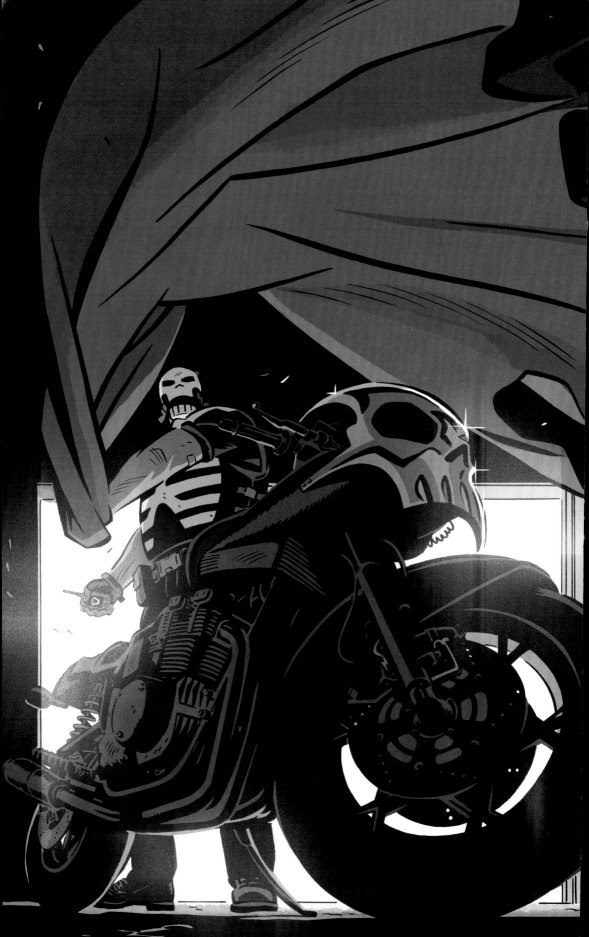

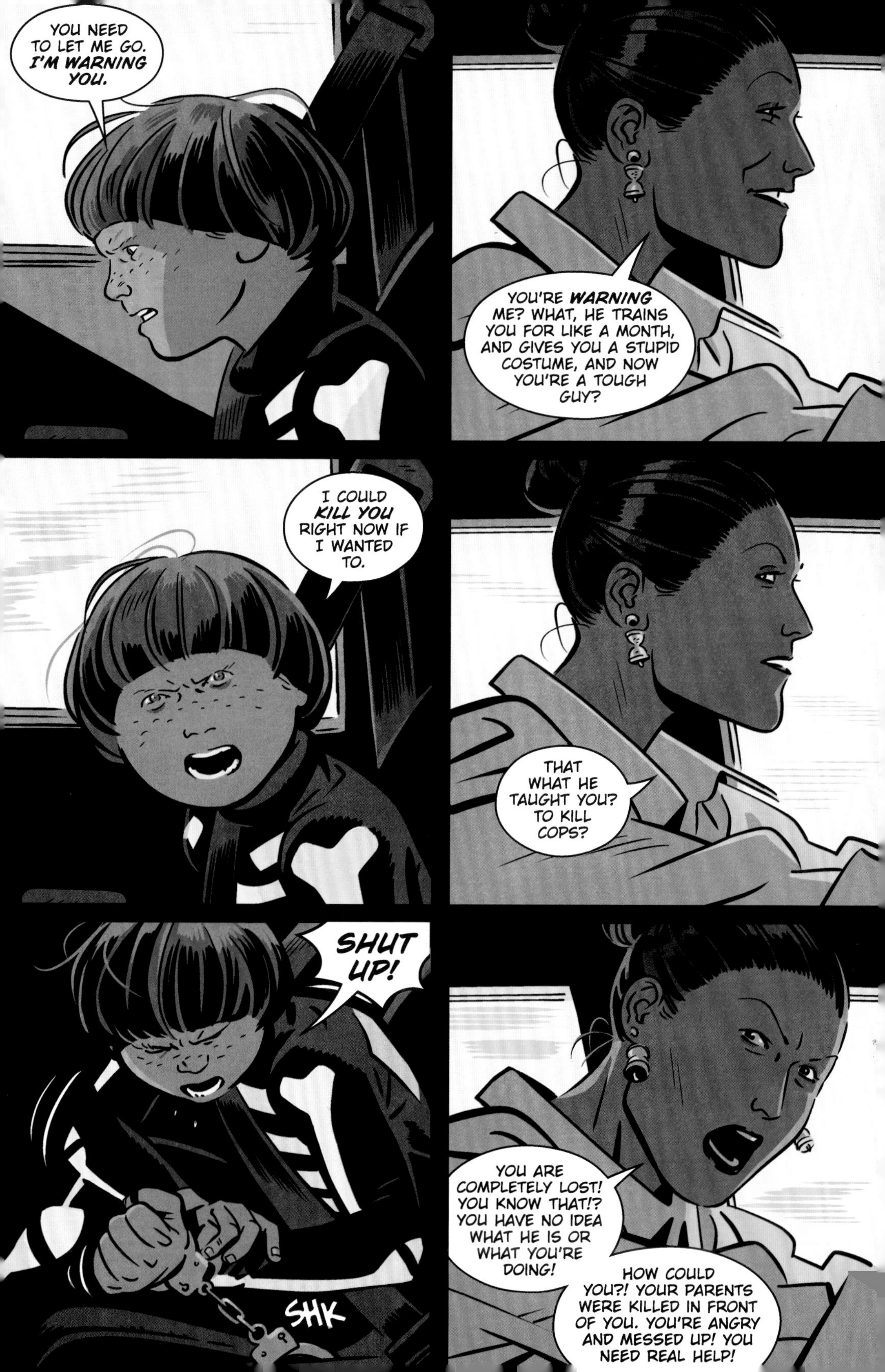
YOU NEED TO LET ME GO. I'M WARNING YOU.
YOU'RE WARNING ME? WHAT, HE TRAINS YOU FOR LIKE A MONTH, AND GIVES YOU A STUPID COSTUME, AND NOW YOU'RE A TOUGH GUY?
I COULD KILL YOU RIGHT NOW IF I WANTED TO.
THAT WHAT HE TAUGHT YOU? TO KILL COPS?
SHUT UP!
SHK
YOU ARE COMPLETELY LOST! YOU KNOW THAT!? YOU HAVE NO IDEA WHAT HE IS OR WHAT YOU'RE DOING!
HOW COULD YOU?! YOUR PARENTS WERE KILLED IN FRONT OF YOU. YOU'RE ANGRY AND MESSED UP! YOU NEED REAL HELP!

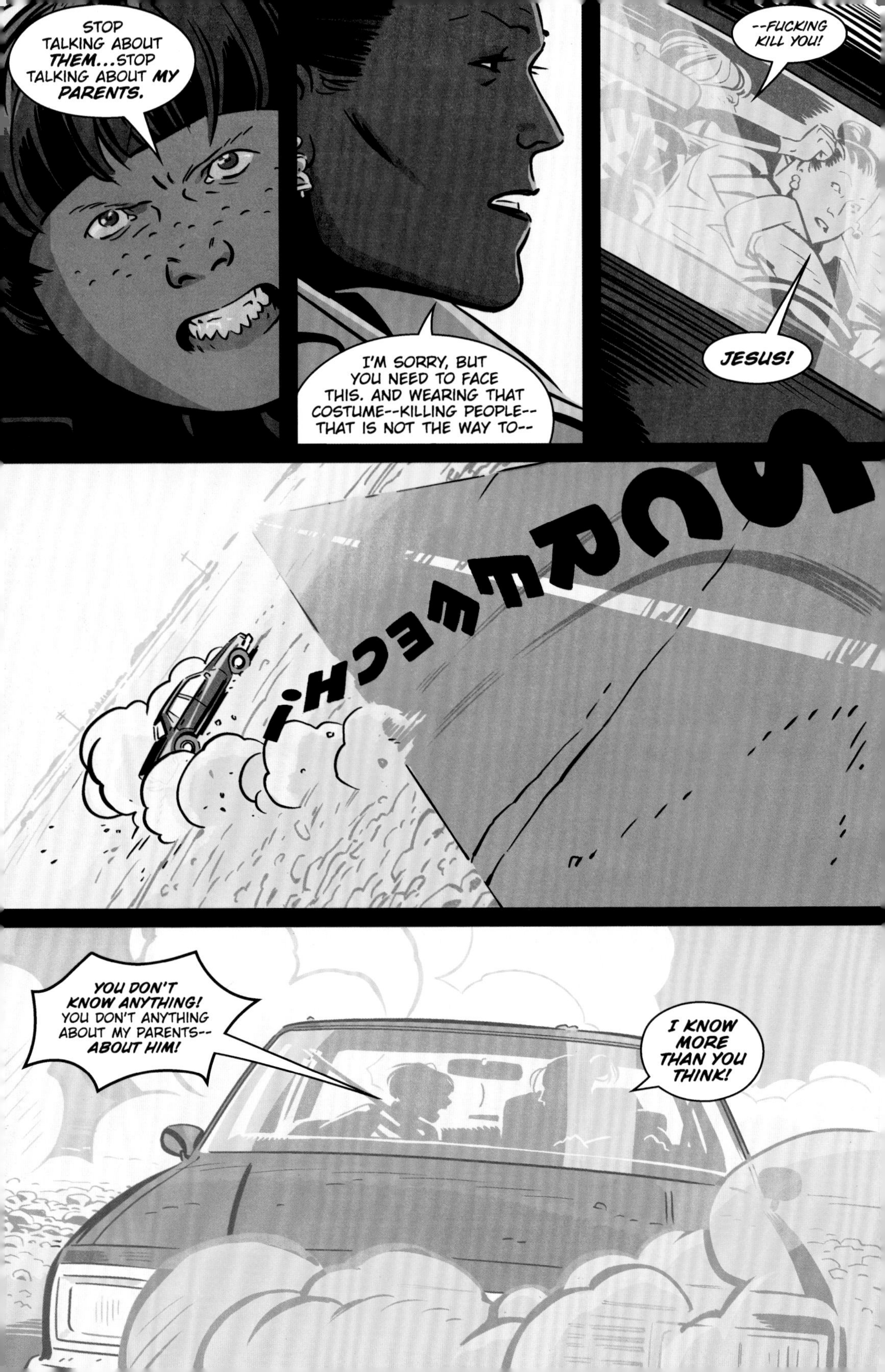

STOP TALKING ABOUT THEM...STOP TALKING ABOUT MY PARENTS.
I'M SORRY, BUT YOU NEED TO FACE THIS. AND WEARING THAT COSTUME--KILLING PEOPLE--THAT IS NOT THE WAY TO--
--FUCKING KILL YOU!
JESUS!
SCREEECH!
YOU DON'T KNOW ANYTHING! YOU DON'T ANYTHING ABOUT MY PARENTS--ABOUT HIM!
I KNOW MORE THAN YOU THINK!

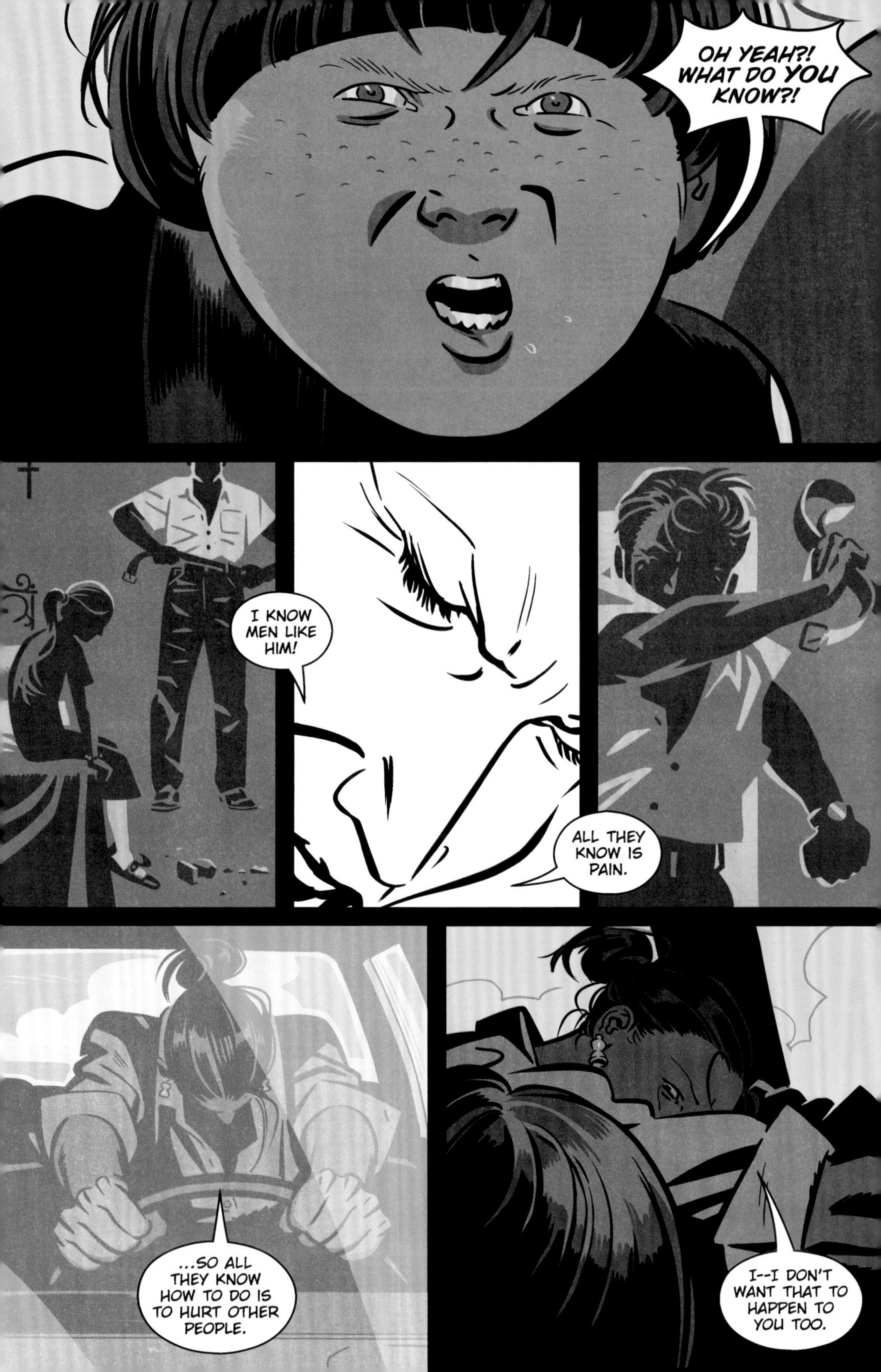
OH YEAH?! WHAT DO YOU KNOW?!
I KNOW MEN LIKE HIM!
ALL THEY KNOW IS PAIN.
...SO ALL THEY KNOW HOW TO DO IS TO HURT OTHER PEOPLE.
I--I DON'T WANT THAT TO HAPPEN TO YOU TOO.

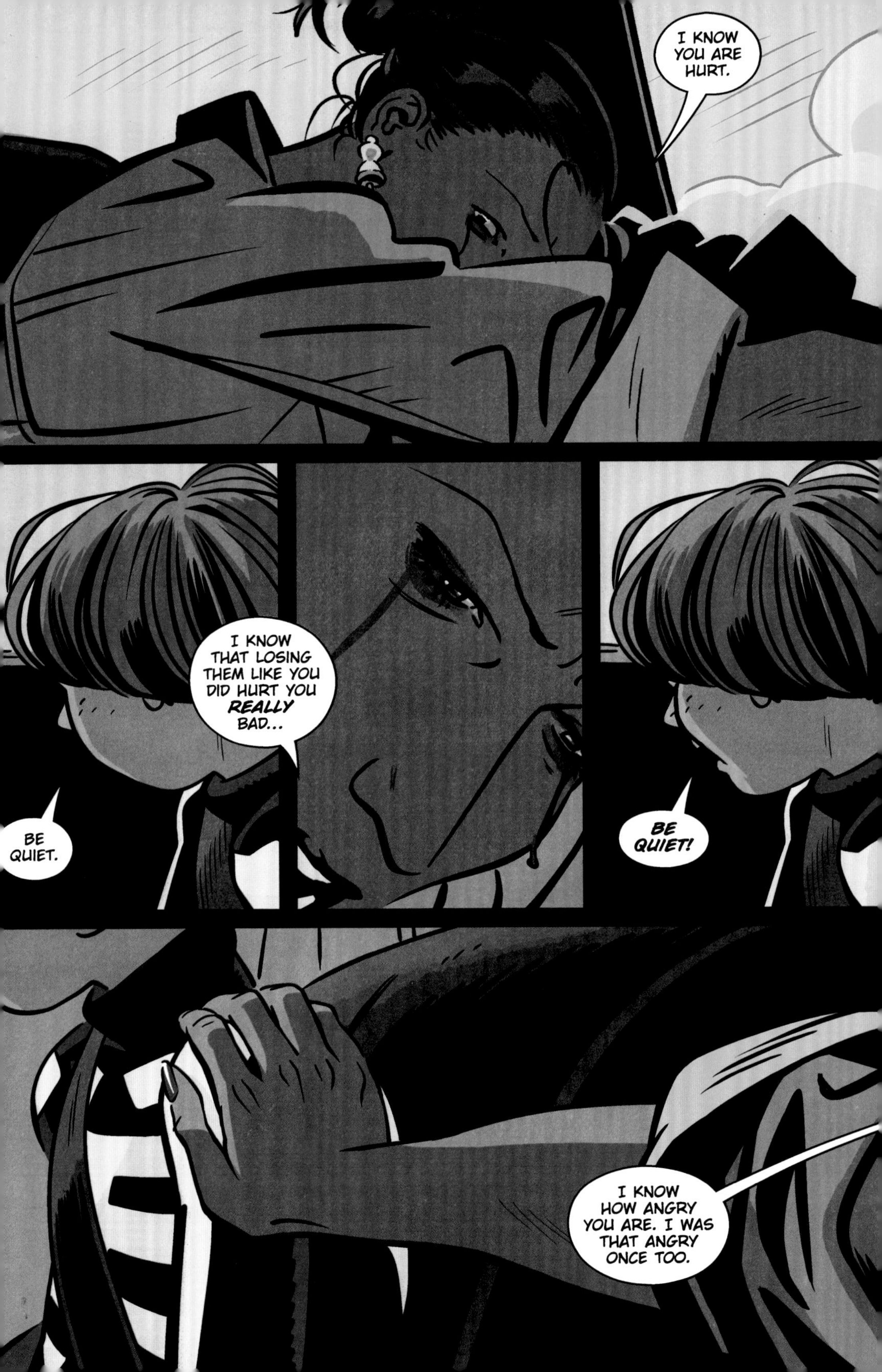
I KNOW YOU ARE HURT.
I KNOW THAT LOSING THEM LIKE YOU DID HURT YOU REALLY BAD...
BE QUIET.
BE QUIET!
I KNOW HOW ANGRY YOU ARE. I WAS THAT ANGRY ONCE TOO.

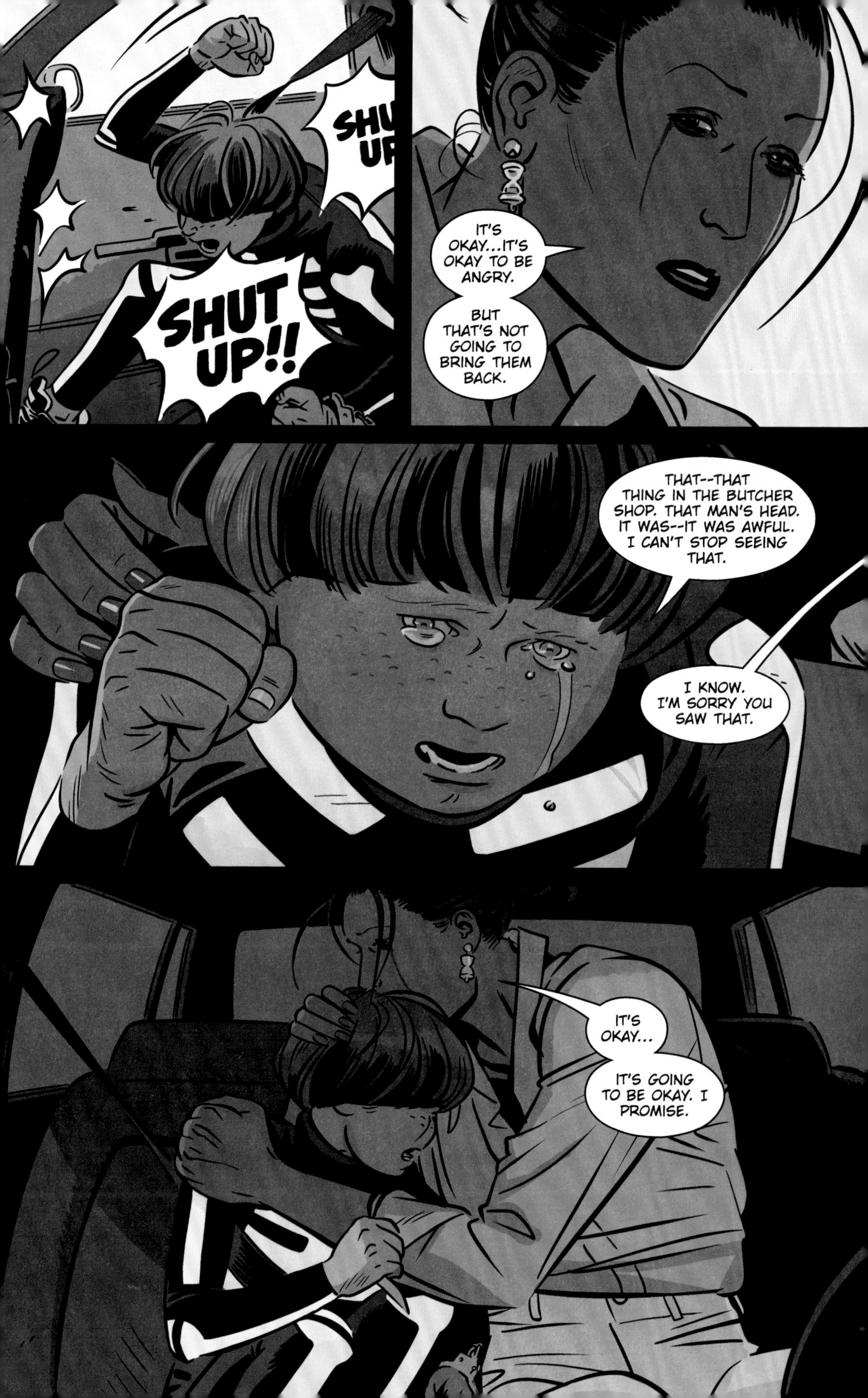
SHUT UP
SHUT UP!!
IT'S OKAY...IT'S OKAY TO BE ANGRY.
BUT THAT'S NOT GOING TO BRING THEM BACK.
THAT--THAT THING IN THE BUTCHER SHOP. THAT MAN'S HEAD. IT WAS--IT WAS AWFUL. I CAN'T STOP SEEING THAT.
I KNOW. I'M SORRY YOU SAW THAT.
IT'S OKAY...
IT'S GOING TO BE OKAY. I PROMISE.

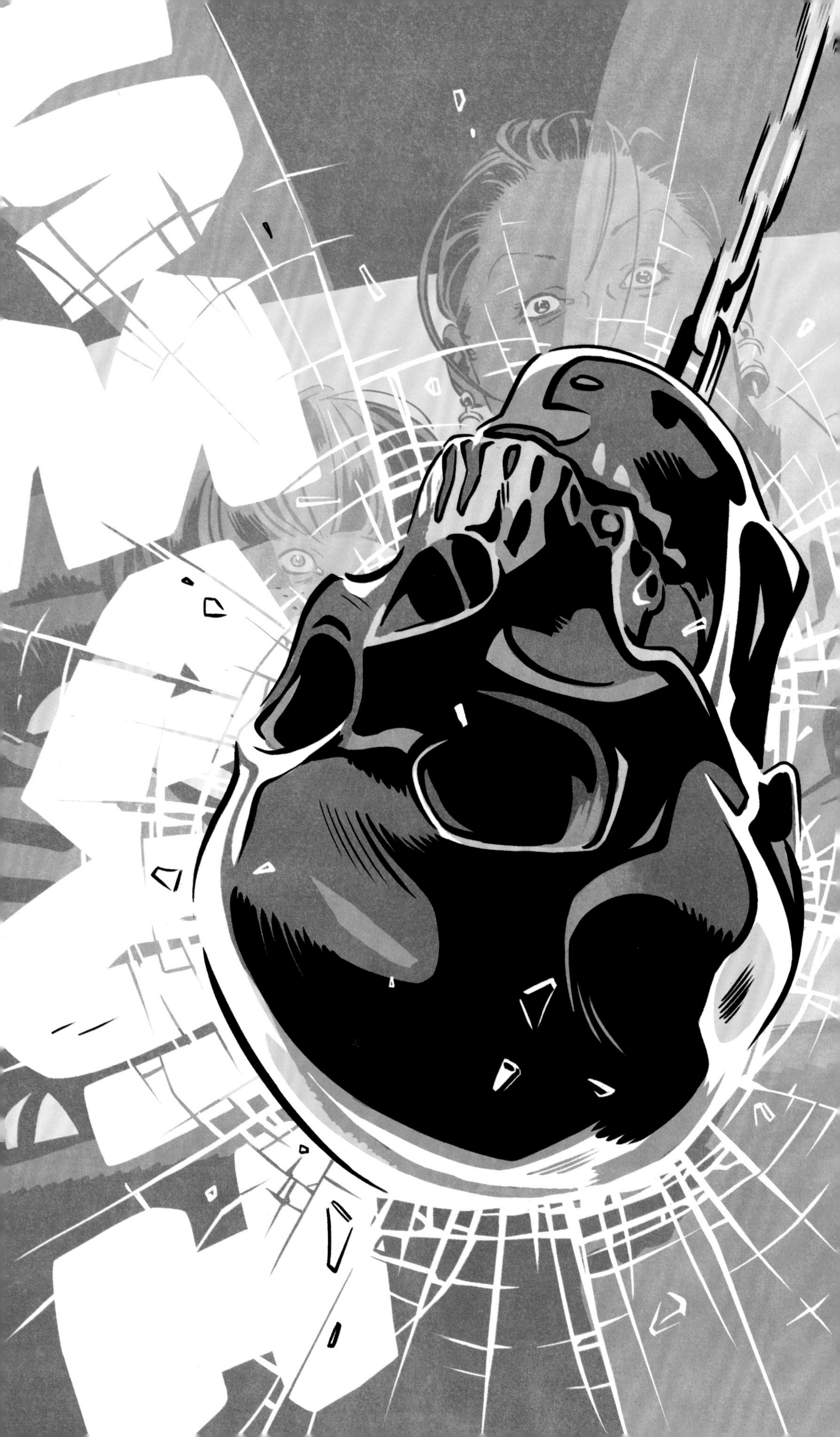

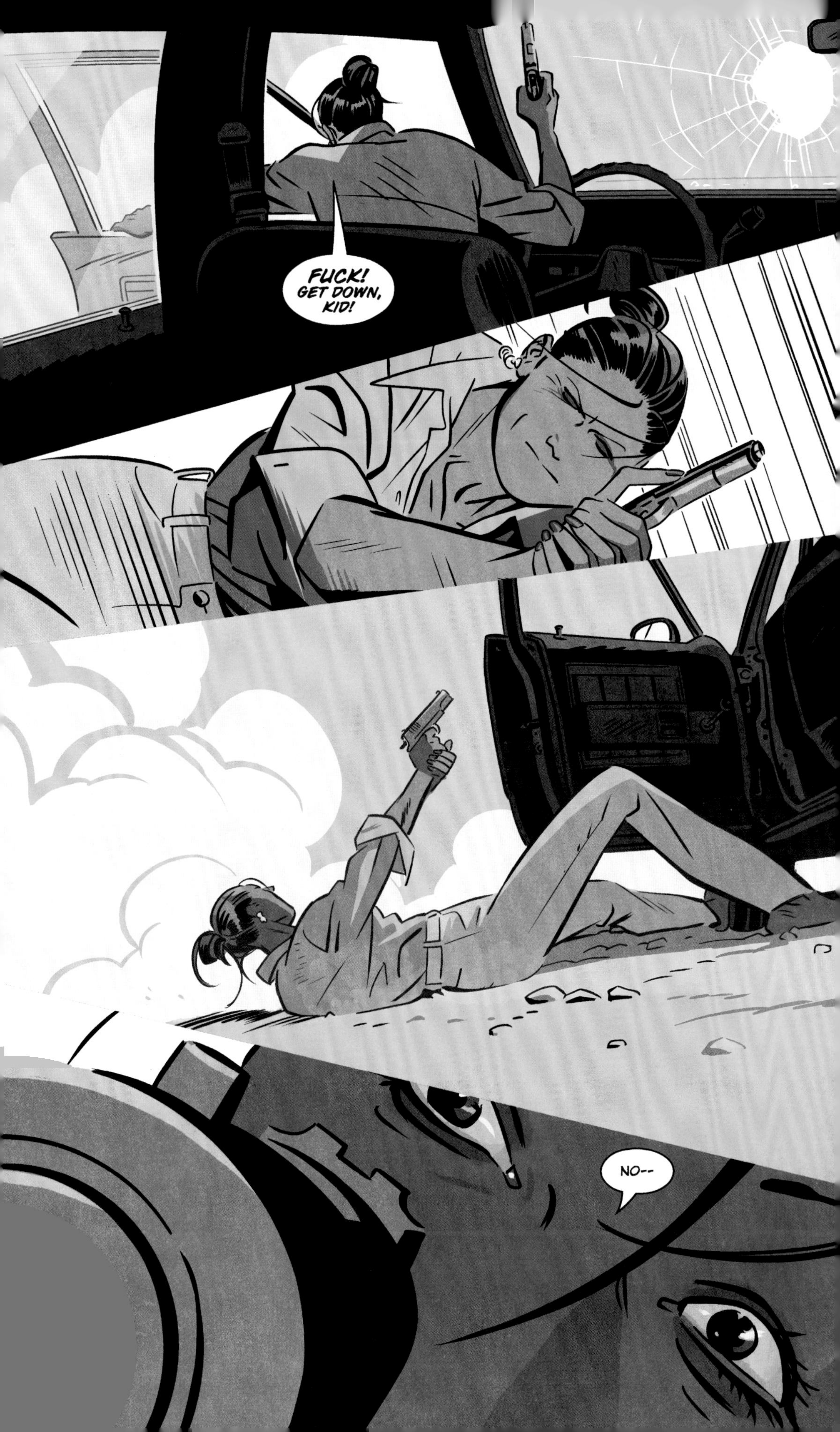
FUCK! GET DOWN, KID!
NO--

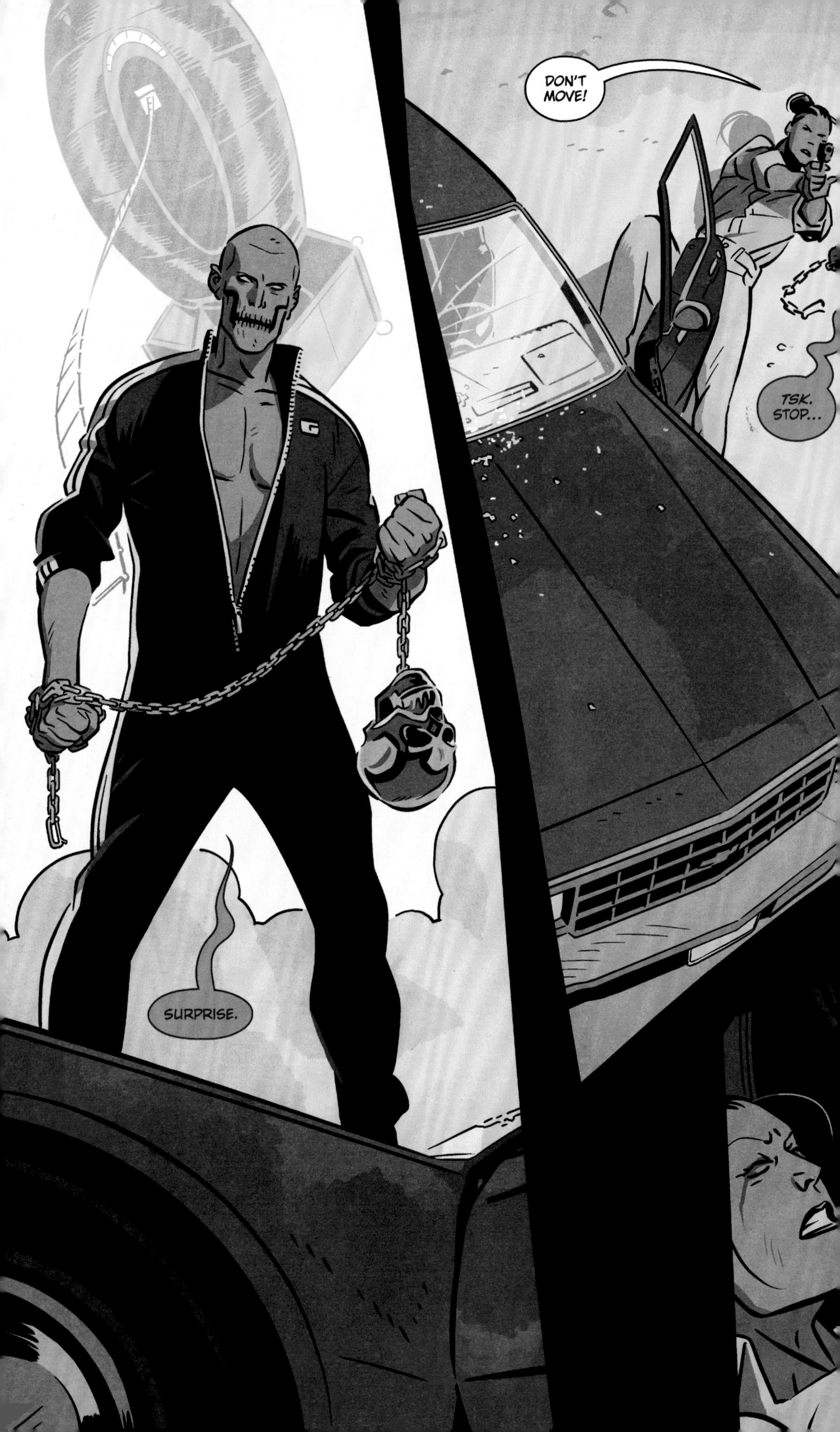
DON'T MOVE!
TSK. STOP...
SURPRISE.

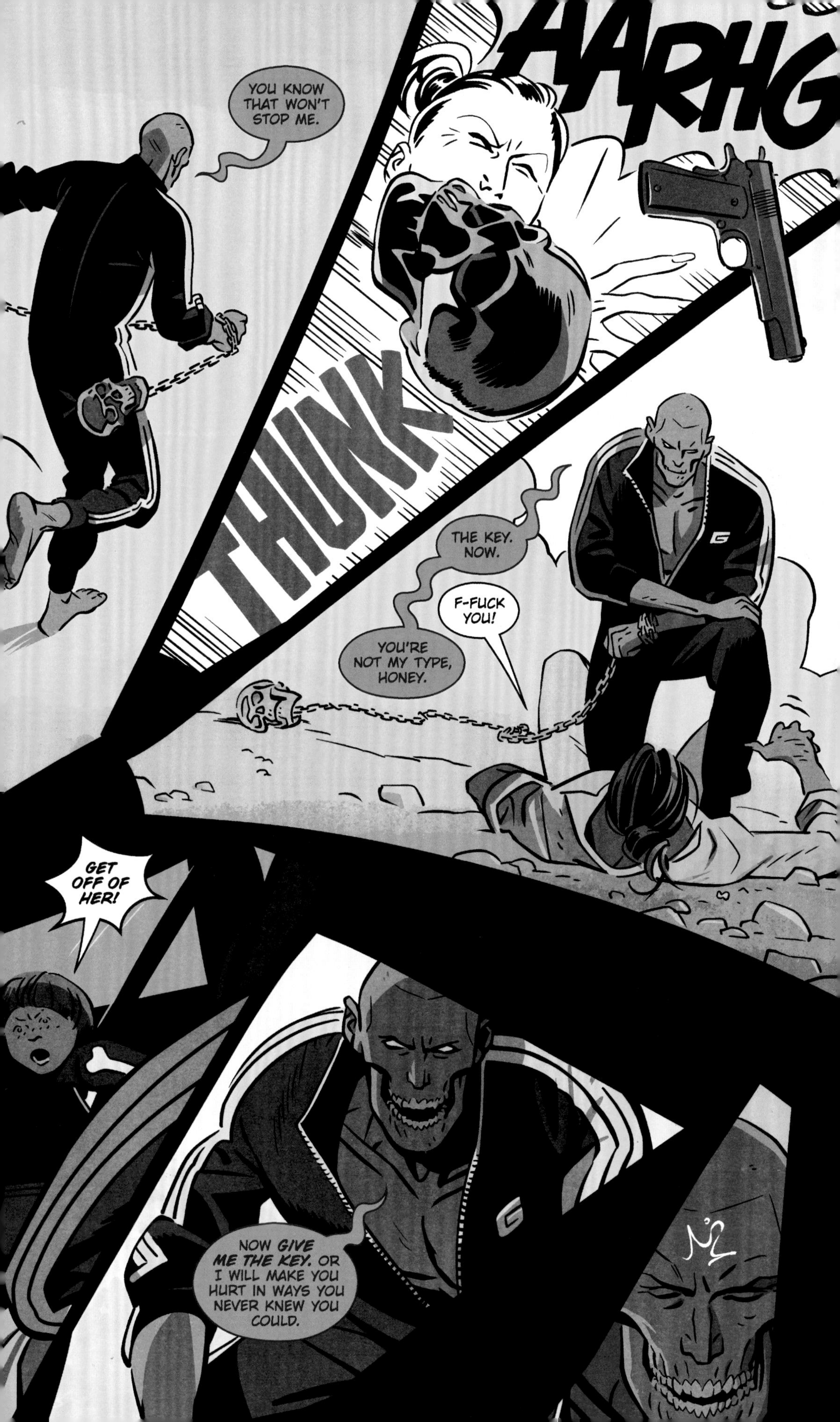
YOU KNOW THAT WON'T STOP ME.
AARHG
THUNK
THE KEY. NOW.
F-FUCK YOU!
YOU'RE NOT MY TYPE, HONEY.
GET OFF OF HER!
NOW GIVE ME THE KEY. OR I WILL MAKE YOU HURT IN WAYS YOU NEVER KNEW YOU COULD.

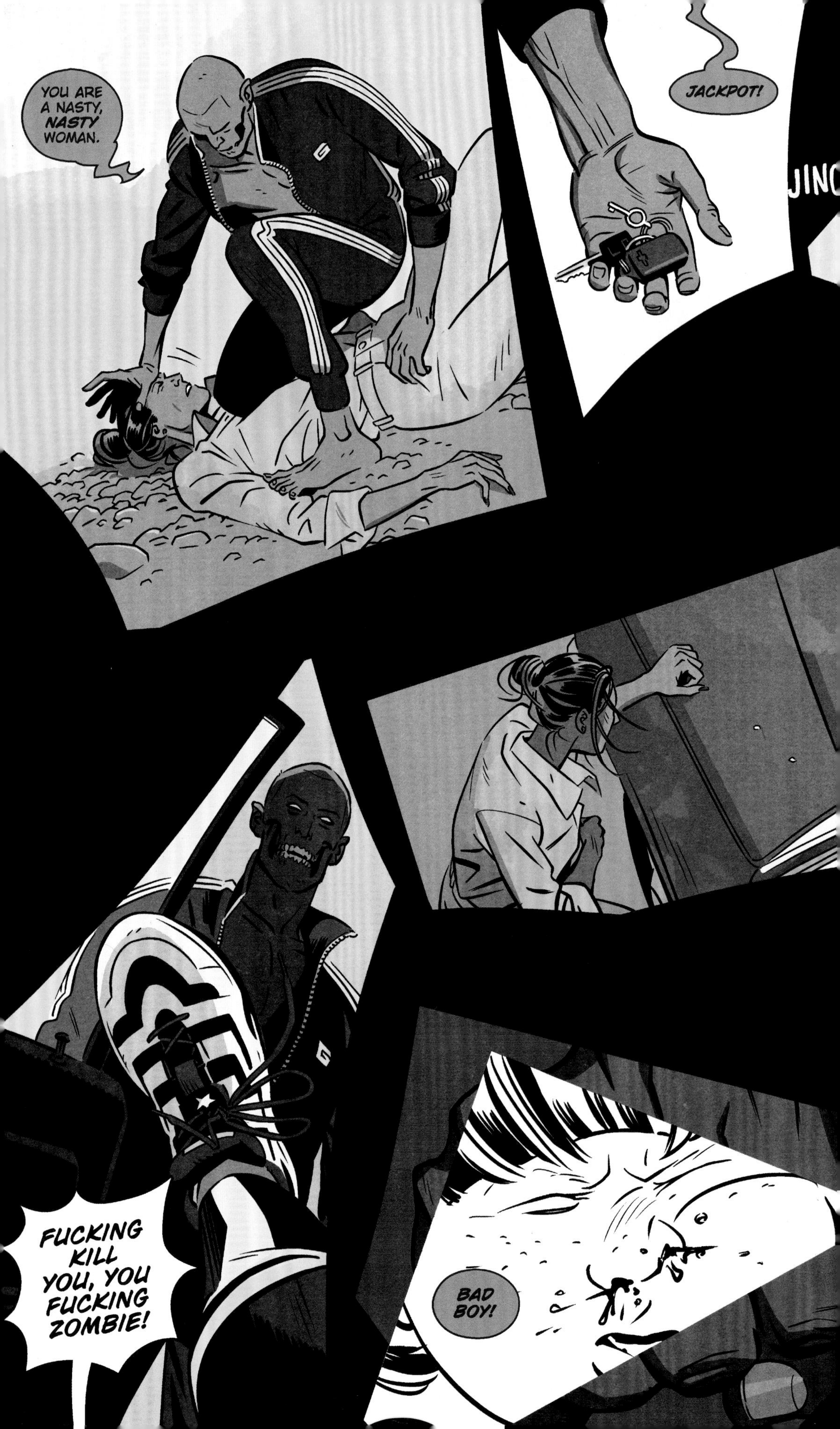
YOU ARE A NASTY, NASTY WOMAN.
JACKPOT!
FUCKING KILL YOU, YOU FUCKING ZOMBIE!
BAD BOY!

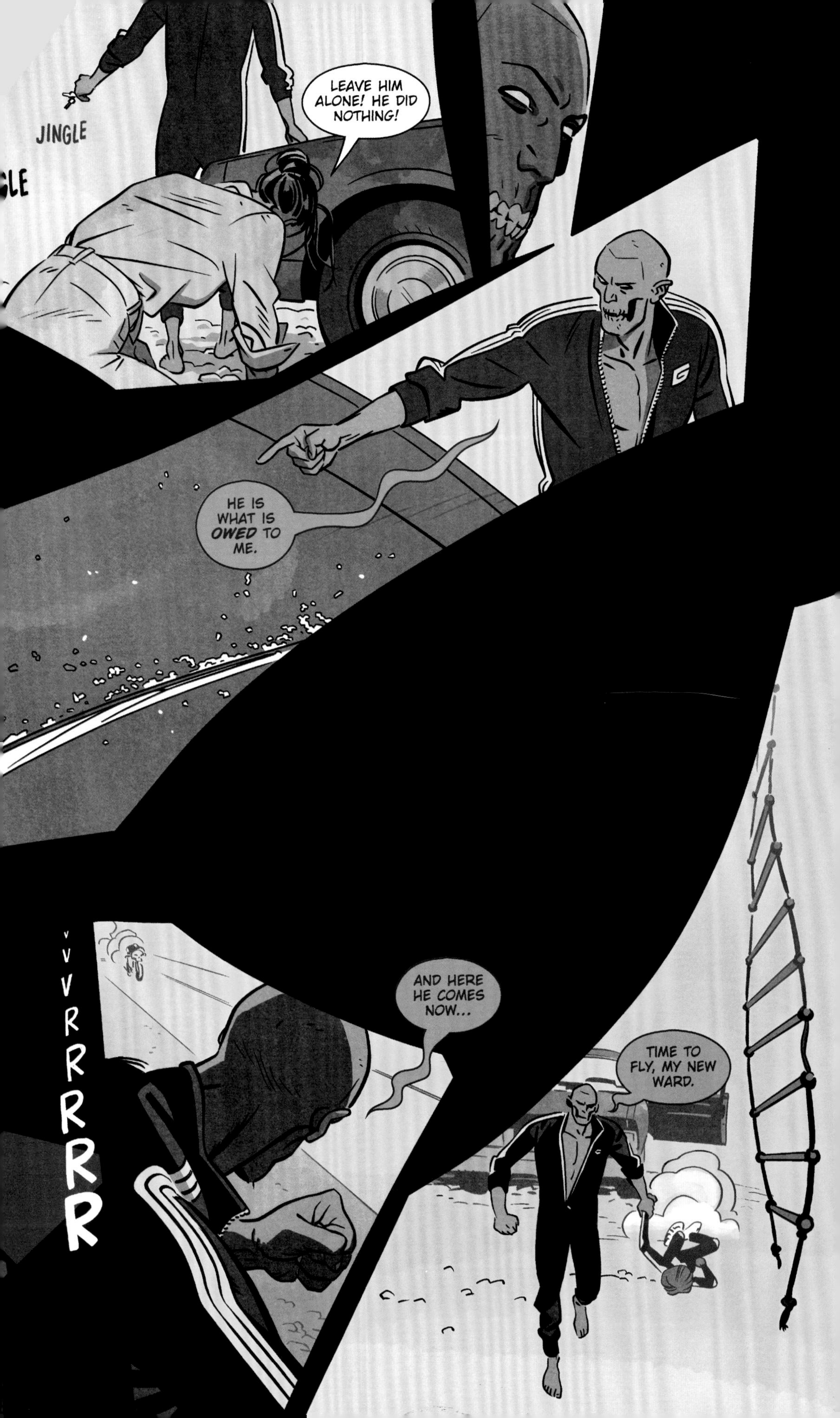
JINGLE
LE
LEAVE HIM ALONE! HE DID NOTHING!
HE IS WHAT IS OWED TO ME.
VVVRRRRRR
AND HERE HE COMES NOW...
TIME TO FLY, MY NEW WARD.

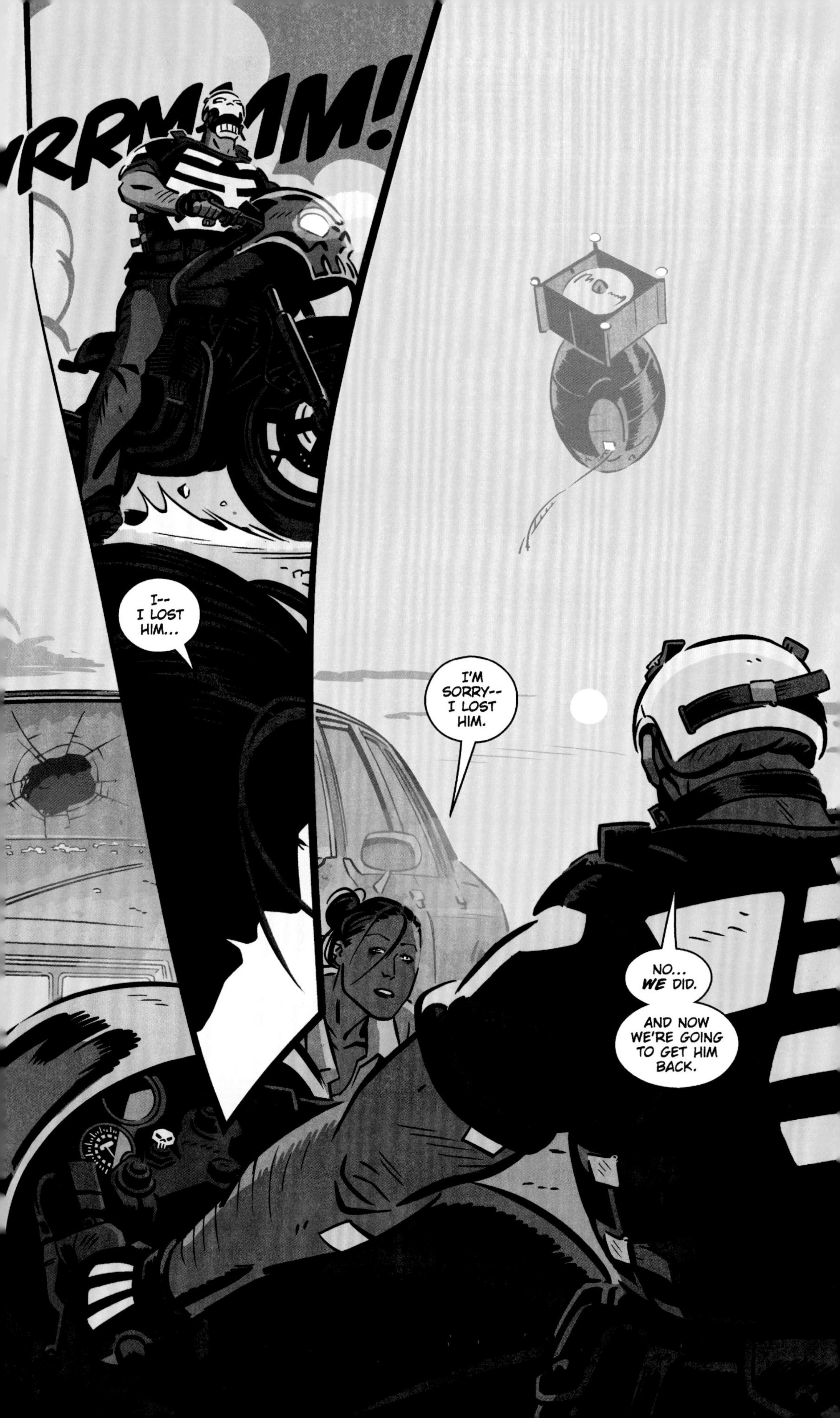

I-- I LOST HIM...
I'M SORRY-- I LOST HIM.
NO... WE DID.
AND NOW WE'RE GOING TO GET HIM BACK.

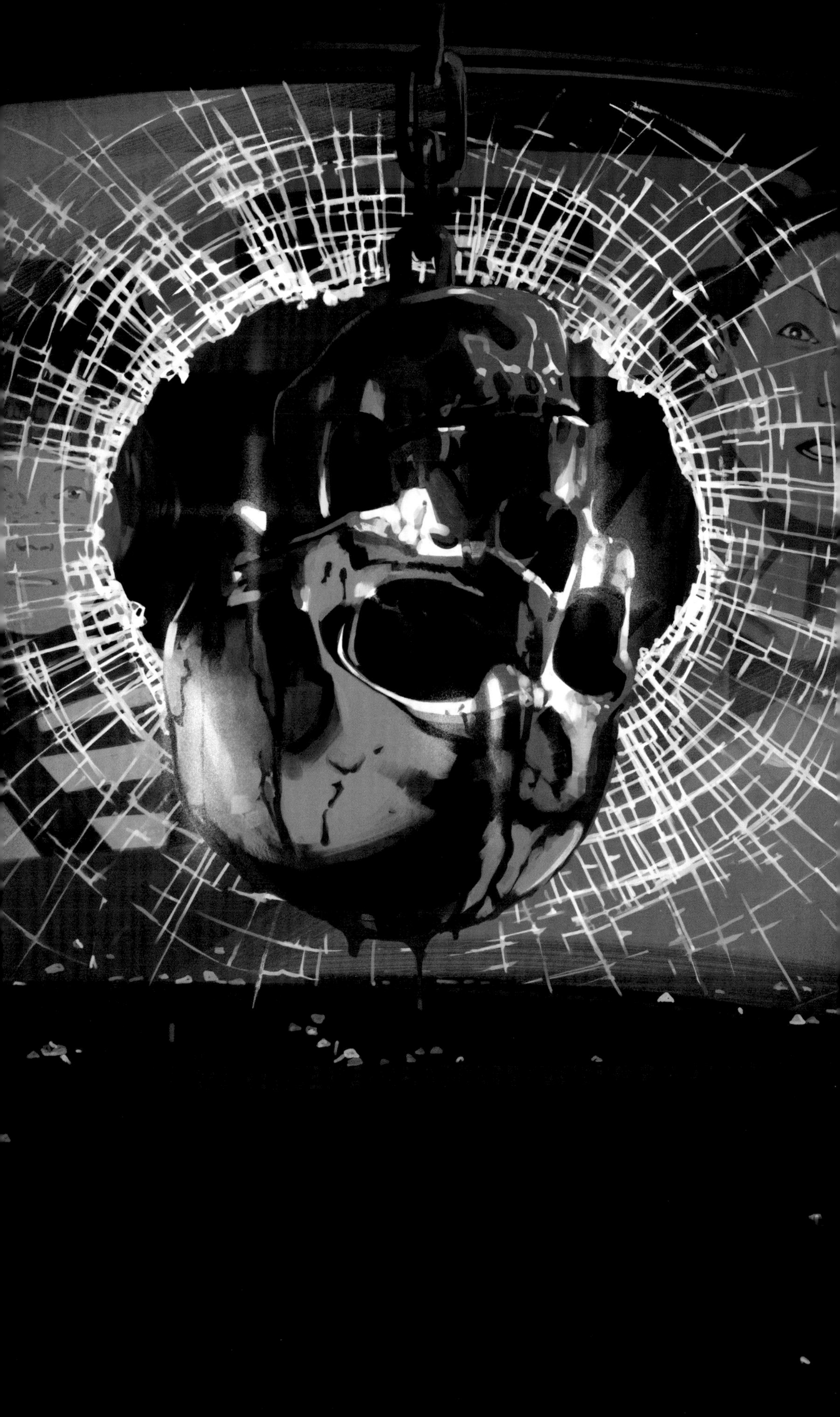

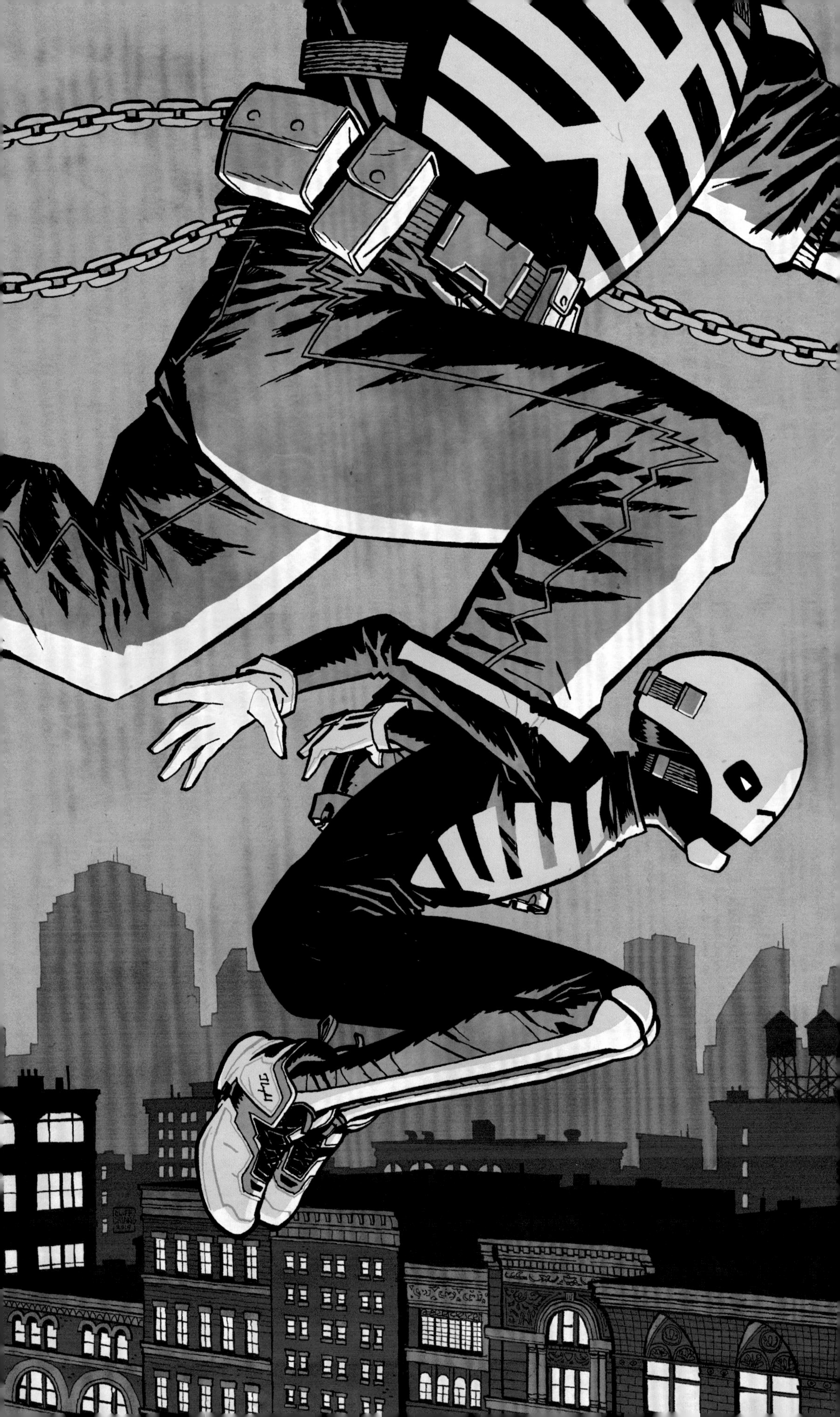

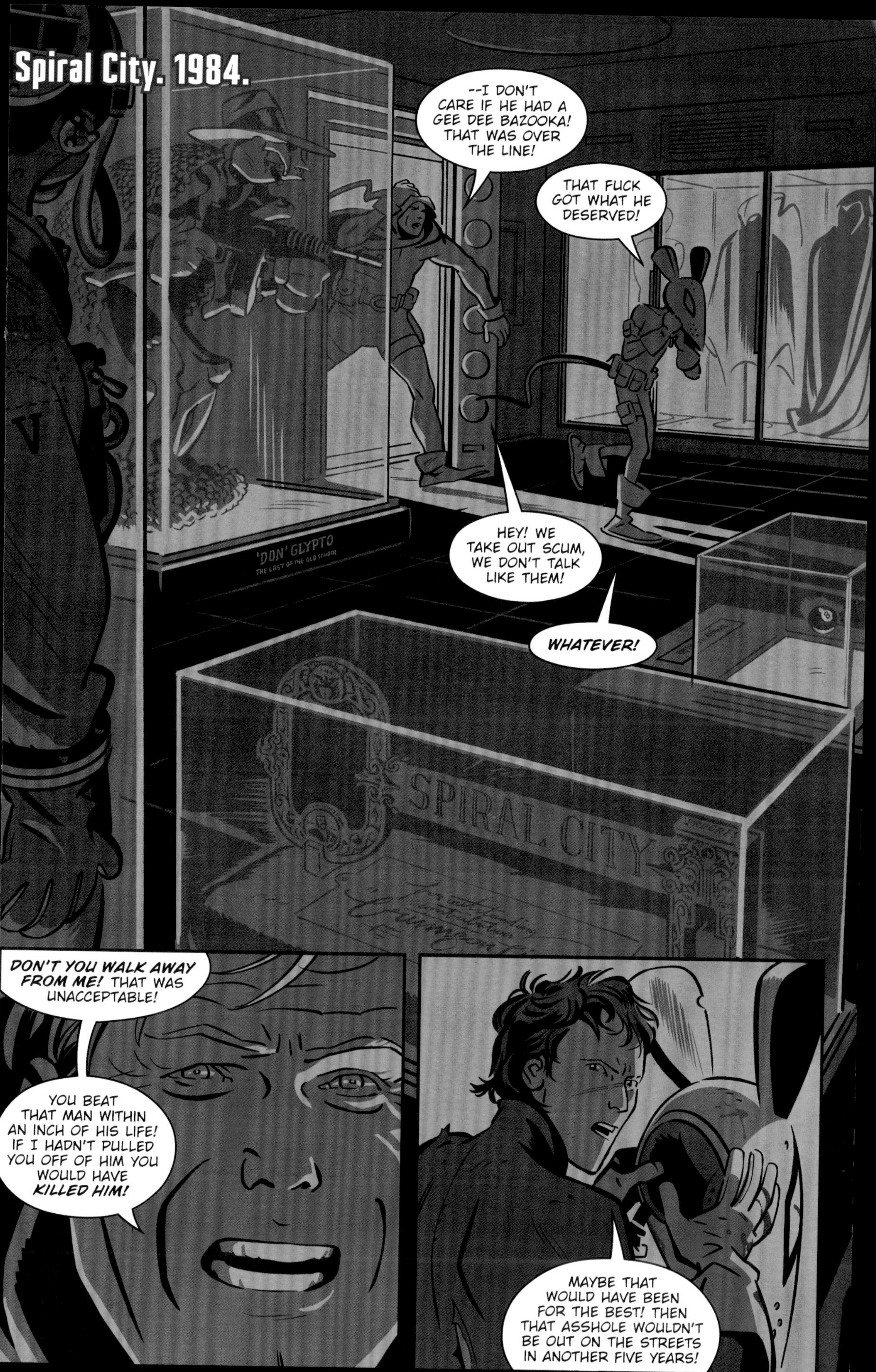
Spiral City. 1984.
--I DON'T CARE IF HE HAD A GEE DEE BAZOOKA! THAT WAS OVER THE LINE!
THAT FUCK GOT WHAT HE DESERVED!
HEY! WE TAKE OUT SCUM, WE DON'T TALK LIKE THEM!
WHATEVER!
'DON' GLYPTO
THE LAST OF THE OLD SCHOOL
SPIRAL CITY
DON'T YOU WALK AWAY FROM ME! THAT WAS UNACCEPTABLE!
YOU BEAT THAT MAN WITHIN AN INCH OF HIS LIFE! IF I HADN'T PULLED YOU OFF OF HIM YOU WOULD HAVE KILLED HIM!
MAYBE THAT WOULD HAVE BEEN FOR THE BEST! THEN THAT ASSHOLE WOULDN'T BE OUT ON THE STREETS IN ANOTHER FIVE YEARS!

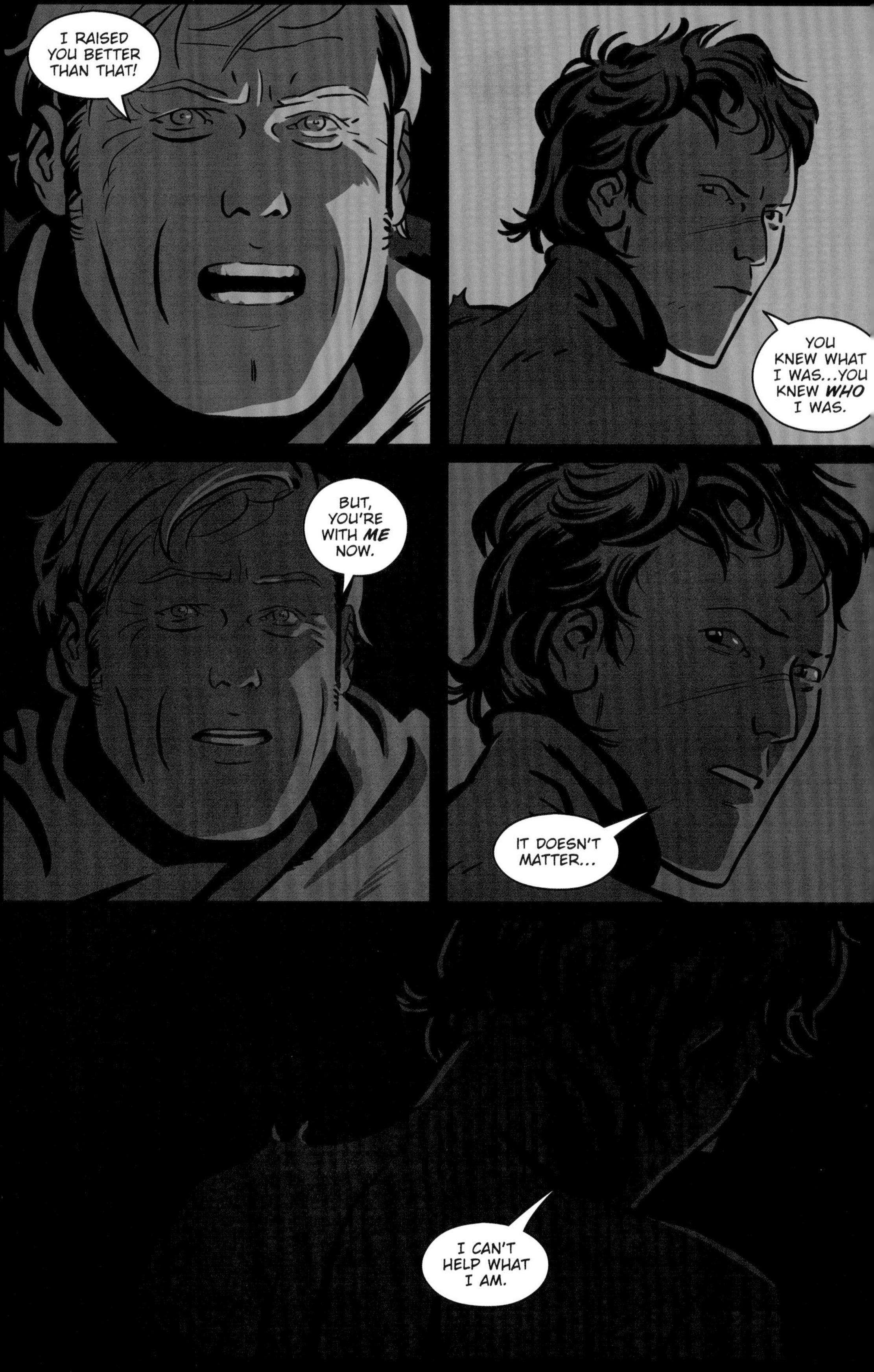
I RAISED YOU BETTER THAN THAT!
YOU KNEW WHAT I WAS...YOU KNEW WHO I WAS.
BUT, YOU'RE WITH ME NOW.
IT DOESN'T MATTER...
I CAN'T HELP WHAT I AM.

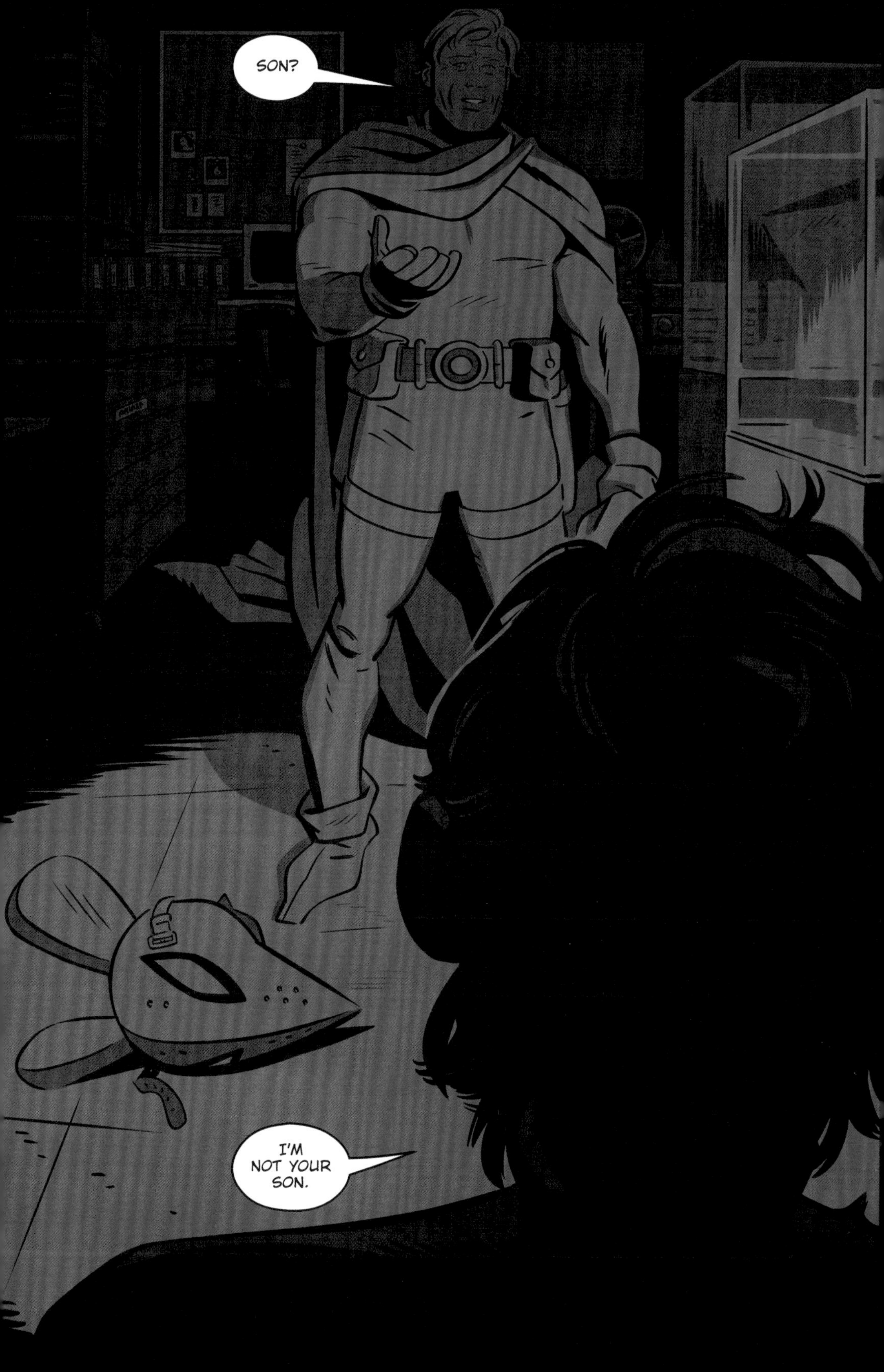
SON?
I'M NOT YOUR SON.

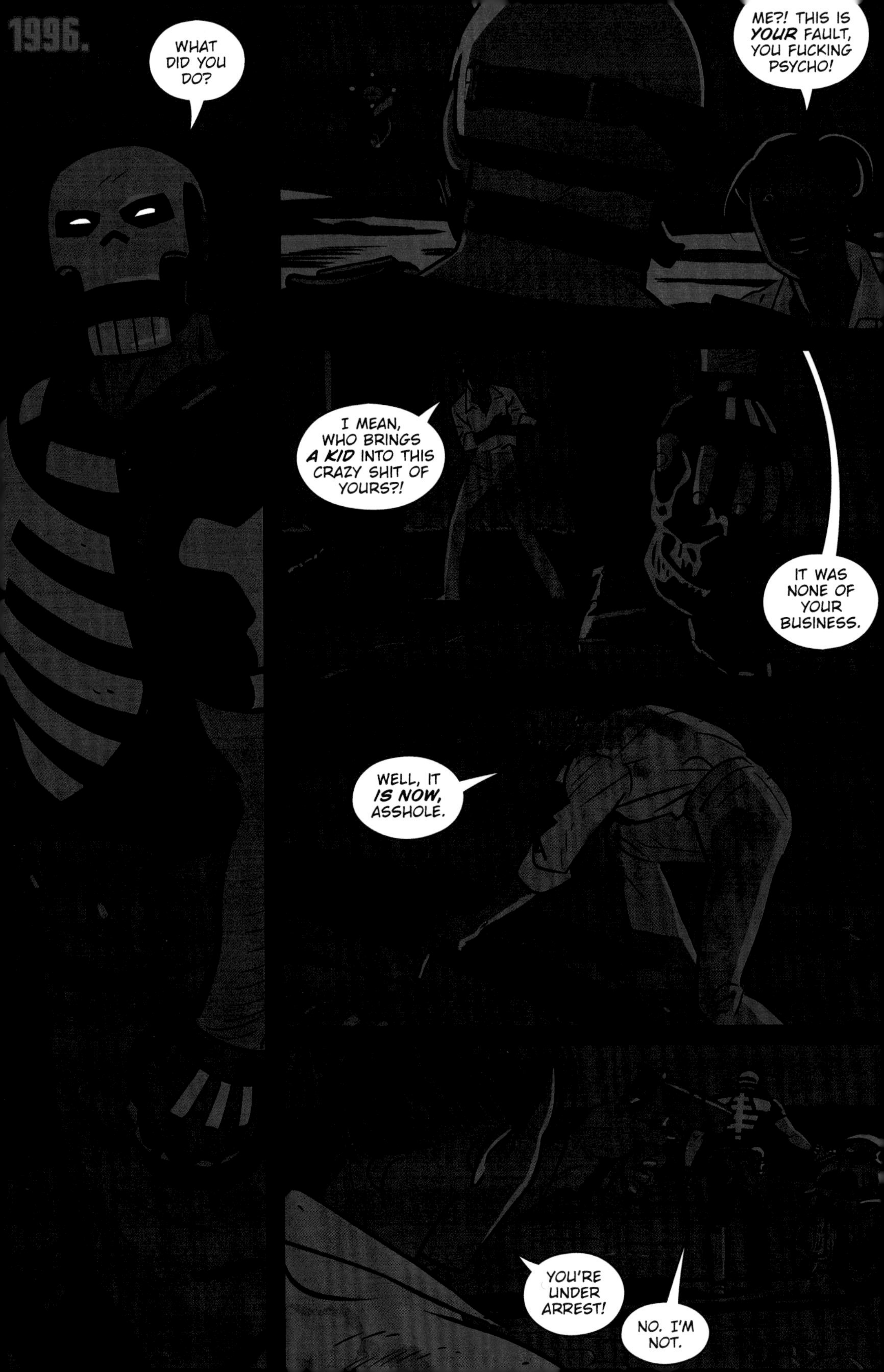
1996.
WHAT DID YOU DO?
ME?! THIS IS YOUR FAULT, YOU FUCKING PSYCHO!
I MEAN, WHO BRINGS A KID INTO THIS CRAZY SHIT OF YOURS?!
IT WAS NONE OF YOUR BUSINESS.
WELL, IT IS NOW, ASSHOLE.
YOU'RE UNDER ARREST!
NO. I'M NOT.

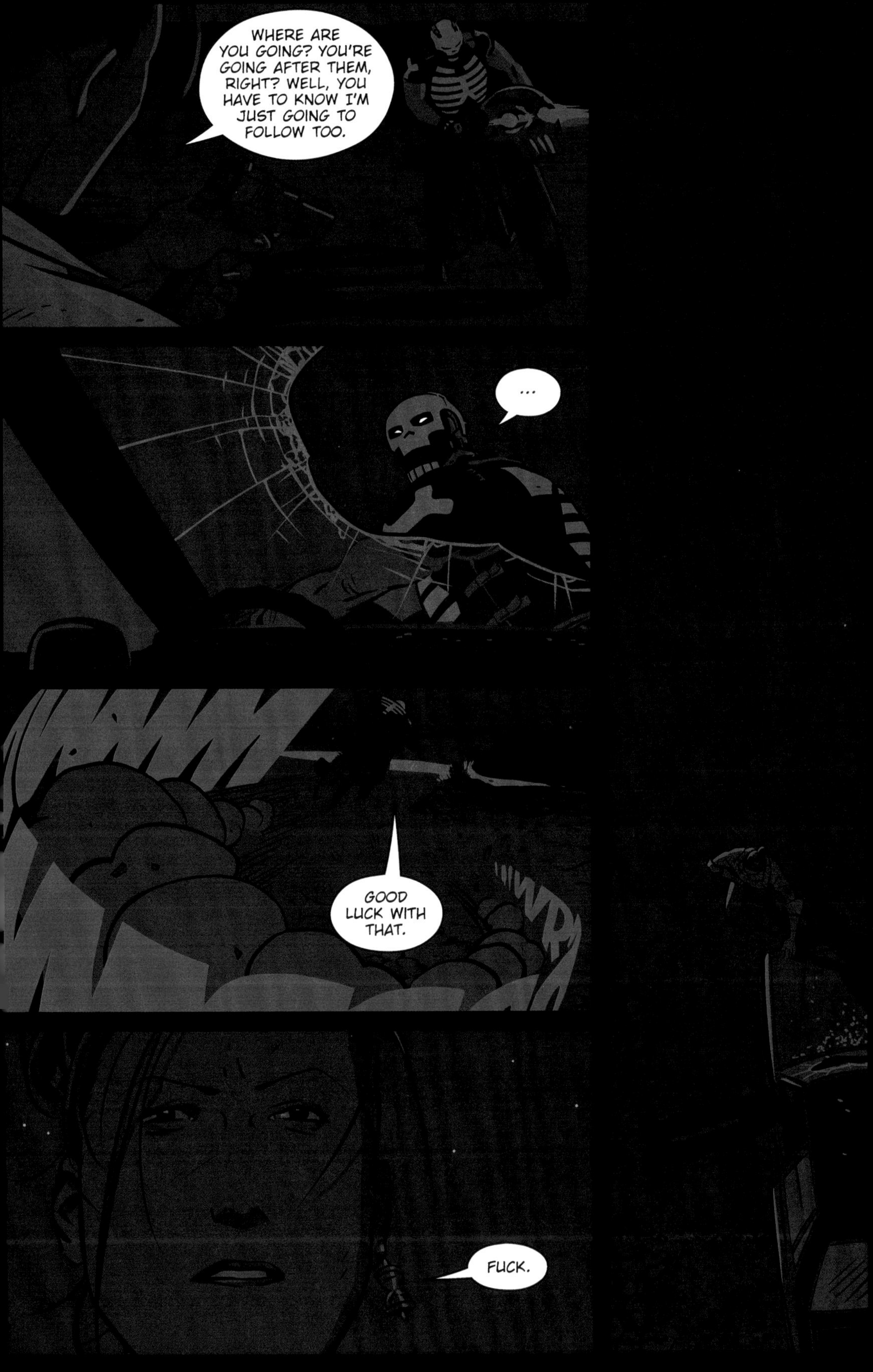
WHERE ARE YOU GOING? YOU'RE GOING AFTER THEM, RIGHT? WELL, YOU HAVE TO KNOW I'M JUST GOING TO FOLLOW TOO.
...
GOOD LUCK WITH THAT.
FUCK.

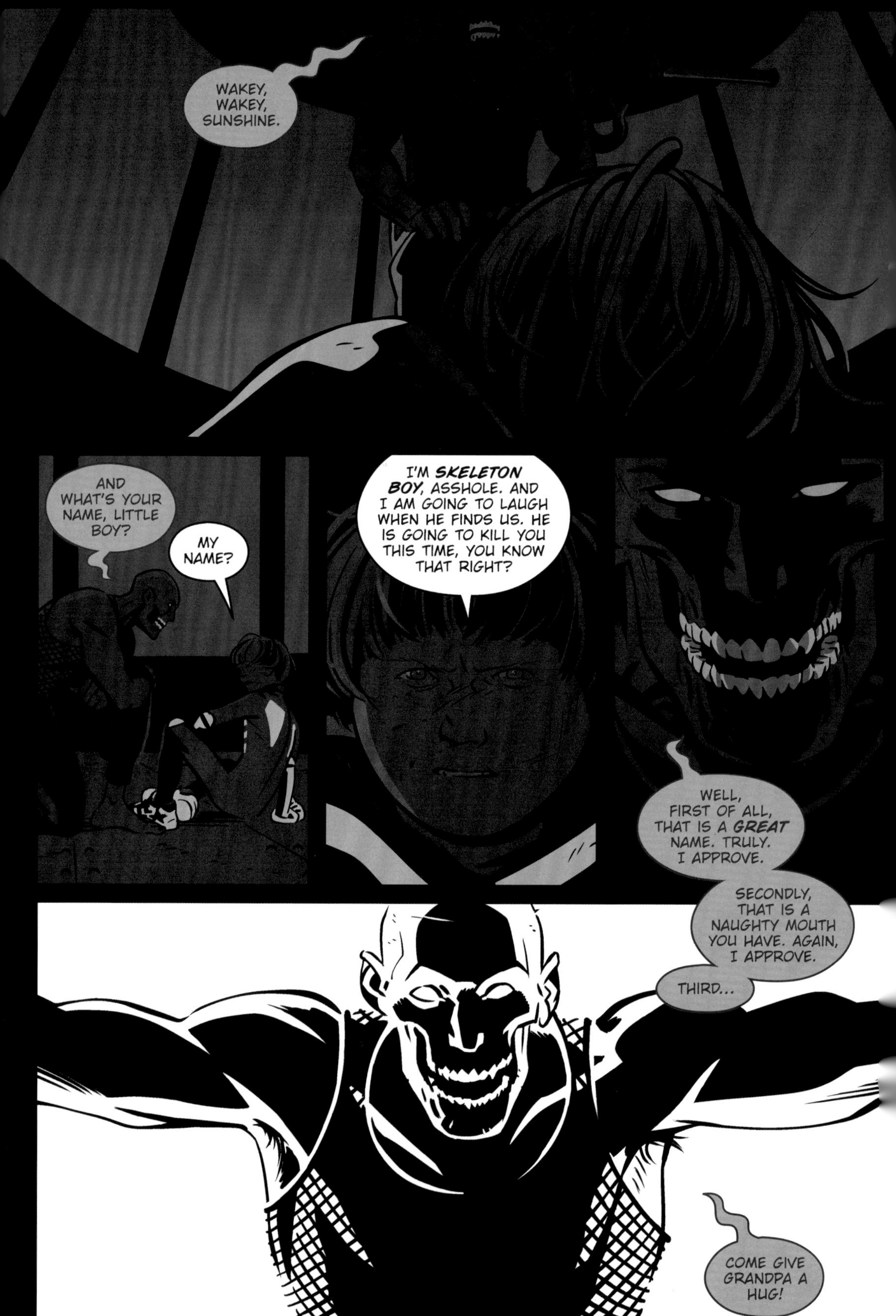
WAKEY, WAKEY, SUNSHINE.
AND WHAT'S YOUR NAME, LITTLE BOY?
MY NAME?
I'M **SKELETON BOY**, ASSHOLE. AND I AM GOING TO LAUGH WHEN HE FINDS US. HE IS GOING TO KILL YOU THIS TIME, YOU KNOW THAT RIGHT?
WELL, FIRST OF ALL, THAT IS A ***GREAT*** NAME. TRULY. I APPROVE.
SECONDLY, THAT IS A NAUGHTY MOUTH YOU HAVE. AGAIN, I APPROVE.
THIRD...
COME GIVE GRANDPA A HUG!

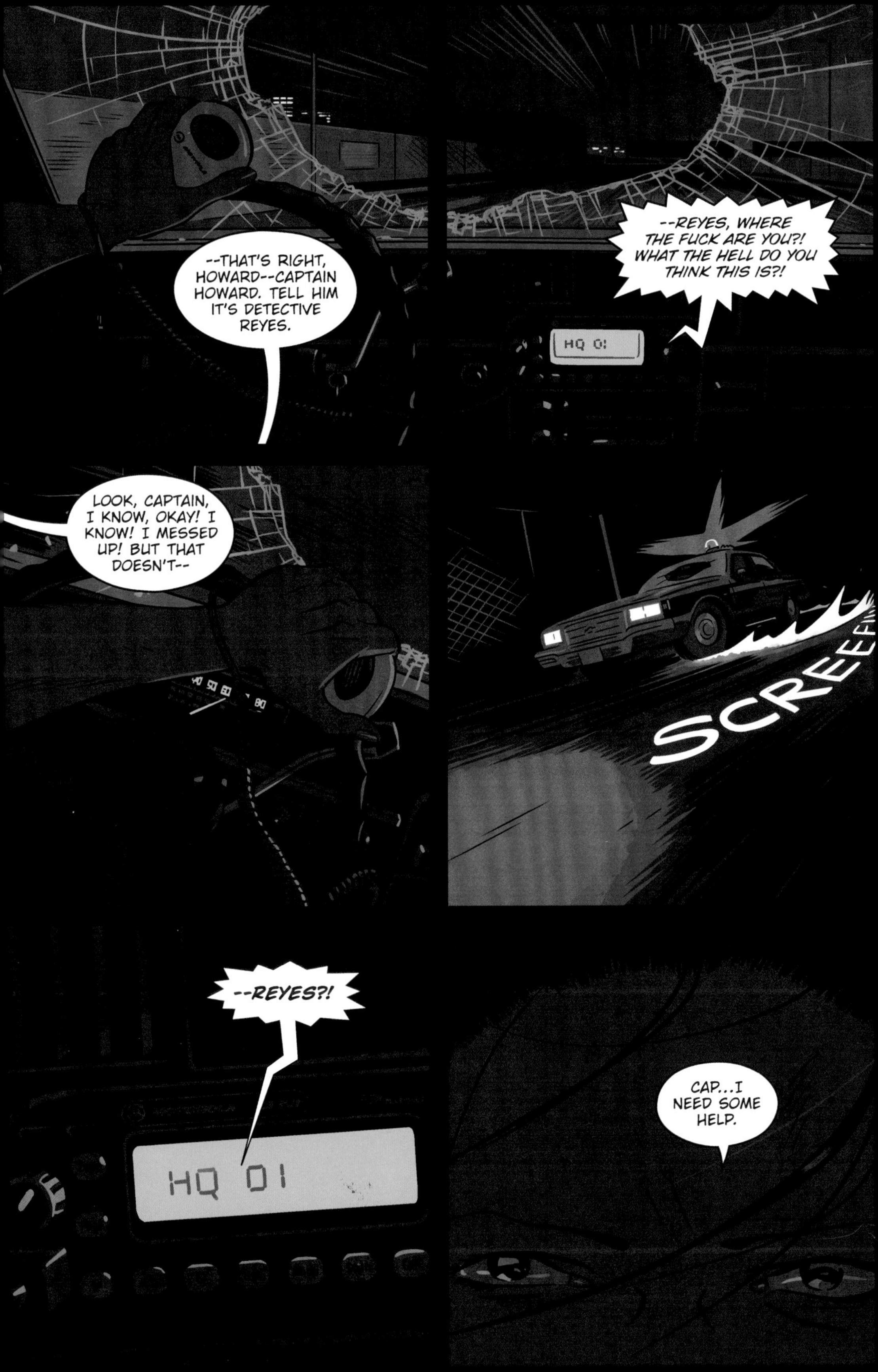
--THAT'S RIGHT, HOWARD--CAPTAIN HOWARD. TELL HIM IT'S DETECTIVE REYES.
--REYES, WHERE THE FUCK ARE YOU?! WHAT THE HELL DO YOU THINK THIS IS?!
HQ 01
LOOK, CAPTAIN, I KNOW, OKAY! I KNOW! I MESSED UP! BUT THAT DOESN'T--
SCREEE
--REYES?!
HQ 01
CAP...I NEED SOME HELP.

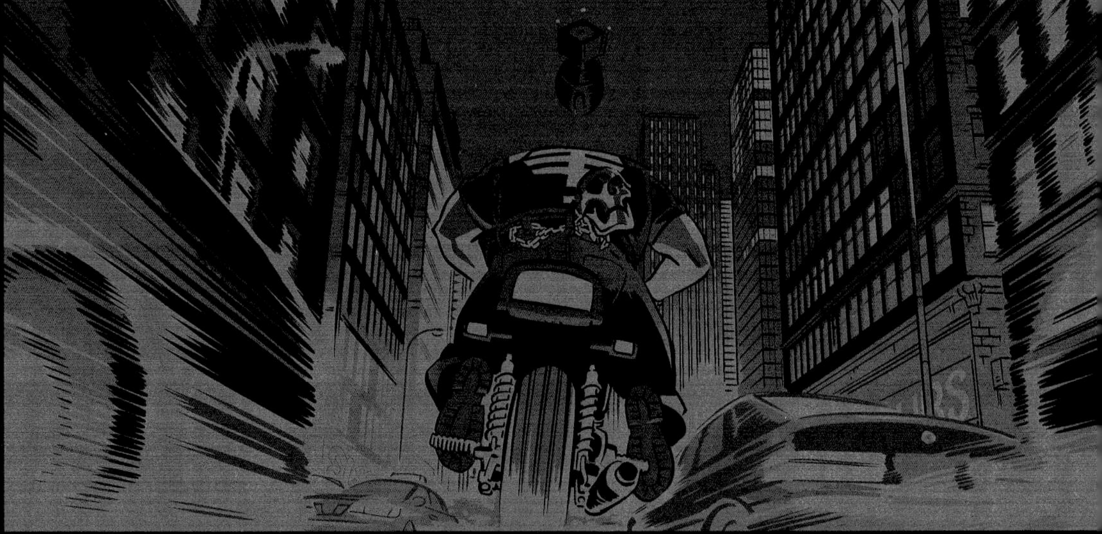

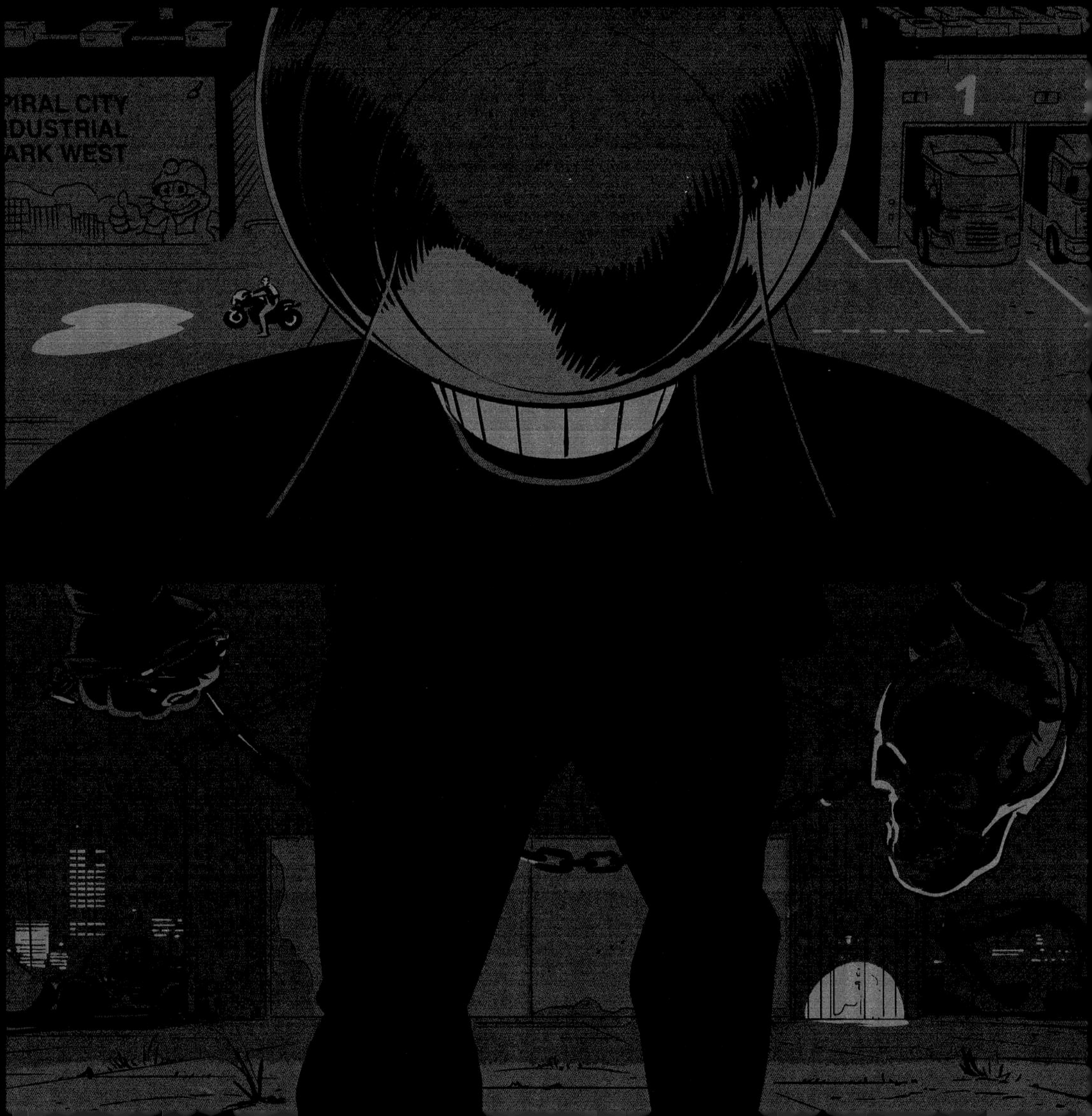
PIRAL CITY
DUSTRIAL
ARK WEST

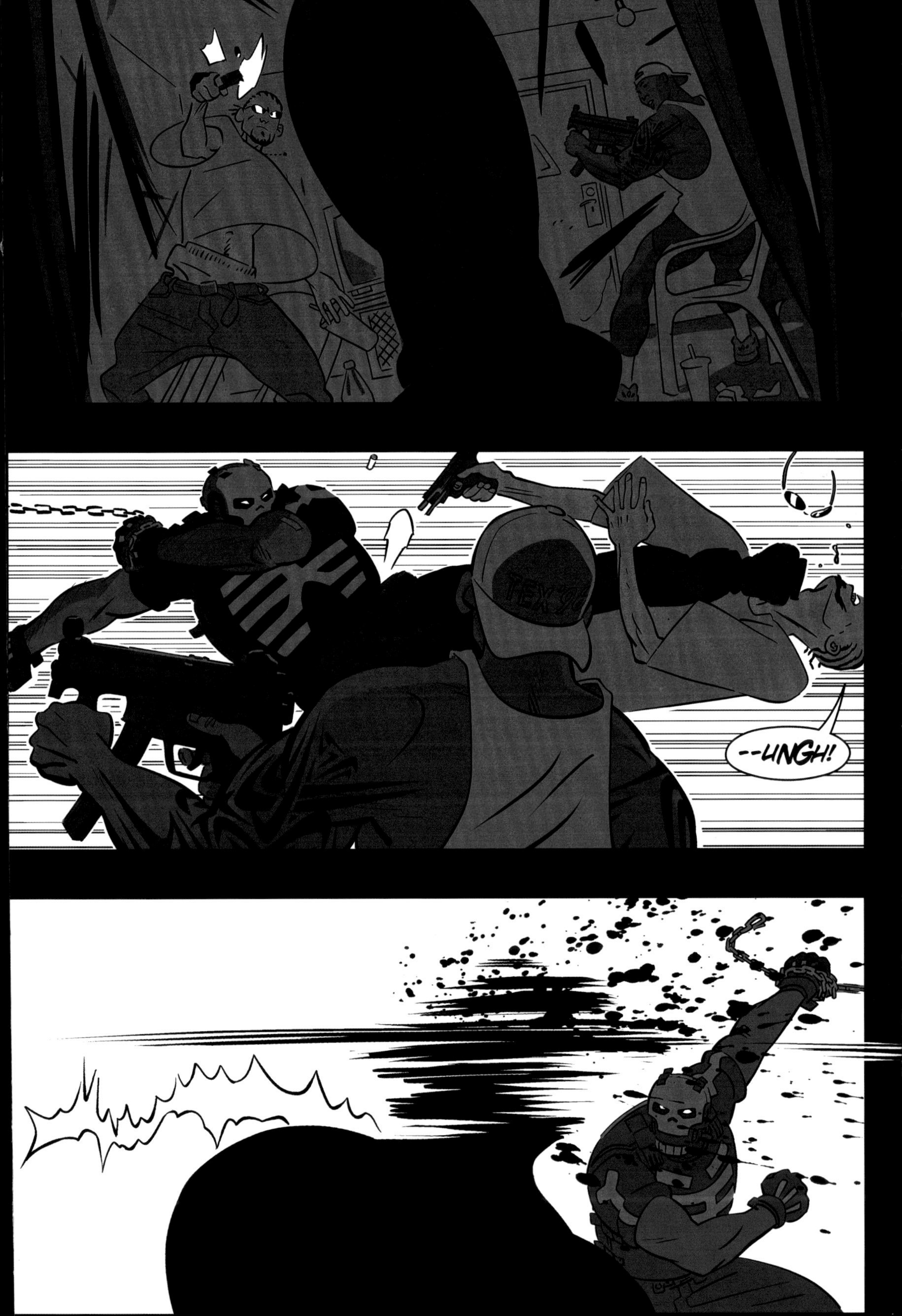

--UNGH!

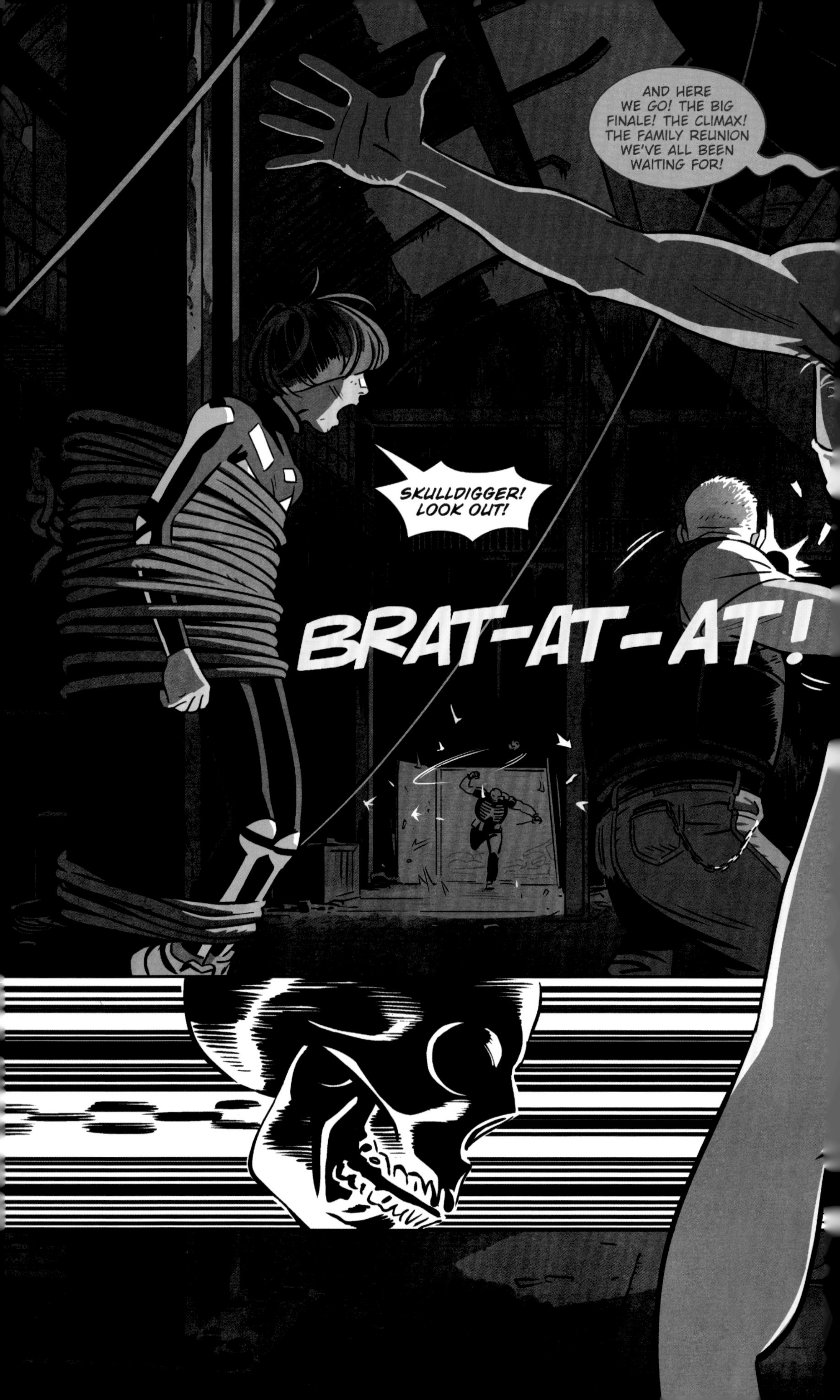
AND HERE WE GO! THE BIG FINALE! THE CLIMAX! THE FAMILY REUNION WE'VE ALL BEEN WAITING FOR!
SKULLDIGGER! LOOK OUT!
BRAT-AT-AT!

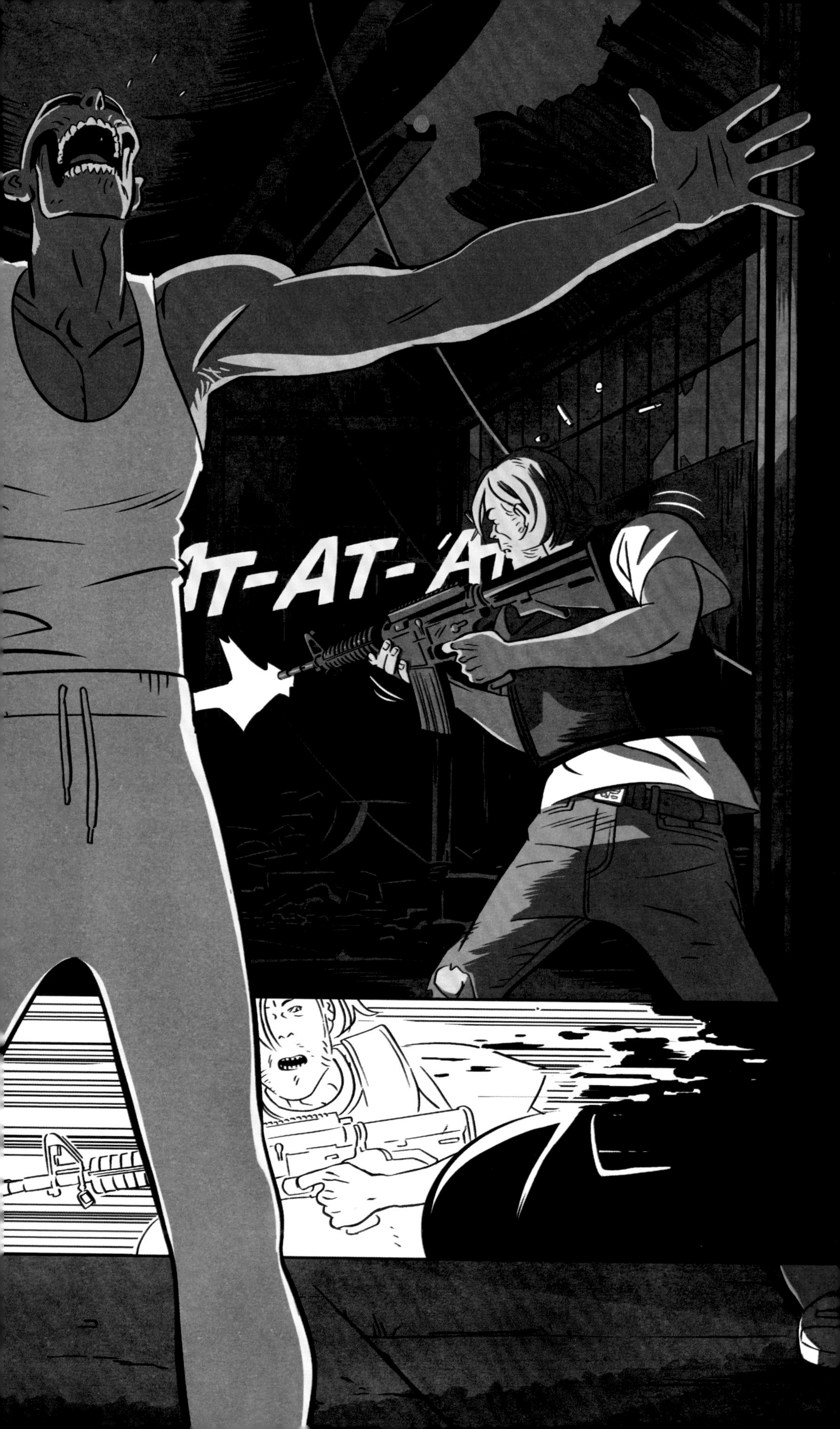
T-AT-'A

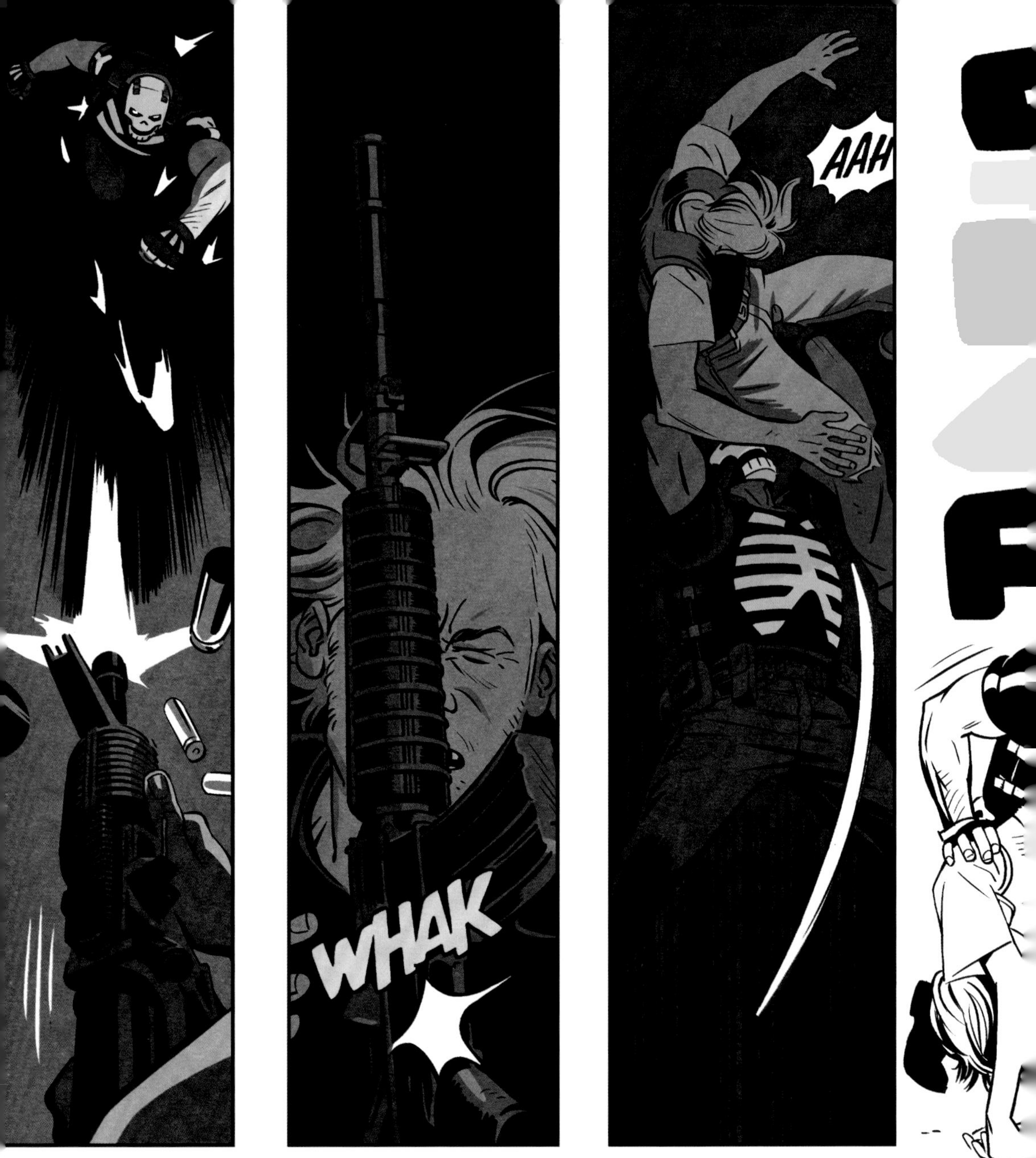
WHAK
AAH

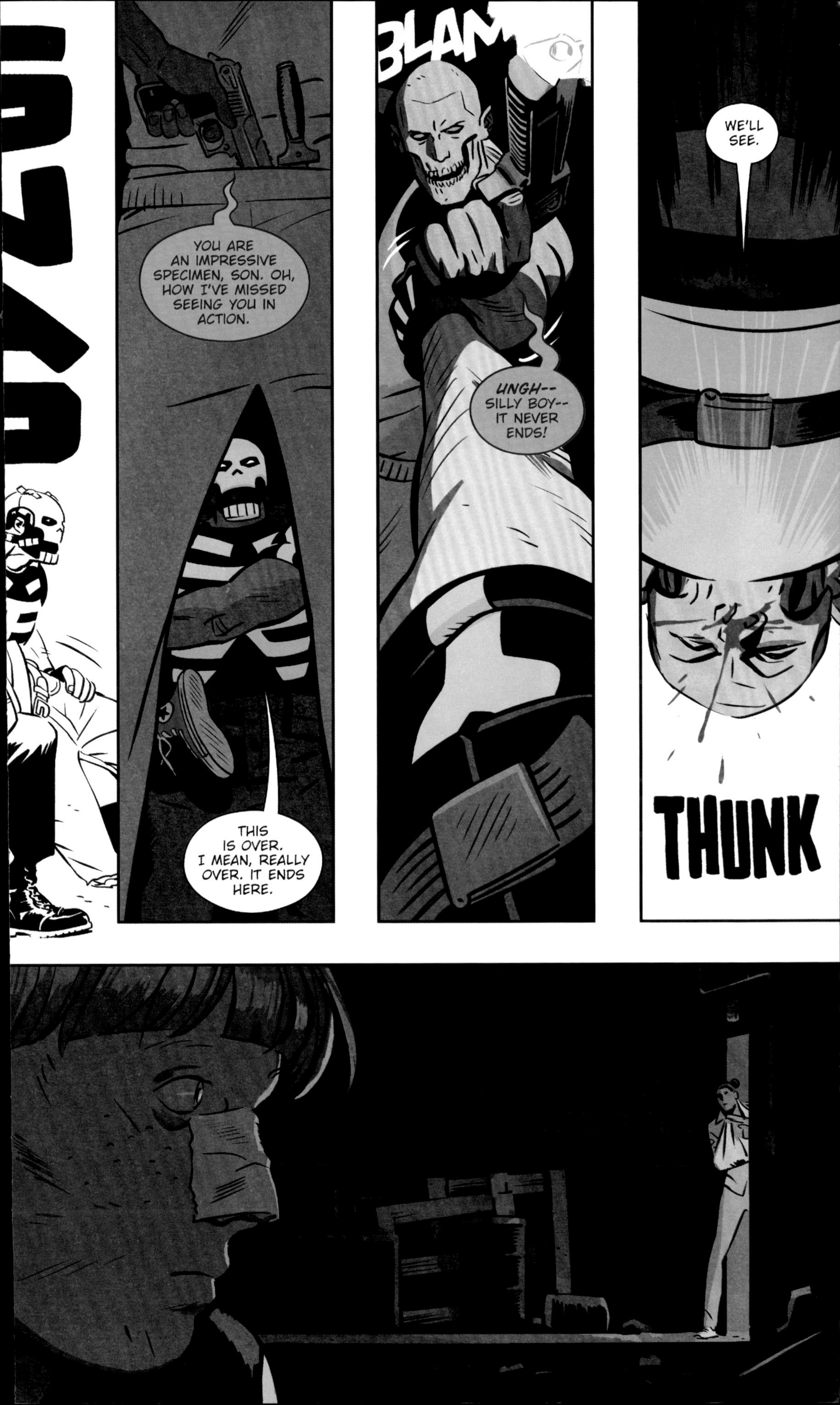

YOU ARE AN IMPRESSIVE SPECIMEN, SON. OH, HOW I'VE MISSED SEEING YOU IN ACTION.
THIS IS OVER. I MEAN, REALLY OVER. IT ENDS HERE.
BLAM
UNGH-- SILLY BOY-- IT NEVER ENDS!
WE'LL SEE.
THUNK

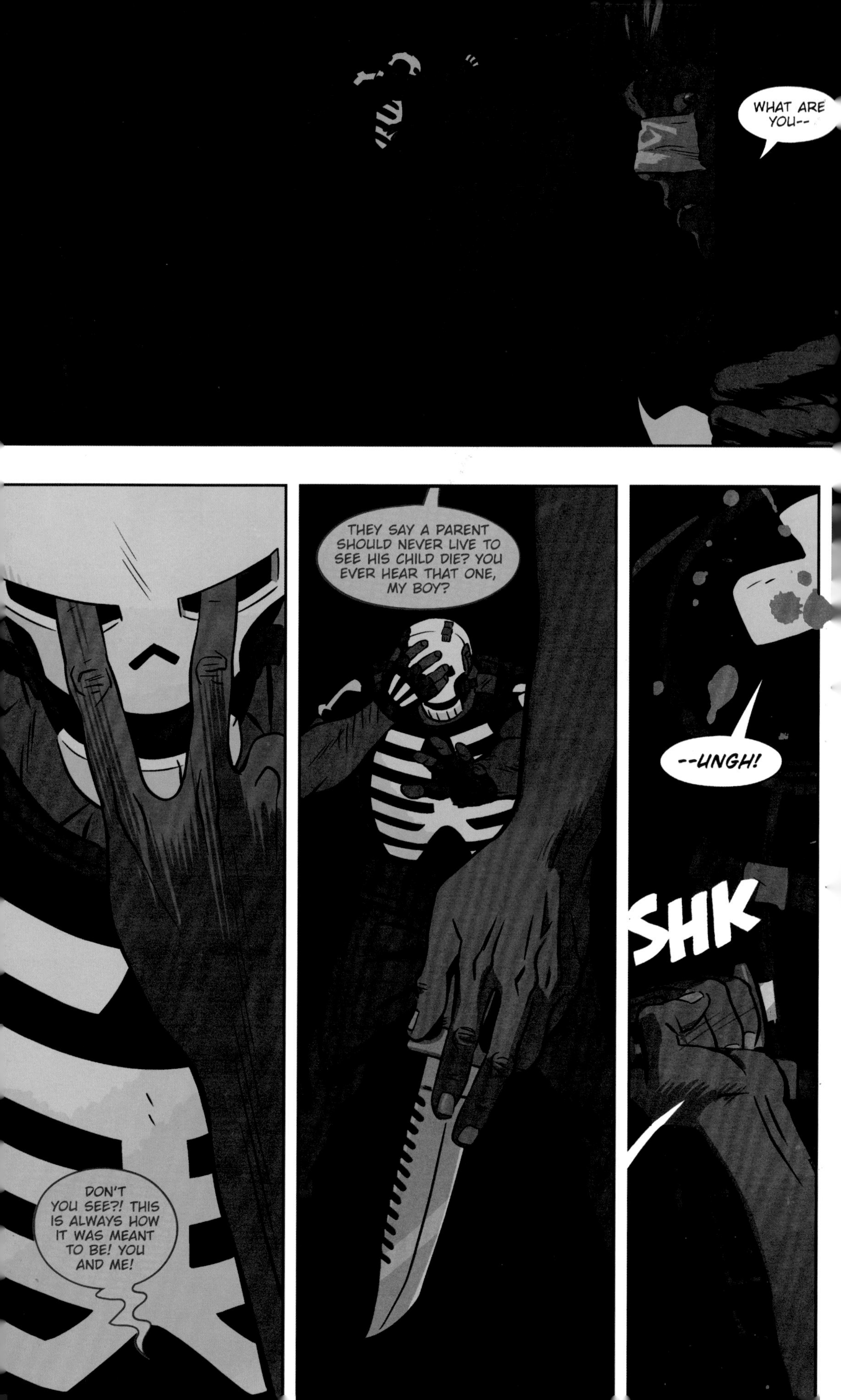

WHAT ARE YOU--
DON'T YOU SEE?! THIS IS ALWAYS HOW IT WAS MEANT TO BE! YOU AND ME!
THEY SAY A PARENT SHOULD NEVER LIVE TO SEE HIS CHILD DIE? YOU EVER HEAR THAT ONE, MY BOY?
--UNGH!
SHK

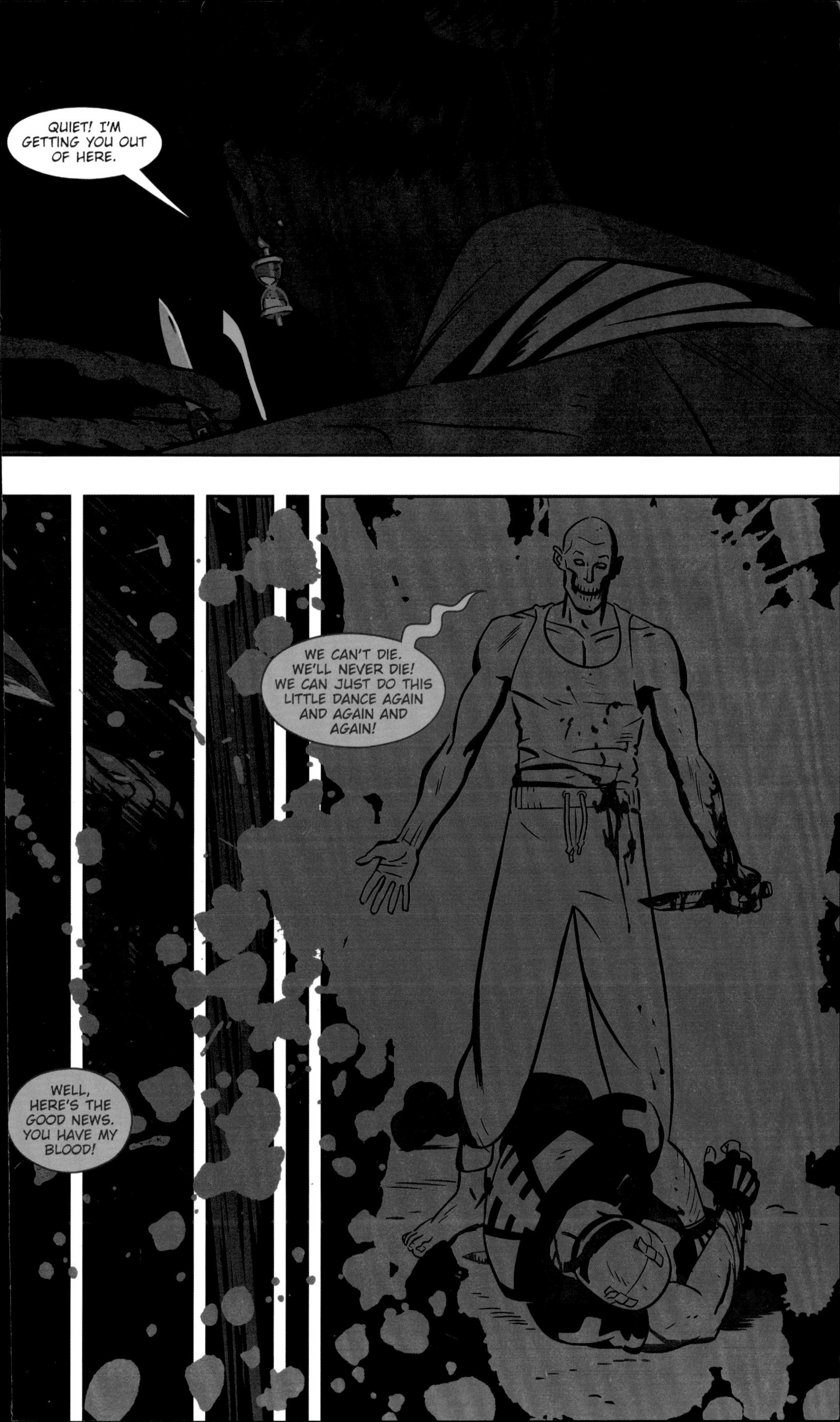
QUIET! I'M GETTING YOU OUT OF HERE.
WE CAN'T DIE. WE'LL NEVER DIE! WE CAN JUST DO THIS LITTLE DANCE AGAIN AND AGAIN AND AGAIN!
WELL, HERE'S THE GOOD NEWS. YOU HAVE MY BLOOD!

THERE! COME ON!

WEEE OOOOO WEEE OOOOO

BUT I--I DO SEEM TO BE A BIT OF A MESS, AND SOME UNWANTED GUESTS ARE ON THEIR WAY.

IT WAS FUN PLAYING WITH YOU TOO, LITTLE BOY. GRANDPA WILL SEE YOU AGAIN REAL SOON. I PROMISE.

WEEE OOOOO WEEE OOOOO

FAREWELL, MY SON.

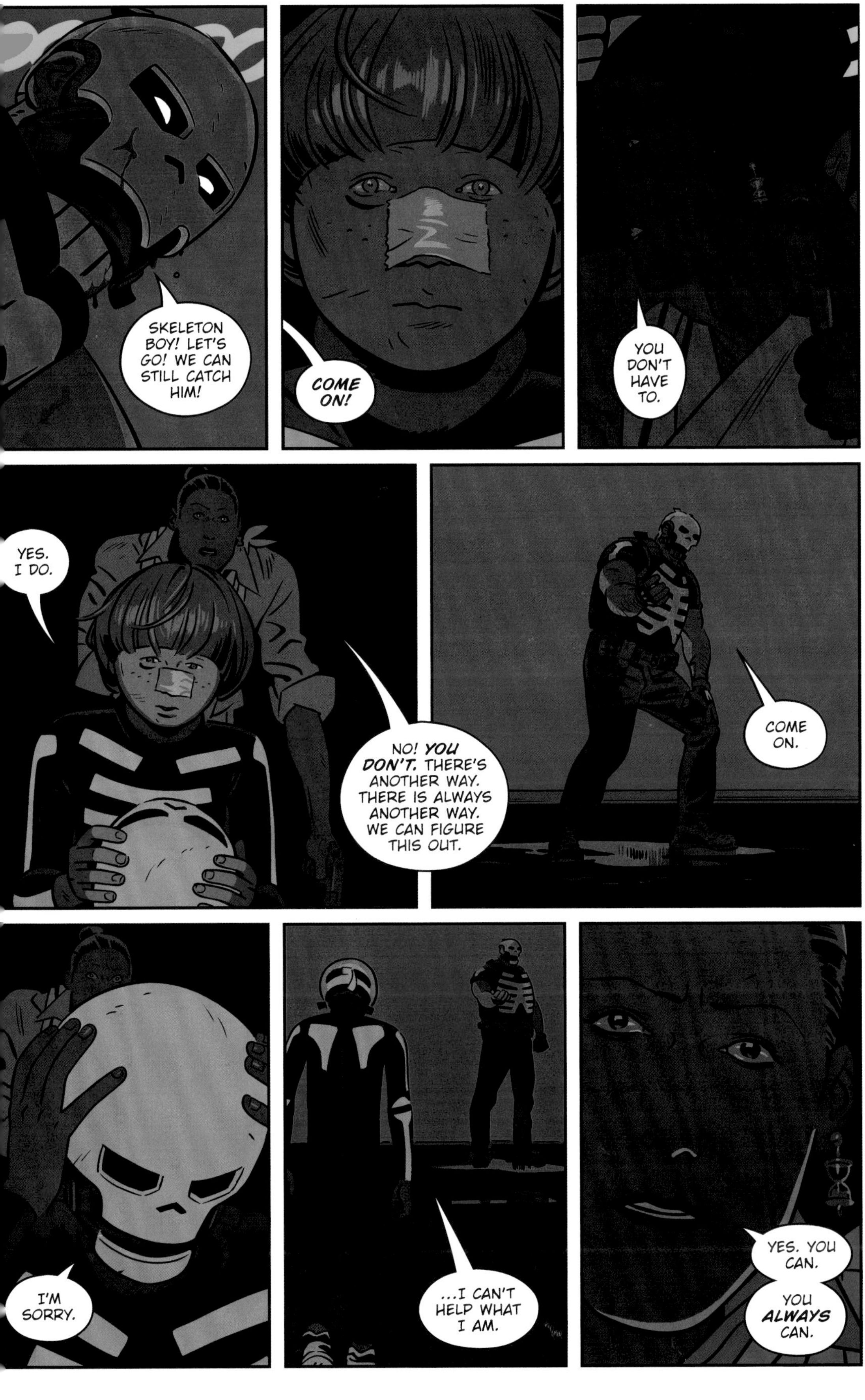
SKELETON BOY! LET'S GO! WE CAN STILL CATCH HIM!
COME ON!
YOU DON'T HAVE TO.
YES. I DO.
NO! YOU DON'T. THERE'S ANOTHER WAY. THERE IS ALWAYS ANOTHER WAY. WE CAN FIGURE THIS OUT.
COME ON.
I'M SORRY.
...I CAN'T HELP WHAT I AM.
YES. YOU CAN.
YOU ALWAYS CAN.

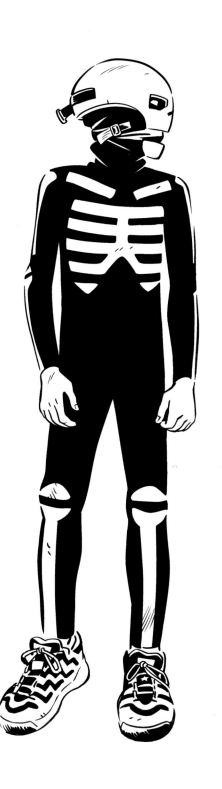

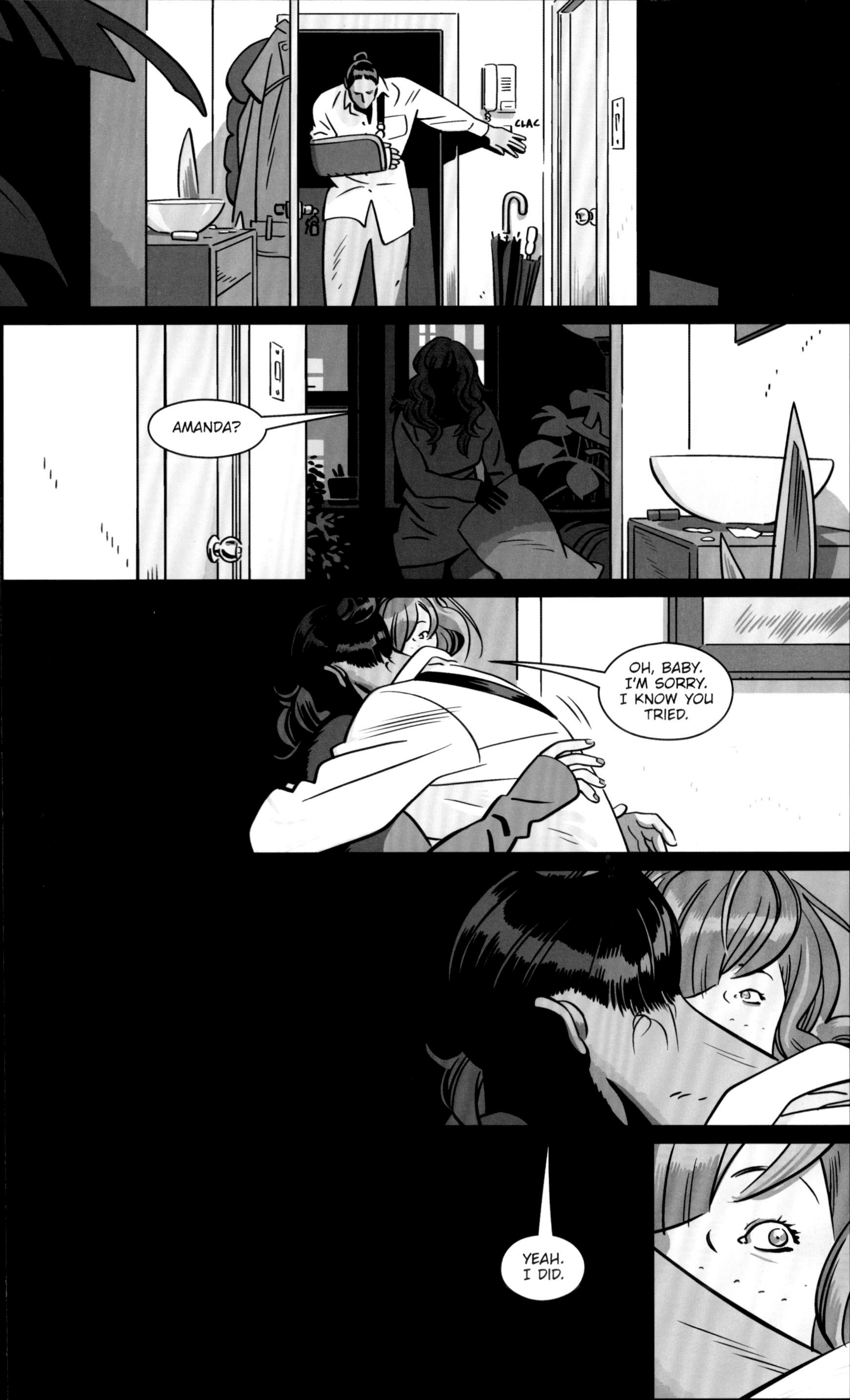
CLAC
AMANDA?
OH, BABY. I'M SORRY. I KNOW YOU TRIED.
YEAH. I DID.

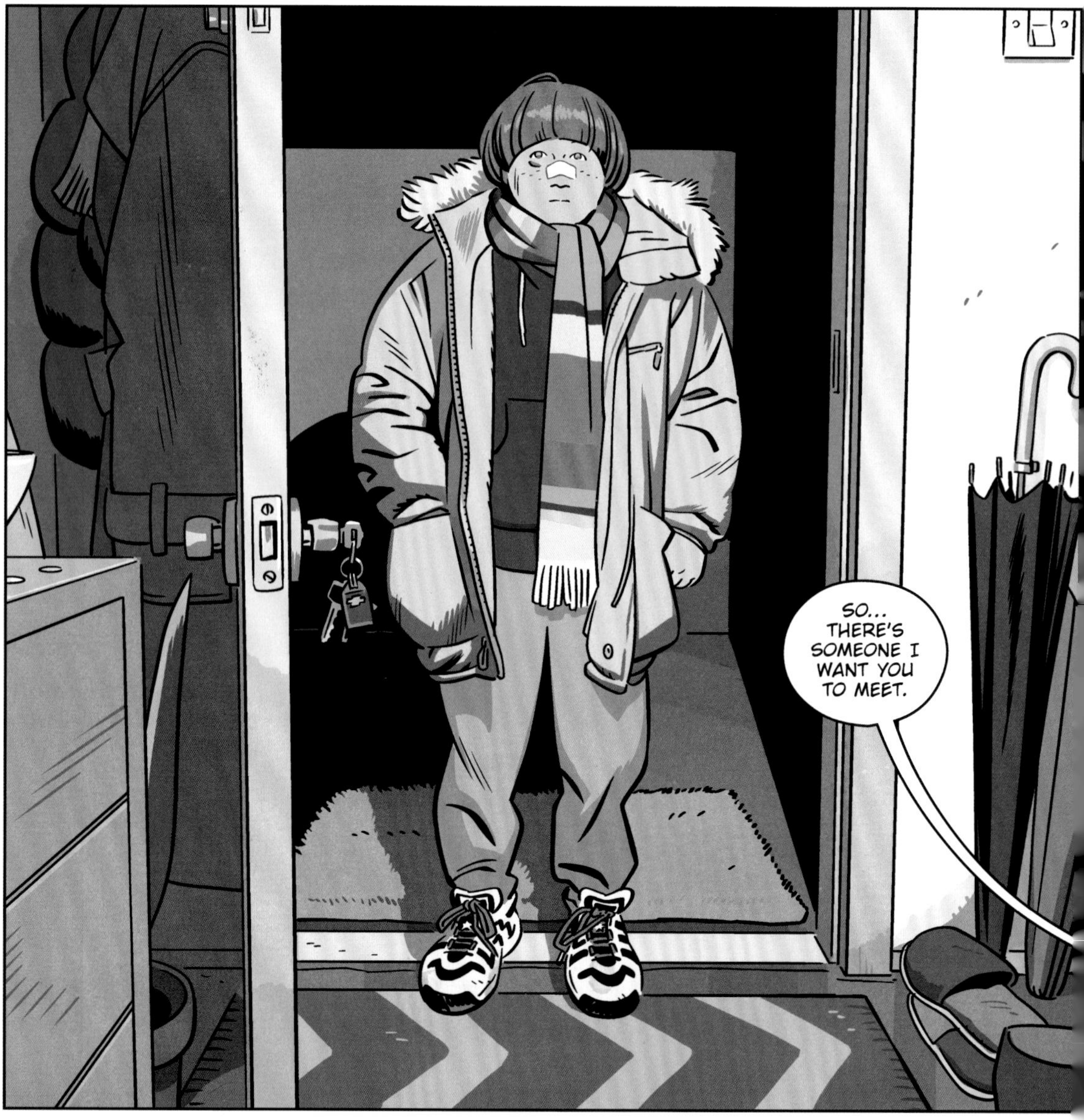
SO... THERE'S SOMEONE I WANT YOU TO MEET.

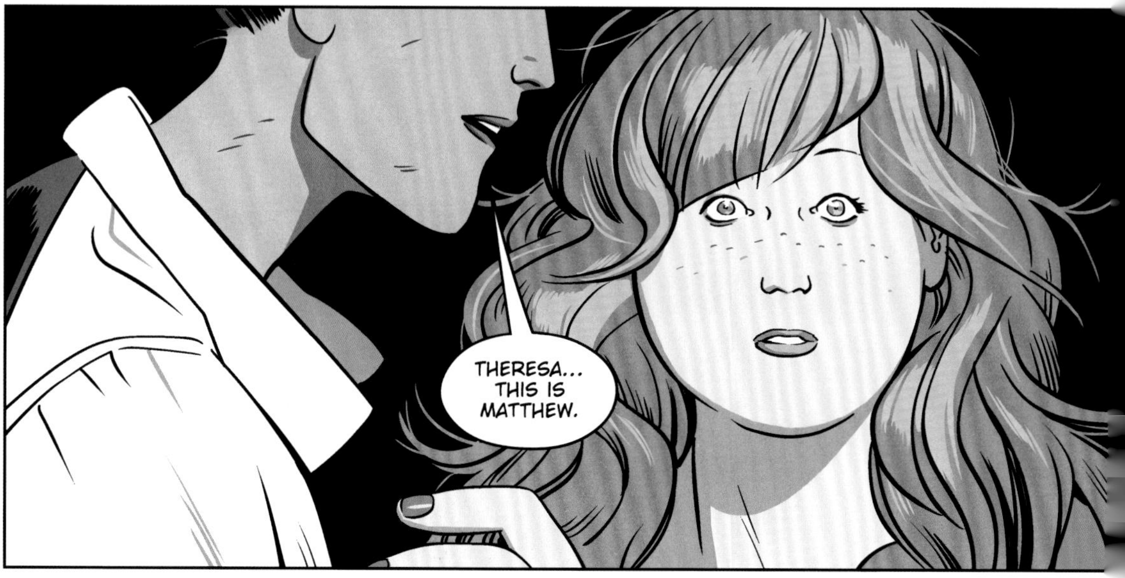
THERESA... THIS IS MATTHEW.

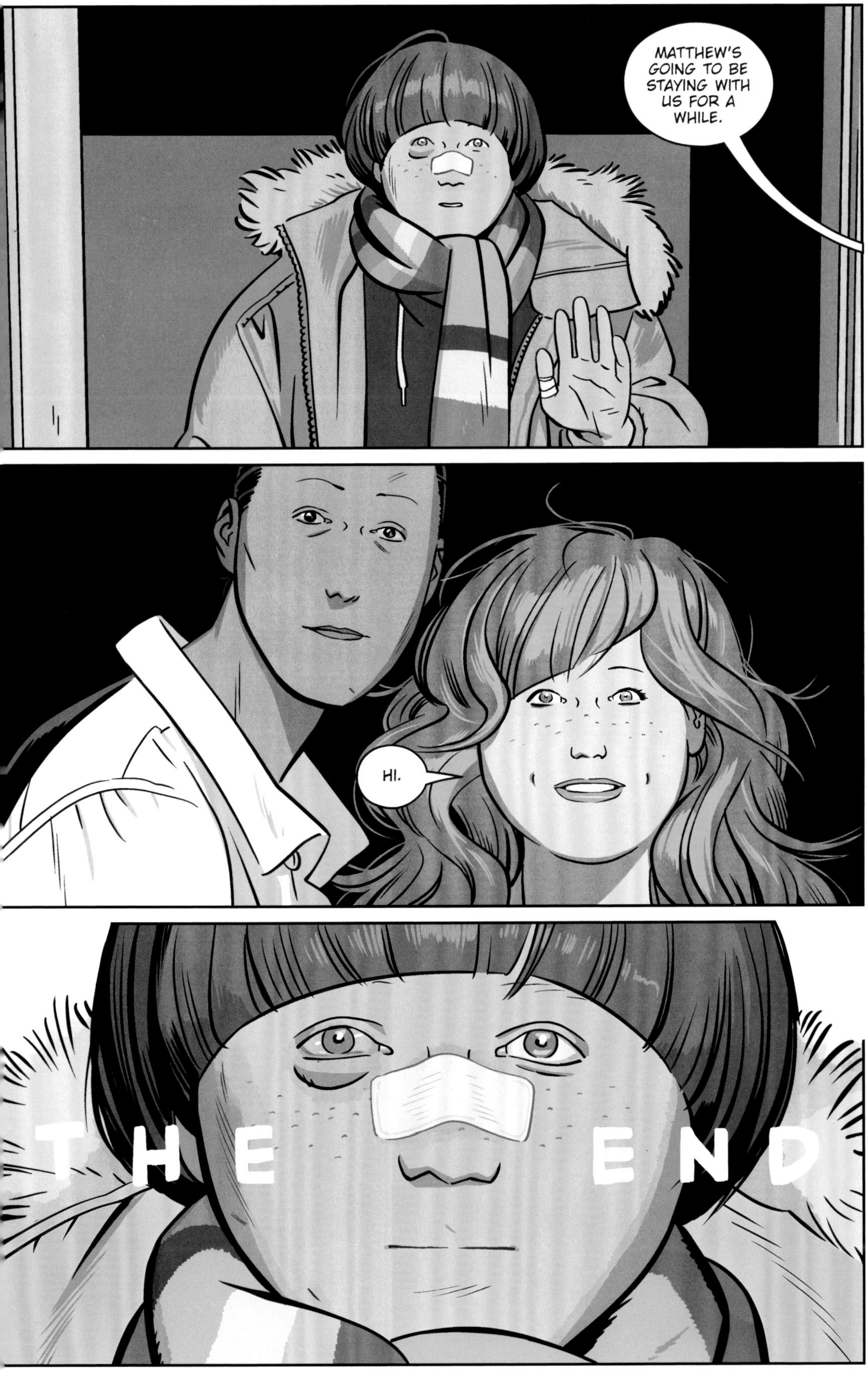
MATTHEW'S GOING TO BE STAYING WITH US FOR A WHILE.
HI.
THE END

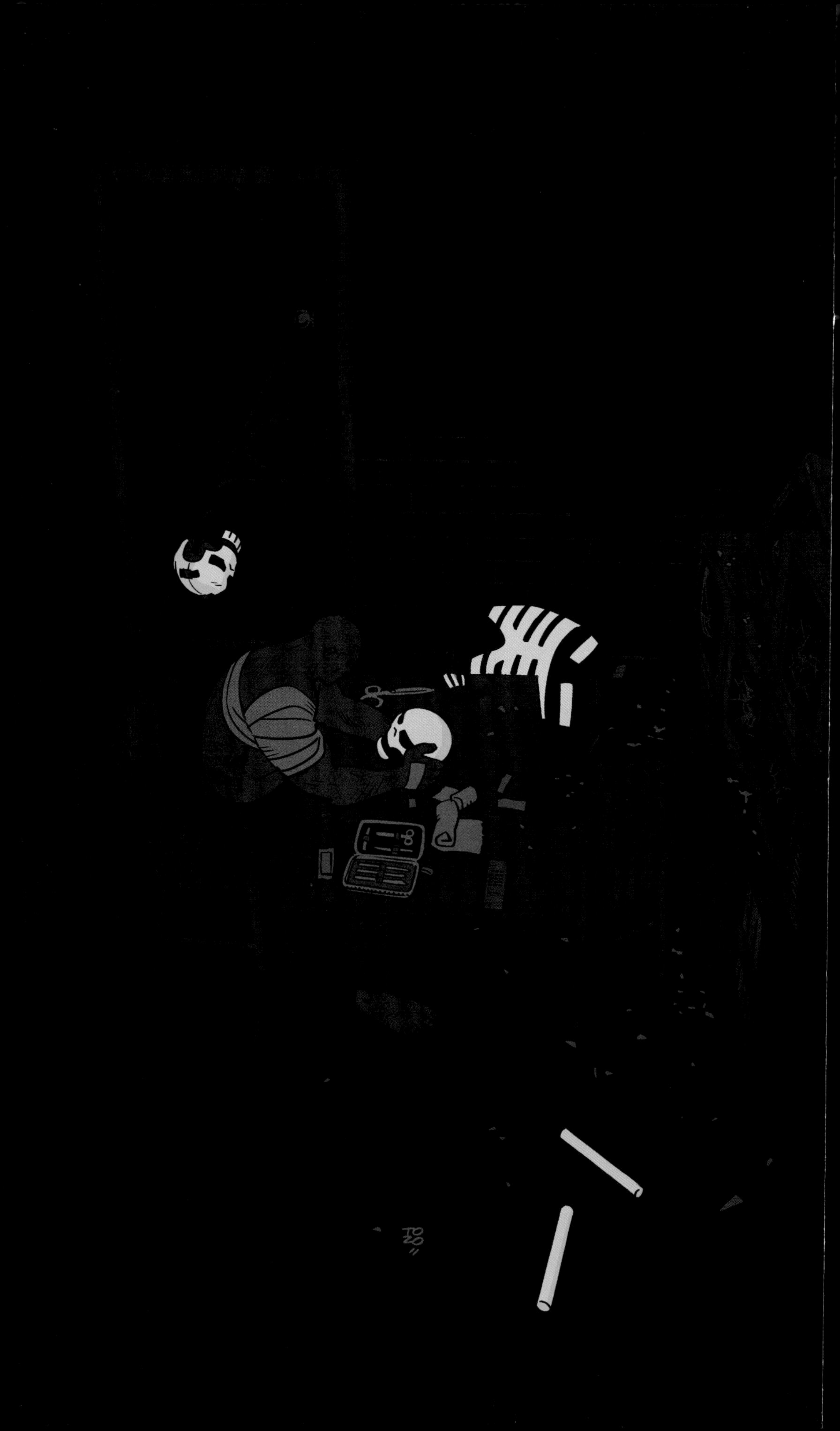

SKULLDIGGER + SKELETON BOY

SKETCHBOOK

Notes by
JEFF LEMIRE AND TONCI ZONJIC

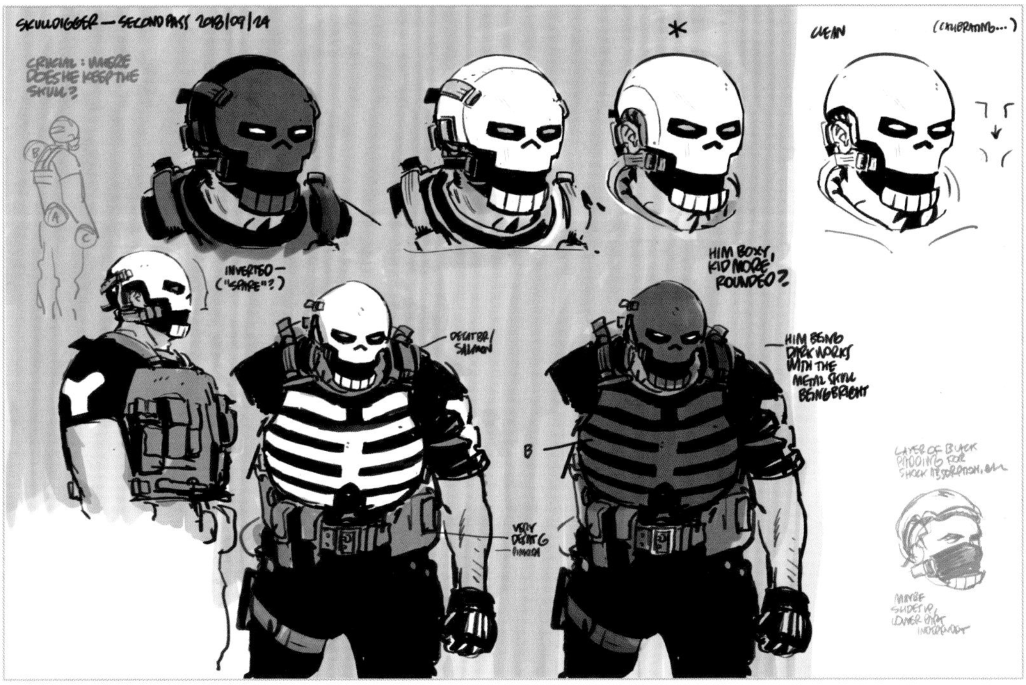

SKULLDIGGER — SECOND PASS 2018/09/24
CLEAN
HIM BOXY, KID MORE ROUNDED?
HIM BEING DARK WORKS WITH THE METAL SKULL BEING BRIGHT

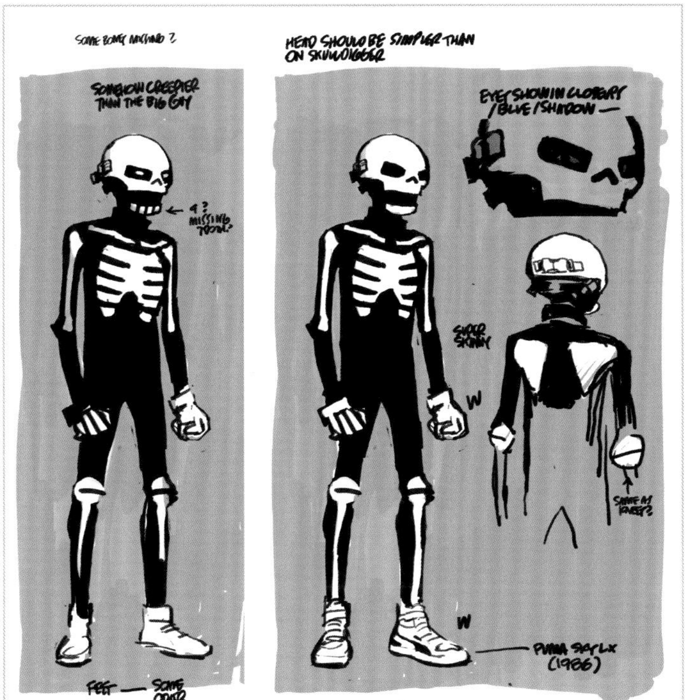

HEAD SHOULD BE SIMPLER THAN ON SKULLDIGGER
SOMEHOW CREEPIER THAN THE BIG GUY
EYES SHOWN IN CLOSEUP / BLUE / SHADOW —
SUPER SKINNY
PUMA SKY LX (1986)
SUPER CREEPY VARIANT
BACK
(REV SEP 24)

Most of the design process was focused on just those two, taking a few months to try and make memorable costumes that would at the same time have been created, within the world of the book, by someone without the resources of Bruce Wayne.

Coming up with "new" skull shapes was also a tall order since the skull motif has been used for, what, at least 125,000 years? I can't say that I checked them against every skull in recorded human history, but I think they do look pretty fun. Adding storytelling detail, such as Skeleton Kid's jaw not having painted "teeth" making him toothless, so to speak, hopefully adds to the fun.

—Tonci Zonjic

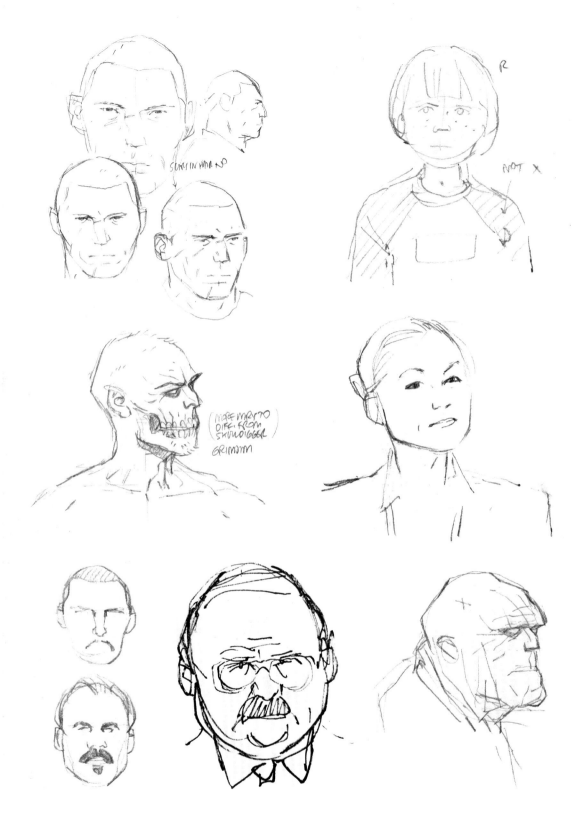

The rest of the characters were mostly designed on the page, or had one or two very quick roughs. The police chief was there in the very first sketch, so was Concretestador with his thousand-mile stare (already designed by David Rubín). The kid, I knew I wanted him to have Susie Derkins hair. Reyes is far too soft in the sketch here. For Skulldigger, my goal was to make him look friendlier *with* the mask on than without it.

And drawing goons is among the most fun times you can have in comics. These two needed to be only recognizable enough to be distinguishable while rappelling down from a blimp—they got killed by Skulldigger within a couple pages.

—TZ

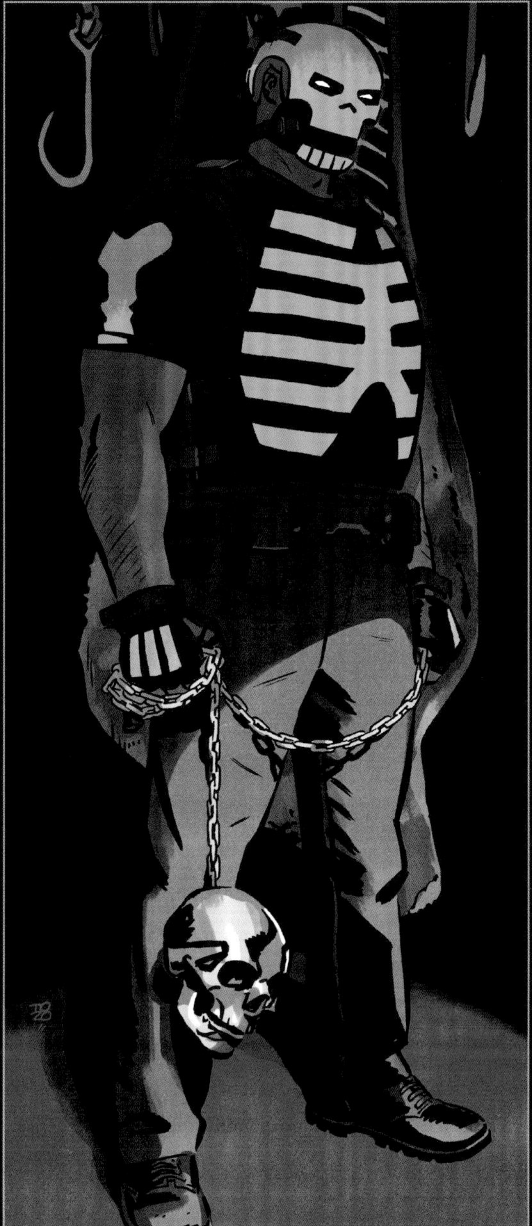

These two images for the special *Black Hammer Encyclopedia* issue were the first finished images of the duo, I think. Pretty much there—the kid now even has his Voltage shoes, which became the most recognizable part of his costume.

—TZ

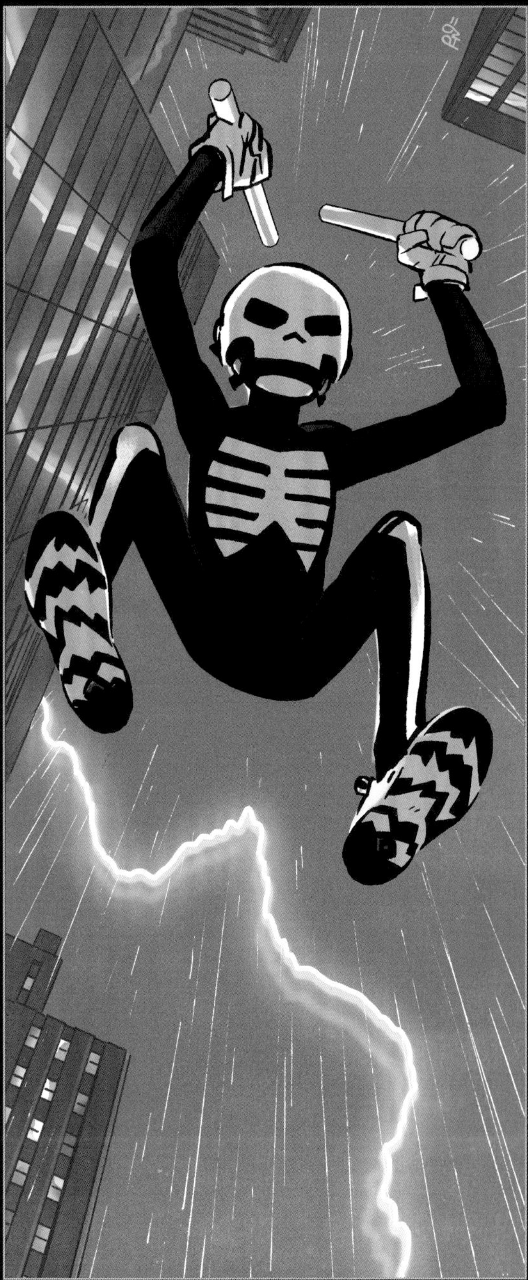

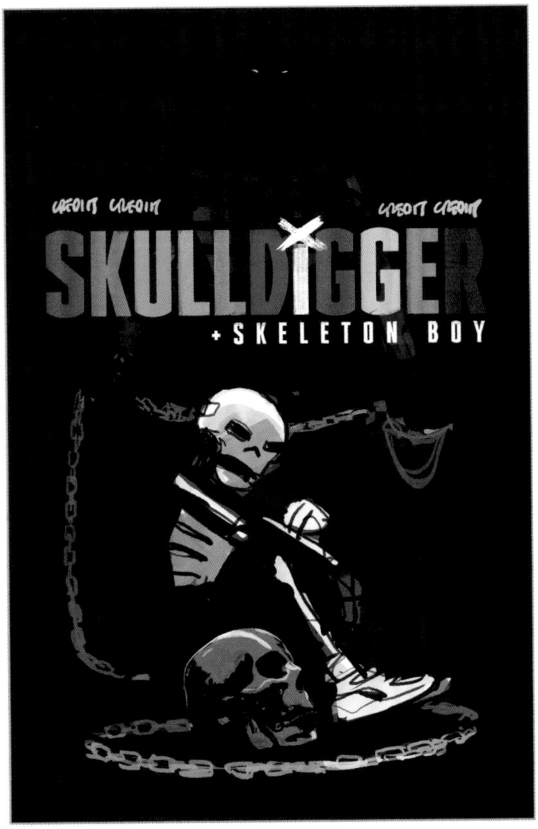

SKULLDIGGER
+ SKELETON BOY

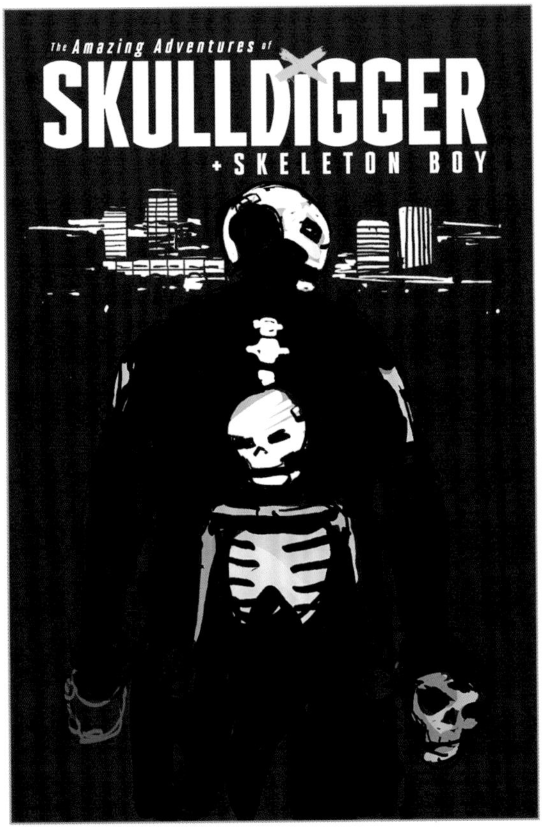

The Amazing Adventures of
SKULLDIGGER
+ SKELETON BOY

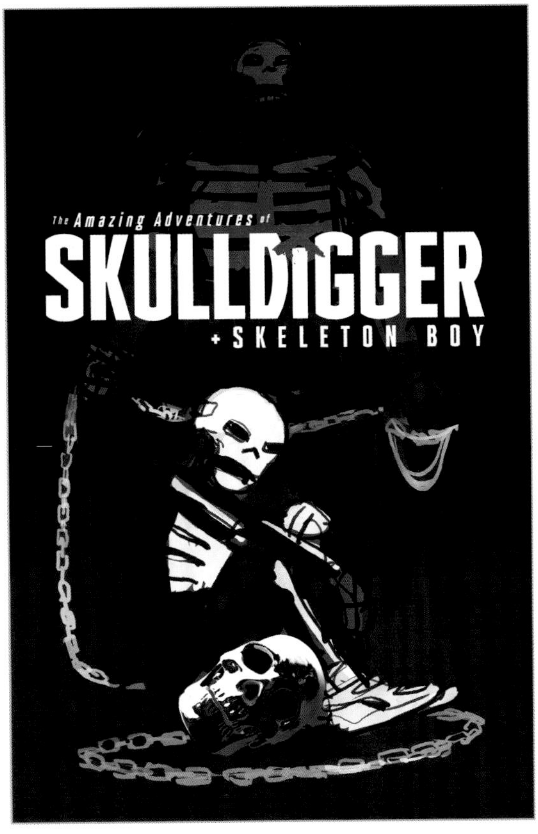

The Amazing Adventures of
SKULLDIGGER
+ SKELETON BOY

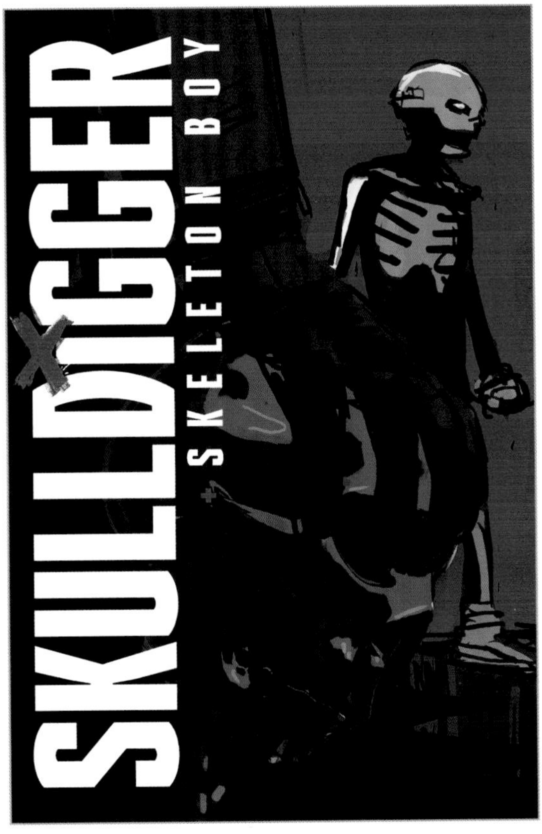

SKULLDIGGER
+ SKELETON BOY

The first cover was done before a single page of the story was drawn. It also had to work as a cover for the collected edition you're reading now, two years later. It's always daunting to work in that inverted order, so here's me trying to figure out what the book even is. The final cover with the candy-colored title had that feeling of "what the hell is this book??," which seemed like the perfect tone for it.

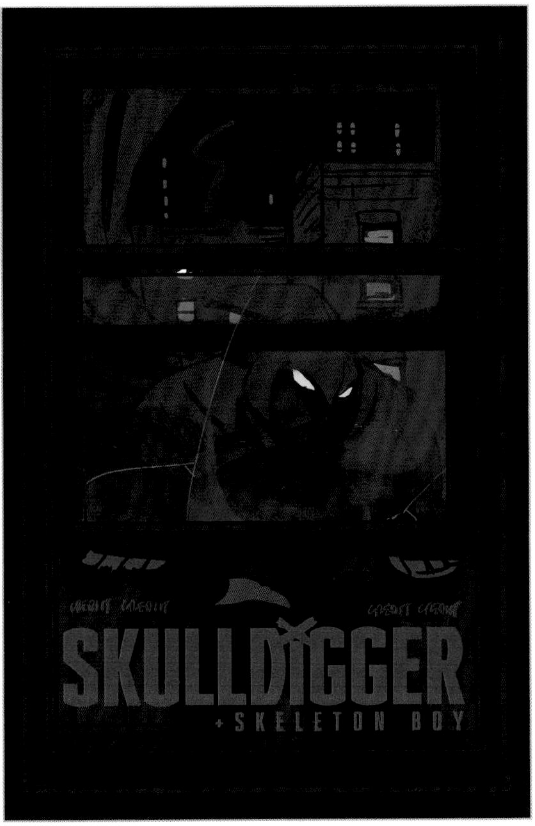
SKULLDIGGER
+ SKELETON BOY

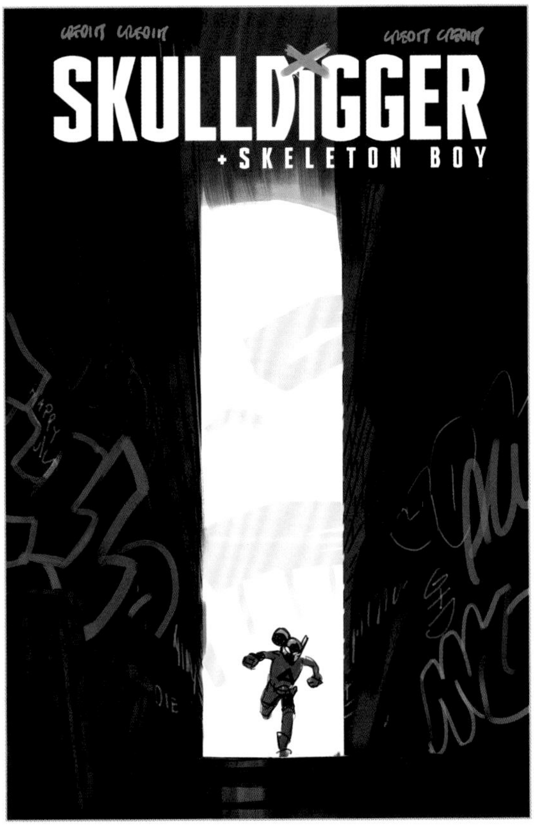
SKULLDIGGER
+ SKELETON BOY

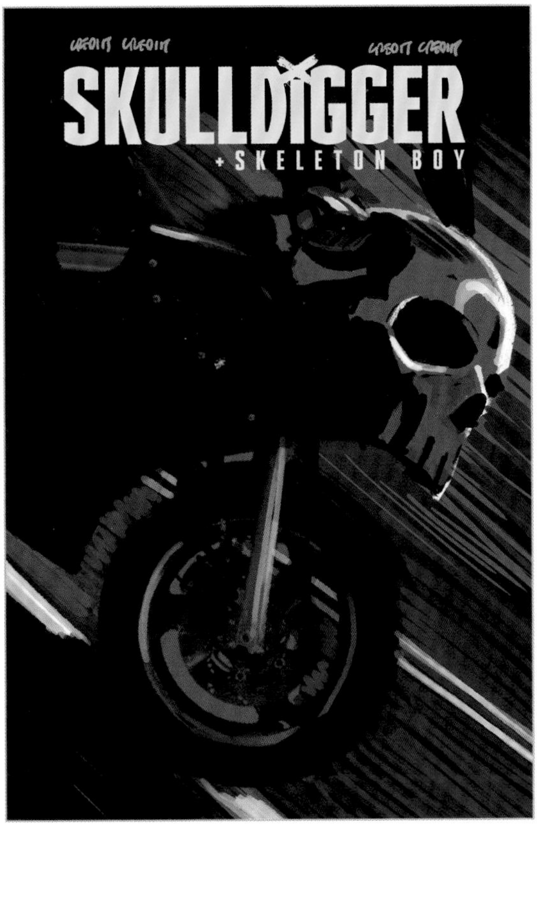
SKULLDIGGER
+ SKELETON BOY

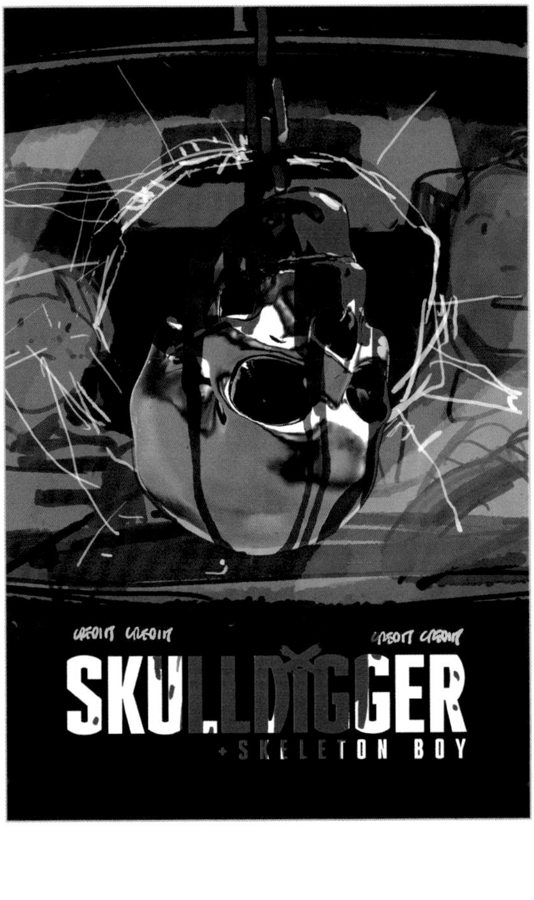
SKULLDIGGER
+ SKELETON BOY

After that, the remaining covers were straightforward. (Some alternate versions included here.)

—TZ

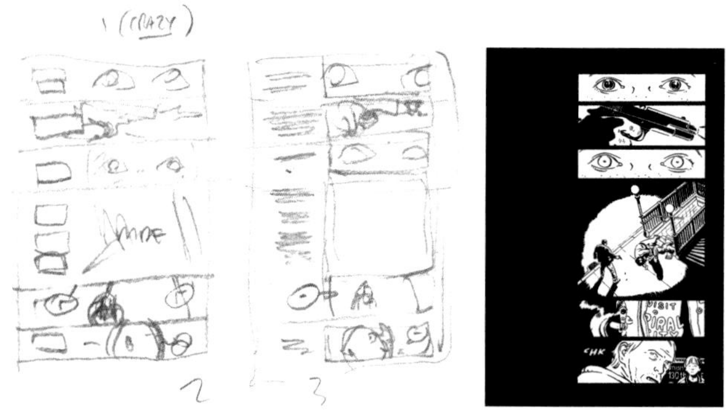
1 (CRAZY)
MORE
CHK
2
3

A comparison of the thumbnails and finished pages for the opening of the first issue (left) and some selected bits from issue two (right). All the actual works happens in this stage, really.

—TZ

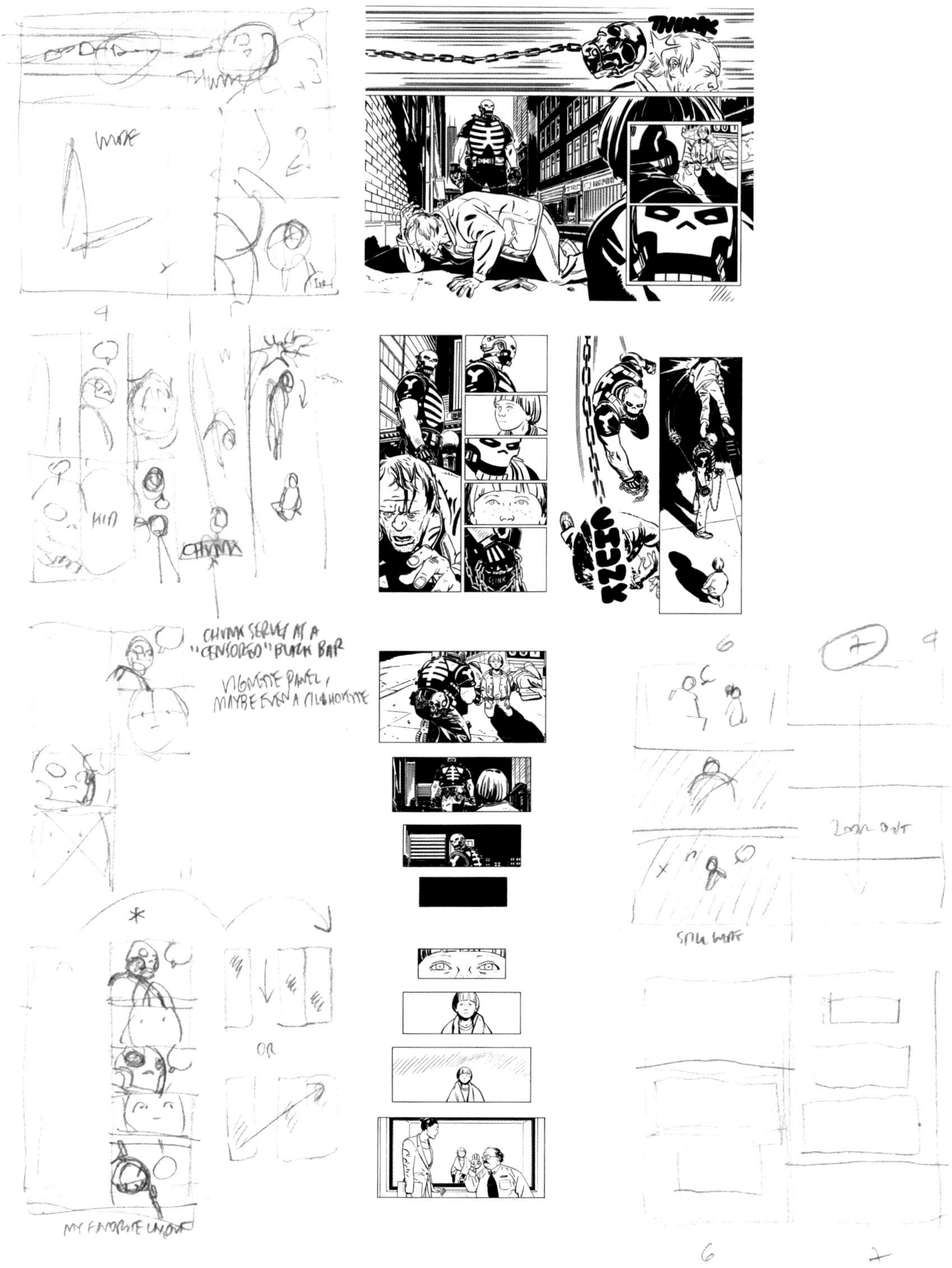
THUNK
THUNK
MORE
KID
CHUNK
CLINK
CHUNK
CHUNK SERVES AS A "CENSORED" BLACK BAR
VIGNETTE PANEL, MAYBE EVEN A SILHOUETTE
OR
LOOK OUT
6
7
6
7

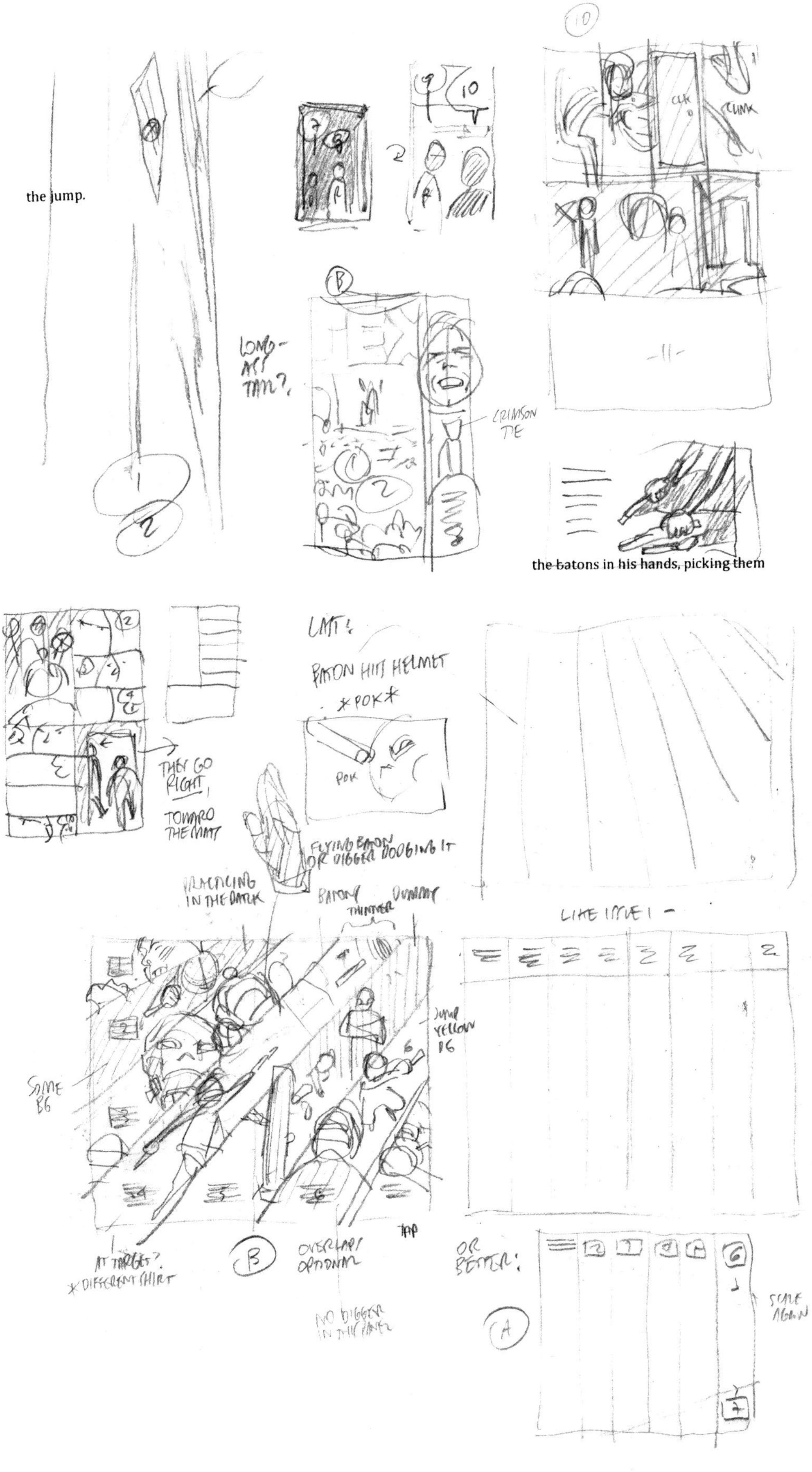

the jump.
10
CLICK
CLUNK
LONG-ARM TAIL?
CRIMSON TIE
the batons in his hands, picking them
LMT!
BATON HIT HELMET
POK
POK
THEY GO RIGHT, TOWARD THE MAT
FLYING BATON OR DIGGER DODGING IT
PRACTICING IN THE DARK
BATON THINNER
DUMMY
LIKE ISSUE 1 -
JUMP YELLOW BG
SOME BG
AT TARGETS?
*DIFFERENT SHIRT
B
OVERLAP OPTIONAL
TAP
OR BETTER:
NO DIGGER IN THIS PANEL
A
SCALE AGAIN

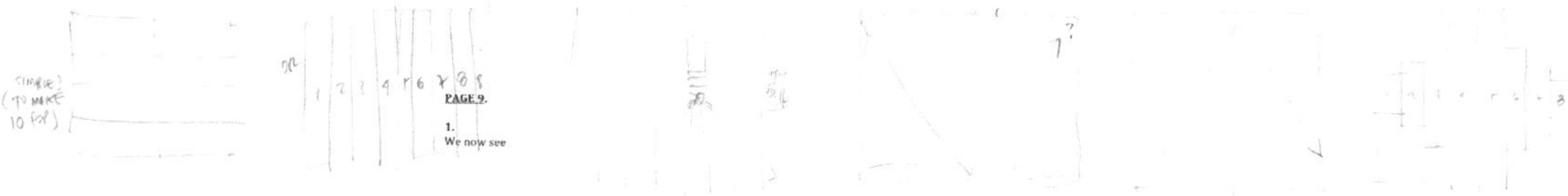
PAGE 9.
1.
We now see

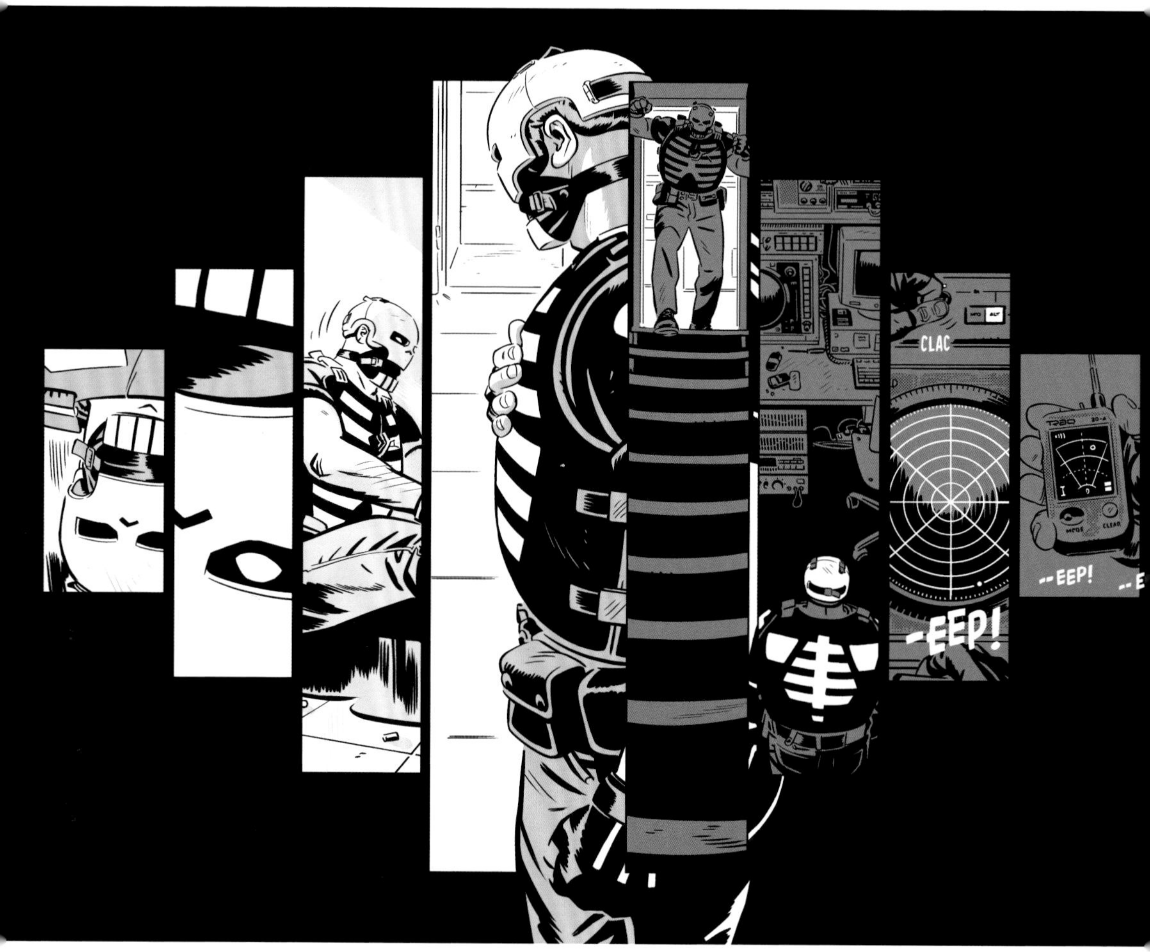
CLAC
-EEP!
--EEP!

Like the previous pages, once the double-page spread has been solved in thumbnail form, drawing the actual pages is the easy part and your reward. The idea with every spread in the book was to emphasize storytelling first—graphic impact was always secondary.

—TZ

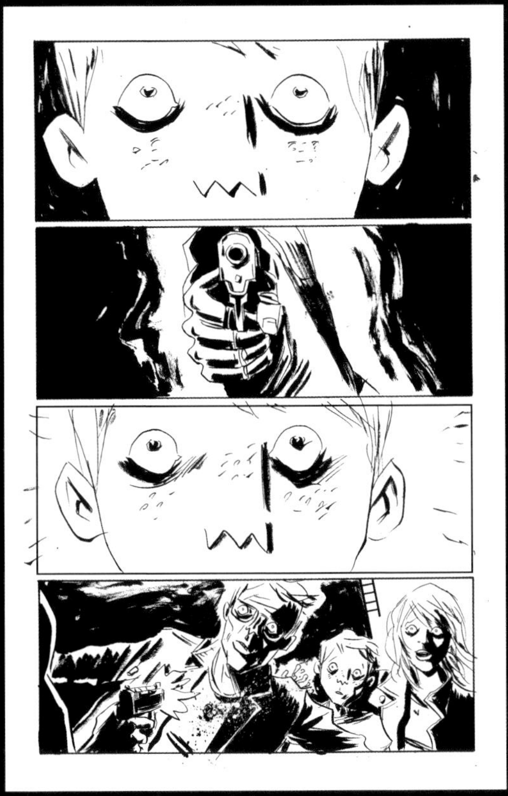

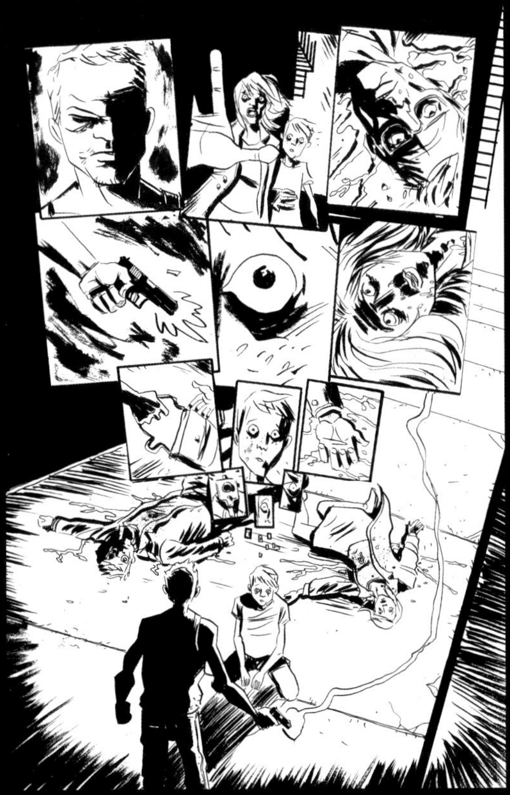

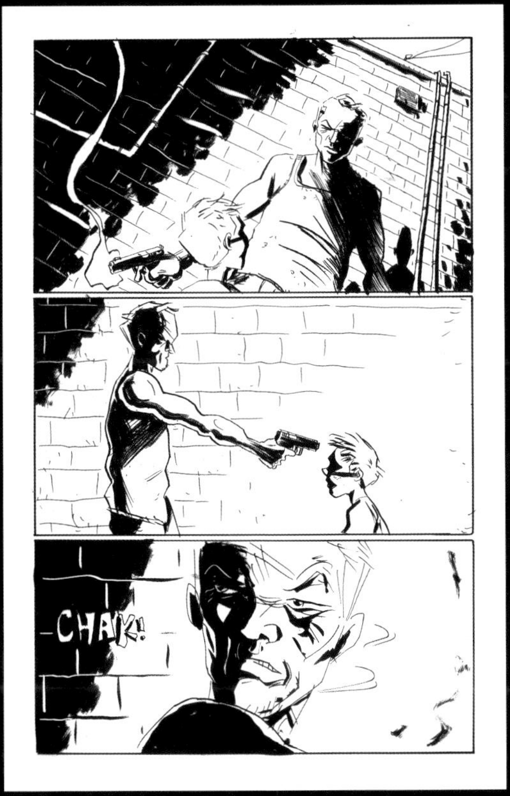

CHAK!

It's safe to say that *Skulldigger & Skeleton Boy* had a much longer and more interesting development period than any of the other Black Hammer spinoffs I've done up to this point. As you can see from the artwork here, there was a long period when I was going to both write and draw this comic myself. I spent the better part of a half of a year working on character designs and started drawing the first issue back in the fall of 2018.

—Jeff Lemire

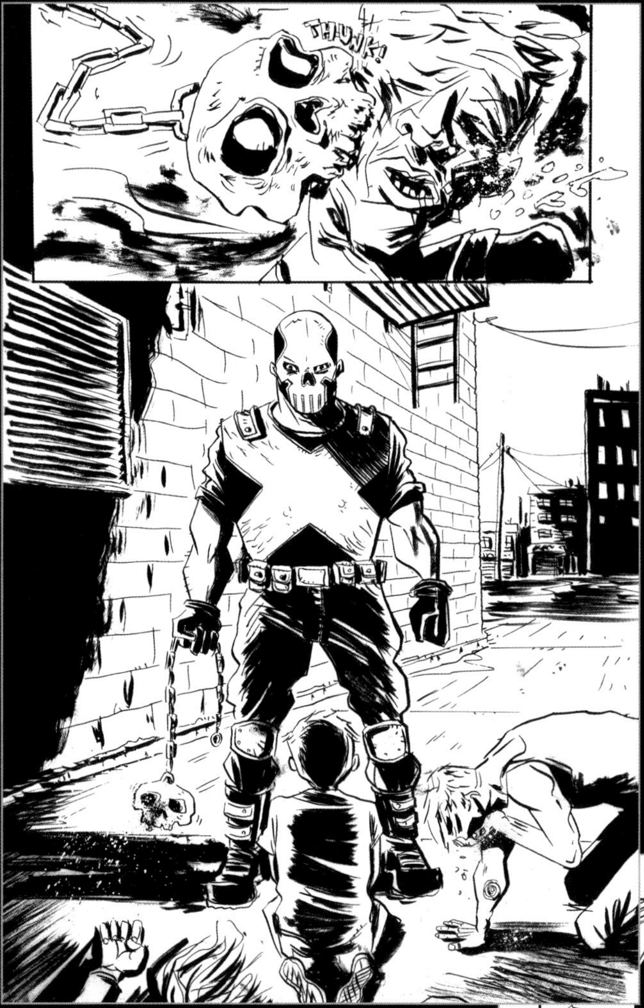
THUNK!

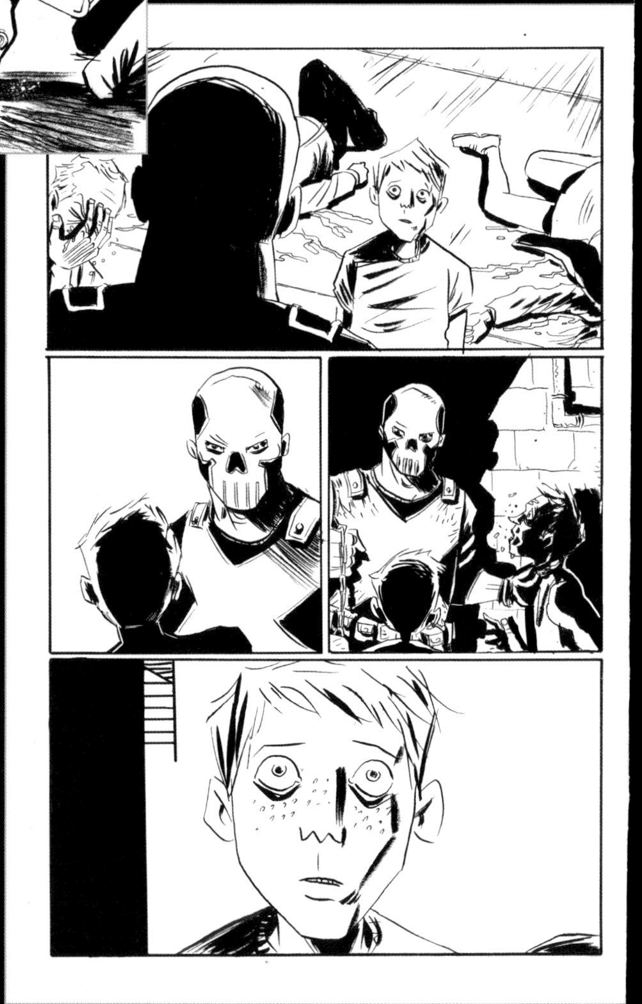

These are all of the pages that I finished before I decided to change course and work with another artist on the project. It was a bittersweet decision. I had always really wanted to draw a *Black Hammer* book myself, and loved this story, but something about it just never quite felt right and there was also another non–*Black Hammer* story that I had been tinkering with that suddenly started to come to life for me. So I moved on and with editor Daniel Chabon's help, we started looking for an artist to draw *Skulldigger*. Luckily for me, and for the readers, that artist turned out to be the incredible Tonci Zonjic.

—JL

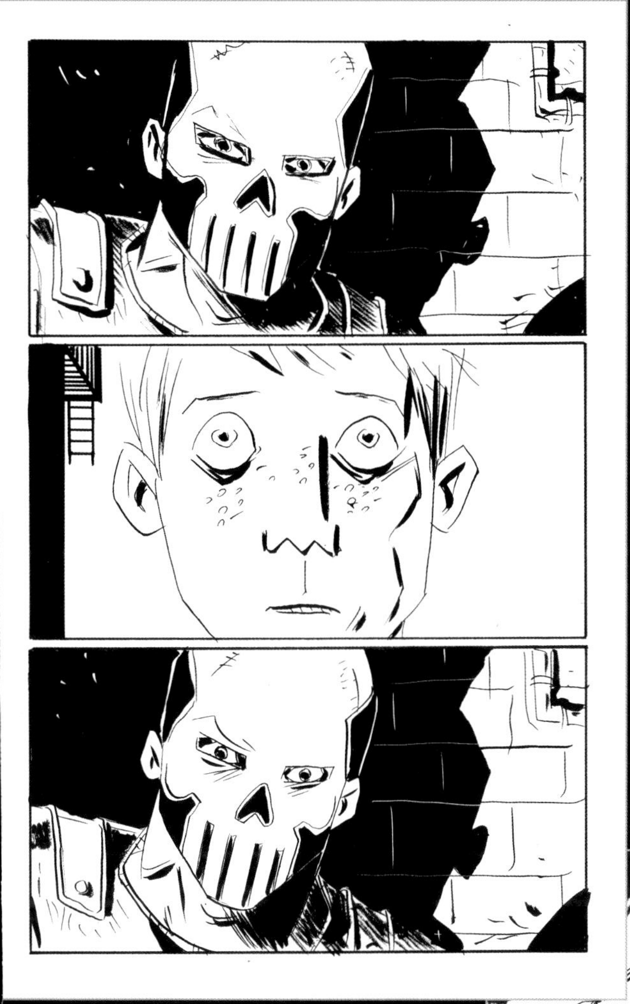

I worked for months and months trying to nail down Skulldigger's mask and costume. I literally have two sketchbooks in my studio filled with nothing but different takes on his mask and costume. But I never quite got it right. And then Tonci came in and totally nailed it within days. You can see here in my pages the difference between the version I was playing with and what Tonci ended up doing. He is such a smart designer.

—JL

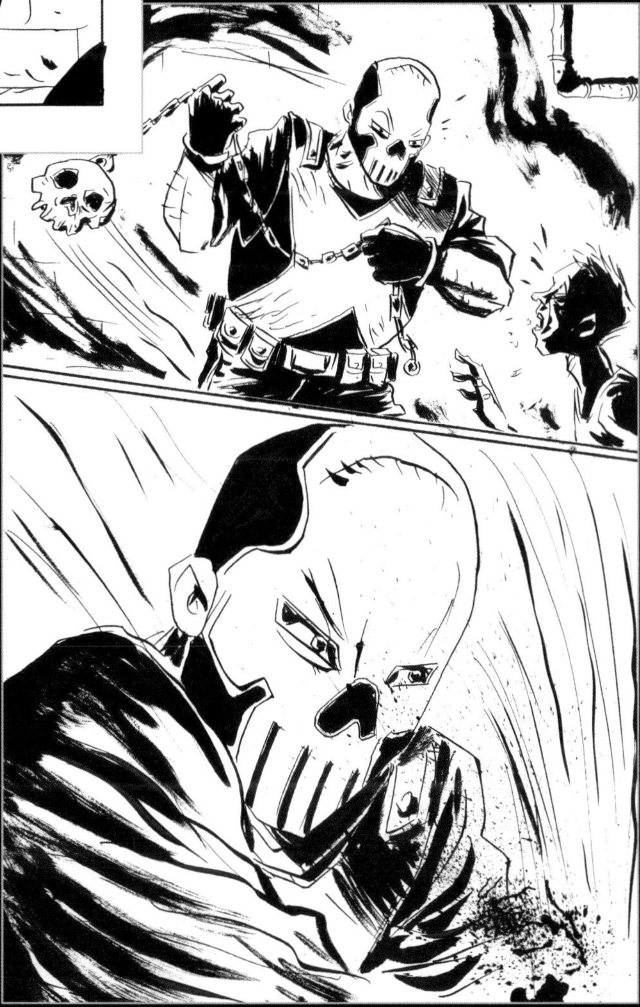

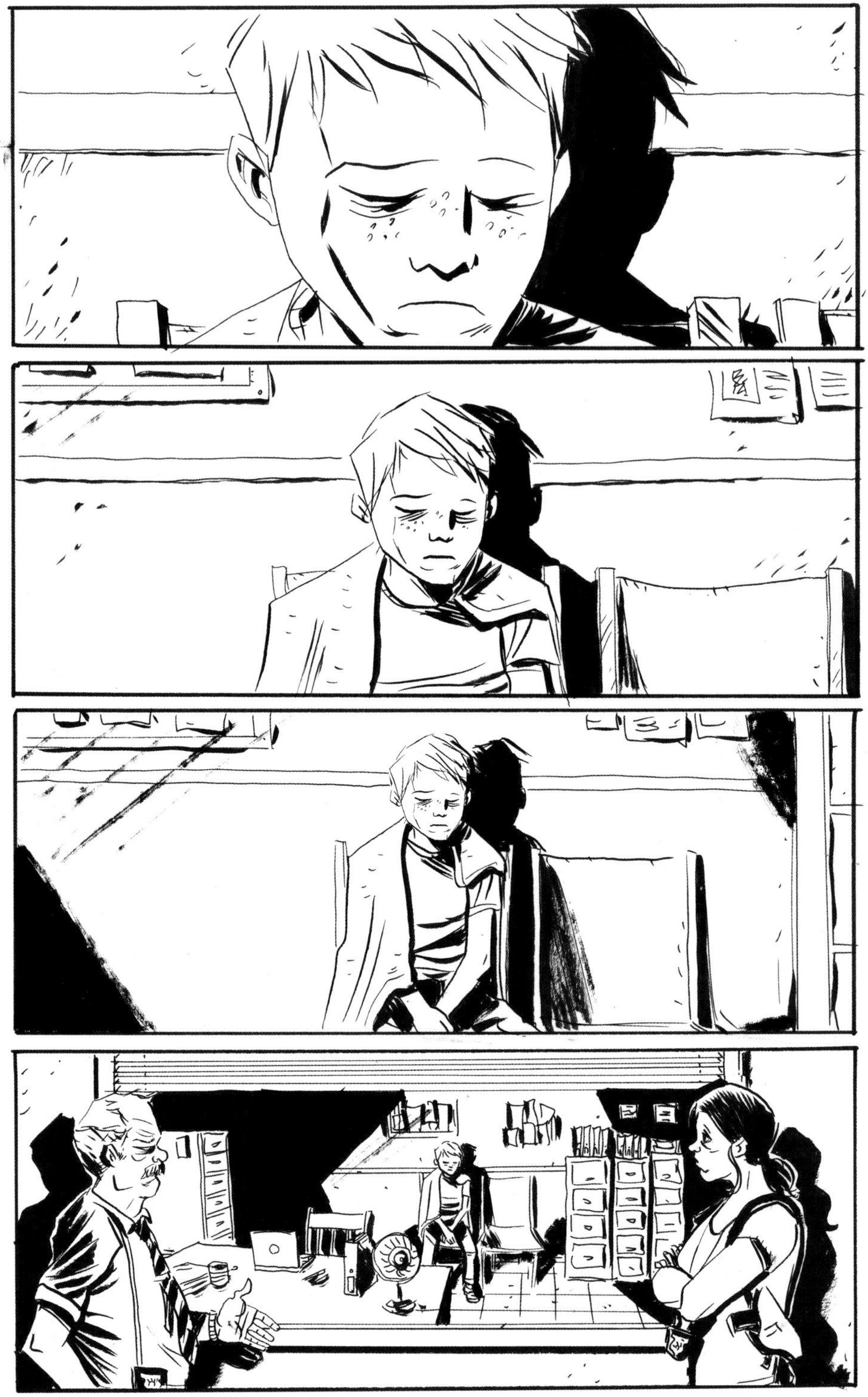

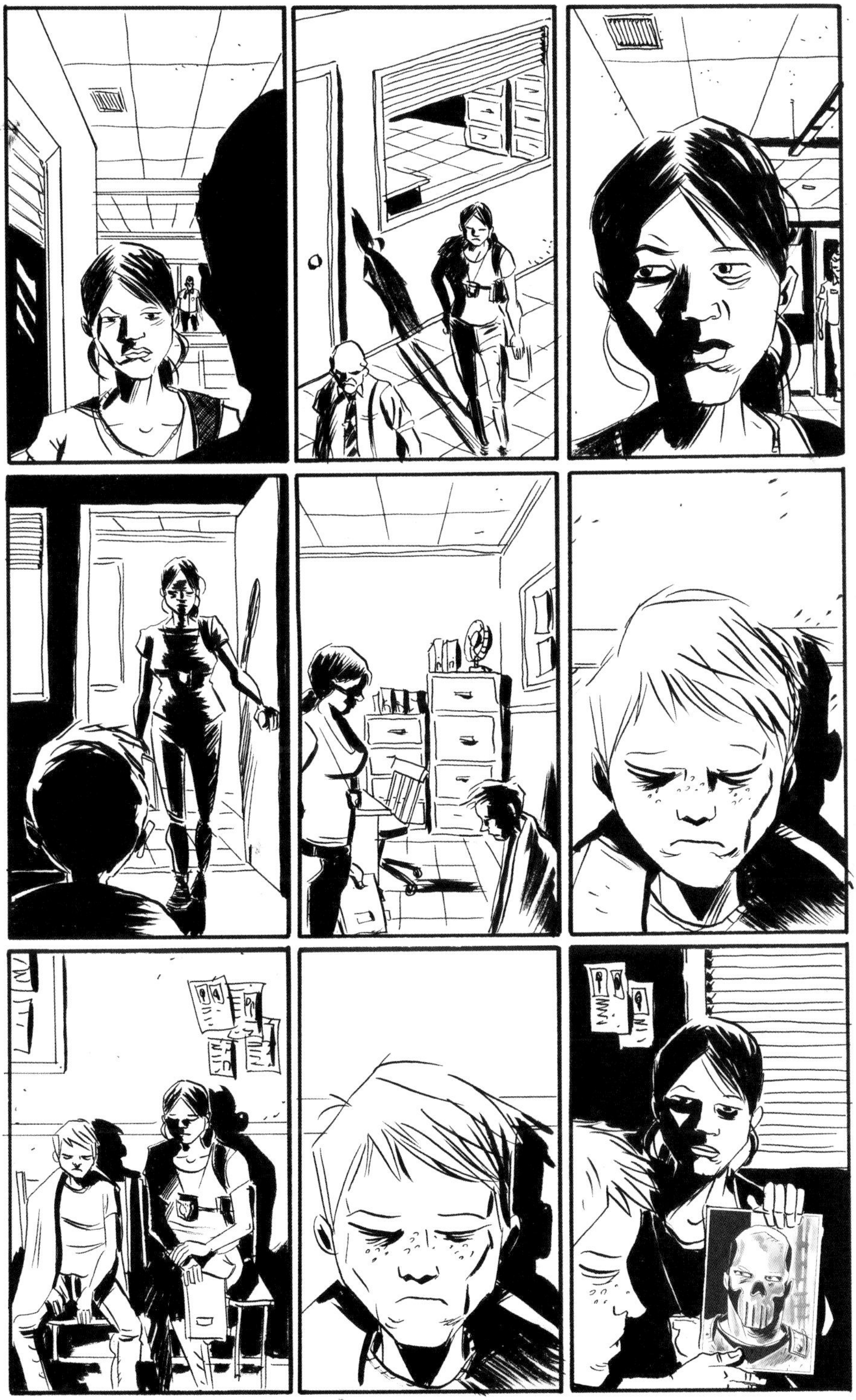

Skeleton Boy's look changed a lot too. My take had the big collar and smiley face mask, but when Tonci reworked it, it really came to life. I especially loved his addition of the sneakers. I really loved what Tonci did with the boy's haircut as well. Tonci is an incredible storyteller too, and he added so much to the "writing" of the book just with his layouts and the way he told the story.

—JL

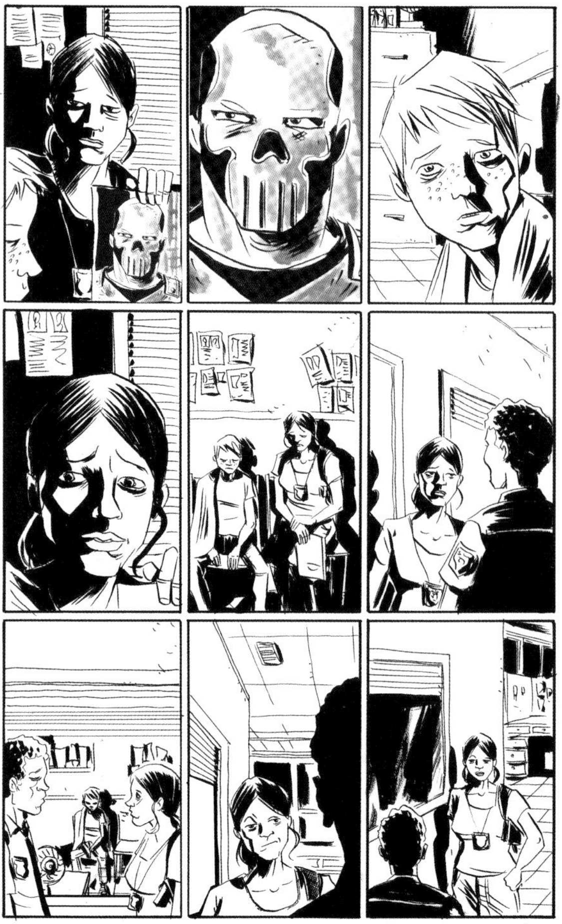

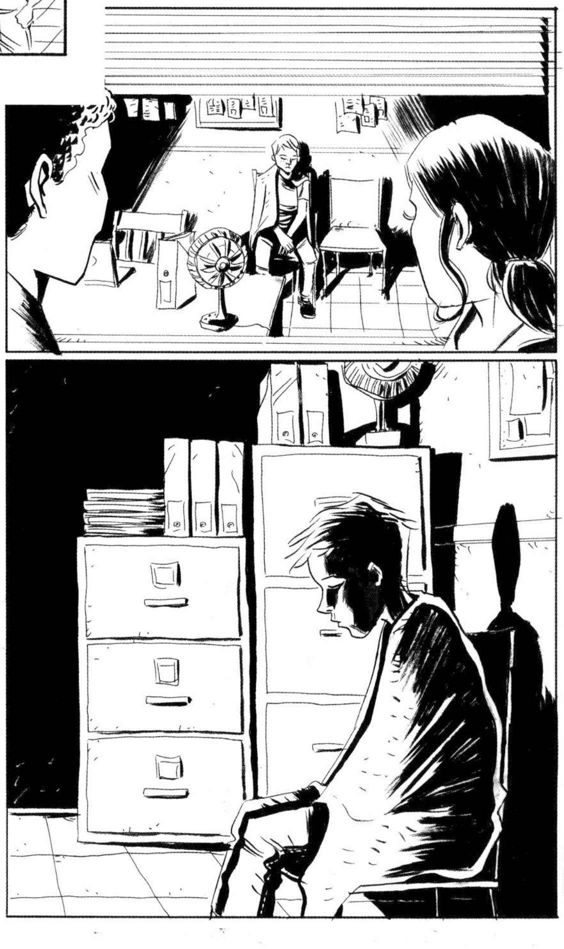

The biggest change in the character from my early design was that Skulldigger was going to use guns. I quickly moved away from that. I didn't want to glorify gun violence in the book, and also the use of the metal skull was so much more visual and visceral. In my mind the skull belongs to Digger's first victim.

—JL

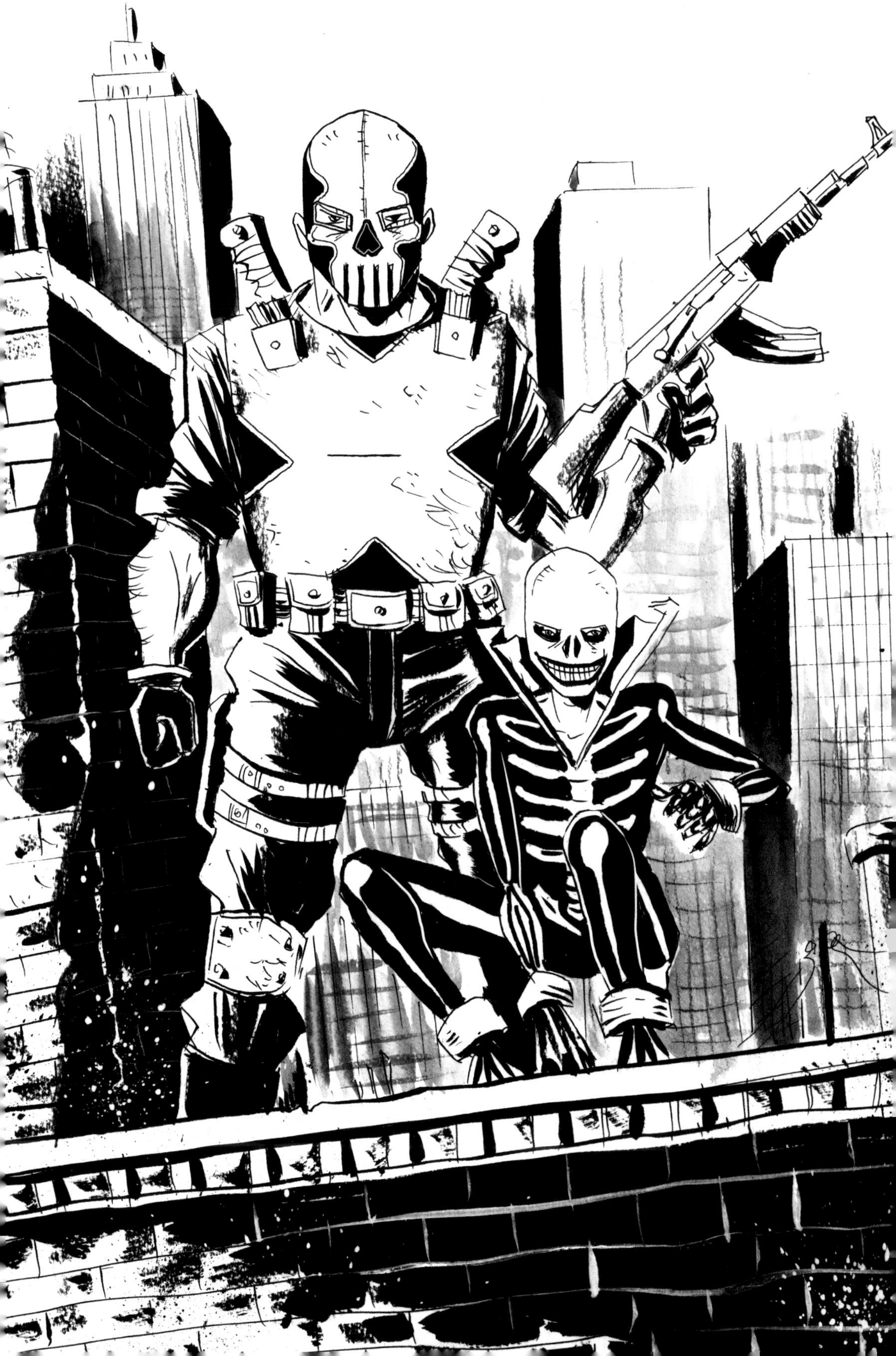

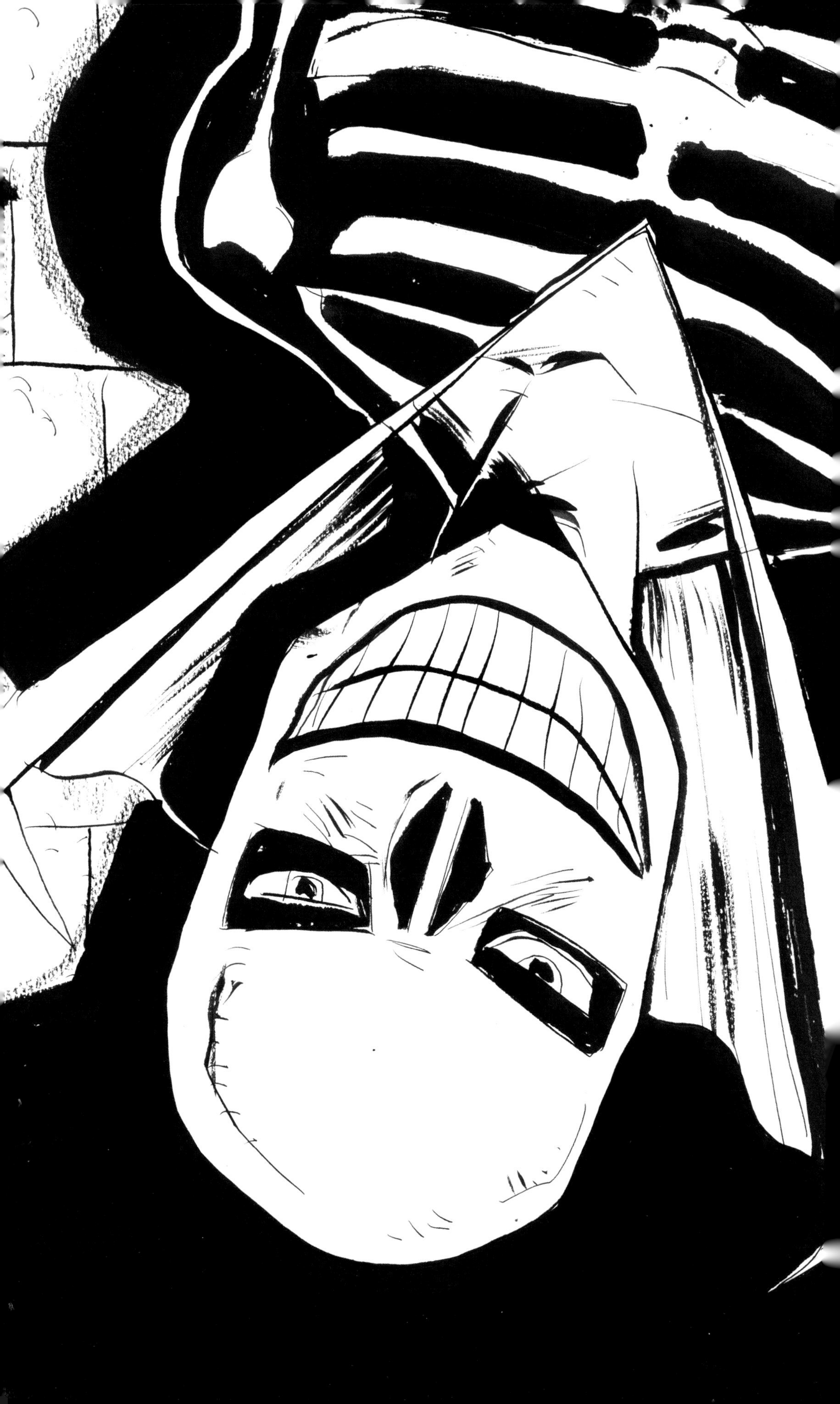

"If you think there's no room left in your life for another superhero comic, *Black Hammer* might just prove you wrong."—IGN

BLACK HAMMER™

ONCE THEY WERE HEROES, but the age of heroes has long since passed. Banished from existence by a multiversal crisis, the old champions of Spiral City—Abraham Slam, Golden Gail, Colonel Weird, Madame Dragonfly, and Barbalien—now lead simple lives in an idyllic, timeless farming village from which there is no escape! And yet, the universe isn't done with them—it's time for one last grand adventure.

FROM THE WORLD OF BLACK HAMMER
SHERLOCK FRANKENSTEIN
AND THE LEGION OF EVIL
JEFF LEMIRE
DAVID RUBÍN

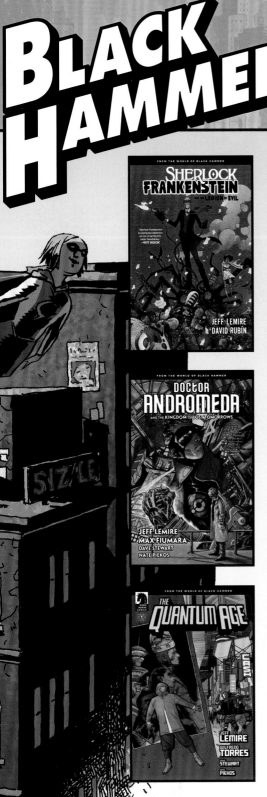

BLACK HAMMER
Written by Jeff Lemire
Art by Dean Ormston

THE WORLD OF BLACK HAMMER LIBRARY EDITION VOLUME 1
978-1-50671-995-5 • $49.99

THE WORLD OF BLACK HAMMER LIBRARY EDITION VOLUME 2
978-1-50671-996-2 • $49.99

VOLUME 1: SECRET ORIGINS
978-1-61655-786-7 • $14.99

VOLUME 2: THE EVENT
978-1-50670-198-1 • $19.99

VOLUME 3: AGE OF DOOM PART ONE
978-1-50670-389-3 • $19.99

VOLUME 4: AGE OF DOOM PART TWO
978-1-50670-816-4 • $19.99

BLACK HAMMER LIBRARY EDITION VOLUME 1
978-1-50671-073-0 • $49.99

BLACK HAMMER LIBRARY EDITION VOLUME 2
978-1-50671-185-0 • $49.99

SHERLOCK FRANKENSTEIN & THE LEGION OF EVIL
Written by Jeff Lemire • Art by David Rubín
This mystery follows a reporter determined to find out what happened to her father, the Black Hammer. All answers seem to lie in Spiral City's infamous insane asylum, where some dangerous supervillain tenants reside, including Black Hammer's greatest foe—Sherlock Frankenstein!
978-1-50670-526-2 • $19.99

FROM THE WORLD OF BLACK HAMMER
DOCTOR ANDROMEDA
AND THE KINGDOM OF LOST TOMORROWS
JEFF LEMIRE
MAX FIUMARA
DAVE STEWART
NATE PIEKOS

DOCTOR ANDROMEDA & THE KINGDOM OF LOST TOMORROWS
Written by Jeff Lemire • Art by Max Fiumara
This dual-narrative story set in the world of *Black Hammer* chronicles the legacy of a Golden-Age superhero wishing to reconnect with his estranged son, whom he hoped would one day take the mantle of Doctor Andromeda.
978-1-50672-329-7 • $19.99

THE QUANTUM AGE: FROM THE WORLD OF BLACK HAMMER
Written by Jeff Lemire • Art by Wilfredo Torres
A thousand years in the future, a collection of superheroes, inspired by the legendary heroes of Black Hammer Farm, must band together to save the planet from an authoritarian regime, while a young Martian struggles to solve the riddle of what happened to the great heroes of the twentieth century.
VOLUME 1
978-1-50670-841-6 • $19.99

FROM THE WORLD OF BLACK HAMMER
THE QUANTUM AGE
JEFF LEMIRE
WILFREDO TORRES
STEWART
PIEKOS

BLACK HAMMER: STREETS OF SPIRAL
Jeff Lemire, Dean Ormston, Emi Lenox, and others
A Lovecraftian teen decides she will do anything to make herself "normal," a bizarre witch guides her guests through her house of horrors, and an all-star slate of guest artists illustrate a bizarre adventure with Colonial Weird on the farm. Also features a complete world guide to the *Black Hammer* universe and its characters!
978-1-50670-941-3 • $19.99

BLACK HAMMER '45: FROM THE WORLD OF BLACK HAMMER
Jeff Lemire, Ray Fawkes, Matt Kindt, and Sharlene Kindt
During the Golden Age of superheroes, an elite Air Force crew called the Black Hammer Squadron bands together to combat the Nazis, a host of occult threats, and their ultimate aerial warrior the Ghost Hunter.
978-1-50670-850-8 • $17.99

BLACK HAMMER/JUSTICE LEAGUE: HAMMER OF JUSTICE!
Written by Jeff Lemire • Art by Michael Walsh
A strange man arrives simultaneously on Black Hammer Farm and in Metropolis, and both worlds are warped as Starro attacks! Batman, Green Lantern, Flash, Wonder Woman, Superman, and more crossover with Golden Gail, Colonel Weird, and the rest of the Black Hammer gang!
978-1-50671-099-0 • $29.99

COLONEL WEIRD—COSMAGOG: FROM THE WORLD OF BLACK HAMMER
Written by Jeff Lemire • Art by Tyler Crook
978-1-50671-516-2 • $19.99

DARK HORSE BOOKS

AVAILABLE AT YOUR LOCAL COMICS SHOP OR BOOKSTORE
TO FIND A COMICS SHOP IN YOUR AREA, VISIT COMICSHOPLOCATOR.COM.
For more information or to order direct, visit darkhorse.com.

BLACK HAMMER™ RECOMMENDED READING ORDER

TRADES

1. **BLACK HAMMER VOL. 1: SECRET ORIGINS TPB**
   Collects *Black Hammer* #1–#6
   ISBN 978-1-61655-786-7 | $14.99

2. **BLACK HAMMER VOL. 2: THE EVENT TPB**
   Collects *Black Hammer* #7–#11, #13
   ISBN 978-1-50670-198-1 | $19.99

3. **SHERLOCK FRANKENSTEIN AND THE LEGION OF EVIL TPB**
   Collects *Black Hammer* #12 and *Sherlock Frankenstein and the Legion of Evil* #1–#4
   ISBN 978-1-50670-526-2 | $17.99

4. **DOCTOR ANDROMEDA AND THE KINGDOM OF LOST TOMORROWS TPB**
   ISBN 978-1-50672-329-7 | $19.99

5. **BLACK HAMMER VOL. 3: AGE OF DOOM PART 1 TPB**
   Collects *Black Hammer: Age of Doom* #1–#5
   ISBN 978-1-50670-389-3 | $19.99

6. **BLACK HAMMER VOL. 4: AGE OF DOOM PART 2 TPB**
   Collects *Black Hammer: Age of Doom* #6–#12
   ISBN 978-1-50670-816-4 | $19.99

7. **THE QUANTUM AGE TPB**
   Collects "The Quantum Age" from *Free Comic Book Day 2018* and *The Quantum Age* #1–#6
   ISBN 978-1-50670-841-6 | $19.99

8. **BLACK HAMMER '45 TPB**
   Collects *Black Hammer '45* #1–#4
   ISBN 978-1-50670-850-8 | $17.99

9. **BLACK HAMMER: STREETS OF SPIRAL TPB**
   Collects *Black Hammer: Giant-Sized Annual*, *Black Hammer: Cthu-Louise*, *The World of Black Hammer Encyclopedia*, and "Horrors to Come" from *Free Comic Book Day 2019*
   ISBN 978-1-50670-941-3 | $19.99

10. **BLACK HAMMER/ JUSTICE LEAGUE HC**
    Collects *Black Hammer/Justice League: Hammer of Justice!* #1–#5
    ISBN 978-1-50671-099-0 | $19.99

11. **SKULLDIGGER AND SKELETON BOY TPB**
    Collects *Skulldigger and Skeleton Boy* #1–#6
    ISBN 978-1-50671-033-4 | $19.99

12. **COLONEL WEIRD: COSMAGOG TPB**
    Collects *Colonel Weird: Cosmagog* #1–#4
    ISBN 978-1-50671-516-2 | $19.99

13. **BARBALIEN: RED PLANET TPB**
    Collects *Barbalien: Red Planet* #1–#5
    ISBN 978-1-50671-580-3 | $19.99

LIBRARY EDITIONS

1. **BLACK HAMMER LIBRARY EDITION VOL. 1**
   Collects *Black Hammer* #1–#13 and *Black Hammer: Giant-Sized Annual*
   ISBN 978-1-50671-073-0 | $49.99

2. **THE WORLD OF BLACK HAMMER LIBRARY EDITION VOL. 1**
   Collects *Sherlock Frankenstein and the Legion of Evil* and *Doctor Andromeda and the Kingdom of Lost Tomorrows*
   ISBN 978-1-50671-995-5 | $49.99

3. **BLACK HAMMER LIBRARY EDITION VOL. 2**
   Collects *Black Hammer: Age of Doom* #1–#12, *Black Hammer: Cthu-Louise*, and *The World of Black Hammer Encyclopedia*
   ISBN 978-1-50671-185-0 | $49.99

4. **THE WORLD OF BLACK HAMMER LIBRARY EDITION VOL. 2**
   Collects *The Quantum Age* and *Black Hammer '45*
   ISBN 978-1-50671-996-2 | $49.99

BLACK HAMMER SECRET ORIGINS
BLACK HAMMER THE EVENT
SHERLOCK FRANKENSTEIN
DOCTOR ANDROMEDA
BLACK HAMMER AGE OF DOOM
BLACK HAMMER AGE OF DOOM
THE QUANTUM AGE
BLACK HAMMER '45
BLACK HAMMER STREETS OF SPIRAL
BLACK HAMMER JUSTICE LEAGUE
HAMMER OF JUSTICE!
SKULLDIGGER + SKELETON BOY
COLONEL WEIRD COSMAGOG
BARBALIEN RED PLANET
BLACK HAMMER
THE WORLD OF BLACK HAMMER
BLACK HAMMER
THE WORLD OF BLACK HAMMER